T0345029

Political Standards

Political Standards

Corporate Interest, Ideology, and Leadership in the Shaping of Accounting Rules for the Market Economy

KARTHIK RAMANNA

The University of Chicago Press
Chicago and London

Karthik Ramanna is associate professor of business administration at Harvard University.

The University of Chicago Press, Chicago 60637
The University of Chicago Press, Ltd., London
© 2015 by The University of Chicago
All rights reserved. Published 2015.
Printed in the United States of America

24 23 22 21 20 19 18 17 16 15   1 2 3 4 5

ISBN-13: 978-0-226-21074-2 (cloth)
ISBN-13: 978-0-226-21088-9 (e-book)
DOI: 10.7208/chicago/9780226210889.001.0001

Library of Congress Cataloging-in-Publication Data

Ramanna, Karthik, author.
    Political standards : corporate interest, ideology, and leadership in the shaping of accounting rules for the market ecomony / Karthik Ramanna.
        pages cm
    Includes bibliographical references and index.
        ISBN 978-0-226-21074-2 (cloth : alk. paper) — ISBN 978-0-226-21088-9 (e-book)
1. Auditing.   2. Consolidation and merger of corporations.   3. Social responsibility of business.   I. Title.
    HF5667.R323 2015
    657—2dc23

                                                                    2015011503

♾ This paper meets the requirements of ANSI/NISO Z39.48-1992 (Permanence of Paper).

For my parents

SCENE: The state opening of Parliament, as the Gentleman Usher of the Black Rod comes calling, c. 1787.

Charles James Fox, opposition leader: Do you enjoy all this flummery, Mr. Pitt?
William Pitt the Younger, prime minister: No, Mr. Fox.
Fox: Do you enjoy anything, Mr. Pitt?
Pitt: A balance sheet, Mr. Fox. I enjoy a good balance sheet.
ALAN BENNETT, *The Madness of King George*

Contents

Abbreviations

AICPA: American Institute of Certified Public Accountants
APB: Accounting Principles Board
ASBI: Accounting Standards Board of India
BRP: blue ribbon panel
CAP: Committee on Accounting Procedure
EC: European Commission
ED: exposure draft
EU: European Union
FAF: Financial Accounting Foundation
FASB: Financial Accounting Standards Board
FTB: fair value to book value
GAAP: Generally Accepted Accounting Principles (United States)
GASB: Governmental Accounting Standards Board
GDP: gross domestic product
IASB: International Accounting Standards Board
IFRS: International Financial Reporting Standards
IGAAP: Indian Generally Accepted Accounting Principles
M & A: mergers and acquisitions
MOF: Ministry of Finance (China)
MTB: market to book
NASBA: National Association of State Boards of Accountancy
NYSE: New York Stock Exchange
PAC: political action committee
PCAOB: Public Company Accounting Oversight Board
PCC: Private Company Council
PCFRC: Private Company Financial Reporting Committee
RICO: Racketeer Influenced and Corrupt Organizations Act of 1970

s a s : Statement on Auditing Standards
s e c : Securities and Exchange Commission
s f a s : Statement of Financial Accounting Standards
s o x : Sarbanes-Oxley Act
w t o : World Trade Organization

Tables

Figures

Preface

In subtle but significant ways, our corporate accounting system has been captured. This is disturbing for at least two reasons. First, because accounting rules are at the heart of our market economy. They define the fundamental notion of profitability, facilitate capital allocation across competing ventures, and ensure the accountability of corporations and their managers. The health of the accounting system impacts the health of the economy and the distribution of wealth and income therein. Second, because the evidence of capture in accounting rule-making can be symptomatic of a broader problem with how the "rules of the game" in our market economy are determined—particularly esoteric and highly technical rules that are outside the understanding and oversight of the general public. For example, the rules around bank governance and supervision, the rules around corporate auditing, and the rules around risk management and disclosure in financial firms.

This book assembles a large body of evidence on the political process of corporate accounting rule-making, particularly in the United States. It studies the role of individual corporations, investment banks, asset-management firms, audit firms, industry associations, and members of the Financial Accounting Standards Board (FASB), the private, not-for-profit body charged with making U.S. corporate accounting rules. It evaluates the workings of the rule-making process. Does the process generate rules that are in the general interest—that is, are they likely to facilitate investment-allocation efficiency and corporate accountability in our market system?

In several instances, I find evidence of rules that benefit one or more special-interest groups (e.g., industrial corporations, financial firms, and audit firms) at the potential expense of the general interest. In other words, the evidence suggests special-interest capture of the accounting rule-making process. But unlike the traditional understanding of capture, where powerful interest groups are able to strong-arm regulators to obtain rules in their favor, several instances of capture in accounting rule-making are more subtle. Capture in these contexts involves selectively co-opting conceptual arguments from academia and elsewhere to advance the views of the special-interest groups. In this sense, the capture can be described as an ideology-enabled capture, or *ideological capture.*

The findings on the state of accounting rule-making are of added import because accounting rule-making is an illustration of a distinctive kind of regulatory challenge: producing public policy in a *thin political market.* Accounting rules cannot be determined without the substantive expertise and experience of special-interest groups that, by definition, also have strong commercial interests in the outcome and enjoy little political opposition from the general interest because of the abstruse nature of the subject matter. The challenge of such a thin political market is producing regulatory policy that is in the general interest.

✶

This book is aimed at sophisticated participants and observers in the market economy, including corporate managers, policy makers, and, particularly, business and social-science scholars. No specialist knowledge of accounting is necessary; the book is self-contained with regard to technical concepts that are relevant to interpreting the evidence. The evidence in this book spans nearly four decades of data and is drawn from both large-sample formal statistical studies and in-depth case studies. A large proportion of this evidence has been vetted through the academic peer-review process and published in scholarly journals in accounting. The basic findings are as follows:

- With the financialization of the U.S. economy, particularly since the 1990s, we see a growing impact of investment banks and asset-management firms in accounting rule-making. These groups are more likely to propose rules that accelerate financial-statement recognition of anticipated economic gains—that is, fair-value accounting rules. Under certain circumstances, this can result in higher compensation to executives in these firms.
- The rules above can be difficult to audit because they require verification of conjectural profits. Large audit firms have responded by lobbying for more check-the-box-style rules (in contrast to rules that require subjective judgment). Check-the-box-style rules can lower auditors' legal and political liability in case the conjectural profits do not materialize; such rules can also lower auditors' overall accountability in the system.
- Members of the FASB generally propose rules consistent with the inter-

ests of the industries from which they hail—in particular, members from investment banking and asset management generally propose fair-value accounting rules.

- Managers in nonfinancial firms lobby on issues of particular relevance to them; they generally lobby for rules that further their private interests. On other issues they are generally silent.

- Some large private firms (firms not listed on stock exchanges), concerned particularly about the compliance costs of fair-value accounting rules, have been part of a successful coalition to create a new accounting rule-maker for themselves: the Private Company Council. This was done despite a dearth of conceptual arguments for separate accounting rules for private companies.

- There is evidence that the impact of special interests on accounting rule-making is not limited to the United States. This appears to be an international and even a global phenomenon.

Three themes emerge from across the findings. First, corporate accounting rule-making is largely determined by a few specialist individuals (mostly corporate executives, bankers, and auditors) with strong economic interests in the outcome. They experience little political opposition in the process, particularly from those representing the interests of individual savers and, more so, ordinary citizens. Second, the outcome is, in several instances, skewed toward the interests of the specialists in ways that can compromise accounting's role in corporate performance evaluation, corporate accountability, and asset allocation. Put differently, there is evidence suggesting that the accounting system has been "captured" by special-interest groups, although this capture is sometimes of a distinct nature better referred to as ideological capture. Third, and perhaps most important, the evidence does not point to systematic and sustained capture by any one special-interest group. There is no single extractive institution, no unequivocal villain in the story. The capture in accounting rule-making appears to be ad hoc and driven by those with the strongest economic incentives in any particular case.

Several books have been written on regulatory capture—or attempts thereof—in different areas of the economy, including federal broadcasting standards, automobile safety standards, and pharmaceutical approval standards. This book adds to the corpus of regulatory appraisals by offering a broad evaluation of the political process in accounting rule-making: a critical market institution that is rarely subject to wide-ranging assessment. But beyond that, the book develops the notion that accounting rule-making is a "thin political market"—a notion that can have implications for several other areas of regulation.

I argue that the three themes emerging from the analysis of accounting's political process together structure a special class of problem in the creation and maintenance of market institutions that underlie capitalism: the problem of a thin political market. I define a thin political market as an area of rule-making or regulation relevant to the functioning of capitalist economies, where corporate managers (a) possess the technical expertise necessary for informed regulation, (b) enjoy strong economic interests in the outcome, and (c) face little political opposition from the general interest. Beyond accounting rule-making, areas such as banking and insurance regulation and rule-making for auditing and actuarial practice are likely thin political markets. They are "thin" in the sense that they are each dominated by a few specialist players with little opposition from the general interest. They are "political markets" in the sense that in each case a *deliberative* process is being used to allocate a scarce and valuable resource—for example, accounting, auditing, or insurance rules for the economy.

Thin political markets are distinct from political processes where the general public is sufficiently informed or incented to participate—for example, the political market for Social Security reform. They are also distinct from political processes where expertise for regulation does not necessarily reside with corporate interests, such as the political market for environmental regulation, where climate scientists possess substantial know-how. In a thin political market expertise germane to developing regulation is experiential in nature—the knowledge is tacit, or a posteriori, residing within the regulated entities by virtue of their day-to-day activities. The comingling of such regulatory expertise and economic interest within corporations, together with the paucity of political representation of the general interest (due partly to the highly technical nature of the underlying subject matter), makes thin political markets particularly challenging.

In a thin political market, it is difficult for nonvested interests to design precise regulation in the general interest. Independent experts—for example, accounting professors in the case of accounting rule-making—have modest impact in thin political markets because their "independence" generally correlates with distance from the substantive experience necessary for regulation. Ex post facto studies—such as the kind in this book—can bring circumstantial evidence to bear on the likelihood of capture. For example, research presented in this book shows that (1) several important accounting rules deviate from what is expected given accounting's role in performance evaluation, asset allocation, and stewardship and (2) that this deviation can be explained by the vested interests of those with relevant experience. But this assessment is after-the-fact, not concurrent and not preventative. This is not to suggest that academics have not played an important role in the development of accounting rules over the past few decades but rather (as I argue later) that academic voices are selectively heard; they are particularly impactful when they can corroborate and advance the positions of prevailing special-interest groups. This process I describe as ideological capture.

So what can we do about the problem of thin political markets?

The various actors in the accounting rule-making game are all individually acting in their own interests, seeking to increase their own profits in a manner that is not obviously illegal. Indeed, on one level, their actions essentially embody the capitalist spirit as articulated in Milton Friedman's famous claim that "the social responsibility of business is to increase its profits." But the logic of profit-increasing behavior is the logic of competitive markets; and, as the evidence in this book demonstrates, this logic breaks down in thin political markets. I argue that when lobbying in a thin political market, corporate managers assume an agency responsibility for the market system as whole and for the citizens in whose interests market capitalism functions. So just as there is widespread recognition among managers of their agency responsibility to corporations and shareholders—recognition that is imbued in them via business schools and corporate codes as a moral and legal duty—so too must managers recognize their agency of the system when lobbying in thin political markets. The problem of thin political markets cannot be solved without a fundamental reexamination of what is the legitimate responsibility of corporate managers in such political contexts. The solution is one that relies just as importantly on reimagining business leadership as on clever institutional redesigns. The book concludes with an urgent call to action in this regard.

1

Introduction

When I first conceived the idea for this book, I imagined it would focus exclusively on making an assessment of the accounting rule-making process for corporations in the United States and beyond. Corporate accounting rules are a critical institution in modern market capitalism, essential to mitigating collusion and information asymmetry and to promoting the efficient allocation of capital across diverse competing projects. I have been studying this process for several years, so a comprehensive report on that investigation seemed appropriate and timely. And indeed, a substantial portion of this book (chapters 2–7) presents such a report.

But the book goes beyond an assessment of the state of accounting rule-making. As I started to put this book together—and reflect on my findings, searching for the "whole" that would integrate the numerous distinct studies I have conducted in this area—I came to realize that the book ought to be much broader. Because the accounting rule-making process offers a window into a central aspect of the functioning of market capitalism: the nature and challenge of what I define as "thin political markets." By this I mean a political process of designing essential technical rules of the game in areas where substantive expertise lies with vested interests and where the general interest is usually not involved. Beyond accounting rule-making, areas such as banking supervision, insurance regulation, and standards for auditing and actuaries can be thin political markets.

Thin political markets present a paradox. There is nothing explicitly illegal about constituents lobbying in the accounting rule-making process for outcomes that are likely to increase their own reported profits. These constituents' actions, as I document in this book, essentially embody the capitalist spirit, as Milton Friedman famously argued: "The social responsibility of business . . . is to increase its profits."[1] But the "invisible hand" that usually aggregates and equilibrates self-interested profit-seeking behavior in markets into a collective prosperity that legitimizes capitalism does not manifest itself in the thin political market of accounting rule-making. By their very nature, thin political markets are one-sided and unrestrained vis-à-vis the general interest. In this sense, they are distinct from "thick" political processes, where the general public is engaged (either directly or through intermediaries) or where expertise for regulation does not necessarily reside largely with vested interests.[2]

Toward the end of the book I introduce in more detail the notion of thin political markets and offer an inductive definition that I hope future research will expand upon and refine. Then I begin to outline a solution to the challenge of thin political markets. I note that in pursuing profit-increasing behavior in the conduct of commerce, managers are acting in the context of the ethical framework that legitimizes capitalism. Without this framework—which lays out the logic for how the individual pursuit of profit aggregates to a collective good—profit-seeking behavior is morally empty. What makes profit-seeking "a social responsibility" (in Milton Friedman's words) is the very sound reasoning at the heart of capitalism—a reasoning powerfully articulated by Adam Smith and, more recently, by economic Nobelists as ideologically diverse as Kenneth Arrow, Friedrich Hayek, Paul Samuelson, and Amartya Sen.[3] This is not to say that corporate managers are not self-interested or that absent some ethical grant made by capitalism, corporate managers would not pursue their own profit but rather that were it not morally virtuous and ethically sound, the pursuit of self-interest would not be so overt and unabashed.

The logic of profit-increasing behavior is the logic of competitive markets. As the empirical evidence in this book will demonstrate, this logic breaks down in thin political markets. Here, the distinction between thin and thick political markets is also germane. In a thick political market (e.g., the political market for universal health care)—with a vibrant, deliberative process, diverse views well represented, and expertise dispersed across interest groups—the profit-seeking approach to lobbying might indeed be ethically tenable. But the absence of competent opposition in a thin political market obviates the ethical foundations for profit seeking. In this specific context, the capitalist spirit of "rent extraction" is no longer virtuous.

When lobbying in a thin political market, corporate managers assume an agency responsibility for the market system as a whole and, eventually, for the citizens in whose interests market capitalism must function virtuously. So just as there is widespread recognition among managers of their agency

responsibility to corporations and shareholders—a recognition that is imbued in them via business schools and corporate codes as a moral duty (in
addition to being a legal duty; in fact, it is a legal duty because it is moral)—so
too must we create a recognition for managerial agency of the system when
lobbying in thin political markets. This is a key takeaway from the book.

What comes next is a detailed introduction to the book. I begin with an
example from the area of accounting rule-making for corporate mergers and
acquisitions (M&A). The example illustrates the phenomenon at the core of
the evidence and analysis in this book: the problem of thin political markets.
Later in the introduction, I provide an outline of the chapters that follow.

✶

Mergers and acquisitions between and across companies are a critical institution of our modern market-capitalist economy. They allow companies to fold
into each other to unleash synergies that can sustain and grow the economy.
Furthermore, they constitute a core element of the "market for corporate
control"—the process by which floundering companies and their manage-
ments are held to account by the rigors of the marketplace, embodying the
creative destruction at the heart of capitalism. From 1980 to 2012, M&A activity in the United States totaled roughly $44 trillion, about 15 percent of U.S.
gross domestic product (GDP) over that period.[4] The central issue in M&A
is the price to be paid in an acquisition; decades of academic research has revealed that managers often overpay in M&A, perhaps because they are over-
confident in their ability to realize synergies or because they are unreasonably
driven to build scale into their existing organizations.[5]

Given that M&A can either generate value for shareholders and society or,
alternatively, be misused by "empire-building" management teams, it is important to hold managers to account for their M&A activities, particularly for
an acquisition's purchase price. This is largely accomplished through corporate financial reporting. Without financial reporting that matches the costs of
an acquisition to its benefits, investors could be led to reward managers who
increase the scale of their companies but decrease their value through over-
priced acquisitions. As such, accounting rules for M&A are a key accountability institution in capital markets. A particularly relevant area of M&A
accounting—relevant to the purchase price of an acquisition—is "goodwill
accounting."

Goodwill is the excess of the purchase price in an acquisition over the
current value of all purchased assets less the current value of all assumed liabilities. In other words, goodwill is premium paid over the verifiable value
of the acquired firm. It generally represents the conjectural "future profits"

that an acquiring manager hopes to realize through an acquisition. Research has shown that, on average, acquiring CEOs overestimate on the date of acquisition the amount of goodwill than can be realized.[6] How goodwill is accounted for is thus critical to the accountability of M&A transactions.

Since 2001, the formal rules or Generally Accepted Accounting Principles (GAAP) in the United States that govern goodwill accounting have compromised this accountability role in subtle ways. To see this requires a brief plunge into accounting principles. "Income" in accounting is defined as revenues minus expenses. A core principle underlying traditional historic-cost accounting income is to match expenses to their associated revenues. In other words, to get a useful income number for a given year, we want the year's revenues to be matched with the costs—including investments from previous years—that were needed to generate those revenues. In the case of measuring income from an M&A deal, the revenues are those generated when imagined synergies become real sales to customers. The corresponding costs are numerous, but they include the value of goodwill acquired—that is, the premium paid in the M&A. Since the revenues from actualized synergies can occur over many years following an M&A in a process that is not measurable with any certainty, the traditional historic-cost way to account for M&A is to take a predetermined proportion of a firm's goodwill balance and treat it as a cost each year (e.g., one-tenth of the goodwill balance each year for ten years). In fact, this was the rule that defined goodwill accounting in several cases prior to 2001—a process known as goodwill amortization (the maximum allowed goodwill amortization period was forty years).

But since 2001, firms have not been required to draw down their goodwill balance each year. Instead, they are required to determine for themselves whether their goodwill is "impaired." Not surprisingly, a CEO who overpays in an M&A is not particularly keen to publicly acknowledge that overpayment, so instances of firms declaring their goodwill as impaired are rare. What this means is that if an M&A was successful—and the acquiring firm generates the synergies it imagined at acquisition—the firm's income recognizes the revenues from those synergies but not all of its costs, resulting in a double-counting of sorts. This violates the basic premise of traditional accounting. Alternatively, if an M&A is unsuccessful, and imagined synergies are for naught, investors and other users of accounting information can be left waiting for true accountability from managers; it takes a particularly earnest CEO to admit that he or she overpaid for an acquisition. In fact, research shows that goodwill impairment is more likely to occur under new CEOs, who take a "bath" on their predecessors' accumulated goodwill balance.[7]

Why would the goodwill accounting rule change matter if even a few sophisticated investors are able to undo its effects, reconstructing what firms' income statements and balance sheets would have looked like under the old rules through some accounting analysis? Partly because summary accounting numbers such as net income and net assets—which are both affected by the rule change—are sometimes predictably associated with stock prices, reflecting market inefficiencies.[8] And partly because such summary accounting numbers are used in a host of formal commercial contracts, such as executive bonus contracts, debt contracts, and supplier contracts. As a matter of economy, these contracts are generally written on GAAP rules; it is costly for contracting parties to redefine accounting rules on an ad hoc basis.[9]

Thus one likely consequence of the goodwill accounting rules since 2001 is compromised accountability for M&A. Then a natural follow-up question is: How did the 2001 accounting rules for M&A come to be?

The answer lies in a deeper understanding of the arcane process through which accounting rules are determined. At the heart of this process is the Financial Accounting Standards Board (FASB), the country's accounting rulemaker. In 1999, the FASB, partly in response to pressure from the U.S. Securities and Exchange Commission (SEC), which oversees the nation's stock markets and publicly listed securities, decided to reevaluate the accounting rules for M&A. What followed was an unusually long and political process that, importantly, involved the country's biggest investment banks: Goldman Sachs, Merrill Lynch, and Morgan Stanley. Investment banks, by the nature of their business, have an interest in issues related to M&A, including the accounting rules used by their prospective clients. As the opportunity to revisit these rules came up, the investment banks became key players in the private rule-making process. First, they saw their allies in the U.S. Congress lambast the FASB for its initial proposed replacement to the extant M&A accounting rules. Then representatives from the banks met with the FASB to advance their own proposals. They lobbied for rules that looked very similar to the ones that eventually ended up as the final FASB standard on goodwill accounting—that is, they advocated the abolishment of goodwill amortization and the introduction of the rules for goodwill impairment.

To be sure, the old rule—goodwill amortization—was far from perfect; treating a predetermined portion of a firm's goodwill balance as an expense each year is arbitrary. Moreover, the SEC had been concerned about abuses of other extant M&A accounting rules (unrelated to goodwill per se), which was part of the impetus for the 2001 rule change. So compromised accountability for M&A under the current goodwill rules is the outcome of complex

bargaining that comingled many issues. But given the repercussions of compromised goodwill accountability to the integrity of M&A and capital markets, there is, nevertheless, cause for concern.

How did a handful of special interests shift such a core accounting rule?
Why was the shift not bigger news as it happened? Who looks out for the
interests of common citizens and retail investors in the political process that
determines the accounting rules?

In this book, I address these questions through a broad analysis of the
corporate accounting rule-making process in the United States and beyond.
Apart from the accounting community, this analysis can be of interest to
scholars of the market economy, policy makers, and executives in business
more generally. After all, accounting rules are at the heart of measuring corporate performance, securing corporate accountability, and facilitating capital allocation in a market economy.

*

Since the early 1970s, corporate accounting standard setting in the United
States has been formally vested in the FASB, a small group of accounting
rule-makers, incorporated as part of a private not-for-profit organization,
the Financial Accounting Foundation (FAF). But neither the FASB nor the
FAF holds a congressional charter to make accounting rules for corporate
America. Rather, this authority comes from the SEC, which has been charged
by Congress since its establishment in the 1930s with the determination of
accounting standards for publicly listed companies in the United States.[10]
The SEC has for almost all its history relied on private bodies to draft and
promulgate accounting standards. This delegation of public responsibility
to private interests implicitly recognizes that neither Congress nor the SEC
have direct substantive knowledge and experience in the matters that inform
accounting standards. The expertise necessary to create accounting rules—
familiarity with ever-mutating business practices, their evolving methods of
account, and emerging technologies to audit such accounts—resides in the
private sector.

But inherent in the idea of private rule-making is the fear that private
interests will come to subvert the public's benefit through opportunistic rule-
setting. In fact, two private bodies were delegated the accounting rule-making
role prior to the FASB—the Committee on Accounting Procedure (1939–59)
and the Accounting Principles Board (1959–73)—and both these bodies met
their demise in part because of concerns about their lack of independence
from private interests.[11] Speaking in 1971 of the need to reevaluate extant institutions of accounting rule-making, the then-president of the American

Institute of Certified Public Accountants (AICPA), the umbrella professional society for all American accountants, noted: "If we are not confronted with a crisis of confidence in the profession, we are at least faced with a serious challenge to our ability to perform a mission of grave public responsibility."[12]

How to deal with the critical tension inherent in the process of creating accounting rules—a process that relies on private interests acting for the public good—was a key theme in the design of the FASB in the early 1970s. There are several notable differences between the FASB and its immediate predecessor institution, the Accounting Principles Board (APB). First, membership in the FASB is a full-time commitment. Members are required to resign all their other positions to serve in the nation's principal corporate accounting rule-making body; members of the APB served part-time. Second, the FASB is part of an independent, not-for-profit organization whose trustees are committed in principle to insulate the FASB from conflicts of interest; the APB was part of the AICPA. And third, the FASB is supported by an independent full-time research staff to assist in technical and administrative matters; the APB relied considerably on the research support of the AICPA and large auditing firms.[13]

As the differences above suggest, the FASB and its supporting infrastructure were created with the goal of making accounting standard setting more independent of groups with strong vested interests in the rule-making outcomes. But of course, the challenge still remains that it is in those very groups that the necessary expertise for accounting rule-making lies. The special committee of the AICPA that proposed the establishment of the FASB in 1972 noted: "The common need we see is for a bold new effort to insure public confidence in the ways in which financial information is reported."[14] So the FASB is an experiment of sorts, to extract a select few technical specialists from corporate interests, endow them with independence from those interests, and empower them to set rules.

More than forty years on, has this experiment delivered on those intentions?

Answering this question requires an evaluation of not only the FASB but rather the entire ecosystem from which accounting rule-making emerges. This ecosystem includes industrial corporations, financial institutions, auditing firms, and, naturally, the FASB members who are drawn from these organizations. A substantial fraction of this book is occupied by a discussion of the results of such an evaluation. Briefly, I find evidence consistent with "capture" of the accounting rule-making process by a number of these groups. The capture appears to be motivated by self-interest in many cases, although idiosyncratic differences across the groups on fundamental questions about the nature and purpose of accounting appear to also precipitate "ideological capture" in certain cases.

Making observations about the social-welfare implications of a regulatory institution, including the costs of its likely capture, is extremely difficult. For example, as seen earlier, there is no definitively "correct" accounting method for acquired goodwill, so it is difficult to assert conclusively that the new goodwill method is the result of capture. Rather, the evidence is suggestive. The goodwill anecdote in all its complexity embodies the broader empirical reality. But relative to other areas where such observations might be made (e.g., the desirability of universal health care or a minimum wage), accounting rules are a relatively clean setting. This is because, as I describe in the next chapter, a well-developed economic theory of financial reporting provides a conceptual benchmark of properties of accounting rules against which outcomes of accounting's political process can be evaluated.

*

The remainder of this introduction is devoted to providing an outline of the chapters that follow. Briefly, chapter 2 develops a framework for essential properties of accounting rules, given their use in generating metrics for corporate performance evaluation, corporate accountability, and asset allocation. The framework is used in the next three chapters to interpret the evidence on each of three key constituents in the accounting rule-making process: chapter 3 focuses on corporate managers, chapter 4 on auditors, and chapter 5 on the FASB members themselves. Chapter 6 brings to bear some international evidence, discussing the political process of accounting rule-making in two settings outside the United States. Chapter 7 broadens the scope from the creation of accounting rules to the creation of accounting rule-making bodies by analyzing the recent establishment of a separate U.S. accounting rule-maker for private (unlisted) companies. Chapter 8 consolidates the evidence from the preceding chapters to discuss their implications. It then inductively develops the notion of thin political markets. Chapter 9 begins an exploration of possible solutions to the problem of thin political markets, charting avenues for future scholarship and practice.

Chapter 2

Interpreting the evidence on the political process in accounting rule-making requires a conceptual basis of comparison. For example, I began this introduction by reasoning that extant accounting rules for acquired goodwill are likely to compromise corporate managerial accountability in M&A. Strictly speaking, making such an evaluation requires a theoretical benchmark of "optimal" accounting rules. Such a pure theory—which anticipates and predicts all business transactions, their interrelations, their context, and correspondingly their ideal methods of account—is impracticable. But decades of academic research in accounting has specified an economic theory of financial reporting from which the general parameters of a conceptual framework for accounting rules can be drawn. This economic conceptual framework, introduced in chapter 2, is used in the analysis of evidence in subsequent chapters.[15] Much of what I discuss in chapter 2 will be familiar to readers with a background in accounting scholarship.[16]

The essence of the economic conceptual framework in chapter 2 is as follows: Financial reporting is a mechanism facilitating contracting with and the flow of information from the firm. For example, current and prospective shareholders and creditors seek to monitor firm managers, measure managerial performance, and value their (potential) investments. Financial reporting facilitates these objectives. Of course, accounting is not the only information and contracting mechanism: for example, qualitative disclosure by managers to current and prospective shareholders is another such mechanism. Accounting's comparative advantages are (1) its relative verifiability—financial reports are audited—and its emphasis on conservative reporting to mitigate managers' incentives to overstate their achievements, (2) its technology to reconcile flows (profits) and stocks (assets) through double-entry bookkeeping, and (3) its technology to match multiperiod investments to corresponding revenues through capitalization, which can increase the relevance of earnings to decision making. The economic conceptual framework developed in chapter 2 is the set of accounting rules that are generally consistent with these properties.

An alternative to the conceptual framework above is the one specified by the FASB itself. Indeed, aspects of the FASB conceptual framework are also found in numerous academic studies as well. In the early 1980s, the FASB completed the development of a set of principles with which it expected its accounting rules to be consistent.[17] This original FASB framework is similar in many respects to the economic framework described above. However, the original FASB conceptual framework itself evolved over time, albeit more gradually than the FASB's accounting rules. By the 2000s, the FASB had produced a new conceptual framework that differs in some significant ways from both its old framework and the economic framework.[18] For example, the FASB's new framework de-emphasizes verifiability, conservatism, and matching, which are all important elements of the economic framework, while being more amenable to fair-value accounting.[19] Thus using the new FASB framework as the benchmark to interpret the evidence in this book could yield a substantially different analysis. I do not use the new FASB framework because, as I discuss in chapter 2, it is likely the result of the very political process in accounting that is the focus of this book; its use as a benchmark would constitute a logical circularity.

Chapter 3

Next, I turn to evidence on the role of corporate managers from both industrial and financial companies in the outcome of accounting rule-making. I do so through the case of accounting for goodwill acquired in M&A, which is the focus of chapter 3.[20] For several years prior to 1999, when the FASB decided to reevaluate M&A accounting rules, the SEC had expressed concerns about those rules. In particular, the SEC was concerned that some firms were abusing a particular M&A accounting method called "pooling of interests" in a way that led to overpayment for acquisitions and decreased M&A accountability. When the FASB first proposed a revision to the M&A accounting rules, it considered eliminating the pooling-of-interests method. Such elimination would result in all acquired goodwill being recognized on an acquiring firm's balance sheet and being expensed annually as amortization, a situation that could increase accountability for M&A. But this situation could also generate a substantial downward "drag" on the postacquisition earnings of firms hitherto using the pooling-of-interests method. Thus perhaps not surprisingly, the FASB proposal met with strident and often exaggerated opposition from such firms. For example, Cisco Systems, a frequent pooling-of-interests user, protested that the FASB proposal would "stifle technology development" and "slow job creation."[21] Soon, Congress got involved, mostly against the FASB proposal. Some members of the House introduced a bill to "impose a moratorium" on the elimination of pooling of interests, an uncommon and potentially dangerous move that inserted congressional politics into the highly technical world of accounting rules.[22]

During and immediately after the congressional intervention on this issue, a small group of corporate managers, which included those from Cisco, other technology firms involved in M&A, and investment banks, met with the FASB to propose an alternative. If the pooling-of-interests method were to be eliminated, they suggested that goodwill amortization be eliminated as well. Their suggestion was accepted for the most part, resulting in the M&A rules for goodwill impairment we see today. Chapter 3 presents this history with additional formal evidence of the special-interest politics underlying accounting rule-making. Specifically, the members of Congress who became involved in this issue can be linked in statistical tests, through a history of campaign contributions, to corporate interests that were opposed to the elimination of pooling of interests. Furthermore, these corporate interests can be linked to lobbying pressure on the FASB to adopt rules—including elimination of goodwill amortization—that eventually became the official M&A accounting standards.

Earlier, I discussed conceptually the consequences of the elimination of goodwill amortization: potentially decreased accountability in the multitrillion-dollar M&A industry. Chapter 3 augments this discussion with more formal evidence. Specifically, firms with strong indications of failed goodwill from M&A are shown to delay accounting for these losses for more than eight quarters. That is, the timeliness of accounting statements in providing accountability for M&A has declined in some cases by at least two years. Additional evidence suggests that average overpayment for acquisitions increased across the U.S. economy after the accounting rules for M&A were changed.[23]

The story of the evolution of goodwill accounting rules is an allegory for the successes of corporate managerial self-interest in accounting rule-making. But corporate managerial interests are mitigated, in theory, by auditors. So an examination of the role of auditors in the process is also necessary. Chapter 4 presents evidence on this matter.

Chapter 4

The auditing industry in the United States (and in many countries worldwide) is an oligopoly—that is, a few large audit firms are responsible for over 95 percent of the audits of listed companies in America. And while an oligopoly has persisted in auditing for the entire history of the FASB, the number of players has declined from eight in the 1970s to four today. The tightening audit oligopoly has been a source of concern in public policy circles, with elements of government, the press, and academia worrying that the existing "Big N" audit firms (where "N" refers to the extant number of large audit firms) are "too big" or "too few to fail."[24]

Chapter 4 discusses evidence on how the tightening oligopoly in auditing has shaped the accounting rule-making incentives of the Big N audit firms over the last four decades.[25] As the number of large audit firms has declined from eight to four, the remaining Big N firms have become more concerned about decreased "reliability" in accounting rules. "Reliability" here refers to a key property of accounting rules, which ensures that information is objectively verifiable and, thus, auditable. At first blush, this result could be consistent with increasing aggregate welfare. But additional analysis is necessary before drawing a conclusion: Why would the fewer remaining large audit firms become more concerned about decreased reliability?

Conceptually, auditors face dual incentives in their roles: (1) catering to clients' demands on the nature of accounting practices—after all, clients retain and pay the auditors—which is accomplished in ways that can decrease reliability, and (2) lowering the likelihood of litigation and regulatory penalties that arise from failing their responsibilities to certify client accounting practices, which is accomplished in large part through accounting reliability. As the number of large audit firms declines, the remaining firms can become increasingly secure in their position vis-à-vis regulators and the law—which is the concern inherent in the "too big to fail" argument—and, thus, more likely to cater to their clients' demands. If true, we would expect to see auditors less concerned about decreased reliability in accounting rules. Alternatively, if, as the number of large audit firms declines, they become more visible targets for political intervention and litigation, they are likely to be more concerned about decreased reliability in accounting rules. The empirical evidence is consistent with this latter explanation.

In other words, over the history of the operation of the FASB, as the number of large audit firms has declined from eight to four while their combined market share has remained largely intact, the auditors have focused their lobbying in accounting rule-making on opposition to decreased reliability in financial reporting. But this emphasis comes from motives to protect their own wealth from political and legal scrutiny. One likely consequence of this emphasis is the increasing incidence of accounting rules that are "check-the-box" or compliance based rather than based on the auditors exercising professional judgment—a phenomenon identified by the SEC as a major source of concern in U.S. capital markets.[26] Check-the-box rules not only lower the value-add of auditors in capital markets; they could decrease the overall accountability of the system unless accounting is somehow substituted by an alternative contracting and information mechanism.

Chapter 5

With both corporate managers and auditors promoting self-interests in accounting rule-making, focus falls on the members of the FASB itself. After all, as discussed earlier, the institutions and due process of the FASB were set up to increase the independence of accounting rule-makers. Chapter 5 discusses the results of an empirical examination of the accounting rule-making tendencies of every FASB member over its thirty-four-year history ending in 2006.[27] Several background characteristics of the FASB members, including their professional experience, their prior employment, and their political tendencies, were studied to see if these characteristics predicted the nature of accounting rules they proposed.

Across a battery of empirical tests, one result in particular stands out as statistically robust. Over time, particularly since the 1990s, the proportion of FASB members from the financial-services industry (defined as investment banking and investment management) has increased, and this increase is associated with accounting rules that deploy fair-value methodologies.

Fair-value accounting is the practice of measuring assets and liabilities at estimates of their current value in contrast to the centuries-old tradition of keeping books at historical cost. The argument for fair-value rules is that they increase the direct association between a firm's accounting numbers and its equity prices. Fair-value rules are consistent with the FASB's new conceptual framework. But fair-value rules can be less reliable than their historic-cost counterparts because they involve estimating conjectural profits. As such, in several circumstances, they are inconsistent with the economic framework for accounting and the FASB's original conceptual framework because they can de-emphasize the role of matching, conservatism, and verifiability in GAAP.

Fair-value accounting was blamed for some dubious practices in the period leading up to the Wall Street crash of 1929 and was essentially banned by the SEC from the 1930s through the 1970s.[28] But the use of fair values in accounting rules has increased over the last twenty years as the proportion of FASB members from the financial services industry has increased. In the early 2000s, fair-value rules were implicated in some of the accounting misdeeds at Enron that led to the firm's collapse.[29] There are numerous complex reasons for individuals from the financial-services industry to support fair-value accounting. Most notably, accounting profits defined on a fair-value basis rather than a historical-cost basis accelerate the recognition of expected gains, particularly in periods of rising asset prices. To the extent that managerial bonuses are based on such profit numbers, financial-services executives reap richer rewards under fair-value rules. In fact, this situation was an incentive for greater securitization of subprime loans by executives at several financial-services firms in the period leading up to the 2008 Financial Crisis.[30]

Thus the principal result in the study of the impact of FASB members on accounting rule-making is the role of members from the financial services industry in promoting accounting rules that can benefit the sector. The growth of financial-services representation on the FASB parallels the financialization of the U.S. economy, and the incentives of finance-sector employees are seen shaping accounting rules at the expense of reliability, a key comparative advantage of accounting.

Interestingly, the Big N auditors' increasing concern about decreased reliability in GAAP proposals (discussed in chapter 4) is not driven by the rising incidence of fair-value accounting. In fact, the auditors appear to support the rules proposed by FASB members from the financial-services industry. This latter result could be due to the fact that auditors' liability under fair-value accounting appears to be limited in some cases, due in part to their own successful lobbying on this matter.[31]

Also endorsing the rise of fair-value accounting are the academics who have served on the FASB. Despite an active debate on fair-value accounting in the academic literature,[32] all academics who have served on the FASB since the mid-1980s appear to be favorably disposed to fair-value rules. The evidence suggests that the selection of academics to the FASB could be conditioned on their pro-fair-value stance.

The narrative that emerges from the growth of fair-value accounting betrays a distinct form of capture that I call ideological capture.[33] While it appears that the rise of fair-value accounting was partly driven by the interests of the financial-services industry, this rise was also facilitated by large audit firms and select academics who provided necessary theoretical arguments for increased fair-value use in GAAP. In fact, the changes to the FASB's own conceptual framework that made it more agreeable with fair-value accounting (described in chapter 2) can be viewed in this light. The fundamental shift in accounting from its traditional historic-cost focus to a greater emphasis on fair values appears to be the result of a complex confederacy of interests and ideas, consistent with an ideology-enabled capture of the FASB on this issue.

Chapter 6

Thus far, I have focused on the institution of the FASB and evidence from the United States. But accounting rule-making, like most business activity, has been globalizing. In fact, one of the biggest developments in accounting over the last fifteen years has been the establishment and growth of the International Accounting Standards Board (IASB), the global equivalent to the FASB. Much has been said and written on this issue, which like all globalization efforts is multidimensional and complex.[34] In chapter 6, I focus on providing evidence for one simple point: the American experience with the FASB is not unique, and special-interest politics has a role in accounting rule-making worldwide.[35]

In 2006, the government of China was in negotiations with the IASB over the country's adoption of international accounting rules (known as IFRS, or International Financial Reporting Standards). A thorny issue arose: IFRS, like its U.S. equivalent, had strict rules on disclosure of transactions between "related parties" (such as firms with substantially overlapping ownership) in corporate financial reports. The notion of disclosing related-party transactions is elementary in and fundamental to accounting: the idea is that transactions between players who are not at arm's length are not reportable transactions at all. These related-party rules were undesirable to the Chinese government because they could call into question the reported profitability of numerous state-controlled enterprises that dominated its economy. State-controlled enterprises, by virtue of their common ownership heritage, qualified under the IASB rules as related parties and thus had to disclose numerous transactions in IFRS-compliant financial reports. Chapter 6 describes how the Chinese government was able to water down the definition of related parties in the worldwide accounting rules as a condition to its adoption of IFRS. The IASB obliged, perhaps because having China on board was a major victory in its goal of global accounting harmonization.

Where large firms from China were able to secure their interests in the global accounting game, large firms from India have had less luck. But even in this case, there is a role for politics in accounting. Chapter 6 additionally documents how a large Indian multinational, Tata Steel, which is part of the Tata Group, one of the country's largest and most respected conglomerates, was able to influence that country's accounting policy on IFRS adoption in a way that fostered its own interests. Specifically, certain IFRS rules for recording gains and losses due to currency fluctuations (when assets and liabilities are held in multiple jurisdictions) were set aside in India due, in part, to Tata Steel's lobbying that the rules needlessly hurt its income statement and balance sheet.

Chapter 7

Here I return to the United States to provide a final piece of evidence on the political market for accounting. The issue in this chapter is not simply the creation of an accounting rule that is in the interest of a particular set of corporate managers, auditors, or standard setters. Rather, it is the creation of an entirely new rule-maker itself. On May 23, 2012, the trustees of the FAF, the not-for-profit organization that oversees the FASB, approved the establishment of a new accounting rule-maker: the Private Company Council (PCC). The PCC is charged with producing U.S. GAAP accounting rules for private companies (i.e., companies not publicly listed on stock exchanges). Previously, private companies used the same accounting rules as public companies. These were the only "GAAP rules" for companies and were largely produced by the FASB under authority from the SEC, which has a congressional charter to this effect. Although there was no explicit mandate for private companies to use these GAAP rules, private companies did so in part due to GAAP's widespread familiarity. Why then was the PCC—an institution for separate private-company GAAP—created?

Chapter 7 aims to answer this question by exploring the economic and political forces behind the creation of the first major corporate-accounting rule-maker in the United States since the FASB was established in 1973.[36] Economically, there are few substantive reasons for separate private-company GAAP; while the nature and levels of financial *disclosure* across private companies and public companies could legitimately differ, the rules for *recognition* of transactions in these companies' financial statements should generally be the same. The lone dissenter—also the only research professor—on a special FAF panel to consider the creation of the PCC noted: "There has . . . been no compelling evidence or framework presented to the Panel to suggest that the objectives of financial reporting differ between private companies and public companies. The Panel has merely been presented with a list of standards that accountants associated with private companies do not find desirable."[37]

The economic arguments against separate private-company accounting notwithstanding, politically, there was a complex coalition behind the creation of the PCC. First, there were the private companies themselves, including large conglomerates such as Koch Industries and private-equity groups such as Bain Capital, who were concerned about the rising costs of complying with FASB rules, particularly since they were not legally obligated to do so. Then there were industry groups, such as the U.S. Chamber of Commerce, that raised philosophical objections to certain FASB rules around disclosure of corporate information; these rules were motivated by the SEC's charge of promoting "fairness" in capital markets particularly for small, retail shareholders. Finally, there was the AICPA, which was sometimes seen as representing the interests of small auditors over the Big Four. Small auditors had long complained about the dominance of the Big N in accounting rule-making.

The creation of the PCC went unnoticed by most Americans, although its existence can have a significant impact on their future. Rules from the PCC will define the measurement of corporate performance and accountability for private companies, which make up about one-half of U.S. GDP. As with the FASB, this rule-making process is likely to be highly technical and largely outside the public eye. Commercial self-interest is likely to have a defining say in PCC rules. It is too soon to tell whether the creation of separate private-company accounting rule-making will help or hurt aggregate welfare. Indeed, the presence of the PCC might offer competition of sorts to the FASB, potentially disciplining the rule-making process from excessive dominance by special-interest objectives. On the other hand, the political process of determining accounting rules is hardly one that receives much attention from the general public; if this process is further bifurcated into private and public company rule-making, relevant special-interest groups may enjoy more concentrated fiefs and thus even less opposition to their agendas. To date there is no robust statistical evidence of which I am aware on these questions, but the absence of strong conceptual arguments for creating the PCC does raise concerns about this venture.

Chapter 8

The implications of the various studies discussed in chapters 3–7 are explicitly and collectively explored in chapter 8.[38] Three themes in particular emerge as salient from the evidence discussed in this book. First, corporate accounting rule-making is largely determined by a few specialist individuals (mostly corporate executives, bankers, and auditors) who benefit from (1) strong experience-based expertise on the issues at hand, (2) strong economic interests in the outcome, and (3) little political opposition in the process, particularly from those representing the interests of individual savers and, more so, ordinary citizens (who might be employees, customers, or suppliers of corporations). In other words, corporate-accounting rule-making is a thin political market. Here, the term "political market" refers to the deliberative process through which a particular scarce resource—for example, the set of rules dictating how businesses should prepare their accounts—is allocated. The analog to a political market is a price-based market, where prices from voluntary exchanges rather than deliberative processes are used to allocate scarce resources.

Second, the outcome of this thin political market in accounting rules is, in more than one instance, skewed toward the interests of corporate managers, auditors, and bankers in ways that are likely to compromise accounting's role in corporate performance evaluation, corporate accountability, and investment allocation. Put differently, there is evidence of capture of the accounting rule-making process by special-interest groups, which could—if persistent in the long run—compromise the functioning and legitimacy of GAAP. Indeed, one major finding in the accounting literature over the past few years is the increasing volatility and declining persistence of GAAP earnings numbers,[39] to the effect that there is some evidence that these numbers are less useful in equity valuation than they were twenty years ago.[40] In a similar vein, there is evidence that GAAP balance sheet numbers have become less useful in debt covenants since the mid-1990s.[41] Eventually, capital misallocation and expropriation resulting from these trends could undermine the legitimacy of the market capitalist system as a whole.

Third, perhaps most importantly, the evidence does not point to systematic and sustained capture by any single special-interest group. That is, investment banks and corporations with strong M&A activity might shape accounting rule-making for M&A, auditors might structure certain accounting rules so that auditing tasks are more check-the-box than judgment based to mitigate their liability, the financial-services industry might propagate fair-value accounting rules that suit their business model, and private companies might seek their own exceptions to rules—but no one group has an absolute say over the entire process. There is no single extractive organization or institution to take down, no unequivocal villain in the story. The capture in accounting rule-making appears to be narrow and targeted toward the interests of those with the strongest economic incentives in each particular case.

There is an implication of this third theme that merits explicit recognition: the nature of thin political markets is such that the FASB is dependent on special interests, and the results suggest no one special interest dominates. My own read of this conclusion is a vindication of the *individuals* at the FASB, although not of the accounting rule-making model itself. There is no evidence in my reading upon which one can impugn or assault the integrity of FASB members and staff. The process is flawed and merits serious change but not for any systematic disingenuity of the rule-making bureaucracy. I make this assertion in part because I do not want the evidence and conclusions in this book to be misinterpreted, exaggerated, or misused to advance a political agenda. Indeed, it would be an unfortunate irony if this book became the vehicle for some special interest to steamroll self-serving institutional changes to an already vulnerable rule-making infrastructure.

Collectively, the three themes described above structure a special class of problem in the creation and maintenance of the esoteric market institutions that underlie capitalism. So what can we do about this problem?

On the one hand, there is some cause for optimism given that despite regulatory capture, some firms continue to differentiate themselves by adopting accounting practices that are consistent with economic principles (e.g., matching, verifiability, and conservatism). And, indeed, these firms are received more favorably by the market in some circumstances.[42] Moreover, there is also some emerging evidence that the political process itself is being used to unravel the costs of regulatory capture. In fact, the emergence of the PCC can be viewed as a response by certain groups disgruntled by the capture of public-company GAAP. But these solutions are ad hoc, limited, or glacial in pace, suggesting that real costs to the economy from capture persist. Thus there is still need for a more general solution.

Chapter 9

I conclude this book with the outline for a solution. But I caution that the solution is by no means intended to be authoritative or exhaustive. Rather, it is presented as a starting point for a conversation about what constitutes appropriate managerial engagement in thin political markets.

At the outset, it is important to reiterate that the nature of thin political markets is such that the expertise necessary for appropriate rule-making or regulation lies with corporate interests broadly defined (in the case of accounting rules, "corporate interests" includes auditors and bankers). The notion of a sophisticated independent regulator who can parse out the bias in lobbying information supplied by corporate interests is infeasible because such a regulator will not have access to the necessary field experience to do so. A sophisticated regulator with such field experience is unlikely to be independent of corporate interests, as the empirical evidence on FASB members' background characteristics demonstrates (see chapter 5). A similar argument applies to any imagined independent third-party expert (e.g., an academic): such "independence" will likely betray a lack of relevant experience. At best, independent analyses can shed light on the likelihood of capture, but even such studies (e.g., the analysis in this book) are ex post facto and based on a postulated conceptual benchmark.

For those who are convinced by the evidence of what the status quo in thin political markets has wrought, the temptation is strong to institutionalize a solution, perhaps by creating new laws to effect and enforce managerial agency of the system or by creating yet another regulatory body in the hopes that it will somehow be independent of special interests.[43] But such institutionalization is realistically a secondary step. Recall that the FASB itself already represents an institutional arrangement that is quite advanced (in theory) in terms of mitigating conflicts of interests: its members serve full time upon resigning prior commitments, they are generously compensated and well supported by a professional research staff, and they are by and large free from concerns about their agency's financial health (due to the FASB's independent funding structure). Here I argue that meaningful proposals to address the problem of thin political markets must begin with changing the managerial mind-set around what is the appropriate limit to profit-seeking behavior in this context. Any first-order solution to the problem of thin political markets has to focus on modifying corporate managers' approach to lobbying.

A skeptical reader might guffaw at this point and assert that it is naïve to imagine a solution that relies on managers "doing the right thing" when it comes to lobbying. Acknowledging this reality, a substantial part of chapter 9 is devoted to considering how such a solution might be practicable. Because if it is not, the legitimacy of market capitalism can be negatively impacted.

I conclude the book with some promising examples of efforts to reframe managerial norms around lobbying in thin political markets. Of particular note is the effort of a small group of business leaders who are innovating in the thin political markets of bank governance standards and pharmaceutical drug approval standards with ways to create "ethical spaces" for managers to engage with their regulators. The idea is to set the tone for what is an appropriate "ask" when lobbying, so as to at least narrow the limit of self-interested regulation that might emerge. Of course, real progress on this front is accomplished when all parties collectively agree that certain areas—those pertaining to the design of the rules of the game—are not domains over which firms should seek to be opportunistic, for example, by erecting competitive barriers. I stress that these emerging innovations are works in progress, with several attendant limitations, but the ventures offer a pivot for serious and sustainable solutions to the problem of capture in thin political markets.

The Benchmark: What Should GAAP Look Like?

Accounting rules are largely determined through a political process. In itself, this is not a cause for concern, particularly if the process yields outcomes that enable the functioning of the market-capitalist system in which accounting is a critical constituent element. To assess the outcomes of the political process in accounting, one requires a basis for comparison. Ideally, such a basis would be drawn from an all-encompassing theory of accounting—one that yields the comprehensive set of accounting rules that optimize the functioning of the market-capitalist system. Then observed outcomes from the political process could be benchmarked to determine if, how, and to what extent those outcomes differed from the desired optimum.

The ideal benchmark—the ideal theory of accounting—would understand every aspect of accounting's impact in a market system: from its role in communicating the most basic economic information, to its role in facilitating the most complex of financial contracts, and everything in between, including enabling opportunity seeking and value creation and mitigating collusion, monopoly, theft, and laziness. And it would do this anticipating all future business transactions that might arise from new technologies and new organizational forms, while also taking into account potential changes in the contexts for business, such as changes in laws or the functioning and interpretations of courts. Such an ideal theory is out of reach given the practical limitations of human understanding. And were it attainable, it would, in the long run, likely obviate the need for any accounting rule-making process, since the theory itself would offer a set of accounting rules close to, if not actually, the optimum.

With the ideal benchmark out of practical reach, I adopt the existing economic theory of financial reporting as a surrogate.[1] The theory is based on an interpretation of the accumulated works of numerous scholars in accounting and related fields, such as economics and finance, based at various American universities, including the University of Chicago, Harvard University, Massachusetts Institute of Technology, the University of Michigan, the University of Pennsylvania, the University of Rochester, and Stanford University. The theory is imperfect in that it does not anticipate all possible uses of accounting, all potential future business transactions, and all conceivable changes to the business context. Furthermore, aspects of the theory have been debated and questioned by several prominent academics, including those from some of the universities above (in fact, such academic criticisms have been used to support the growth of fair-value accounting, as I argue in chapter 5). That said, the theory reflects a scholarly understanding of the role of accounting in the market system, particularly as understood through an economics-based analysis. It is analytically rigorous and has been subject to decades of empirical testing, where it is found to explain several key accounting practices—such as the traditional historic-cost rules on revenue recognition and expenditure capitalization—that evolved in an unregulated context and that have, in some cases, persisted for over a century. In this sense, the theory is "second best."

From the theory, I develop the general parameters of a conceptual framework for accounting rules. This economics-based conceptual framework is used in interpreting the evidence on outcomes of the accounting rule-making process presented in subsequent chapters. The economic conceptual framework is particularly useful in evaluating the political process that yields fair-value accounting methods at the expense of traditional historic-cost methods—a key development in U.S. GAAP over the past several decades.

The core of what I present in this chapter will be familiar to those within accounting academe and accordingly can be skimmed. For nonacademic readers and readers from outside accounting, I have sought to avoid technical jargon and present the conceptual framework in a logical, self-contained manner.

Toward the end of this chapter, I consider an alternative conceptual framework for accounting rules: the one provided by the FASB itself. The FASB conceptual framework is a constitution of sorts "to set forth fundamentals on which financial accounting and reporting standards" should be based.[2] FASB members are expected to be guided and limited in their rule-making activities by this conceptual framework. I discuss the similarities and differences between the two conceptual frameworks—the economic framework and the FASB framework—and their implications for financial reporting. I discuss how the FASB's *original* conceptual framework, issued in 1980, is broadly similar to the economic framework presented here. I also discuss why the FASB's *current* conceptual framework, as it evolved and was reissued in the 2000s, differs from the economic framework in important ways and why it is unsuitable for use as a benchmark to evaluate the evidence presented in this book.

The Economic Framework for Accounting Rule-Making

The economic theory of financial reporting views accounting practices and principles as having emerged organically to meet the demands of various firm stakeholders. The stakeholders include shareholders, bondholders, suppliers, customers, employees, regulators, and politicians.[3] All these stakeholders demand financial information in connection with conducting their business with the firm. But financial information is produced by managers who might act in their own interests or—as agents of shareholders—in the shareholders' interests.[4] Moreover, financial information requires incorporating some expectation of the future, which is inherently uncertain.[5] Thus the procedures under which financial information is supplied in equilibrium reflect both the information asymmetry between managers and stakeholders and the shared uncertainty about the future.

For expositional purposes, I begin by considering shareholders as the only source of demand for financial information. Later, I discuss how the properties of accounting derived under this assumption can be generalized to a more realistic setting that includes other stakeholders such as bondholders, suppliers, and regulators.

The cornerstone of the economic theory of financial reporting is the separation of management and ownership, which is a common feature of the modern corporation.[6] Shareholders delegate the operation of the firm to managers, because the former have better uses for their time or because the latter are better skilled. Given this delegation of decision rights to managers, shareholders require information from managers about the firm's prospects. To supply this information, managers must make some estimates about the future. This is in essence the purpose of accruals. Given managers' understandings of the firm and its competitive environment, they are well placed to make the estimates that underlie accruals. Indeed, accruals are informative because they incorporate such management estimates. In the parlance of the economic theory of accounting, accruals are informative because they are "relevant" to shareholders and other financial statement users. "Relevance" is thus a key economic property of accounting. The alternative to accruals is simply reporting the cash flows and cash position of the firm, which is also available to constituents of publicly listed companies. But despite such cash-basis information, investors continue to demand accrual information because it is relevant to their investment decision making: accruals contain valuable insights into the firm's future that are not available in cash flows.[7] They provide shareholders with managers' insights into the uncertainty faced by the firm.

To summarize, in the context of the delegation of firm decision making from shareholders to managers, shareholders demand information about the firm's prospects, and this information necessarily incorporates managers' estimates about the future. The emergence and continued existence of the two major accrual-based financial statements—the balance sheet and the income statement—can be seen as meeting this information demand. The balance sheet and income statement provide information about the firm's prospects and enable shareholders to evaluate the quality of their investments in the firm.

Also in the context of the delegation of decision making from shareholders to managers, shareholders have two additional concerns. The first concern is that some managers might become overly aggressive with the resources (assets) under their control and take excessive risks. This is because managers are operating with others' capital, and their own liability for loss is limited, except generally in cases of breach of fiduciary duties.[8] To mitigate this concern, shareholders need periodic measures of the stock of resources under the managers' control. Such measures help shareholders keep tab on their assets and mitigate excessive risk taking on the part of managers.[9] The balance sheet is seen as addressing (in part) the demand for such periodic stock reporting.

The second concern is that some managers might underperform in their roles—that is, exert insufficient effort. This is because, absent performance-based incentives, the benefits of such effort will not accrue to managers.[10] To mitigate this concern, shareholders need periodic measures of firm (i.e., managerial) performance. Periodic performance reports help shareholders evaluate managerial effort and the outcomes of such effort. Moreover, incenting and rewarding managers on performance reports can mitigate concerns that managers will shirk on their responsibilities.[11] The income statement is seen as addressing (in part) the demand for such periodic flow reporting.

The discussion thus far suggests that the balance sheet and the income statement can be seen as satisfying shareholders' demand for information from managers about the firm's prospects while also mitigating shareholders' concerns about potential managerial expropriation (ranging from over-aggressive risk taking to shirking). The properties of accruals in the balance sheet and income statement are likely to reflect these various demands. This is the central insight of the economic theory of accounting, and I build on this insight below.

Consider first the income statement. The primary challenge to measuring performance in the income statement is the disconnect between the investment horizon and the accountability horizon. Put differently, income-statement performance is generally assessed yearly, whereas investments can require several years to materialize. The technology in accounting to resolve this disconnect is the "matching principle." The idea behind matching is to archive (or "capitalize") on the balance sheet expenditures that are expected to yield benefits ("revenues") beyond the current year; the archived expenditures are then drawn into the income statement as the benefits accrue. Thus expenditures are "matched" to revenues, creating a more meaningful measure of performance. Matching is fundamental to achieving "relevance" for the income statement and is, as such, an important part of the economic theory of financial reporting.[12]

Just as relevance is a desirable property of the income statement, so too is it desired of the balance sheet. Absent any concerns about managerial misreporting or misvaluation, a "relevant" balance sheet is one that provides shareholders with managers' current estimates of the firm's assets and liabilities. But such concerns are real, so as a practical matter, a relevant balance sheet cannot always incorporate managers' current estimates of asset and liability values—a point on which I will expand later.

Double-entry bookkeeping reconciles the flow reporting in the income statement to the stock reporting of the balance sheet. This reconciliation process ensures that expenditures that are deferred to the future (by capitalizing them on the balance sheet) eventually pass through the income statement and thus are considered in the primary performance evaluation metric: earnings. (Again, as a practical matter, there are certain limited exceptions to this pass-through rule.[13]) Analogously, earnings—the flow metric of performance— are aggregated over time and archived as a stock on the balance sheet as "retained earnings," a resource for managers to steward until the earnings are paid out as dividends to shareholders.

Any information supplied by managers to shareholders, including the accrual information in the income statement and balance sheet, is still colored by the concern that managers have the information advantage and can use such advantage to their benefit.[14] An additional related concern in this context is managers' proclivity to emphasize good news and de-emphasize or delay bad news.[15] This is particularly likely in contexts where managers are being evaluated, such as in reports of their financial performance (i.e., the income statement).[16] There is considerable empirical evidence consistent with these concerns—in fact, a large proportion of empirical accounting research over the past thirty years has found evidence consistent with these concerns. Thus financial reporting practices that evolve in an economic equilibrium are expected to incorporate procedures to mitigate managers' proclivity to (1) use their information advantage to their benefit and (2) emphasize good news over bad news. These are additional key premises (beyond "relevance") of the economic theory of financial reporting.

The primary procedures observed in accounting practice that address the two concerns discussed above are the conditions that accruals be "verifiable" and "conservative." Verifiability, in the legal sense, means that the estimates can be "objectively determined to be true or false."[17] In reality, some accrual estimates are more objectively determinable than others (e.g., accrual estimates relating to inventory are usually more objective than those pertaining to intangibles). Verifiability, in a practical sense, lowers the subjectivity in accruals and thus the likelihood that accruals will be misused by managers. Even absent the intent to misuse, verifiability can improve the quality of accruals by subjecting management estimates about the future to a test for objectivity. In this sense, verifiability mitigates the likelihood that accruals are skewed by unrealistic (even if unbiased) management estimates. Verifiability is accomplished in large part by having an independent evaluator issue an opinion on financial reports, which is what the auditing profession originally evolved to do.[18] Although auditing is currently mandated of publicly listed companies and the nature of auditing has changed over the course of its regulation (more on this point in chapter 4), auditing emerged absent regulation, suggesting verifiability through auditing is the result of an economic equilibrium rather than a political process.[19]

"Conservatism" is the condition that imposes a higher standard for recognizing good news, relative to bad news, in financial statements. Put differently, conservative accounting procedures accelerate the recognition of bad news into accounting estimates, whereas the recognition of good news is delayed until it is verifiable.[20] An example of conservative accounting practice is the allowance created in banks' financial statements for expected loan losses. This allowance may not be verifiable to the degree necessary for recognition of good news events, but it is recognized nonetheless because doing so is conservative.

The conditions that estimates in financial reporting be verifiable and conservative enhance the credibility of management-supplied accrual information by mitigating the likelihood that the information is biased and that bad news is being delayed. Thus verifiability and conservatism—together with relevance, particularly as effected via matching—are central features of equilibrium accounting rules, as predicted by the economic theory of financial reporting. These basic properties of accounting can be used to explain long-standing historic-cost accounting procedures such as those that govern when revenue and its corresponding expenditures are to be recognized in the income statement and, relatedly, when expenditures can be capitalized on the balance sheet as assets.

Consider the traditional revenue-recognition rule, which states that revenue is to be recognized when it is "earned and realizable." The "earned" criterion in this rule ensures that performance is not recognized until the underlying managerial effort necessary to generate that performance has been exerted. (Managerial "effort" is used here in a broad sense. Some of the activities that may be necessary to satisfy the "earned" criterion, for example, ensuring the delivery of a product, do not necessarily involve managers breaking a sweat.) This requirement, consistent with the verifiability principle, mitigates the likelihood of moral hazard from rewarding managers before they do what is expected of them.[21]

Similarly, the "realizable" criterion in the revenue-recognition rule ensures that performance is not recognized until verifiable outcomes materialize. "Realizable" means cash or a claim to cash must be received from an arm's-length transaction before revenue is recognized. Since managerial effort itself is sometimes unobservable and the consequences of such effort are uncertain, the "realizable" rule errs toward the principle of verifiability by requiring that the firm enjoy at least some legal claim to cash before recognizing performance. At the same time, the standard is not that cash itself be received before revenue is recognized. Such a standard would be overly burdensome and would potentially compromise accounting relevance.

In cases where cash or claims to cash are realized in advance of effort being exerted (such as with prepayments on a cell phone service contract), the application of the verifiability principle results in the cash or its equivalents being archived as a "liability" until effort is exerted and verified. This latter treatment is also consistent with the principle of conservatism in that it implies a higher standard for recognizing as revenue the "good news" of cash received. Thus the principles of verifiability, conservatism, and relevance can explain the nature of traditional rules on revenue recognition.

Analogously, consider the traditional rules that govern the recognition of expenditures in the income statement. The general idea behind the matching principle is to capitalize expenditures expected to generate future revenues on the balance sheet until those revenues are recognized. Such matching makes the income statement more relevant. The matching is generally done either at the product level (e.g., with inventories, where the expenditures on inventories are recognized on the income statement as those inventories are sold) or on a periodic basis (e.g., with the depreciation of plant, where expenditures are recognized over the time frame when corresponding benefits are expected to accrue). However, here too, the application of the key countervailing principles, such as verifiability and conservatism, govern. In cases where revenues are highly uncertain, such as with expenditures on basic research, the expenditures are immediately recognized in the income statement as an application of the verifiability and conservatism principles (the associated revenues are unverifiable, so traditional historic-cost rules are conservative about recognizing the expenditures).[22] And in cases where the revenues associated with previously capitalized expenditures are no longer expected to accrue ("bad news"), the expenditures are written off immediately in the income statement, again as an application of the conservatism principle.[23]

The traditional rules that govern the definition of an asset on the balance sheet mirror the rules that govern the recognition of expenditures on the income statement. Again, the application of verifiability and conservatism, together with the desire for relevance, primarily explain the asset-recognition rules. Under traditional historic-cost accounting, expenditures are recognized as assets when they are associated with "probable future economic benefits" that are "obtained or controlled" from a "past transaction or event." These rules, as discussed below, seek to ensure that items recognized as "assets" actually do satisfy the economic demands for a balance sheet.

The balance sheet is expected to produce periodic measures of the stock of resources under managerial control to help shareholders both keep tab of their investments and mitigate excessive risk taking by managers. As noted earlier, absent any concerns about managers' misvaluing assets or misusing their information advantage over shareholders to their benefit, managers' current-value estimates of the firm's assets would provide "relevant" information. But given that such concerns are reasonable, assets on the balance sheet must additionally be verifiable and conservative. Absent verifiability and conservatism in asset recognition rules, managers' incentives to circumvent shareholder control could lead them to overstate assets and mislead shareholders on the status of their investments.[24]

The requirement that assets represent "probable"—as opposed to "possible"—future economic benefits is consistent with the higher standard of objectivity required by the verifiability principle. Moreover, a decline in the likelihood of realizing the "future economic benefits" that an already recognized asset represents generally precipitates a write-off, consistent with the conservatism principle. And as another manifestation of conservatism, assets previously written off are not usually written up again, even in the presence of objective information suggesting the assets have increased in value. Similarly, the requirement that assets be "obtained or controlled"—that is, have a legal basis—facilitates objective auditing. As does the requirement that assets result from "past transactions or events" (this requirement also mitigates the moral hazard that can arise from recognizing future management effort in attempts to monitor managers).

✶

Thus far, I have focused on the simplified case of demand for financial information arising out of the delegation of firm decision-making responsibilities by shareholders to managers. The key takeaway from the preceding discussion is the centrality of relevance (particularly earnings relevance through the matching principle), verifiability, and conservatism in explaining longstanding accounting practices that govern the recognition of accruals.

The inclusion of other stakeholders such as bondholders, suppliers, and regulators is likely to increase the demand for verifiability and conservatism, without substantially diminishing the demand for relevance and matching. This is because, like shareholders, these stakeholders expect the firm (i.e., managers) to meet certain implicit or explicit contractual obligations to them (e.g., meeting interest payments and repaying principal in the case of bondholders). To monitor the firm in this context, these stakeholders, like shareholders, seek information on the performance of the firm and on the stock of the firm's assets. And like shareholders, while they seek information from managers on the firm's prospects, they worry about managers' incentives to opportunistically shape such information.[25] Moreover, in addition to *managers'* incentives to manipulate financial reports, these stakeholders have to be concerned about similar incentives among *shareholders,* to whom managers are fiduciaries.[26] Indeed, it is this latter observation that predicts an increase in the equilibrium supply of verifiability and conservatism in financial reports in a setting that includes other stakeholders beyond shareholders.[27]

Thus relevance, verifiability and conservatism are key properties of accounting under the economic theory of financial reporting. Put differently, financial reports that meet the economic demands of stakeholders are likely to be shaped by these principles. The particular emphasis on verifiability and conservatism is not to diminish the role for management discretion or judgment in the accrual process. Indeed, it is because of such discretion that verifiability and conservatism in accruals are warranted. Thus the optimal accounting system, from an economic perspective, is one that affords managers the discretion necessary to provide relevant metrics of firms' financial performance and position (through income statements and balance sheets) while ensuring that such discretion is subject to the principles of verifiability and conservatism. This conclusion is the basis of the conceptual framework for financial reporting that I use in subsequent chapters to evaluate the outcomes of the political process in accounting. In particular, I do not expect accounting outcomes that are inconsistent with verifiability and conservatism to be economically efficient; the evidence in subsequent chapters explores whether such outcomes are instead the result of special-interest politics.

I close this section by noting that the economic theory of financial reporting does not presuppose audited financial statements as the only source of information from the firm (i.e., managers) to stakeholders. Indeed, alternative sources of information, such as additional qualitative disclosures by management, are important complements to the income statement and balance sheet.[28] That is, in addition to quantitative accrual-based measures of current managerial performance and of the stock of resources under management control, shareholders need qualitative information (e.g., information about upcoming investments or sales contracts) to evaluate their continued investment in the firm.[29] Such information is neither auditable nor conservative. Thus such information is usually supplied outside of the financial statements. To be sure, the income statement and the balance sheet complement such additional disclosures by providing objective ex post facto confirmation of these projections.[30] In this sense, matching, verifiability, and conservatism likely survive in financial reporting partly because they complement and are complemented by alternative channels for information transfer, such as qualitative disclosure.

The FASB's Conceptual Framework

A potential alternative to the conceptual framework from economic theory presented above is the FASB's own conceptual framework for financial reporting. This framework is the basis for much of the FASB's rule-making activities, although in specific instances final rules can deviate from the framework. The FASB conceptual framework was developed early in the history of that organization to serve as a guide for the FASB board and staff. In principle, this conceptual framework would limit the set of possible accounting treatments for a given transaction by specifying some broad, generalizable principles and properties of accounting rules. As such, if applied consistently and faithfully, the FASB conceptual framework could serve to limit the scope of special-interest lobbying in accounting rule-making because exceptions driven by political forces would likely be apparent violations of the conceptual framework. The FASB's conceptual framework is well known—

particularly among accountants, auditors, and financial executives—and is certainly germane to accounting practice. This raises the question: Why not use the FASB's conceptual framework as the basis to evaluate the outcomes of the political process in accounting?

In this section, I briefly describe the FASB's conceptual framework in its current manifestation and as it was originally formulated, discussing both versions' similarities to and differences from the economic framework presented above. I then explain why the FASB framework, as it currently exists, is unsuitable for use as a basis to evaluate the political process underlying GAAP that is described in this book.

Unlike the economic framework, which views financial reporting practices as having emerged to meet the needs of various stakeholders who demand financial information from the firm, the FASB's current conceptual framework views existing and potential shareholders as the primary users of financial information.[31] Creditors are also considered users under the FASB framework, although the degree of the FASB's emphasis on structuring financial information as a direct measure of equity valuation (discussed below) suggests a lesser emphasis on the needs of creditors.[32] The FASB framework does not explicitly consider other stakeholders. The emphasis on current and potential shareholders and on creditors is driven by the assumption that these groups "have the most critical and immediate need for the information in financial reports."[33]

The FASB conceptual framework, as it stands today, is perhaps most significantly characterized by a standard known as CON 8 (although another standard known as CON 7, which introduces techniques for fair-value measurement, is also an important part of the FASB's current conceptual framework). CON 8 discusses two "fundamental" characteristics of financial information: relevance and faithful representation. Relevance refers to the property that financial information has either predictive value, confirmatory value, or both. Predictive value means that the information is itself a forecast or it can be used by stakeholders to generate forecasts. Confirmatory value means that the information provides confirmation of prior forecasts. In addition, "relevant" information is expected to be "material," in that its omission or misstatement would change the decision of stakeholders.[34] The notion of relevance in the FASB framework is similar to that in the economic framework along some dimensions, but important differences also exist. In particular, as discussed later, the matching principle, which is core to achieving earnings relevance in the economic framework, is de-emphasized to advance fair-value accounting in the FASB framework.

Faithful representation in the FASB framework means that the financial information is complete, neutral, and free from error. In requiring information to be "complete," the FASB framework suggests that any supporting explanation necessary to interpret an accounting estimate must also be provided in financial reports (e.g., relevant facts about the quality of an estimate, including critical assumptions). The requirement that financial information be "neutral" asserts that it should be free from bias—that is, there should be no emphasis or slant to the information, even if to increase credibility, as with conservatism. Finally, the FASB framework asserts that to the extent possible, financial information should be error free.[35]

Beyond the two fundamental characteristics—relevance and faithful representation—the FASB conceptual framework also encourages as enhancing characteristics the comparability, understandability, timeliness, and verifiability of financial information. Comparability suggests that the information presented be suitable for comparison across similar or different items (such comparisons are a key element of financial analysis). Understandability suggests that the financial information is accessible to a user with a "reasonable knowledge of business and economic activities." The timeliness property asserts the importance of avoiding delay in presenting relevant financial information.[36]

"Verifiability" in the FASB framework has parallels to the concept from the economic framework. It suggests that financial estimates should be such that "knowledgeable and independent observers" could reach a consensus—although not complete agreement—on those estimates. Verifiability is to be ensured through direct observation or through indirect means such as by "checking the inputs to a model, formula, or other technique." Importantly, the FASB framework recognizes that some "relevant" information may be unverifiable. This is noteworthy because relevance, as a "fundamental" characteristic, appears to take precedence over verifiability (an "enhancing" characteristic) in the FASB framework.[37]

As is evident from the description above, the FASB conceptual framework is similar in some respects to the economic framework of financial reporting; however, there are also important differences between the two. Several characteristics of financial information from the FASB framework—in particular, completeness, freedom from error, comparability, understandability, and timeliness—are consistent with properties desirable from an economic view of financial reporting. Other characteristics—notably, the emphasis of relevance over verifiability, particularly as these concepts apply to good news events, and of neutrality over conservatism—contradict the economic framework in important ways.

The FASB framework affords preeminence to relevance over verifiability even in cases of good news events,[38] which is in direct contrast to the equilibrium properties of financial reporting expected under economic theory. This distinction has the effect that certain prospective financial information with speculative value (e.g., fair-value estimates of a thinly traded asset) that can be incorporated in financial reports under the FASB framework would not be incorporated in financial reporting that emerges in an economic equilibrium because such information cannot be objectively certified.[39]

Moreover, relevance, particularly earnings relevance, in the economic framework is achieved in large part through the matching principle, which, as seen from the discussion in the previous section, is closely linked to verifiability and conservatism. In contrast, the FASB framework has de-emphasized the role of matching in favor of fair-value accounting.[40] Fair values can be consistent with the economic framework, provided the fair-value estimates are obtained from active, liquid markets and are thus verifiable. (In GAAP parlance, these are usually included in a category known as "Level 1" fair values.) In the FASB framework, however, the emphasis on relevance over verifiability and the de-emphasis on matching permits the use of fair-value accounting even if the fair values are generated absent liquid markets. (In GAAP parlance, these are usually known as Level 2 and Level 3 fair values.)

A similar contrast between the FASB's current framework and the economic framework exists over the former's emphasis on neutrality above conservatism.[41] In the economic view of financial reporting, stakeholders protect themselves from managers' proclivity to emphasize good news over bad news by insisting on a higher verifiability standard for good news. In effect, this results in an accelerated recognition of expected bad news and a downward bias on financial information. Such conservatism is explicitly rejected by the FASB's current conceptual framework because, in the words of CON 8, it "would be inconsistent with" the adopted goal of "neutrality."[42]

These differences between the FASB's current framework and the economic framework are particularly salient to fair-value accounting, as already alluded to above. Fair value accounting, which is one of the major developments in U.S. GAAP over the past two decades, is the practice of measuring assets and liabilities at estimates of their current value in contrast to the traditional practice of keeping books at historical cost. Fair-value rules can increase the direct association between accounting metrics and current equity values. They are consistent with the FASB framework's emphasis on a brand of "relevance" that excludes matching and de-emphasizes verifiability and conservatism.[43]

When fair-value estimates can be objectively verified, such as in cases where the underlying assets and liabilities are actively traded, their use can be expected under the economic framework for financial reporting. Fair-value estimates can also be expected under the economic framework when used to calculate certain asset write-downs following bad news, even if such estimates cannot always be objectively certified, because the write-downs are conservative.[44] In most other cases, fair-value rules are unlikely to be sustainable in an economic equilibrium because they are susceptible to misuse by managers. Thus the choice of the economic framework or the FASB framework as the benchmark to evaluate outcomes of the political process in accounting rule-making can yield very different inferences, particularly given the proliferation of fair-value rules in U.S. GAAP. Below I explain why I do not use the FASB's current framework as the benchmark in this book.

✶

At its core, the differences between the FASB's current framework and the economic framework can be traced to their differential emphasis on the concern that managers can misuse their information advantage to their benefit. In the economic framework, as noted earlier, this concern is a prime determinant of accrual properties. In the FASB's current framework, this concern is seemingly less central. The wealth of empirical evidence on managers' use of accounting choice suggests that the concern over managerial misuse is well founded.[45] This is not to suggest that accrual discretion is entirely or even substantially abused but that concerns about its potential for misuse bear out in the data. Thus a framework that incorporates the notion that accounting properties should attempt to address potential management misuse of discretion seems better suited to the practical reality. Beyond this pragmatic reason to use the economic framework over the FASB's current framework as the benchmark in this book, there is also a conceptual reason to do so: using the FASB's current framework as the benchmark would constitute a logical circularity, as I will describe next.

The FASB's current conceptual framework, as represented by CON 8, emerged in the 2000s after nearly two decades of a shifting emphasis toward fair-value accounting (this process is described further in chapter 5). CON 8 replaced the FASB's original conceptual framework (substantively described in a document known as CON 2) that appeared in 1980, about seven years after the FASB first started issuing accounting rules.[46] CON 2 differed in several important ways from CON 8.

Most notably, "reliability" was one of the two "fundamental" characteristics of financial information, together with relevance.[47] In fact, relevance and reliability were regarded as two key potentially countervailing properties shaping financial reporting properties, with reliability serving as a check against an excessive thrust toward "relevant" financial information.[48] "Faithful representation" was an element of reliability in CON 2 but so too was "verifiability."[49] Thus verifiability, which is currently considered secondary to relevance in the FASB conceptual framework, was regarded as a coequal prime property of financial information. Moreover, in contrast to the current FASB conceptual framework, CON 2 also recognized "a place for a convention such as conservatism," although it disapproved of the bias inherent in conservatism.[50] Finally, although CON 2 did not directly discuss the matching principle, documents associated with CON 2 and part of the FASB's original conceptual framework did consider matching as contributing to the relevance of earnings.[51]

In all these regards, the FASB's original conceptual framework was not very different from the economic framework for financial reporting, perhaps the most interesting difference being its tolerance—but not endorsement—of conservatism. In fact, for many practical purposes CON 2 and the economic framework could be considered equivalent.

Over time, as the prevalence of fair-value accounting rules in U.S. GAAP grew, the distance between the ideals espoused in CON 2 and actual GAAP standards also grew, particularly making the "reliability" principle in CON 2 seem inconsistent with the direction in which the political economy was driving GAAP.[52] In fact, an empirical study of the evolution of the FASB's own ideology over thirty-five years beginning 1973 finds that over time, particularly since the 1990s, FASB members, through their emphasis on fair-value accounting, grew distant from their own original conceptual framework.[53] In 2000, the FASB introduced its first new conceptual framework document in about fifteen years, CON 7, partly with the objective to introduce fair-value accounting to its conceptual lexicon. In justifying the need for CON 7, the FASB noted that in "recent years, the Board [had] identified fair value as the objective for most measurements at initial recognition" but that its original conceptual framework did "not use the term fair value."[54]

Then in 2002, the FASB and the still nascent International Accounting Standards Board (IASB) signed a memorandum of understanding to harmonize their rules to facilitate eventual U.S. adoption of International Financial Reporting Standards (IFRS).[55] Although conceived as an international body, the IASB was at its founding substantially influenced on conceptual matters by accounting developments in the United States, including on the use of fair values.[56] Fair-value accounting was thus a key component of IFRS from the very start, creating added pressure on the FASB particularly over the principle of "reliability" in CON 2. A 2006 article by an IASB board member stated, "In almost every standard-setting project of the FASB and IASB, the boards consider fair value as a possible measurement attribute."[57]

By 2005, FASB board members and professional staff were explicitly recognizing the tension between fair-value accounting and "reliability" in public documents.[58] Around that time, the FASB initiated a project to again revise its conceptual framework.[59] The revision, CON 8 (described above), was implemented in 2010. In explaining its "basis for conclusions" in CON 8, the FASB stated that the term "reliability" in its original conceptual statement was being interpreted in practice in two competing ways. The first view (consistent with the economic framework for financial reporting) "focused on verifiability." The second view "focused more on faithful representation." Tellingly, the FASB rejected the first view and decided to embrace the second—rejecting its original position that "reliability" meant "verifiability." The FASB went on to state "prudence (conservatism), and verifiability, which were aspects of reliability in [CON 2], are not considered aspects of faithful representation [in CON 8]." Thus CON 8 brought the FASB's conceptual framework in line with the growth of fair-value accounting: it eliminated verifiability as a "fundamental" characteristic of financial information and explicitly eschewed conservatism.[60]

To be sure, elements of the FASB's new conceptual framework in CON 8 have appeared in U.S. GAAP as far back as the 1970s. For example, the FASB demonstrated its belief in the primacy of the balance sheet over the income statement—which is implicit in the fair-value approach to accounting—in some of its earliest standards.[61] But these commitments notwithstanding, the FASB did not reveal any bias toward fair-value accounting in its original conceptual framework. The first significant commitment to fair-value accounting in the conceptual framework came with the issuing of CON 7 in 2000, after nearly a decade of substantial growth in fair-value-based standards.

As seen from the description of events above, the FASB conceptual framework is itself shifting: it has evolved over time to reflect the growth of fair-value accounting in U.S. GAAP. The very political process that has precipitated the growth of fair-value accounting could thus also be responsible for the evolution of the FASB conceptual framework (more on this point in chapter 5). This observation suggests that the FASB framework is unsuitable for use as a benchmark in evaluating outcomes of accounting's political process, particularly over long periods. The use of the FASB conceptual framework in such an evaluation would constitute a logical circularity.

The economic framework for financial reporting, by contrast, is relatively stable, being shaped by the basic demands of numerous stakeholders in the firm who are at an information disadvantage relative to managers. This is not to suggest that the economic framework is inadaptable to changing technologies. Indeed, changing audit and information technologies could shift the relative emphasis on relevance, verifiability, and conservatism on specific rules. But the conditions that give rise to the economic framework for financial reporting—information asymmetry and uncertainty about the future—are longstanding and innate to the nature and organization of corporations.[62] In fact, the concern that managers can misuse their information advantage to their benefit, which is the basis for much of the difference between the FASB's current framework and the economic framework, has not diminished in any systematic way over time. In other words, there is no general evidence (of which I am aware) to suggest that managers are any less likely to abuse their discretion in accruals today than they were thirty-four years ago when the FASB's original framework was put in place. This raises the question of why the FASB's conceptual framework has changed and what role, if any, special-interest politics played in that process. Moreover, the economic framework is similar in many respects to the FASB's own original conceptual framework. For these reasons, I use the economic framework—in particular, the idea that matching, verifiability, and conservatism are cornerstones of financial reporting—as the benchmark in the remainder of this book.

Goodwill Hunting: The Political Economy
of Accountability for Mergers and Acquisitions

On March 2, 2000, Dennis Powell, then the corporate controller of Cisco Systems, appeared before the Senate Committee on Banking, Housing, and Urban Affairs to testify on a recent FASB proposal to abolish the pooling-of-interests method of accounting for M&A. Mr. Powell expressed his opposition to the FASB proposal, arguing that the accounting method firms would be required to use in lieu of pooling (i.e., the purchase method) would "stifle technology development, impede capital formation and slow job creation."[1] The Senate heard from eight other expert witnesses that day; all but one—then-FASB chairman Ed Jenkins—argued against the proposal to abolish pooling.[2] Two months later, Mr. Powell prepared testimony for the House Finance Subcommittee on the same matter, again arguing for the retention of the pooling-of-interests method, which he said, together with the purchase method, had "for the past 50 years, generated and supported the strongest capital markets in the world."[3]

The substance of Mr. Powell's testimony was not surprising given his public letter to the FASB in December 1999, where he had expressed "serious concerns" with the proposed elimination of pooling accounting in favor of the purchase method. "While we understand that pooling accounting has its critics," he wrote, "we believe on balance, for equity funded transactions, it is less problematic than the purchase accounting model in representing the economic reality of operating results of the combined entity."[4]

At the time of Mr. Powell's testimony and writings, U.S. GAAP had two methods to account for M&A: the purchase method and the pooling-of-interests method. Under the purchase method, acquired tangible assets, certain acquired intangible assets (e.g., contracts, patents, franchises, customer and supplier lists, and favorable leases), and all acquired liabilities were revalued to their current fair values before being added to the acquiring firm's books. Any excess of the total price paid for the acquisition over the sum of the revalued net assets was added to acquirer's books as "goodwill." In the years following the acquisition, goodwill was amortized in the acquirer's income statement.

Under the pooling method, the surviving firm in an acquisition simply added the book value of all acquired assets and liabilities to its own assets and liabilities. There were no asset and liability revaluations, and no goodwill was recorded. Firms were required to use the purchase method unless they met certain criteria to qualify for pooling accounting. The most important of these criteria were (1) that each of the companies in an acquisition was independent of the other and (2) that the acquiring firm issued only common stock with rights identical to its own outstanding common stock in consideration for the acquired firm.[5]

Mr. Powell's support for the pooling method over the purchase method appeared to be based on the idea that "goodwill," the account created only under the purchase method, was not an "asset." U.S. GAAP defined "assets" as "probable future economic benefits obtained or controlled by a particular entity as a result of past transactions or events."[6] "Goodwill is simply the amount of purchase price that is left over after allocating value to identifiable assets," Mr. Powell noted. "It has no value on its own; it can't be borrowed against, sold separately or generate any cash flow."[7] Mr. Powell continued: "The purchase method of accounting was designed for accounting for tangible assets that have reliable measurable fair values. However, in the acquisitions of New Economy technology companies, an overwhelming portion of the purchase price is attributable to intangibles. It is this situation that makes the purchase method inadequate. Identifying intangibles is difficult, but determining the fair value of identified intangible assets with some level of consistency or reliability is impossible."[8]

Accounting rules for M&A were particularly critical to a company such as Cisco, whose growth was fuelled in large part by acquisitions. Cisco effectively farmed out its research and development activities by acquiring and then integrating emerging technology companies into its core marketing and operations capabilities.[9] After going public in 1990, Cisco made its first acquisition in 1993. From then through the end of 2000, Cisco acquired seventy-five other companies at a combined price of over $36 billion. Most of these deals were to acquire intangibles (i.e., emerging technologies and human capital). Of the combined purchase price of Cisco's acquisitions through February 2000, Mr. Powell attributed 95 percent to goodwill and other intangible assets.[10] (See table 3.1 for a summary of Cisco's acquisition history from

TABLE 3.1. Summary of Cisco Systems' acquisition history, 1993–2000

	Purchase-method deals		Pooling-method deals		All deals	
Year	Value (in millions of U.S. $)	# of deals	Value (in millions of U.S. $)	# of deals	Value (in millions of U.S. $)	# of deals
1993	0	0	89	1	89	1
1994	423	3	0	0	423	3
1995	31	2	462	2	493	4
1996	275	2	5,275	4	5,550	6
1997	586	5	0	0	586	5
1998	1,070	9	84	1	1,154	10
1999	4,969	13	10,218	7	15,187	20
2000	5,617	23	7,114	4	12,731	27

Source: Adapted from Karthik Ramanna, The Politics and Economics of Accounting for Goodwill at Cisco Systems (A) (HBS No. 109-002) (Boston: Harvard Business School Publishing, 2008).

1993 to 2000.) Given this strategy, Mr. Powell noted the disadvantage to the purchase method in his December 1999 letter to the FASB: "While Cisco continues to grow our business by combining with similar companies with the same long term strategic goals, our operating results would decrease because of the amortization of goodwill."[11] Effectively, Mr. Powell was arguing against having a goodwill charge drag down Cisco's reported earnings.

Mr. Powell concluded his letter to the FASB with a passionate defense of pooling accounting, citing its role in the roaring information-technology economy of the time (the late 1990s): "We believe the retention of pooling of interests accounting is particularly critical considering the adverse impact its elimination will have on the merger activity in the United States, which in turn will negatively impact the ecosystem that is driving technology development in this country today."[12]

But these arguments and rhetoric notwithstanding, less than a year later, by September 2000, Mr. Powell had abandoned his support for the pooling method. In leading a group of industry representatives at a meeting with members of the FASB, Mr. Powell argued for a regime that permitted only the purchase method, provided that goodwill recognized under that method was solely subject to an impairment test based on estimating from time to time the fair value of goodwill rather than subjecting goodwill to amortization as the FASB had originally proposed.[13]

The FASB, after some field testing, issued a revised proposal that effectively abolished the pooling method and accepted the purchase method with goodwill impairment as the new rule for M&A.[14] This revised proposal met with additional opposition from the set of firms that had previously championed pooling, including Cisco Systems. But their concern with the revised proposal was not the abolishing of the pooling method but rather the cost of implementing the fair-value-based impairment test for goodwill. These firms argued for a revised impairment test that would be less costly to comply with but that would also make timely goodwill impairment less likely. In June 2001, the FASB formally promulgated new accounting rules that abolished pooling accounting, requiring all firms to use the purchase method, with an impairment test that closely resembled the one sought by the erstwhile pooling-method supporters.[15]

Why did Mr. Powell—who had at first passionately defended the pooling method by suggesting that abolishing the method would "stifle technology development, impede capital formation and slow job creation"—and others like him abruptly abandon their support for pooling in favor of a fair-value-based impairment test for acquired goodwill? And how has this new accounting rule for M&A performed since it was put in place? In this chapter, I discuss evidence addressing each of these two questions. The discussion in this chapter is intended to illustrate in the specific context of M&A accounting the complex political economy of special-interest lobbying in accounting rule-making at the FASB.

First, I show that firms such as Cisco that were initially opposed to the FASB proposal to abolish pooling accounting can be linked via a history of campaign contributions to the members of the House and Senate who became involved in the issue and threatened legislation overriding the FASB proposal. Congressional intervention in accounting rule-making is rare, although not unheard of, so it is important to understand the conditions under which Congress becomes involved in technical accounting matters. Next, I show that the propooling firms were among those who encouraged the FASB to abandon goodwill amortization under the purchase method in favor of a fair-value-based impairment test. In fact, the rules that eventually became U.S. GAAP for M&A emerged from the lobbying by former propooling firms.

To understand why firms might support an impairment-only approach to goodwill under the purchase method, in lieu of the pooling method, I study whether firms' lobbying support for the impairment-only approach varies in their abilities to misuse the subjectivity inherent in that approach to delay timely goodwill impairment. As Mr. Powell himself argued before he abandoned support for the pooling method, "Determining the fair value of identified intangible assets with some level of consistency or reliability is impossible." I find evidence consistent with the proposition that support for the impairment-only approach increased in the ability to misuse that approach.

Finally, drawing on joint work with Professor Ross Watts of the Massachusetts Institute of Technology (MIT), I discuss how firms are actually using the new M&A accounting rules. I find that among firms with strong market indications of impaired goodwill, delays in recording impairment on the books are seen among firms with the abilities to misuse the subjectivity in the new M&A rules. In the specific case of Cisco Systems, despite a nearly 70 percent decline in its market capitalization from 2000 to 2001—a decline that has largely persisted through 2013—the company has not recorded any substantial goodwill impairment on its books. As of the fiscal year that ended July 2013, the company had a goodwill balance on its books of nearly $22 billion against total assets of about $101 billion.[16]

Given the evidence abstracted above, it is important to understand why the FASB chose to take on a project to abolish the pooling method. Did the FASB not anticipate the potential opposition and its ability to rally Congress? What was the FASB's own interest in undertaking the rule change? The following subsection explores these background issues as a way of establishing the context for a detailed discussion of the evidence on the political economy of M&A accounting.

Background to the 2001 Revision of M&A Accounting Rules

When the FASB first added a potential revision to the accounting rules for M&A to its agenda in 1996, there was already a contentious history to the subject dating back at least fifty years. The FASB's two predecessor bodies, the Committee on Accounting Procedure (CAP) and the Accounting Principles Board (APB), both grappled with the issue during their respective regimes. Although there is evidence of the use of the pooling method dating back to the 1920s, its use was limited and potentially controversial. In 1950, the CAP first formally recognized the pooling-of-interests method for M&A. The method had been advocated by acquiring companies who were reluctant to revalue their assets and recognize acquired goodwill, the amortization of which would reduce future income. The CAP's decision to introduce the pooling method was contentious at the time, and the CAP introduced a number of criteria to limit the kinds of acquisitions that could qualify for pooling accounting.[17] But as accounting historian Professor Steve Zeff notes, "It was not long before these criteria were largely ignored and only weakly enforced by the SEC."[18]

In 1959, a few years after the CAP's decision on pooling, it was replaced by a new accounting rule-maker, the APB.[19] In part because the CAP had been routinely subject to corporate lobbying, the APB was reconstituted to include corporate financial executives as members; the CAP's membership had been limited to accounting practitioners and academics.[20] At first, the APB let stand the CAP's decision on pooling of interests, deciding not to address the charged issue. But the 1960s witnessed a growing number of acquisitions—by one estimate M&A in 1968 were twelve times the level in 1950—and critics of these acquisitions argued that abuses and misuses of the pooling method were partially responsible for the increase. The APB responded with a proposal that would considerably limit the scope of pooling method usage. Among other criteria, the proposal suggested that the pooling method be permissible only when neither target nor acquirer was less than one-third the size of the other. The idea was to limit the pooling method to "mergers of equals."[21]

The proposal was met with fierce opposition from both supporters and opponents of pooling. The then Big Eight audit firms were themselves divided on the issue.[22] Arthur Andersen, then part of the Big Eight, released a competing proposal that would effectively eliminate pooling.[23] Concurrently, supporters of pooling launched a campaign critical of the APB that involved members of Congress and the financial press.[24] As a result of this pressure, the APB dropped the relative-size requirement to qualify for pooling.[25] Finally, in 1970, the APB issued two new standards relating to M&A, designated APB Opinions 16 and 17. These standards let stand the pooling of interests method, although they clarified the circumstances under which firms were permitted to elect for pooling. Furthermore, the standards set out a generous forty-year maximum amortization period for goodwill recognized under the purchase method, thus mitigating to an extent the negative annual charge on earnings from goodwill amortization.[26]

The intensely political process leading up to APB Opinions 16 and 17, and the political compromises necessitated thereof, were partly responsible for a decline in public trust in the APB. Within a year of the issuance of Opinions 16 and 17, three of the eight major audit firms had publicly announced their lack of confidence in the rule-maker.[27] By 1971, two high-profile national committees had been constituted to consider alternative rule-making principles and institutions.[28] By 1973, the APB was out of business and the FASB had taken over.

Criticisms of the pooling accounting method continued to gnaw at the FASB for attention. In 1974, the FASB added accounting for M&A to its agenda. But the young agency postponed consideration of the subject several times before dropping the issue from its agenda in 1981.[29] As the number and visibility of M&A grew in the 1980s and 1990s, so too did pressure on the FASB to reevaluate M&A accounting rules. As part of its due process, the FASB routinely polled members of its professional advisory council for issues to add to its formal agenda. From 1990 through 1996, revising accounting rules for M&A was a top issue suggested by the advisory council.[30] But the FASB resisted taking on the issue, likely because it was aware of its contentiousness and its role in the demise of its predecessor body. Then finally, in 1996, the issue was added to the FASB's formal agenda.

It is difficult to conclusively say why the FASB finally decided to revisit M&A accounting in the late 1990s, but at least two factors likely played an important role in this decision. First, the SEC had become increasingly concerned about the "abuses" of the pooling method: There was growing evidence that firms were engineering M&A deals simply to qualify for pooling and thus avoid a goodwill amortization "drag" on their earnings. For example, one study in 1995 estimated that AT&T overpaid somewhere between $50 million and $500 million in its acquisition of NCR Corporation just so that the deal would meet the conditions for pooling method usage.[31] The SEC saw such maneuvers as being value destroying for shareholders. The SEC chief accountant at the time, Lynn Turner, noted that he often saw pooling transactions that "clearly [did] not meet the spirit or the intention of [APB Opinion 16]."[32] His then-deputy, Jane Adams, called the practice that had evolved around APB Opinion 16 a "quagmire" and remarked that "[a]n incredible amount of resources of preparers, practitioners, standards setters and regulators [was] consumed daily by APB 16."[33] Moreover, firms unable or unwilling to engineer M&A deals to qualify for pooling had to report amortization costs under the purchase method, leading to, in the FASB's words, situations where "two transactions that [were] not significantly different [could] be accounted for by methods that produce[d] dramatically different financial statement results."[34]

Second, as part of its efforts to harmonize U.S. GAAP with accounting rules in other countries, the FASB had been working closely with rule-makers from Australia, Canada, New Zealand, the United Kingdom, and the International Accounting Standards Committee. This international group of accounting rule-makers, known as the G4+1, had initiated a joint project to develop a single set of accounting rules for M&A.[35] The joint project was motivated in part by the growing cross-border nature of business combinations, the inconsistencies across countries in the practices used to account for such business combinations, and the desire to address concerns by securities regulators such as the SEC that the pooling-of-interests method was being misused.

Thus, by 1996, a combination of SEC pressure over pooling-method abuse and the forces of international convergence had pushed the FASB to formally reconsider accounting rules for M&A. If the APB's history with the issue was any indication, the FASB was entering treacherous terrain.

Revising M&A Accounting Rules: Round One

Between 1996 and 1999, the FASB exposed to public comment two documents with proposals on accounting for M&A. The first, in June 1997, was a "special report" on "issues associated with" M&A.[36] This document received over fifty comment letters from various FASB constituents. The second, in December 1998, was part of a G4+1 effort on the subject. This document proposed eliminating the pooling-of-interests method.[37] It received nearly 150 comment letters from various FASB constituents. Investment banks and high-technology industrial companies, in particular, expressed opposition to any abolishing of the pooling method.[38] The active constituent response to both documents suggested that there was considerable interest in the subject. But neither document was part of the FASB's official due process to revise accounting rules, so neither document indicated an imminent threat to the pooling method.

Then, in September 1999, the FASB issued a formal exposure draft, called ED 201, on M&A accounting. The ED proposed eliminating pooling and requiring all business combinations to use the purchase method. Furthermore, any acquired goodwill under the purchase method was to be amortized, with the maximum amortization period reduced from forty to twenty years.[39]

ED 201 provided for a ninety-day comment period; over two hundred comment letters were sent in by various constituents, about half of which came from corporations. About 60 percent of corporate respondents to the ED opposed abolishing pooling. This opposition, as the previously discussed example of Cisco Systems documents, deployed strong, if not incredulous, language in defense of the pooling method. Several of the corporate comment letters cited the prevalence of the pooling method in acquisitions involving the "New Economy" companies that were driving the stock-market boom of the late 1990s. One firm, InCert, noted that "killing pooling would . . . be a mortal blow to our free enterprise system" and a "major disaster for our economic well-being."[40] Another firm, Guidant Corporation, noted, "Eliminating pooling will discourage the desirable consolidation that is now occurring in certain industries, thereby reducing the flow of capital to them which in turn will stifle the entrepreneurial culture, impede the development of new products, and impair job growth."[41] A third firm, Flextronics International, went further in its comment letter, arguing that "purchase accounting is a terrible blight on the accounting profession" and that the "elimination of Pooling [sic] will distort the allocation of resources in the very industries that are driving the growth of this country."[42]

The debate over M&A accounting rules, particularly the proposed abolishing of the pooling method, soon reached the U.S. Congress. In March and May of 2000, the Senate Banking Committee and the House Finance Subcommittee, respectively, held hearings on the issue.[43] Many of the firms and industry associations that had already expressed their opposition to ED 201 through comment letters or testimonies at FASB public hearings also testified at the congressional hearings. In fact, apart from the FASB itself, there were no supporters of ED 201 at the Senate hearings.

Almost all congressional pressure on the FASB over its business combinations ED was in support of propooling firms' interests. For example, then-senator Phil Gramm of Texas spoke of hearing from the "victims" of the FASB proposal, adding his opposition to periodic goodwill amortization by assuming away the theory of competitive strategy, "I don't see any immutable law of economics that says goodwill must decline."[44] Similarly, Rick Lazio, a member of the House from New York argued that without pooling, the economy "would have been deprived of the synergy" of the then recently completed AOL-Netscape merger.[45] House member Bill Tauzin of Louisiana, in arguing against goodwill amortization under the purchase method, called on the FASB to "propose something more creative than simply forcing companies to amortize goodwill."[46] Those few members of Congress who did not actively make the case for supporters of the pooling method did not support the FASB's position either: they only expressed concern over the dangers of congressional involvement in accounting standard setting. For example, then-senator Paul Sarbanes of Maryland noted, "Congress would be entering into very dangerous ground if we begin to move in to try to make these determinations ourselves."[47]

Notwithstanding this counsel from Senator Sarbanes, in October 2000, several members of the House introduced a bill, HR 5365, the Financial Accounting for Intangibles Reexamination Act. The stated purpose of the bill was to "impose a moratorium on the elimination of . . . pooling" until a congressionally appointed commission reported on the economic impact of eliminating pooling and on methods to better account for intangible assets.[48] Also in October 2000, the FASB received a letter from a bipartisan group of thirteen U.S. Senators who wrote expressing "reservations" over the FASB's plan to eliminate pooling. The letter asked the FASB to "take no conclusive action" on the business combinations project until Congress "had the opportunity to review the economic impact of the FASB's plans."[49]

Congressional hearings on accounting standards are, in the words of former FASB Chair Dennis Beresford, "relatively infrequent."[50] By the year 2000, Congress had become directly involved in FASB rule-making in only a handful of other cases, including lease accounting and accounting for oil and gas exploration costs in the 1970s and accounting for financial assets and for employee stock options in the 1990s. And since 2000, Congress has become involved in accounting matters on employee stock options, accounting for financial assets, and lease accounting.[51] But as sporadic as such intervention might be, Mr. Beresford notes that such hearings, when they do occur, are taken "very seriously" by the board.[52] And moreover, as noted earlier, the FASB's predecessor, the APB, had met with its demise in part due to its perceived mishandling of accounting for M&A.

Given the circumstances described above, it is plausible that the congressional intervention for the pooling method and against goodwill amortization was motivated by propooling firms and industry groups. To test this proposition more formally, I examine whether a statistical association can be made between those congresspersons who became involved in the pooling issue and the firms and industry groups that opposed abolishing pooling (i.e., propoolers). The idea is to test whether the propoolers used their allies in Congress to pressure the FASB to rethink its original proposal to abolish pooling and amortize goodwill.

For the purposes of this statistical test, congresspersons pressuring the FASB over pooling are defined as those involved against the board in at least one of the following events (all discussed earlier): the March 2000 Senate hearings, the May 2000 House hearings, the October 2000 House bill to create a federal commission on intangibles accounting, and the October 2000 Senate letter seeking a moratorium on the FASB's original proposal.

I use political action committee (PAC) contributions to link congresspersons to propooling firms and industry groups.[53] I use PAC money although it represents only one component of money used to lobby congresspersons because the other major sources of money (namely, soft money and direct lobbying money) cannot be directly traced from source organizations to congresspersons under extant political-spending disclosure laws. Moreover, prior political-science research has shown a high correlation between PAC money from nonideological PACs, such as corporations, and direct lobbying money.[54] Formally, I hypothesize that PAC contributions received from firms and industry groups opposed to the FASB's pooling decision increase the likelihood of a congressperson self-selecting into the group pressuring the FASB over pooling.

There are forty-three distinct congresspersons involved in at least one of the four congressional intervention events described above. I compare these propooling congresspersons to all other members of the 106th Congress (1999–2000). For this combined set of congresspersons (propooling and others), I obtain data on contributions made by the PACs of all firms and industry associations that lobbied for or against the original FASB proposal (i.e., ED 201 to abolish pooling and amortize goodwill). For each congressperson, I aggregate PAC contributions from firms and associations by lobbying position. Thus I obtain two data points for each member of Congress: PAC contributions from the propooling group and PAC contributions from the antipooling group. For each congressperson, the total group contributions are scaled by total PAC receipts. I run a probit-model regression on the combined sample of congresspersons, where the dependent variable is coded as "1" for propooling congresspersons and "0" for all other congresspersons. The primary explanatory variables are scaled PAC contributions from the pro- and antipooling lobbying groups.[55]

To address alternative hypotheses, I include several control variables in the regression. First, an indicator for members of the House Finance Subcommittee or Senate Banking Committee controls for the likelihood that only congresspersons with relevant finance expertise became interested in the pooling issue. Second, I include two variables capturing congresspersons' ideologies to control for the possibility that congressional positions on pooling can be explained by political beliefs. The ideology variables are the "Common Space Scores" obtained from congresspersons' roll-call records, which are commonly used in political science studies. The first ideology variable roughly captures a congressperson's partisanship, whereas the second roughly captures nonpartisan voting blocks.[56]

It is widely held in the political science literature that firms' relations with congresspersons are developed over long periods and that firms likely give to congresspersons who are already predisposed to supporting them (i.e., PAC giving is likely endogenous).[57] To address this concern, the probit model of congressional positions is estimated simultaneously with a model for propooling PAC contributions received by each congressperson. The explanatory variables in this latter model are the ideology variables and committee-membership indicator described above, together with the following additional controls. First, a control for whether the congressperson is a Senator or House member to address the likelihood that Senators receive on average more PAC money because they have larger constituencies. Second, a control for the congressperson's seniority in her or his respective chamber to address the likelihood that more senior members of Congress receive more PAC money.[58] Third, a control for the size of the state the congressperson rep-

TABLE 3.2. Univariate evidence on the association between propooling-method organizations and congresspersons involved in the issue

	Propooling congresspersons (%)	Other congresspersons (%)
$ from antipooling PACs ÷ Total PAC receipts	4.84	3.43
$ from propooling PACs ÷ Total PAC receipts	13.36	8.86

All percentages are means.

Source: Adapted from Karthik Ramanna, "The Implications of Unverifiable Fair-Value Accounting: Evidence from the Political Economy of Goodwill Accounting," Journal of Accounting and Economics 45, nos. 2–3 (2008): 253–81.

resents to address the likelihood that representatives of larger states receive more PAC money.

Table 3.2 reports univariate evidence on the association between propooling firms and industry groups and congresspersons involved in the issue. The mean PAC contribution from propooling groups to propooling congresspersons was 13.36 percent of those congresspersons' total PAC receipts. This number is statistically greater than (1) the mean PAC contribution from propooling groups to *other* congresspersons (8.86 percent), (2) the mean PAC contribution from antipooling groups to propooling congresspersons (4.84 percent), and (3) the mean PAC contribution from antipooling groups to other congresspersons (3.43 percent). Some examples of the top givers among propooling groups include Arthur Andersen, Citigroup, Eli Lilly, General Electric, Goldman Sachs, Morgan Stanley, PricewaterhouseCoopers, and the National Venture Capitalists Association.[59] Some examples of the top recipients among propooling congresspersons include Representative Chris Cox of California (later SEC chairman), Representative Anna Eshoo of California, Representative Bob Goodlatte of Virginia, Senator Phil Gramm of Texas, Senator Joe Lieberman of Connecticut, and Senator Chuck Schumer of New York.[60]

Table 3.3 reports the results of the probit regression model, estimated in the simultaneous system described above. The coefficient on PAC contributions from propooling groups is positive and significant; the marginal effect suggests that a two-standard-deviation change in propooling PAC money about its mean value increases the probability that a congressperson is propooling by 29.5 percent. Thus the formal evidence is consistent with the proposition that congressional intervention for the pooling method and against goodwill amortization was motivated by propooling firms and industry groups. Among the control variables, the ideology variables are significant. The first of the two ideology variables captures partisan voting with

TABLE 3.3. Multivariate evidence on the association between propooling-method organizations and congresspersons involved in the issue

		Variable	Prediction	t-statistic	Marginal effect (%)
Control equation: Dependent variable is $ from propooling PACs ÷ Total PAC receipts		Intercept		4.49	
		Ideology dimension 1		7.45	6.7
		Ideology dimension 2		0.06	0.1
		Indicator: House/Senate Finance-Committee membership		4.74	5.7
		Indicator: Senate membership		2.96	2.9
		Congressional seniority		0.73	0.6
		State size		−0.33	−0.3
Probit equation: Dependent variable is "1" if congressperson supported pooling, "0" otherwise		Intercept		−7.08	
		$ from antipooling PACs ÷ Total PAC receipts		0.87	2.8
		$ from propooling PACs ÷ Total PAC receipts	+	2.91	29.5
		Ideology dimension 1		−2.49	−16.2
		Ideology dimension 2		−2.07	−8.6
		Indicator: House/Senate Finance-Committee membership		1.10	19.8

Source: Adapted from Karthik Ramanna, "The Implications of Unverifiable Fair-Value Accounting: Evidence from the Political Economy of Goodwill Accounting," *Journal of Accounting and Economics* 45, nos. 2–3 (2008): 253–81.

Democrats having negative values. The negative coefficient on this variable suggests that Democrats are more likely to be propooling, consistent with strong Democratic representation in states with high-technology companies that supported pooling (e.g., California, Connecticut, and New York). In the model explaining congresspersons' propooling PAC receipts, the first ideology variable, the committee-membership dummy, and the Senator indicator dummy are statistically significant. This is, respectively, consistent with Republicans, finance committee members, and Senators receiving on average more PAC money.

It is important to clarify that the main result above—associating congressional intervention for the pooling method to propooling firms and industry groups—does not imply that PAC contributions were used to *buy* congressional positions on pooling. PAC contributions can be used to establish donors' *association* with, but not *causality* of, specific congressional decisions. Relations with congresspersons are likely developed over long periods, and firms likely give money to their allies in Congress.[61] Thus the results more appropriately suggest that congresspersons pressuring the FASB over pooling are likely allies of propooling firms and associations.

Revising M&A Accounting Rules: Round Two

During the period of congressional intervention over ED 201, the idea of an impairment-only approach to goodwill was simultaneously being proposed to the FASB. First, in May 2000 (shortly after the House hearings), the FASB heard from representatives of Morgan Stanley Dean Witter, Goldman Sachs, Arthur Andersen, and PricewaterhouseCoopers, among others.[62] These organizations had previously written comment letters in favor of retaining the pooling method. Later, in September 2000, the FASB heard from another team from the American Business Conference, Cisco Systems, Merrill Lynch, TechNet, and UPS.[63] This team also included groups that had previously supported the pooling method. Both teams in their meetings with the FASB discussed the merits of implementing an impairment-only test for goodwill. They proposed that goodwill impairment in periods after an acquisition be determined based on acquiring managers' estimates of the fair value of goodwill, a highly subjective procedure. In February 2001, with the threat of direct congressional intervention still looming, the FASB unanimously issued a revised exposure draft, called ED 201-R, that did not change the board's stance on abolishing pooling but now proposed replacing goodwill amortization with the impairment-only approach.[64]

Over two hundred comment letters were received on ED 201-R. This revised proposal to abolish pooling and impair goodwill was considerably more popular than the original one (to abolish pooling and amortize goodwill). About 70 percent of corporate respondents to ED 201-R supported the impairment-only approach. Although the FASB had left its decision on abolishing pooling intact, there was little mention of the pooling issue in firms' comment letters: only 14 percent of corporate respondents on ED 201-R expressed support for pooling. Congressional interest in retaining pooling had also waned: there were no comment letters by congresspersons on ED 201-R.

In June 2001, the FASB issued its new rules on M&A accounting—these were labeled SFAS 141 and 142 (SFAS refers to Statement of Financial Accounting Standards, the formal term for a new FASB accounting standard[65]). The former abolished the pooling method in favor of the purchase method.[66] The latter introduced impairment-only accounting for goodwill.[67] The goodwill impairment method in SFAS 142 differed, however, in one important way from the method initially introduced by the FASB in ED 201-R. It is through this difference that additional insights into the political economy of M&A accounting rules can be gleaned.

ED 201-R detailed the following procedure for goodwill accounting:

(A) Goodwill from an acquisition is initially allocated among the "reporting units" of a firm based on estimates of how that goodwill will be realized across those units. Reporting units are divisions of the firm that regularly produce financial information for management review. In subsequent periods, goodwill is tested for impairment at this reporting unit level.

(B) A reporting unit's goodwill is considered impaired if the goodwill's "implied fair value" is less than the goodwill's book value. The goodwill's "implied fair value" is calculated as the excess of the reporting unit's estimated total fair value over the estimated fair value of the reporting unit's non-goodwill net assets.

(C) Goodwill impairment losses from various reporting units in a firm are aggregated and presented in a separate line item in the income statement.

The final rules in SFAS 142 are similar to those described above with the following notable addition: The "implied fair value" of a reporting unit's goodwill is calculated only when the unit's estimated total fair value is less than the book value of the unit's net assets. In other words, under SFAS 142, firms are spared the expense of estimating the fair-value of their nongoodwill assets and liabilities, unless the book value of those assets and liabilities exceeds the estimated fair value of the unit as a whole.[68] This is a subtle but important difference for at least two reasons. First, limiting goodwill write-offs to only those situations where the total fair value of a reporting unit is less than the unit's book value is likely to lower the observed frequency of goodwill impairment. Second, estimating the total fair value of a reporting unit is potentially more subjective than estimating the fair value of the units' net assets. This is because the unit's assets and liabilities are more likely to be fungible than the unit itself, thus there are more likely to be observable comparables for current value estimates of the unit's assets and liabilities than for the unit as a whole. As such, any current value estimate of the unit can be manipulated by changing unverifiable assumptions in a valuation model.

This discussion suggests goodwill impairment effected under SFAS 142 rules can be subject to more gaming than that under the ED 201-R rules. In other words, the subtle rule change between ED 201-R and SFAS 142 could have addressed a primary concern of supporters of the pooling method and opponents of the purchase method: the "drag" of goodwill expenditures in the income statement.

It so happens that the idea of limiting goodwill impairment to situations where a reporting unit's estimated total fair value is less than the book value of the unit's nongoodwill net assets emerged during the meetings in May and September of 2000 where representatives of several investment banks, technology firms, and industry associations met privately with the FASB. Furthermore, among the constituent comment letters filed in response to ED 201-R, over one-third of respondents proposed this idea. Accordingly, I call the FASB's goodwill impairment procedure in ED 201-R the "Revised ED Position" and the goodwill impairment procedure that made it into SFAS 142 the "Comment Letter Position."

Given the FASB's observed acquiescence to the Comment Letter Position in SFAS 142 and the considerable political power of propooling interests in this rule-making process, it is plausible that propooling organizations were associated with the proposal and eventual acceptance of the Comment Letter Position. Put differently, the politically connected propooling interests are unlikely to have let a proposal become the final standard if they did not support it. I formally test this proposition. Specifically, I examine whether firms opposing the FASB's original proposal (ED 201, abolish pooling and require goodwill amortization) are more likely to have supported the Comment Letter Position in ED 201-R, which eventually became the rule in SFAS 142.

Anecdotally, the role of the investment banks during the process that resulted in SFAS 142 is consistent with this proposition. Investment banks, by the nature of their business, have a lot to gain from keeping the volume of M&A activity high. M&A accounting rules that would create a "drag" on clients' earnings, such as goodwill amortization, and therefore potentially discourage clients from aggressive M&A activity are unlikely to be popular with investment banks. Not surprisingly then, the three biggest investment banks at the time, Goldman Sachs, Morgan Stanley, and Merrill Lynch, all supported the pooling method in the FASB's original ED. These banks were also among the largest contributors to the congresspersons who became involved in the issue in support of pooling. The investment banks were then part of the groups that met privately with the board to propose an impairment-only alternative to goodwill accounting. Finally, these investments banks supported the rules for estimating goodwill impairment that eventually became SFAS 142.

It is plausible to imagine that the investment banks would prefer the goodwill impairment rules in ED 201-R over those in SFAS 142 because the former precipitate more frequent impairment testing: such testing can be a source of revenue to investment banks that also provide valuation services. However, as revealed from their actual lobbying, it appears that the investment banks focused instead on lessening the "drag" on their clients' earnings from goodwill charges—presumably because the lower drag is likely to precipitate more M&A activity, which can be a larger source of revenue than valuation services for impairment testing.

As noted earlier in this chapter, the proposal to abolish the pooling method and require the purchase method was due in part to SEC concerns over the pooling method's abuse. If the SEC was correct about pooling being abused, and if abusers are among the propoolers predicted above to have influenced the goodwill impairment rules in SFAS 142, it is likely that potential for abuse has been retained in those rules. To test this proposition, I further examine whether firms' abilities to misuse the subjectivity in SFAS 142 goodwill impairment rules explains their lobbying support for the rules.

The potential to misuse the goodwill impairment rules arises due to the rules' reliance on unverifiable fair-value estimates. To be sure, all fair-value estimates—and many accrual estimates—are to some degree subjective, but the rules for goodwill impairment require estimates on several assets, liabilities, and units for which there are unlikely be reasonable comparables. This situation increases the concerns about subjectivity and misuse. Indeed, Mr. Powell of Cisco Systems had himself raised the difficulty of verifiably estimating the fair value of intangibles before he abandoned support for the pooling method. And firms lobbying against goodwill impairment in ED 201-R also raised such concerns (although their motives for doing so were plausibly strategic, i.e., to prevent M&A-intensive competitors from enjoying such accounting discretion). For example, IBM in its comment letter noted: "Ongoing assessments of [goodwill's] value would be arbitrary and subjective at best . . . [we] want to ensure that the degree of subjectivity and therefore customization of financial results from any revised goodwill accounting guidelines is minimized."[69] Similarly, M&T Bank noted: "The requirement . . . to 'compute' fair value of reporting units . . . would be arbitrary and subject to manipulation."[70]

Through an assessment of the SFAS 142 goodwill impairment rules, I identify three firm characteristics that increase the potential for abuse of the rules' discretion: (1) larger and more numerous business segments, (2) higher market-to-book (MTB) ratios, and (3) higher proportions of net assets without observable market values. I expand on the logic underlying these three characteristics below.

1. Under SFAS 142, goodwill recognized in an acquisition must be allocated across the acquirer's "reporting units" based on fair-value estimates of how that goodwill will be realized. As such, acquired goodwill usually represents future economic profits (i.e., "rents") expected by the acquirer, and any allocation of such rents across units is arbitrary and unverifiable.[71] All else equal, the larger and more numerous an acquirer's reporting units, the greater the acquirer's flexibility in allocating goodwill and thus the greater its discretion in determining future impairment. Since data on "reporting units" (as defined in SFAS 142) are not publicly dis-

closed, I use data on firms' "business segments," which are disclosed under GAAP rules,[72] in computing an empirical proxy for this characteristic.

2. After acquired goodwill is allocated to reporting units, acquirers must periodically evaluate whether it is impaired. As already discussed, SFAS 142 requires such impairment testing only for reporting units with fair-value-to-book-value (FTB) ratios less than one. This rule implicitly assumes that all the excess of a unit's fair value over its book value is due to acquired goodwill; internally generated rents and the understatement of book value are not accounted for at this step. All else equal, units with high FTB ratios can absorb losses to acquired goodwill, giving them greater discretion to avoid future impairments. Since units' FTB ratios are unobservable, I use firm-wide MTB ratios in computing an empirical proxy for this characteristic.

3. For units with FTB ratios less than one, SFAS 142 requires recording impairment losses when the extant value of goodwill is less than its historical book value. Since there is no observable market price for goodwill, the extant value of a unit's goodwill is calculated as the difference between the unit's estimated total fair value and the estimated fair value of its non-goodwill net assets. In a firm, the fair values of some nongoodwill assets and liabilities (e.g., cash, investments, payables, etc.) can be verified more readily than the fair values of others (e.g., firm-specific assets such as a specialized plant and equipment). Indeed, some nongoodwill assets and liabilities are unverifiable. All else equal, the greater the proportion of unverifiable net assets, the greater the flexibility in estimating the current value of net assets and thus the greater the potential for abuse in the goodwill impairment test.

I test whether lobbying support for ED 201-R, which proposed the impairment-only approach to goodwill, varies with these firm characteristics. There are three firm lobbying positions on ED 201-R. The first position is anti-impairment: I call this the Amortization Position since firms supporting this position (about 28 percent of corporate lobbyists) wanted the practice of goodwill amortization to continue. The other two positions are both proimpairment. These are the Revised ED Position and the Comment Letter Position described earlier. They were supported by about 38 percent and about 34 percent of corporate lobbyists, respectively. Given the history of the Comment Letter Position—in particular its potential origin among propooling firms—I especially focus on whether the firm characteristics expected to facilitate abuse of the impairment rules increase the likelihood of companies supporting this position over the Amortization Position.

In testing the propositions discussed in this section, I jointly model the decision to lobby on ED 201-R and the positions upon lobbying using a two-level nested multinomial logit model. The first level models the probability that firms lobby; this is a binary choice (i.e., lobby or not). For those firms that lobby, the second level models the probability of choosing a given lobbying position, which is a multinomial choice among three options (i.e., the Comment Letter Position, the Revised ED Position, and the Amortization Position).[73] As control variables in the regression on the decision to lobby, I include proxies for firm size and for the potential effects of goodwill accounting changes on debt contracts, executive-compensation contracts, and asset-pricing concerns. Prior research has shown that these variables can affect firms' lobbying positions.[74] I also include a variable that captures the magnitude of a firm's concern with goodwill issues.

Table 3.4 shows the distribution of firms across lobbying positions in both the original ED 201 and the revised ED 201-R. I identified 186 distinct firms lobbying on either of the two proposals: of these, fifty-two firms lobbied on both. Thirty-one firms lobbying for the pooling method in the original ED also lobbied on the revised ED: of these, only five supported the Amortization Position, whereas eighteen supported the Comment Letter Position (consistent with the prediction in this section). Twenty-one antipooling firms from the original ED also lobbied on the revised ED: of these, eight supported the Comment Letter Position. Half of all lobbyists from the original ED did not lobby on the revised ED. Increased certainty about the project's outcome following congressional intervention may have made it unnecessary for these firms to lobby. Eighty-two firms lobbying on the revised ED did not lobby on the original ED, but these newly lobbying firms supported goodwill impairment over amortization by nearly a two-to-one margin.

I perform chi-square tests on two subsamples in table 3.4. The first sub-

TABLE 3.4. Distribution of firms across lobbying positions in the original exposure draft 201 and the revised exposure draft 201-R

		Original ED (201)			
		Antipooling	Propooling	Didn't lobby	Total
Revised ED (201-R)	Amortization Position	5	5	28	38
	Revised ED Position	8	8	35	51
	Comment Letter Position	8	18	19	45
	Didn't lobby	21	31		
	Total	42	62		

Source: Adapted from Karthik Ramanna, "The Implications of Unverifiable Fair-Value Accounting: Evidence from the Political Economy of Goodwill Accounting," Journal of Accounting and Economics 45, nos. 2–3 (2008): 253–81.

sample is all firms lobbying on the original ED. The chi-square for this sample is not significant (*p*-value is 0.57), consistent with a random clustering of lobbying decisions and positions among original ED lobbyists. The second subsample is all firms lobbying on the revised ED. The chi-square for this sample is statistically significant (*p*-value is 0.01), consistent with a nonrandom clustering of lobbying decisions and positions among revised ED lobbyists. I further explore this finding below.

Table 3.5 presents results of the second level of the two-level nested multinomial logit regression model described earlier. Here, I use the Comment Letter Position as the "base case"—that is, the decision to lobby on the two other positions is contrasted with lobbying for the Comment Letter Position. Thus results from the regression model are interpreted as the effect of

TABLE 3.5. Multivariate evidence on firms' lobbying positions on the revised exposure draft 201-R

	Variable	Prediction	t-statistic	Marginal effect (%)
Level 2: Support for the Amortization Position over the Comment Letter Position	Intercept		5.564	
	Proxy for the number and size of reporting units	−	−4.564	−18.8
	Proxy for fair-value to book-value ratio of reporting units	−	−2.147	−21.1
	Proxy for unverifiability of reporting units' net assets		1.011	2.2
	Proxy for magnitude of a firm's concern with goodwill	−	−2.307	−11.3
	Indicator: Firm lobbied for the pooling method on the original ED	−	−3.960	−9.0
	Indicator: Firm opposed by its industry association		2.134	10.4
Level 2: Support for the Revised ED Position over the Comment Letter Position	Intercept		7.390	
	Proxy for number and size of reporting units	−	−4.624	−29.0
	Proxy for fair-value to book-value ratio of reporting units		0.105	2.2
	Proxy for unverifiability of reporting units' net assets	+	3.539	52.6
	Proxy for magnitude of a firm's concern with goodwill		−0.641	−2.4
	Indicator: Firm lobbied for the pooling method on the original ED	−	−3.344	−11.3
	Indicator: Firm opposed by its industry association		−4.160	−43.1

Source: Adapted from Karthik Ramanna, "The Implications of Unverifiable Fair-Value Accounting: Evidence from the Political Economy of Goodwill Accounting," *Journal of Accounting and Economics* 45, nos. 2–3 (2008): 253–81.

explanatory variables on the choice of the Amortization Position or Revised ED Position over the Comment Letter Position. Since parameter estimates from the nested model cannot be directly interpreted, I report t-statistics and marginal effects. The marginal effect of a continuous variable is the change in outcome probability when the continuous variable is increased from one standard deviation below its mean value to one standard deviation above its mean value. The marginal effect of an indicator variable is the change in outcome probability when the indicator is increased from zero to one. When calculating the marginal effect of a given explanatory variable, all other explanatory variables are set to their mean values.

The data in table 3.5 suggest that the probability that a firm supports the Comment Letter Position over the Amortization Position is 9 percent higher if the firm supported the pooling method in the original ED. Furthermore, the probability that a firm supports the Comment Letter Position over the Revised ED Position is 11.3 percent higher if the firm supported the pooling method in the original ED. These results are consistent with the hypothesis that the unverifiable fair-value-based impairment test in SFAS 142 (represented by the Comment Letter Position) is partially the outcome of pressure by propooling firms.

Three other results from table 3.5 are of note. First, the number and size of reporting units decreases the probability of supporting the Amortization Position over the Comment Letter Position by 18.8 percent. Second, proxies for the FTB ratios of reporting units are negatively associated with supporting the Amortization Position over the Comment Letter Position; the marginal effect is 21.1 percent. Third, proxies for the unverifiability of fair-value estimates of a reporting unit's nongoodwill net assets are positively associated with supporting the Revised ED Position over the Comment Letter Position, with a marginal effect of 52.6 percent. This result is to be expected given that it is under the Revised ED Position that the potential for misusing the goodwill impairment test relies principally on unverifiability of nongoodwill net assets' fair-value estimates. (Recall that under the Comment Letter Position, fair-value estimates for a reporting unit's nongoodwill net assets need not be generated unless the unit's FTB ratio is less than one.) These three results together suggest that lobbying support for SFAS 142 goodwill impairment rules is increasing in the potential to abuse those rules.

Overall, the formal evidence presented in this section suggests that the unverifiable (or difficult-to-audit) fair-value-based impairment test in SFAS 142 is partially the outcome of pressure by propooling firms and that corporate lobbying support for the fair-value-based impairment approach increases in firms' potential to abuse that approach. When interpreted in conjunction with the evidence from the prior section, which links propooling firms to the congressional intervention on this matter, the results indicate the following. Propooling firms, already under the SEC's eye for abuse, used their allies in Congress to pressure the FASB to accept a fair-value-based impairment test, which due to its unverifiable nature is also susceptible to abuse.

A brief note on an alternative interpretation of the results discussed in this section follows. It is possible that the FASB was determined to eliminate the pooling method due to SEC pressure or because it was keen on converging with international practices (related to its G4+1 project).[75] Under this view, offering goodwill impairment in lieu of goodwill amortization in ED 201-R was the FASB's way of achieving this goal (given the political pressure from Congress on ED 201). The tests presented herein do not rule out this narrative. However, this narrative cannot explain why firms' lobbying support for ED 201-R varies with their potential to abuse goodwill impairment rules. Rather, the evidence presented in this section suggests that firms who supported the pooling method, suspected by the SEC of abuse, lobbied to create goodwill impairment rules that are also subject to abuse. The result is a potential compromise of a key accountability mechanism for M&A. The following section explores this notion in greater detail.

The Performance of SFAS 142

When the FASB issued SFAS 142 in June 2001, the board predicted that the standard "will improve financial reporting because the financial statements of entities that acquire goodwill and other intangible assets will [now] better reflect the underlying economics of those assets."[76] The board expected that managers would, on average, use the opportunity to generate estimates of the fair value of acquired goodwill to convey their private information on future cash flows to investors and other financial-statement users. The result, the board concluded, would be "a better understanding of [managers'] expectations about and changes in [goodwill and other intangible assets] over time."[77]

The idea that managers will use the unverifiable discretion in SFAS 142 to provide private information to external financial-statement users is tempered by the findings from decades of empirical research on managers' use of accounting choice. A substantial body of research has found that absent governance mechanisms, managers use accounting discretion in self-serving ways.[78] This is consistent with the central prediction of agency theory as applied to corporate managers' accounting choices. In fact, as discussed in chapter 2, the institutions of matching, verifiability, and conservatism in financial reporting practice—which are lacking in the goodwill impairment rule in SFAS 142—have evolved to mitigate self-serving and potentially value-destroying accounting choices. Of course, it is possible that other governance mechanisms, such as tighter monitoring by auditors and the board, can mitigate the self-serving use of unverifiable accounting discretion. Thus evaluating the FASB's view against the agency-theory view on SFAS 142 is a matter for empirical testing.

In this section, I report on tests of these competing views on how SFAS 142 goodwill-impairment rules will be applied. Such tests are particularly relevant given the contentious political economy of SFAS 142. These tests were conducted jointly with Professor Ross Watts of MIT in previously published work.

To test the effectiveness of the goodwill impairment rules, one needs an objective indication that such impairment is in fact due. In the tests that follow, Professor Watts and I rely on market indications of goodwill impairment—in other words, we rely on firms whose stock prices suggest that an accounting charge to goodwill is due. We begin with a sample of firms that have at least $1 million of goodwill recorded on their books and market-equity values greater than book-equity values. Then we retain only those firms that end the following *two* fiscal years with market-equity values less than book-equity values, where book-equity values are calculated after the effect of all nongoodwill write-offs but before the effect of any goodwill impairment. Among such firms, goodwill impairment is likely due, particularly at the end of the second fiscal year.

Certain other GAAP rules, such as those related to contingent losses, deferred taxes, and impairment of nongoodwill assets, could generate conditions where a firm's book-equity value exceeds its market-equity value, but these rules are unlikely to explain eight quarters of the condition. Rather, firms that meet the criteria described above very likely have economically impaired goodwill. Thus we assume that among such firms a write-off to goodwill is due.

We identify 124 U.S. listed companies that meet the above-described sample selection criteria between the years 2003 and 2006, the first four years of general implementation of SFAS 142. At first blush, this sample might appear small and unrepresentative of the population of firms. After all, firms with two successive years of market-equity values less than book-equity values are rare. Perhaps it is more appropriate to study goodwill nonimpairment in more representative firms (i.e., those with market-equity values greater than book-equity values). But this reasoning ignores the fact that it is precisely in the sample of firms with two successive years of depressed market values that we would expect the goodwill impairment rules in SFAS 142 to work. An analogy is investigating the effectiveness of brakes in cars. One could argue that testing for brake failures in cars should be conducted at speeds of about 40 miles per hour since this is the average speed of cars on the road. By this logic, studying break failures at speeds of 80 miles per hour is peripheral. But cars can—and some cars do—travel at 80 miles an hour, and they can do much damage if their brakes fail at this speed. So a study of brake failures— and impairment rules—under acute conditions is a good indicator of the effectiveness of relevant controls.

Among the 124 firms with two successive years of market-equity values less than book-equity values in our sample, the frequency of goodwill nonimpairment in the second consecutive fiscal year of book-equity values exceeding market-equity values is 69 percent. Given our expectation that a goodwill write-off is due for these firms, the frequency of nonimpairment appears high.

Managers of these nonimpairing firms may have avoided goodwill write-offs if they had or believed they had private information on positive future cash flows, consistent with the FASB's expectation of how SFAS 142 would be used. Such information is "private" to the extent that it is not incorporated in stock prices (otherwise market-equity values would not be less than book-equity values). Information can be "private" because it is difficult for managers to credibly communicate anticipated future cash flows to investors. If private information on positive future cash flows motivated nonimpairment, it would be prudent for such managers to engage in share repurchases and legal insider share buying. Thus we can use instances of net share repurchases or positive net insider buying to test the FASB's hypothesis.

There is the potential for a selection bias in our sample if firms using share repurchases and insider buying successfully communicate their private information to the market, see their equity values rise above book values, and are thus excluded from the sample. To address this concern, we investigate firms that after one year of equity values below book values see their equity values rise above book values in the second year. A higher incidence of share repurchases and insider buying during the second year among such firms would be consistent with selection bias concerns. We find that this is not the case.

We find the frequency of firms with positive net share repurchases among nonimpairers in the sample (24 percent) is statistically indistinguishable from that among impairers (24 percent). Furthermore, the frequency of firms with positive net insider buying among nonimpairers (22 percent) is also statistically indistinguishable from that among impairers (18 percent). The data are inconsistent with the proposition that managers are withholding goodwill impairment because they have private information on positive future cash flows.

Share repurchases and legal insider share buying are costly activities that our sample firms may be unable to afford to signal their favorable private information. Thus as an additional test of the private-information hypothesis, we examine the one-year-ahead stock-price performance of sample firms. The purpose is to determine whether, on average, nonimpairers are more likely to have higher one-year-ahead stock returns than impairers. If so, nonimpairment is consistent with managers having positive private information (which is subsequently revealed in stock prices). Of the 124 firms in the sample, one-year-ahead stock returns data are available for ninety-six firms. The mean and median one-year-ahead stock returns across nonimpairers and impairers are not statistically distinguishable, which is again inconsistent with the private-information hypothesis and the FASB's expectation of how SFAS 142 would be used.

To investigate whether goodwill nonimpairment is associated with motives predicted by agency theory to affect management's accounting choice, we consider proxies for the following effects based on related prior literature:[79] whether impairment would trigger debt covenants, whether impairment would affect CEO bonus targets, and whether impairment would trigger stock-exchange delisting thresholds. We find a statistically higher proportion of firms with goodwill-inclusive debt covenants among sample nonimpairers (78 percent) than among sample impairers (63 percent). Similarly, the proportion of firms whose CEOs are likely to have goodwill-inclusive bonus contracts is statistically higher among nonimpairers (57 percent) than among impairers (39 percent). Both results are consistent with predictions from agency theory. But we find no statistical difference between the proportions of nonimpairers (51 percent) versus impairers (53 percent) with exchange-delisting concerns.

We further examine whether the goodwill nonimpairment is associated with concerns that a write-off would trigger a larger-than-average decline in stock prices due to a functional relation between net income and stock returns. We also examine how CEO tenure—in particular the likelihood that a CEO was responsible for the M&A that generated the goodwill now deemed impaired—affects impairment. A CEO is likely to be less forthcoming in accepting that a merger he or she personally engineered has failed. Additionally, we test whether nonimpairment varies in some of the proxies for the potential to abuse the discretion in SFAS 142. These proxies are those used to explain firms' lobbying positions on ED 201-R, described in the previous section, specifically, the number and size of reporting units and the unverifiability of a reporting unit's net assets. For brevity, with all these variables I only discuss the results of multivariate tests. These multivariate tests also include the proxies for the private information hypothesis described earlier.

In the multivariate tests, we find some evidence that proxies for debt-covenant concerns and CEO bonus incentives are associated with nonimpairment. Additionally, we find that nonimpairment increases in CEO tenure, consistent with CEOs attempting to shield their reputations in making write-off decisions. These results are consistent with agency theory as applied to corporate managers' accounting choice. We also find nonimpairment increases in the proxies for the potential to abuse the discretion in SFAS 142. In the multivariate tests, none of the other proxies, including those for managers' positive private information, are statistically associated with nonimpairment. The nonresult on the proxy for asset-pricing concerns is consistent with firms' stock prices already reflecting goodwill as impaired, a condition on which we selected the sample. The multivariate tests include controls for firm size, firm stock-price performance, and the proportion of a firm's book goodwill to total assets.[80]

Broadly, the evidence is consistent with some managers opportunistically avoiding timely goodwill write-offs under SFAS 142. This is to be expected given the unverifiable nature of the standard's goodwill impairment rules. The results complement the findings from the political economy of SFAS 142 discussed in the earlier sections. The results suggest SFAS 142 is generating financial reports that do not reflect economic reality with respect to goodwill. Even if the stock markets can completely unravel the effects of opportunistic nonimpairment, SFAS 142 is likely imposing costs on the market economy. These include distortions to debt and compensation contracts written on accounting numbers, as well as the costs to investors from managers continuing negative net-present-value operations (related to failed acquisitions) simply to avoid goodwill write-offs.

Given that the conclusions above are based on a small sample of distressed firms, I also examine more systematic evidence on the nature of M&A deals since the implementation of SFAS 142 in 2002. After all, if SFAS 142 did indeed lower the standard of accountability for acquired goodwill, we would expect to see more overpayment on acquisitions after 2002. One method to infer overpayment commonly used in the academic literature is negative stock-price returns for the acquiring firm around the three days when an acquisition is first announced. The negative announcement-period returns can reflect the market's expectation that value will be destroyed from the acquisition. A study of acquisitions by U.S. companies between 1993 and 2007 found that announcement-period returns in the 2003–7 period (after SFAS 142 went into effect) were more negative than announcement-period returns in the 1993–99 period (before the political process on SFAS 142 was initiated). The difference is statistically significant. This result also holds when comparing acquisitions using only cash, only stock, or combinations of cash and stock as the purchase instruments.[81] The data suggest that the market expects greater overpayment (more value destruction) in acquisitions post-SFAS 142, a result consistent with the hypothesis that SFAS 142 has decreased accountability for M&A.[82]

The impairment-only approach to goodwill acquired in M&A, which resulted from a contentious and self-serving political process, is thus potentially generating costs to society. Interestingly, this approach—with its de-emphasis on matching and verifiability—is consistent neither with the economic framework for accounting nor with the FASB's own original conceptual framework (described in chapter 2). Prior to the regulation of accounting rule-making under the SEC, when firms did not rely on a political process to endorse their accounting practices, a variety of practices for M&A accounting coexisted. An analysis of these practices suggests that the purchase method with goodwill amortization or with an immediate write-down of all acquired goodwill was widely accepted.[83] Such rules would likely introduce greater accountability for acquired goodwill than the impairment-only approach in SFAS 142. But as the evidence in this chapter shows, these rules did not survive the turbulent political process that underlies accounting rule-making.

This is not to suggest that abolishing the pooling method was undesirable or that amortization is the "correct" way to account for acquired goodwill. After all, straight-line amortization is a mechanical rule that does not permit individual firms the ability to reflect the unique economics of their acquisitions. Furthermore, even under a regime that requires goodwill amortization, goodwill must still be tested for write-offs—consistent with the conservatism principle—so there is an important role for goodwill impairment under the economic framework for accounting. What makes the impairment-only regime of SFAS 142 especially costly is its exclusive emphasis on unverifiable estimates to the exclusion of amortization—in violation of the matching principle. It is this situation that depletes the accountability of purchase premiums in M&A resulting in value destruction.

The accounting treatment underlying SFAS 142—that goodwill recognized on the balance sheet is not subject to expensing unless impaired—assumes that acquired goodwill has indefinite life. This assumption violates the basic premise of competitive strategy, which holds that rents cannot be sustained without continual investment.[84] If goodwill is to be capitalized as an asset, then—under the economic framework for accounting—there must be some income-statement accountability (via amortization) arising from that capitalization. If straight-line amortization is too noisy, then one option is for acquiring firms to define an amortization schedule that better matches the economic depletion of the rents represented by goodwill. Such a schedule can be tied to the acquiring firm's strategy for the acquisition and specified at the time of capitalization.[85]

Of course, there are likely to be costs to this approach as well. Indeed, there is unlikely to be a silver-bullet solution to this and other contentious accounting issues. But the main takeaway from this chapter is that there is evidence on the costs of a major existing accounting rule, SFAS 142, which detracts in important ways from the economic framework for accounting. This is reason to consider why that rule is in place.

The story of the evolution of goodwill accounting rules, discussed in detail in this chapter, is a window into the political process of accounting rule-making. It particularly highlights the successes of corporate managerial self-interest and the power of investment banks in accounting rule-making. And the power of corporate political interests in accounting rule-making is not unique to the case of goodwill accounting, as several other studies on the subject have shown. Over the past three-and-a-half decades, research-ers in accounting have documented how different corporate interests have shaped U.S. GAAP accounting rules on subjects as diverse as (1) inflation adjustments to reported accounts, (2) recognition and expensing of the costs of interest on borrowings, (3) translation of foreign currency transactions and foreign operations into an entity's home currency, (4) recognition of unfunded pension obligations as a liability, (5) exploration costs for oil and gas companies, and (6) recognition of employee stock-option grants as an expense.[86] In each of these cases, a handful of corporations most affected by the proposed rules expressively shaped outcomes of the rule-making process. While the implications of these rules are experienced broadly, the evidence suggests that the rules themselves are shaped more narrowly. To paraphrase Winston Churchill tongue-in-cheek, "Never was so much owed by so many to so few."[87]

Take, for example, the case of accounting for employee stock options. As the salience of stock-options-based compensation in the economy rose in the late 1980s and early 1990s, so too did the strength of the case for treating these options as a real compensation expense. After all, in many cases, the options were used as a surrogate for cash compensation, which had to be expensed.

The accounting rule in place at the time (APB Opinion 25) prescribed recognizing options-related expenses at their "intrinsic value," generally defined as the excess, if any, of the price of the underlying stock on the grant date over the option's exercise price.[88] Because, for most options, the exercise price was at least equal to the grant-date stock price, the intrinsic value was zero, and the rule had the effect that there would be no stock-option expense. In June 1993, the FASB issued an exposure draft requiring options to be expensed at their "current value" on the grant date.[89] While this current value was an estimate, the estimate was used to generate a timely expense—an application of conservatism and matching principles.

The FASB proposal almost immediately met with sharp opposition, particularly from technology companies in the increasingly powerful Silicon Valley area, which used options abundantly. These companies, many of which were unprofitable, were concerned about the additional drag on their earnings from options expensing. The technology companies rallied support from elements of the financial-services industry and other industries using options. Soon members of Congress with ties to these industries also became involved. In 1993 and 1994, at least four major actions were proposed in Congress to counter the FASB's proposal, including one that would require FASB rules to be expressly approved by a majority vote of the SEC commissioners, who are political appointees.[90] This latter bill would have significantly weakened the FASB and was likely intended as a threat. Soon, even the American Institute of Certified Public Accountants, which had previously supported the FASB's position, switched sides.[91]

Eventually, in 1995, the FASB gave in and allowed companies the choice to record option expenses at either their intrinsic value or their current value.[92] Companies electing to use the intrinsic-value method could continue, in practice, to record no options-related expense. This situation persisted for about seven years until, in 2002, the Enron and WorldCom scandals surfaced concerns about the potential distortionary impact of options as executive compensation. Quickly, members of Congress, eager to appear responsive to the scandals, introduced bills to effect the expensing of stock options.[93] Although there was still some opposition to this idea, the political tide had turned. Finally, in 2004, the FASB was able to introduce the rule requiring stock-options expensing at current-value estimates.[94]

So the case of accounting for employee stock options is similar to the case of SFAS 142: the corporations most affected by the proposed rules coalesced into special-interest groups to capture the rule-making process. With stock options, it took nearly a decade for the effects of the special-interest capture to unravel. With goodwill accounting under SFAS 142, it also appears, as of this writing, that a reversal of the impairment-only regime might be on the horizon. In February 2014, the FASB issued a communiqué that the board was considering reintroducing the principle of amortization for acquired goodwill.[95]

I conclude this chapter by returning briefly to its core focus: the political evolution of SFAS 142, in particular its embrace of fair-value rules for goodwill accounting. In this narrative, auditors—especially the "Big N" audit firms who have constituted the oligopoly in auditing over at least the past forty years—are relatively silent. Furthermore, over the course of events leading up to SFAS 142, the FASB members themselves appear somewhat hapless and hustled—buffeted by the fickle winds of evolving self-interests. I highlight these observations because these are not entirely accurate portrayals of the positions of auditors and FASB members in accounting rule-making. This point should become amply clear over the course of the following two chapters, which explore, respectively, the role of Big N auditors and FASB members over more than three decades of the FASB's history.

The Shrinking Big N: Rule-Making Incentives of the Tightening Oligopoly in Auditing

As noted in chapter 2, the accrual process at the heart of accounting information is highly discretionary—it requires considerable exercise of judgment on the part of corporate managers to produce informative financial reports. All else equal, corporate managers have incentives to abuse the judgment inherent in the accrual process when preparing reports of corporate financial performance and position. After all, managers are evaluated, compensated, promoted, and fired based on these reports.[1] Furthermore, the information asymmetry between corporate managers and users of financial statements, such as equity and debt holders, gives corporate managers the ability to abuse the discretion in the accrual process. Perhaps the most famous example of these phenomena is the great crash of 1929. Historians of the crash have argued that abuses of accrual discretion played a role in the inflation of stock prices that led to the crash.[2] Without a systematic mechanism to hold managers accountable on their accrual judgments, it is likely that public trust in those judgments would dissipate, eventually unraveling the capital-market system.

Chapter 2 discusses how "verifiability" is a key mechanism of accountability that has evolved in financial-reporting practice. The idea behind this mechanism is to ensure that accrual estimates can be, in the legal sense, "objectively determined as true or false."[3] In practice, of course, there is a continuum of objectivity—and thus verifiability—associated with accrual estimates: for example, certain receivable assets with liquid markets are more verifiable than intangible assets such as goodwill. Auditors operate along this continuum of verifiability and certify that accruals are being recorded in accordance with GAAP rules, thus mitigating concerns that emerge from managers' information advantage.[4] Thus auditors are perhaps the most important of the intermediating institutions related to accounting and financial reporting.

Auditors function as the first line of defense, so to speak, when it comes to publicly issued financial reports. In fact, the role of auditing is so tightly integrated with accounting that the economic theory of financial reporting predicts that auditing and the accrual process—particularly its grounding in "verifiability"—evolve jointly (see chapter 2). And, indeed, historical evidence on the subject is generally consistent with this prediction, at least in the modern era of the corporation and capital markets beginning in the mid-1800s. For example, in early corporate America during the second half of the nineteenth century, as U.S. companies sought to raise capital in London (then the preeminent stock market in the world), they faced an obvious credibility problem. This problem was gradually addressed as British auditing firms started opening up offices in America to audit U.S. companies. The introduction of professional auditing in America has also been tied to the growth of U.S. stock exchanges and capital markets more broadly.[5]

In practice, a corporation's board of directors, particularly its audit committee, exercises much sway over the retention and removal of auditors. At first, this might appear like a curious arrangement—the (potential) fox appoints the guard to the henhouse. But this arrangement is meaningful if the board is independent of corporate managers, who actually make the accrual judgment decisions. In fact, in general, boards, as much as external financial-statement users, rely on auditors to ensure the quality of financial reporting. Of course, from time to time, the independence of boards and the independence of auditors from corporate management have been questioned. The most significant recent evidence in this regard emerged in the early 2000s, after corporate accounting scandals such as those at Enron and WorldCom shook public confidence in financial reporting.[6] The result was a highly significant piece of regulation—the Sarbanes-Oxley Act (SOX)—that introduced, among other measures, considerable change to the nature and organization of auditing. Until the passage of SOX, auditing in the United States was largely a self-regulated profession. Many of the institutions and practices in modern auditing had emerged over a century and a half of evolution in the marketplace. SOX, for the first time, created a public regulator—the Public Company Accounting Oversight Board (PCAOB)—to monitor, assess, and shape the nature of auditing practice.[7]

The focus in this chapter, however, is not on the nature of auditing practice but rather on the role of the auditing industry in accounting rule-making under the FASB. The various institutional features in auditing, such as those described above, are considered insofar as they are relevant to this focus. Perhaps the most important institutional feature of contemporary auditing is that the industry, for better or worse, is organized as an oligopoly.[8] For the entire history of the FASB, since 1973, auditing in the United States has been dominated by a handful of players, whom are often referred to as the "Big N" auditors. The reason for the "N" is that the precise number of players has decreased over the FASB's lifetime. In the 1970s and 1980s, there were eight big auditors who collectively audited the vast majority of public companies. In 1988, the Big Eight were estimated to audit 98 percent of public companies by sales.[9] Over the following decade, the number of Big N auditors decreased through consolidations, first to six and then to five. Then in 2002, in the wake of the Enron scandal, Arthur Andersen, perhaps the most storied of the Big N auditors, collapsed and the oligopoly shrank further to four players. By this point, the combined market share of the Big N was estimated at 99 percent of public companies by sales.[10] (See table 4.1 for a tabular representation of the evolution of the Big N audit oligopoly from Big Eight to Big Four.)

This tightening auditing oligopoly has been a source of considerable concern in public policy circles. The Government Accountability Office—the U.S. Congress' key watchdog—has from time to time written public reports about the issue.[11] And the financial press and business academics have also tried to raise alarm. In particular, these groups are concerned that the Big N auditors are now "too few" and "too big" to fail.[12] In fact, in 2005, when Big N audit firm KPMG was found to be "peddling illegal tax shelters" among its clients, the government did not seek criminal prosecution, which could have put KPMG out of business—rather it allowed the firm to reach a settlement.[13] But the consolidation of the Big N auditors may not be all bad. For

TABLE 4.1. Tabular representation of the evolution of the Big N audit oligopoly from Big Eight to Big Four, 1973–2006

Big Eight 1973–1989	Big Six 1989–1998	Big Five 1998–2002	Big Four 2002–2006
Arthur Andersen	Arthur Andersen	Arthur Andersen	
Arthur Young	Ernst & Young	Ernst & Young	Ernst & Young
Ernst & Whinney/Ernst & Ernst			
Deloitte, Haskins & Sells	Deloitte Touche	Deloitte Touche	Deloitte Touche
Touche Ross			
Peat Marwick	KPMG	KPMG	KPMG
Price Waterhouse	Price Waterhouse	PwC	PwC
Coopers Lybrand	Coopers Lybrand		

Source: Adapted from Abigail Allen and Karthik Ramanna, "Towards an Understanding of the Role of Standard Setters in Standard Setting," *Journal of Accounting and Economics* 55, no. 1 (2013): 66–90.

one, the consolidation could mean that these large auditors now have more bargaining power vis-à-vis their clients—that is, the corporate boards (and managers) who hire and fire them. With less competition to worry about, the auditors could become less focused on catering to their clients' short-term interests and more focused on their key role in assuring the integrity of accounting and financial reporting.

The discussion above suggests that there is an open empirical question about how the consolidation among the Big N has affected the nature of auditing. This question is the focus of a recent paper I coauthored with Professor Abigail Allen of Harvard Business School and Professor Sugata Roychowdhury of Boston College. That paper addresses the question by looking at the changing nature of Big N auditor lobbying at the FASB. In this chapter, I draw on the results of that paper to address an issue more relevant to this book: the role of the Big N auditors in the FASB's rule-making process. As it happens, the changing industrial organization of the auditing industry is a useful feature in addressing this issue because the decreasing number of audit firms changes the surviving firms' incentives when lobbying on accounting rules. The remainder of this chapter discusses the research design, evidence, and implications of my paper with Professors Allen and Roychowdhury as they are relevant to this chapter's focus. But before that discussion, in the following section, I introduce some hypotheses on auditors' incentives in lobbying on accounting rule-making that are the basis for subsequent tests and conclusions.

The Role of Big N Auditors in Accounting Rule-Making at the FASB

In the late 1970s and early 1980s, an empirical academic literature on the role of audit-firm lobbying at the FASB began to emerge. This literature was likely motivated by a 1976 report by the U.S. Senate that alleged that the FASB was "dominated" by the interests of the then Big Eight auditors.[14] The report was troubling news for the fledgling FASB, which had been created with the aim of establishing greater independence from special-interest groups in accounting rule-making. In 1978, following up on the Senate report, the U.S. House even introduced a proposal that would federalize accounting rule-making.[15] The academic literature that followed these congressional positions specifically investigated the influence of audit firms in their lobbying of the FASB.

The academic studies found no evidence of a systematic association between the positions of the Big N auditors and those of the FASB on substantive accounting issues.[16] In other words, there was no evidence of *systematic* capture of the FASB by the auditors. While the FASB did indeed agree with the Big N on some issues, there was dissonance on others. Moreover, the

Big N auditors themselves were not homogeneous in their assessments of substantive accounting matters. The general conclusion from these studies was a vindication for the FASB. That, together with the arrival of a generally antiregulation U.S. presidential administration in the 1980s, put to rest the threat of potential nationalization of accounting rule-making.

The academic literature on the lobbying of the Big N auditors at the FASB continued into the mid-1980s. The literature began to focus on the incentives of the auditors in their lobbying positions. Broadly, there were two hypotheses being evaluated: first, that the audit firms largely represented their clients' interests when lobbying, and second, that the audit firms represented their own interests, even if at the expense of client interests, when lobbying. The evidence in the literature was broadly consistent with the latter hypothesis.[17] Since these studies in the 1980s there has been no direct empirical work on the lobbying of auditors at the FASB (of which I am aware) until the study with Professors Allen and Roychowdhury described earlier.[18] In the nearly thirty years that have elapsed, there have been considerable changes in accounting and auditing institutions, in the industrial organization of auditing, and in the nature of the U.S. economy, including its globalization. Thus another look at the role of audit firm lobbying at the FASB is warranted.

Auditors have dual incentives in performing their fundamental verification task in accounting and financial reporting. First, their job involves the exercise of professional judgment around the certification of client firms' accounting practices. This job inherently carries the potential for legal liability and reputational penalty. While, in a perfect world, these costs manifest only if auditors deliberately err or show substantial negligence in their exercise of judgment, in practice, auditors might incur these costs even in cases where they were genuinely mistaken or where events outside their control subsequently revealed their judgment to be flawed. Thus auditors have an incentive to be risk averse in their exercise of professional judgment.[19]

Second, in practice, auditors are hired, fired, and paid by their client firms. As such, this generates a preference to keep clients happy. Client firms, all else equal, prefer greater discretion in the accrual process. Such discretion is not necessarily for nefarious purposes.[20] Greater accrual discretion helps firms prepare financial reports that more accurately reflect the underlying economics of their businesses. This is especially important to firms with novel strategies, new technologies, or new business models, to which existing accounting rules might be ill-suited.

For example, when Apple first launched the iPhone, extant accounting rules did not allow the company to appropriately communicate the volume and profitability of the iPhone business. Specifically, GAAP rules at the time required Apple to recognize revenue from most iPhone sales over eight quarters, because most customers purchased their iPhone with a two-year cell phone service contract. Apple argued that performance obligations under the two-year contract largely applied to its partners—the cell phone service providers. Apple's own obligations over the two years—largely to maintain software for the iPhone—were minimal. Thus Apple argued that accounting rules requiring the firm to recognize its own iPhone-related revenues over two years distorted its financial statements. Instead, the firm sought rules that permitted it to recognize most iPhone-related revenues in the quarter of the sale. Apple, at first, resorted to preparing supplementary non-GAAP financial disclosures for its investors to this effect. Eventually, Apple successfully lobbied the FASB to change the relevant accounting rules to reflect the innovations in strategy, technology, and operations that the iPhone represented.[21]

Given client firms' preferences for greater discretion in the accrual process and auditors' preferences to satisfy their clients, auditors have an incentive to cater to clients' demands for greater accounting discretion. Such discretion can have the added benefit to auditors of increasing the scope of their work and thus, all else equal, fees they can charge clients.[22]

The two incentives described above can be at odds with each other. Greater risk aversion on the part of auditors can constrain the discretion in the accrual process that clients seek, resulting in displeased clients and, in the extreme, in client defections. Eventually, in equilibrium, auditors are likely to choose some degree of risk aversion in their professional judgment that optimally trades off their concerns over litigation and reputation with the desire to keep clients happy. This basic equilibrium characterization of auditors' incentives in the exercise of their professional judgment is also likely to affect their incentives in lobbying for accounting rules. That is, auditors are likely to seek accounting rules that improve their ability to trade off the risk aversion that emerges from potential litigation and reputational costs with the need to satisfy clients' desires for greater discretion in the accrual process.[23]

In this chapter, I focus especially on how this equilibrium auditor preference for risk aversion in accounting rules has changed over time, in particular over the life of the FASB. Numerous institutional changes to auditing over the period since 1973, including the changing litigation environment in the United States and the changing industrial organization of the audit industry described earlier, could have altered the equilibrium degree of risk aversion among auditors. By studying how Big N auditor lobbying on risk aversion in accounting rules has changed, we can glean an insight into the role of Big N auditors in the accounting rule-making process.

To conduct such an empirical study over the nearly four-decade time period, one requires a metric of Big N auditor preferences on accounting rules that is meaningful across a broad range of accounting issues and that also maps onto the auditors' demand for risk aversion. In my paper with Professors Allen and Roychowdhury, we use Big N auditors' concerns about the decreased "reliability" in FASB exposure drafts as the metric. The metric is extracted from a computational linguistic analysis of the auditors' comment letters on the exposure drafts. (More details on the construction of this variable, including assumptions, strengths, and weaknesses, are available in the following chapter, where the variable is again used in an assessment of the role of FASB members in accounting rule-making.)

As noted in chapter 2, "reliability" is a fundamental property of accounting under both the economic theory of financial reporting and the FASB's own original conceptual framework.[24] Thus by focusing on reliability, we are able to study a substantive dimension of accounting rules that is likely to be pertinent to most, if not all, exposure drafts over our relatively long time series. Moreover, reliability is closely related to verifiability, which is the core task in auditing and is related to auditor risk aversion, as described above. On the one hand, more reliable accounting rules are easier to verify: accrual estimates generated under these rules are more likely to be objectively certifiable. This, in turn, mitigates the likelihood of litigation and reputational costs to auditors. On the other hand, more reliable accounting rules—through their emphasis on objectivity—can temper the discretion in accruals that auditors' clients seek. Thus our metric of the Big N auditors' perceptions of decreased reliability in FASB exposure drafts can help us understand how auditor lobbying on risk aversion in accounting rules has changed over time. This, in turn, provides insights into the role of Big N auditors in the accounting rule-making process.

In the period since the FASB's inception in 1973, the U.S. litigation environment, particularly as it relates to the audit firms, has changed significantly several times. In particular, in 1983, two major court cases increased the standard of auditor liability from "privity" to "reasonable foreseeability."[25] Under the doctrine of privity, auditors were only liable to parties with whom they had a direct contractual relationship; reasonable foreseeability indicated that auditors were liable to any party that might reasonably be expected to rely on audited financial statements. The year 1983 saw another reason for increased auditor liability, as courts held that audit firms could be sued under the Racketeer Influenced and Corrupt Organizations (RICO) Act of 1970, hitherto generally limited to punishing organized crime syndicates.[26] Furthermore, in 1988, the U.S. Supreme Court upheld important elements of the doctrine of reasonable foreseeability in its landmark ruling on the fraud-on-the-market theory.[27] Then in 1992, auditors won a respite as courts introduced the doctrine of "known users" in lieu of reasonable foreseeability—auditors were now only liable to parties whom the auditors *knew* relied on financial reports.[28] That year also saw the introduction of limited liability partnerships for audit firms, which reduced auditors' legal exposure.[29] Shortly thereafter, in 1995, legislation in Congress reduced the liability of auditors under the Securities Act of 1934 and the RICO Act of 1970.[30] Finally, in 2002, the Sarbanes-Oxley Act was introduced, which, as discussed earlier, brought increased regulation and oversight to auditors, increasing the likelihood of detecting auditor malfeasance and thus increasing, in expectation, auditors' potential liability.[31]

These changes to the litigation environment are likely to affect the risk aversion of the Big N auditors and their preference for discretion in the accrual process. Thus the changes in the litigation environment are also likely to affect auditors' expressed concerns over decreased reliability in their comment letters on FASB exposure drafts. By studying how auditors expressed concerns over decreased reliability change with changes in the litigation environment, we can gain an insight into auditors' incentives when lobbying the FASB. Specifically, if we find that the Big N auditors are more likely to express concerns over decreased reliability in periods of heightened litigation (relative to periods of diminished litigation), then we can conclude that the auditors lobby in their own interests, consistent with the first studies of auditor lobbying behavior from the early 1980s.

Just as changes in the litigation environment can be used to shed light on auditors' incentives in lobbying on accounting rules, so too can the changes in the industrial organization of auditing. As noted earlier, the consolidation of the Big N from eight to six to five and finally four audit firms has created competing pressures on the auditors. On the one hand, the auditors are increasingly perceived as being too big and too few to fail. If true, this can increase their hubris as it relates to their exposure to litigation and reputation risk, which in turn frees up the auditors to focus on their clients' demands for greater flexibility in accruals. In this case, the auditors would still focus on client interests because that is their basis for competition among each other. The result, in this scenario, would be a diminished concern over decreases in the reliability of proposed accounting rules as the auditing oligopoly tightens. On the other hand, the consolidation in the audit industry could indicate that the auditors are increasingly secure vis-à-vis their clients, who have fewer options. Furthermore, the fewer the number of audit firms, the more visible each surviving firm is as a target for litigation and regulatory scrutiny.[32] The result would be a heightened concern over decreases in the reliability of FASB exposure drafts.

Thus the changes to the industrial organization of the auditing industry provide competing predictions on Big N auditor lobbying over decreased reliability. But both predictions allow us to investigate whether auditors are self-serving in their lobbying on accounting rules. The implications of such self-serving lobbying behavior, particularly as they relate to the eventual level of discretion versus verifiability in GAAP accruals, are of particular interest to the objectives of this book. In the final section of this chapter, I discuss those implications. The interceding sections discuss the research design and the evidence for the hypotheses described above.

The Research Design

The purpose of the empirical tests in this chapter is to investigate how Big N auditors lobby on accounting rules proposed by the FASB. The tests focus on the Big N auditors' expressions of concerns over decreased reliability in FASB exposure drafts. In particular, the tests examine how the concerns over decreased reliability have changed over the lifetime of the FASB, a period in which the litigation environment for auditors and the industrial organization of auditing have changed significantly.

To undertake these tests, one requires a benchmark measure of decreased reliability in FASB exposure drafts—that is, some indication of the "true" concern over decreased reliability to which the Big N auditors' concerns can be compared. One possible benchmark is to use the assessments of other groups lobbying at the FASB (e.g., financial institutions). But, of course, these groups have their own incentives in lobbying; thus their assessments are biased. Another possibility was for my coauthors and me to evaluate the FASB exposure drafts ourselves to determine their impact on decreased reliability. But as researchers aware of the underlying research questions, we are also potentially biased. Thus to obtain the benchmark assessment, we relied on two research associates who possess considerable expertise and experience in accounting-related matters (over thirty years of combined experience) but who were blind to the study's objectives. In evaluating exposure drafts for decreased reliability, the research associates relied on the formal definition of reliability offered by the FASB in its original conceptual framework—a definition also used by many accounting textbooks in our sample period and thus familiar to auditors lobbying over that period. The evaluations of these research associates serve as our proxy for the true incidence of decreased reliability in FASB exposure drafts.[33]

The regression strategy is to examine how the correlation between the Big N auditors' assessments of decreased reliability in FASB exposure drafts and the assessments of the research associates change over time, particularly over the changing litigation and audit oligopoly periods. Thus the auditors' assessments are the dependent variable in the regressions, and the research associates' assessments are the primary independent variable. Our sample period for these tests runs from 1973 to 2006. Our tests do not include data from 2007 and beyond because these data were not available when we first initiated sample collection procedures in 2009. There are 126 distinct exposure drafts in our sample period after data limitations. Each of these exposure drafts, which resulted in a final accounting rule, has an assessment on decreased reliability by the research associates. In addition, there are 774 distinct Big N auditor assessments of those exposure drafts that serve as the regressand.

Because several factors are likely to affect the Big N auditors' assessments of decreased reliability, we include in the regressions fixed effects for each year in the sample. These fixed effects control for temporal variation in the dependent variable unrelated to the benchmark or "true" variation in decreased reliability. Additionally, since we are interested in how the correlation between the Big N auditors' assessments and those of the research associates change over time, we interact the research associates' assessments with the year fixed effects. Thus the coefficient on the interaction between the year indicator and the research associates' assessments is the key regression output of interest for each year. To examine how this coefficient has changed over time, we average the coefficients for a given time period—for example, the "reasonable foreseeability" period (1984–92), the "known users" period (1993–2002), the Big Eight period (1973–89), the Big Six period (1989–98)—and compare the averages across these periods in formal statistical tests described in the following section.

The research design described above attributes the changes in the correlation between the Big N auditors' assessments and the research associates' assessments over various periods to the changes in the auditors' incentives across those periods. But substantive changes in accounting over time could also affect these correlations to the extent that such substantive changes manifest in a time series similar to the various periods we have identified. The most obvious of these substantive changes is fair-value accounting: the growing incidence of fair-value-based accounting rules could be responsible for the changing correlations between the Big N auditors' assessments and the research associates' assessments that we attribute to the auditors' changing incentives around their changing oligopoly. Thus we include in the regressions controls for the incidence of fair-value-based accounting rules.

In particular, we are interested in isolating that part of the concordance between the Big N auditors' and the research associates' assessments on decreased reliability that is attributable to fair-value-based proposals. On the one hand, fair-value proposals can increase auditor liability because they can increase unverifiable judgment in accruals. In this case, auditors are more likely to emphasize their concerns about decreased reliability of fair-value proposals. On the other hand, if auditors are able to limit their liability on fair-value rules by circumscribing the nature of their audit tasks, they are likely to support fair-value proposals because such proposals can increase the scope of their work and thus their fees. In this case, auditors are less likely to emphasize their concerns about decreased reliability of fair-value proposals.

In this vein, we also include controls for the proportion of FASB members from the financial-services industry. As discussed in the following chapter, FASB members from this industry are particularly associated with the incidence and growth of fair-value accounting in GAAP, especially over the past two decades.

The Evidence

Before presenting the evidence from the regressions, I discuss some descriptive univariate evidence relating to the variables introduced above. Figure 4.1 presents the average annual values of the Big N auditors' assessments of decreased reliability in FASB exposure drafts from 1973 to 2006.[34] As seen from the figure, there is considerable variation in the values over time. That figure

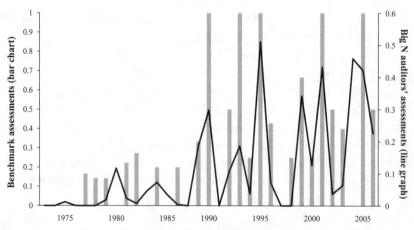

FIGURE 4.1. Graph of the Big N auditors' assessments and benchmark assessments of decreased reliability in FASB exposure drafts, 1973–2006

Source: Adapted from Abigail Allen, Karthik Ramanna, and Sugata Roychowdhury, "The Auditing Oligopoly and Lobbying on Accounting Standards" (working paper 13-054, Harvard Business School, Boston, MA, 2013).

TABLE 4.2. Multivariate evidence on Big N auditors' lobbying on decreased reliability across four auditor-litigation periods, 1973–2006

Auditor-litigation period		Coefficient	Difference from coefficient on		
			Foreseeability	Known users	SOX
1977–1983	Privity	−0.03 ***	***	***	***
1984–1992	Foreseeability	0.31 ***	***	*	
1993–2002	Known users	0.18 ***	***		*
2003–2006	SOX	0.34 ***	***		

*, **, and *** denote statistical significance at the 90 percent, 95 percent, and 99 percent confidence levels, respectively.

Source: Adapted from Abigail Allen, Karthik Ramanna, and Sugata Roychowdhury, "The Auditing Oligopoly and Lobbying on Accounting Standards" (working paper 13-054, Harvard Business School, Boston, MA, 2013).

also includes the average annual values of the research associates' assessments of decreased reliability. These latter assessments also show variation over time, although there is no obviously visible mapping between the time variations across the two variables.

Turning to the results of the regressions, here, for brevity, I only report the correlation coefficients between the Big N auditors' and research associates' (benchmark) assessments of decreased reliability across various periods of interest. These are, respectively, the four auditor-litigation periods and the four auditing-oligopoly periods. In table 4.2 the correlations are averaged within each of the four auditor-litigation periods that emerge across the sample time series through 2006. The first litigation period, defined by the doctrine of privity, extends from 1977 to 1983, when privity was overturned.[35] This is the benchmark period against which correlations from other litigation periods are compared. The second period extends over the time of "reasonable foreseeability" in auditor litigation from 1984 to 1992. The litigation risk in this period is expected to be higher relative to the prior period. The third litigation period covers 1993 through 2002 and is characterized by the doctrine of "known users." The litigation risk in this period is expected to be lower relative to the prior period. Finally, the fourth period extends from 2003 onward and is characterized as the post-SOX era, when the auditors are under increased scrutiny, including from their new overseer, the PCAOB. Here, litigation risk is expected to be higher relative to the "known users" period.

The data in table 4.2 show that the correlations between the Big N auditors' assessments and the benchmark assessments of decreased reliability vary as predicted across the four litigation periods. The correlation coefficient is lowest under the doctrine of privity; it then rises under the doctrine of rea-

TABLE 4.3. Multivariate evidence on Big N auditors' lobbying on decreased reliability across four auditing-oligopoly periods, 1973–2006

| Auditing-oligopoly period | | Coefficient | | Difference from coefficient on | | |
				Big Six	Big Five	Big Four
1973–1989	Big Eight	0.08		**	***	***
1989–1998	Big Six	0.46	***		**	**
1998–2002	Big Five	0.68	***			***
2002–2006	Big Four	1.22	***			

*, **, and *** denote statistical significance at the 90 percent, 95 percent, and 99 percent confidence levels, respectively.

Source: Adapted from Abigail Allen, Karthik Ramanna, and Sugata Roychowdhury, "The Auditing Oligopoly and Lobbying on Accounting Standards" (working paper 13-054, Harvard Business School, Boston, MA, 2013).

sonable foreseeability, decreases again under the doctrine of known users, before finally rising in the SOX period. Moreover, all the correlations are statistically distinguishable from those of immediately adjacent periods. The data are consistent with the proposition that Big N auditors' lobbying over decreased reliability in accounting rules varies with their own private incentives, as characterized by the changing litigation regimes. More broadly, auditors appear to be lobbying in their self-interest, consistent with the empirical findings of studies of auditor lobbying in the early 1980s.

Table 4.3 presents the correlations between the Big N auditors' assessments and the benchmark assessments of decreased reliability averaged within each of the four auditing-oligopoly periods. These are the Big Eight period from 1973 to 1989, the Big Six period from 1989 to 1998, the Big Five period from 1998 to 2002, and the Big Four period from 2002 to 2006. The data in table 4.3 show that the correlation coefficients increase consistently as the auditing oligopoly tightens—the correlation coefficient for each oligopoly period is statistically higher than that of the preceding period. This result suggests that Big N auditors are increasingly expressing concerns about decreased accounting reliability in their lobbying. The result is consistent with the tightening audit oligopoly generating greater visibility on the surviving Big N firms, making them more prominent targets for litigation and regulatory scrutiny. The results are inconsistent with claims that the Big N, now too big or too few to fail, are less focused on risk aversion. More broadly, the result corroborates the findings from table 4.2 that the Big N auditors appear to lobby in their own interests during the accounting rule-making process.

The regressions underlying the results described in table 4.3 also include control variables to capture the association between the Big N auditors' assessments and the benchmark assessments that can be attributable to either

(1) fair-value-based proposals or (2) the proportion of FASB members from financial-services industry. The purpose of the first variable is to determine if the incidence of fair-value proposals per se is driving the increased association between Big N auditor assessments and benchmark assessments over time—after all, the incidence of fair-value proposals has also increased over the sample period. The purpose of the second variable is to examine whether the nature of the composition of the FASB, particularly the presence of members from the financial-services sector, affects the association between Big N auditors' assessments and benchmark assessments. The reason for including this variable is the finding in the following chapter that FASB members from this sector are particularly associated with the incidence and growth of fair-value GAAP proposals.

The coefficient on the first control variable is statistically insignificant. This finding is interesting because it suggests that the increasing manifestation of Big N auditors' concerns over decreased reliability in GAAP proposals is not driven by their opposition to fair-value accounting per se. The coefficient on the second control variable is negative and statistically significant, indicating that Big N auditors are less likely to be in concordance with the benchmark assessment on decreased reliability when GAAP proposals emanate from FASB boards with higher financial-service representation. This finding is consistent with the first finding when interpreted in the context of the result that FASB members from the financial-services sector are associated with the rise of fair-value accounting.

A caveat on the results in table 4.3 follows: changes in the auditing oligopoly—from Big Eight to Big Four—are likely precipitated by more fundamental changes such as changes in the litigation environment, technological changes, globalization, and so on.[36] Put differently, the consolidation of the audit industry is likely to be effected by several macroeconomic and technological trends that are not accounted for in the research design implemented above. Instead, the design takes as given the consolidating audit industry and studies its effects on Big N auditor lobbying behavior. A full specification of the determinants of auditor consolidation is likely to subsume the effects documented in table 4.3. This suggests that the results in table 4.3 are part of a broader story that is presented here in the narrower context of auditor incentives in lobbying at the FASB.

Implications

The focus of this chapter is to shed some light on the role of the auditing industry, particularly the Big N auditors, in accounting rule-making under the FASB. The key takeaway from the results above is that, in the political process that determines U.S. GAAP, Big N auditors appear to lobby in their self-interest. To the skeptical reader, this result likely comes as no surprise; but given auditors' stewardship role in the market economy, it betrays a broader question about who is looking out for the interests of the system as a whole in the determination of accounting rules that are so critical to market capitalism. This is a theme that I more fully consider in chapter 8. The remainder of this section is devoted to exploring the implications of the substantive direction of Big N auditor lobbying over time—that is, toward an increasing emphasis on decreased reliability in GAAP proposals but not in fair-value-based GAAP proposals. The discussion that follows builds on the formal statistical study presented thus far, but my coauthors from that study are not implicated in this exposition.

Substantively, the results in this chapter suggest that as the auditing oligopoly has tightened and the litigation environment for auditors has become more severe, the Big N auditors have increasingly focused their lobbying on GAAP reliability. At first blush, this finding might appear promising. After all, reliability is a key mechanism of integrity in GAAP. Thus the auditors' emphasis on reliability in GAAP proposals could suggest that they are seeking to preserve and enhance GAAP integrity. But there is an alternative interpretation to consider: recall that the results are obtained relative to the baseline or "true" level of reliability in GAAP, which is to say that the Big N auditors' increasing emphasis on reliability could in fact be an *overemphasis*—that is, the auditors, lobbying opportunistically to protect themselves from litigation and regulatory scrutiny, could be seeking to decrease the level of judgment in GAAP below what is optimal for the system as a whole. Too much of an emphasis on "reliability" can strip the accrual process of the discretion necessary to keep financial reports meaningful and relevant to the varying economic and technological situations of industrial companies. The auditors, given their increasing risk aversion, could be lobbying for a socialization or collectivization of the risks of auditing.[37]

In fact, in the decade leading up to 2007, the SEC had become increasingly concerned about the growing proportion of accounting rules and practices that were "check-the-box" rather than judgment based. Numerous preparers and users of corporate accounting reports had complained that financial reporting had migrated from being informative in decision making and contracting to becoming simply a compliance exercise. The SEC even put together a high-level commission on the "future of financial reporting" to help find ways to restore greater judgment in the accrual process.[38] When auditors were questioned before this committee, not surprisingly, they complained that greater discretion in accounting opened them up to greater litigation risk.[39]

If the Big N auditors' increased lobbying emphasis on reliability in fact manifested in the final accounting rules that constitute GAAP, then the evidence discussed in this chapter could provide an explanation for the increased proportion of check-the-box GAAP rules that concerned the SEC and other financial-reporting constituents. Such rules suggest that the level of discretion in GAAP could be less than what is necessary for the efficient allocation of capital in our market system. The result could be a net loss to social welfare. The self-serving role of auditor lobbying in potentially generating this outcome is germane to the thesis of this book.

But how does one reconcile this shift toward more check-the-box rules and the evidence on Big N auditors emphasizing concerns about decreased GAAP reliability in their lobbying with the growth of fair-value accounting, which can be highly discretionary? To shed some light on this question, consider two relevant findings from the previous section. First, note that the data suggest that the increasing manifestation of Big N auditors' concerns over decreased reliability is not driven by the auditors' opposition to fair-value accounting per se. Anecdotal evidence from the auditors' comment letters corroborates this conclusion. While from time to time the Big N audit firms have expressed some concern about certain fair-value measurements, they have generally endorsed the expansion of fair-value accounting, particularly since the early 1990s. Consider, for example, the Big N auditor lobbying in response to the FASB proposal, in 2006, that eventually became SFAS 159—one of the most sweeping fair-value rules intended, in the FASB's words, to "expand the use of fair value measurement . . . consistent with the Board's long-term measurement objectives."[40] The comment letter from KPMG remarked that the audit firm "agree[d] with the Board's stated objective of establishing standards to require reporting financial assets and financial liabilities at fair value in the financial statements."[41] Likewise, the comment letter from Ernst & Young noted that it "generally support[ed] the issuance of this statement,"[42] and the letter from Deloitte expressed its "support [for] the Board's effort to broaden the use of fair value as a measurement attribute."[43]

The Big N's positions on fair-value accounting might be driven by assurances they have secured in relevant auditing standards on the issue. Indeed, Statement on Auditing Standards (SAS) 101, which defines standards for the auditing of fair-value measurements, makes it explicit that corporate managers, not their auditors, are "responsible for making the fair value measurements and disclosures included in the financial statements." The auditor's task is limited to providing "reasonable assurance that fair value measurements" are made in "conformity with GAAP." Recognizing that fair-value measurements are "inherently imprecise," SAS 101 makes it clear that auditors are "not responsible for predicting future conditions" implicit in making fair-value estimates and thus cannot be held liable as such. The standard goes on to provide a detailed set of activities—a checklist of sorts—that would provide the "reasonable assurance" required of fair-value audits, should the auditor engage in them.[44]

Moreover, a recent U.S. federal court ruling on fair-value measurements suggests that the unverifiability of certain fair-value estimates might excuse auditors and their clients from litigation risk altogether. In a case involving a class action against a company for not writing down its goodwill during the 2008 Financial Crisis, the Second Circuit Court of Appeals found that the fair value of acquired assets, an important component of goodwill, is not a matter of "objective fact" and "that there is no universally infallible index of fair market value." As a result, the court reasoned that for the suit to proceed, plaintiffs had to allege that "defendants [i.e., corporate management] did not believe" their own fair value estimates "at the time they made them."[45] Of course, establishing this fact is nearly impossible—it would take a particularly foolish manager to leave a paper trail to this effect—which is why the court rejected the plaintiffs' suit. This court ruling has attracted the attention of several corporate law firms that have explicated on its important implications for liability under fair-value accounting.[46]

The second relevant empirical finding that can help reconcile auditors' focus on check-the-box rules and decreased GAAP reliability with the growth of fair-value accounting is as follows. Recall that the results in the previous section indicate that Big N auditors are less likely to be in concordance with the benchmark assessment on decreased reliability when GAAP proposals emanate from FASB boards with higher financial-service representation. As noted earlier, this finding is consistent with the first finding on fair-value proposals when interpreted in the context of the result (discussed in chapter 5) that FASB members from the financial-services sector are associated with the rise of fair-value accounting.

The overall narrative that emerges from these findings is as follows. Big N auditors have expressed increasing concerns about decreased reliability in GAAP proposals as their incentives to protect themselves from litigation and regulatory risk have increased. But the Big N have not opposed the rise of fair-value accounting, in fact deemphasizing concerns about decreased reliability when proposals emanate from the financial-services sector, which itself is associated with fair-value accounting. Auditors have incentives to support fair-value rules, if such rules can be seen as increasing the need for their services and if their liability from auditing such rules is limited. The narrative points to a powerful political wind behind the rise of fair-value GAAP rules, a theme more fully explored in the following chapter.

Why Fair Value Is the Rule: The Changing
Nature of Standard Setters

One of the central reasons for replacing the Accounting Principles Board (APB) with the FASB, in 1973, was the desire to afford greater independence and autonomy for accounting rule-makers in the rule-making process.[1] The APB was constituted of members who served part time and who had primary full-time affiliations to other organizations, particularly audit firms.[2] FASB members, by contrast, are required to resign their prior commitments and are generously compensated and supported in their activities.[3] A motivating philosophy in the design of the FASB has been the establishment of an environment that allows board members the freedom to frame accounting rules that reflect economic realities rather than political pressures.[4] In this spirit, board members are expected to issue accounting rules that are generally consistent with the FASB's conceptual framework.

As the FASB completes forty years of existence, it is worth asking how this experiment at independent rule-making has performed. The two preceding chapters show constituent pressure in FASB rule-making is alive and well. But this result notwithstanding, it is conceivable that board members, freed from allegiances to various special interests, have, by and large, been able to stem the effects of political pressure in accounting rule-making. Here I report on the results of an examination of the role of FASB members in the determination of accounting rules over the first thirty-four years of the FASB's existence—that is, 1973–2006. The study also examines the role of SEC commissioners who served concurrently during this period, given the SEC's regulatory relationship with the FASB, although the study's primary focus is FASB members. The analysis ends in 2006 due to data limitations that were in place when the study was initiated.

Although there has been some research on the political process in accounting over the last several decades, very little of this work has focused on FASB members or other regulators per se. The likely reason for this neglect is that until recently, most economics-based research viewed "individuals" as largely unimportant in explaining large-scale, complex decisions such as regulatory policy making; the expectation was that individual idiosyncrasies would be averaged out in processes that involved multiple participants.[5] Since the 2000s, however, there has been growing evidence that individual effects do matter even in complex decision-making contexts. For example, research has shown the impact of individual CEOs in explaining major, persistent firm decisions related to strategy, finance, external reporting, and internal control.[6] In this spirit, in 2012, I published with my colleague Professor Abigail Allen a study of the role of individual FASB members and SEC commissioners in accounting rule-making. The results I report here are based on that study.

The study assembles a database of certain key background characteristics of all thirty-nine individual FASB members and all forty-one SEC commissioners who served during the period from 1973 to 2006. The background characteristics include their professional experience, their tenure on the board, and their political leanings, if any. These background characteristics are used to explain the nature of the nearly 150 exposure drafts (EDs) proposed by the FASB over that period. All these EDs eventually resulted in final FASB rules (known as SFAS). The study focuses on EDs rather than the final FASB rules because, as seen from the previous two chapters, these final rules can be influenced by a number of constituents, including industrial, financial, and audit firms.[7] Although EDs themselves can also be shaped by constituent pressures, when compared to the final rules, EDs offer a relatively unadulterated insight into the preferences and impact of FASB members in the rule-making process.

The primary conclusions from the study are drawn from multivariate regressions of the nature of EDs proposed by FASB members on those members' background characteristics. The regressions control for numerous alternative explanations that could affect inferences, as discussed later, and for the background characteristics of SEC commissioners who served concurrently. Briefly, the evidence across thirty-four years of FASB rule-making suggests that the background characteristics of individual FASB members explain in part the nature of accounting rules they propose. Put differently, individual idiosyncrasies of FASB members appear to matter in accounting rule-making. This result is interesting given that the board members should, in theory, be guided by the FASB's conceptual framework and not their own idiosyncrasies. If the individual characteristics of board members matter, then the door is open both for "ideology" in accounting rule-making and for the potential "capture" of the FASB. The remainder of this chapter discusses the evidence and these implications in greater detail. I begin in the next section by explaining how my coauthor and I assessed the nature of the numerous FASB EDs over the sample period to prepare the dependent variable in the study.

Assessing the Nature of FASB EDs

In examining the EDs over the thirty-four-year period from 1973 to 2006, we focus on two accounting properties in particular: "reliability" and "relevance." As noted in chapter 2, "reliability," being closely related to both verifiability and conservatism, is a fundamental characteristic of GAAP, as predicted by the economic theory of financial reporting. It is the basis for the analysis of the Big N auditors' role in accounting rule-making discussed in chapter 4. "Relevance" is similarly central to accounting theory, being the second of two "fundamental qualitative characteristics" of accounting (besides "reliability") according to the FASB's original conceptual framework.[8] And although, as also noted in chapter 2, the FASB's revised conceptual framework in 2010 de-emphasized the centrality of reliability in its accounting theory, this change is less germane to the analysis herein because it postdates the period of that analysis.[9] Moreover, beyond the economic theory of financial reporting and the FASB's own original conceptual framework, relevance and reliability have been identified as critical accounting properties by numerous accounting textbooks used in basic undergraduate and graduate accounting education.[10] Of course, the focus on relevance and reliability in this analysis of EDs suggests that there are numerous opportunities to expand and verify its findings across other accounting properties such as "comparability" and "consistency."

To evaluate all EDs from 1973 to 2006 for their impact on relevance and reliability is a mammoth undertaking, which also requires a certain degree of consistency and objectivity. Assessments of the EDs by me and my coauthor could be corrupted by "researcher bias" since we approach the data with hypotheses to be tested. To avoid this kind of bias, we used assessments by the Big N audit firms. These assessments—in the auditors' comment letters on the EDs—were the dependent variables in the analysis described in the previous chapter. There are 149 EDs and 908 Big N auditor assessments (comment letters) in our sample period after data limitations.[11]

The primary advantage to using assessments of the Big N auditors, over assessments by other constituents such as industrial or financial firms, is that the Big N auditors consistently comment on most FASB EDs over the sample period. Industrial firms tend to comment only on those issues that are particularly salient to their own interests—on other issues, they are usually silent. Financial firms tend to comment more frequently than industrial firms; however, the changing industrial dynamics of the financial-services industry over the past four decades (including the consolidation of brokerage, financial research, investment banking, and investment management firms) means that very few of the same financial firms consistently comment over the thirty-four-year period in the analysis. By contrast, the auditing industry, as the prior chapter discusses, has been organized as an oligopoly over the entire sample period allowing us a relatively homogeneous set of assessors of the FASB EDs.

There are two other important advantages to using the Big N auditors' assessments. First, they are contemporaneous with the EDs. In other words, the assessments were made at the time the EDs were written, keeping in context extant macroeconomic and political issues, together with the extant conceptual understanding of the role of accounting.[12] Second, the Big N auditors are, of course, sophisticated FASB constituents whose comment letters are likely to have meaningful information content.

We convert the Big N auditors' qualitative assessments of EDs into quantitative metrics that can be used in multivariate regressions using the same procedure as in chapter 4. The details of this procedure are discussed in our article published in 2013 in the *Journal of Accounting and Economics*. Briefly, the procedure is as follows. First, for each Big N auditor comment letter, we identify—through a partially computerized search algorithm—the first substantive occurrence of word stems related to "reliability" and "relevance" in each comment letter. Next, a research assistant trained in accounting but blind to the study's objectives determined whether "relevance" is used in a context that suggests the ED would increase GAAP relevance and whether "reliability" is used in a context that suggests the ED would decrease GAAP reliability. Finally, the metrics of increased relevance and decreased reliability for each comment letter are weighted to account for the salience of those sentiments in the comment letter. That is to say, we attempt to give greater weight to the Big N auditors' sentiments about increased relevance and decreased reliability if they are part of the auditors' overall assessment of an ED rather than related to a narrow concern about some part of the ED. Thus, substantively, the quantitative metrics capture the Big N auditors' assessments of each EDs' potential to increase relevance and decrease reliability in GAAP.

Descriptively, the largest value of the measure for increased relevance is found for the ED, from 2006, that resulted in SFAS 159, "The Fair Value Option for Financial Assets and Financial Liabilities." SFAS 159, as the title suggests, is the rule that introduced the ability for firms to use fair-value accounting in reporting their financial assets and liabilities. It is one of the most widely applicable fair-value accounting rules in the FASB's history. In the FASB's own words, the rule was intended to "improve relevance of financial statements."[13] Thus it is not surprising that the ED resulting in SFAS 159 generates the highest value for increased relevance.

Similarly, the largest value of the measure for decreased reliability is found for the ED, from 2005, that resulted in SFAS 141R, "Business Combinations," an amendment to SFAS 141 discussed in chapter 3. A major provision of this ED was to allow the acquiring firm in an M&A the ability to recognize acquired net assets at their fair values without regard to the purchase price of the acquisition. As noted in chapter 3, the prior rule, SFAS 141, limited the fair values of net assets recognized to the acquisition's purchase price. Eliminating the acquisition purchase price as the upper bound for net-asset-value recognition can introduce additional subjectivity to the already subjective M&A accounting rules. Thus it seems reasonable that the ED resulting in SFAS 141R generates the highest value for decreased reliability.

The ED resulting in SFAS 157, "Fair Value Measurements"—arguably the FASB's keystone proposals on fair-value accounting, which established "a framework for measuring fair value in generally accepted accounting principles"[14]—also scored highly on the measures for increased relevance and decreased reliability. Both measures for this ED were over one standard deviation above the respective mean values across all EDs.

The Big N auditors' assessments of FASB EDs are likely to reflect their own private incentives, for example, catering to the demands of their clients or lowering the litigation risk inherent in GAAP rules, as chapter 4 discusses. As such, this feature of the data does not pose a problem to drawing inferences as long as one expects these incentives are not jointly determined with and not affected by the explanatory variables in our study (e.g., the background characteristics of FASB members). Although there is no obvious reason to expect otherwise, we also conduct our analyses using a second assessment of FASB EDs. This assessment is made by two seasoned research associates who are blind to the study's objectives—it was used as the "benchmark" assessment in the analyses in the prior chapter. The research associates both have MBAs from top-tier business schools and have together about thirty years of experience in accounting-related matters. The research associates first independently evaluated the EDs for their impact on accounting relevance and reliability, as defined in the FASB's original conceptual framework. Then the research associates met to compare and reconcile their assessments with each other to produce a joint assessment of each ED. These research-associate assessments are available on 126 of the 149 EDs in our sample. Thus they allow for verification of the results across a substantial portion of the sample. The main drawback to these research-associate assessments is that unlike the auditors' assessments, they are not contemporaneous with the EDs and accordingly could suffer from a hindsight bias.

We examine the correlations between the Big N auditors' assessments of increased relevance / decreased reliability and those of the research associates. We find that increased relevance as assessed by auditors is positively and significantly correlated with increased relevance as assessed by the research associates. The same is true for decreased reliability, as is already evident from the analyses in the prior chapter. Both results suggest that the metrics based on the auditors' assessments and the research associates' assessments capture similar underlying constructs, although the auditors' assessments are also likely colored by their incentives. Furthermore, we find that increased relevance is positively and significantly correlated with decreased reliability across both sets of assessments. This result suggests that relevance and reliability, as manifested in GAAP, are trade-offs, as the FASB's original conceptual framework had intended.

The Background Characteristics of FASB Members

The assessments of the EDs described above are the variables of interest in the multivariate regressions of the impact of individual FASB members on accounting rule-making. The primary explanatory variables in these regressions are the FASB members' background characteristics. Drawing from other studies of the impact of individual regulators in determining regulation,[15] in our tests we focus on three background characteristics in particular. These are described below.

First, we consider the tenure of the FASB members. The classical economic theory of regulation, first articulated by Professor George Stigler of the University of Chicago, predicts that longer regulatory tenures facilitate greater "coziness" between regulators and the regulated.[16] As regulatory tenures get longer, the relationships between regulators and special-interest groups are expected to deepen and the regulators' empathy for the general interest in regulation is expected to deteriorate. This situation is eventually expected to result in regulatory "capture" by special-interest groups. Applying this logic to the context of the FASB, longer tenures on the FASB could be an indication of capture. If the special-interest groups capturing the FASB include financial-statement preparers and financial intermediaries who benefit from decreased reliability/increased relevance in GAAP (on this point, see chapter 2), one outcome of longer FASB tenures could be rules with these effects. Thus a positive association between FASB EDs assessed as decreasing reliability/increasing reliability and longer FASB tenures would be consistent with the predictions of the classical theory of regulation.

Next, we consider the professional backgrounds of FASB members, specifically their immediate prior employment. Prior studies on regulatory backgrounds have focused on employment in industries most closely related to the matter being regulated—for example, a study of members of the Federal Communications Commission focused on prior employment in the broadcasting industry.[17] In the case of the FASB, we accordingly focus on members' immediate prior employment in the auditing and financial-services industries (the latter is specifically defined as the investment banking and investment management industries). We view these as "front line" industries on accounting issues. All else equal, we expect FASB members from the auditing industry to be more focused on preserving and augmenting accounting reliability—at the potential expense of accounting relevance, consistent with the discussions in the prior chapter.[18] In contrast, we expect FASB members from the financial-services industry to be more focused on preserving and augmenting accounting relevance—at the potential expense of accounting reliability, consistent with their interest in fair-value accounting.[19] To summarize, we predict a negative association between EDs assessed as increasing relevance/decreasing reliability and the proportion of FASB members with an auditing background, and we predict a positive association between EDs assessed as increasing relevance/ decreasing reliability and the proportion of FASB members with a financial-services background.

Finally, we consider the political leanings, if any, of FASB members. Prior research on the impact of regulators on regulations has generally found regulators affiliated with the Democratic Party to be less business friendly than regulators affiliated with the Republican Party.[20] This kind of political polarization could translate into the realm of accounting rule-making as well, although it is difficult to clearly specify from theory how FASB members' political leanings might translate to decreased reliability and increased relevance in EDs. Moreover, unlike with public agencies such as the SEC and the Federal Communications Commission, where members' political affiliations are generally widely known, the political leanings of FASB members are unclear. This is because the FASB is not a public body and members are not required to disclose political affiliations. To overcome this issue, my coauthor and I studied the campaign contributions logs of the Federal Elections Commission to determine any political donations by FASB members over our sample period (the logs archive contributions over $200 by U.S. persons). For this study, the FASB members' net campaign contributions are used to determine their political leanings: net contributions to the Democratic Party are used to indicate that the member leans Democratic and similarly for members leaning Republican.

In addition to the FASB members' background characteristics described above, we obtain similar data on the background characteristics of concurrently serving SEC commissioners—specifically, the commissioners' tenure; their backgrounds, if any in auditing and financial services; and their political affiliations. The FASB's authority to determine U.S. GAAP comes from the SEC, which is also eventually responsible for the enforcement of FASB rules. Given this strong regulatory relationship between the FASB and the SEC, our regressions include background characteristics for SEC commissioners as additional explanatory variables.

Some descriptive statistics on the various explanatory variables described above follows. We find that the average tenure of FASB members is 4.2 years, which indicates that, on average, an ED in our sample period is issued by a board with 4.2 years of individual service experience. For comparison, note that the average tenure of SEC commissioners, similarly calculated, is 3.1 years, suggesting that on average FASB members have had an additional year of regulatory experience when an ED is issued. (See figure 5.1 for a graph of the average tenure of FASB members and SEC commissioners by ED over the 1973–2006 period.[21])

The average proportion of FASB members with prior employment in auditing is about 40 percent. This proportion appears to have held steady over the sample period. By contrast, the average proportion of FASB members with prior employment in financial services (defined as investment banking and investment management) is only 4 percent. But this proportion has increased dramatically over the sample period: it was zero through about the mid-1990s and had risen to just under 30 percent by 2006.[22] For comparison, the corresponding statistics for SEC commissioners are as follows. Only one SEC commissioner over the sample period was employed in auditing prior to serving on the commission, while the average proportion of SEC commissioners with prior employment in financial services is 15 percent. This latter figure, like its corresponding FASB figure, shows considerable variation over the sample period. (See figure 5.2 for a graph of the average proportion of FASB members and SEC commissioners with prior employment in auditing and financial services over the 1973–2006 period.)

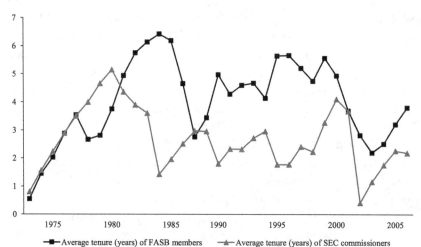

FIGURE 5.1. Graph of the average tenure of FASB members and SEC commissioners by exposure draft, 1973–2006
Source: Adapted from Abigail Allen and Karthik Ramanna, "Towards an Understanding of the Role of Standard Setters in Standard Setting," *Journal of Accounting and Economics* 55, no. 1 (2013): 66–90.

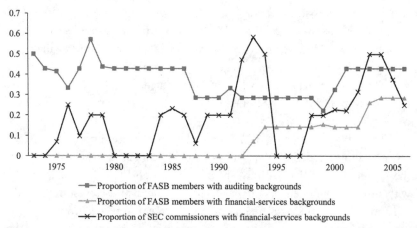

FIGURE 5.2. Graph of the average proportion of FASB members and SEC commissioners with prior employment in auditing and financial services, 1973–2006
Source: Adapted from Abigail Allen and Karthik Ramanna, "Towards an Understanding of the Role of Standard Setters in Standard Setting," *Journal of Accounting and Economics* 55, no. 1 (2013): 66–90.

The average proportion of FASB members leaning Democratic—that is, contributing to the Democratic Party—is 17 percent. The statistic is similar for FASB members leaning Republican at 18 percent. For comparison, the average proportion of Democratic SEC commissioners is 45 percent, and the corresponding statistic for Republican SEC commissioners is 55 percent.

Overall, the partisan proportions for SEC commissioners are higher than those for FASB members because the former are collectively exhaustive in the sample and are known with certainty—the SEC commissioners are political appointments.[23] With regards to the variation in these metrics over the sample period, the proportion of FASB members leaning Democratic is higher than that leaning Republican in the first few years of the FASB's existence; but, between 1995 and 2002, when several fair-value accounting rules were issued, the proportion leaning Republican is higher. The variation over time of the political identity of SEC commissioners represents White House control. (See figure 5.3 for a graph of the average proportion of FASB members and SEC commissioners by political identity over the 1973–2006 period.)

Some additional descriptive data on FASB members' background characteristics over the sample period follow. The FASB members employed by audit firms immediately prior to serving on the board were all employed at Big N auditors, but no particular Big N firm enjoyed a disproportionate influence in this regard. Five of the thirty-nine FASB members over the sample period were employed at universities just prior to serving on the board, and the proportion of academics on the FASB has remained roughly constant over time. Three of the thirty-nine FASB members were employed by the U.S. government immediately prior to their board appointment, although all three served in the first twenty years of the FASB—the last of the three left the FASB in the early 1990s, suggesting that the idea of public employees be-

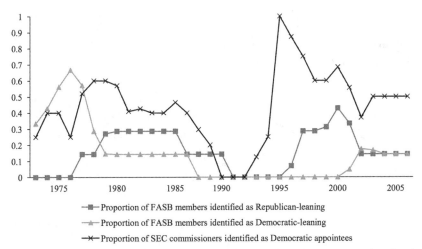

FIGURE 5.3. Graph of the average proportion of FASB members and SEC commissioners by political identity, 1973–2006
Source: Adapted from Abigail Allen and Karthik Ramanna, "Towards an Understanding of the Role of Standard Setters in Standard Setting," *Journal of Accounting and Economics* 55, no. 1 (2013): 66–90.

ing appointed to the board fell out of favor over time. Although a substantial proportion of FASB members were employed at industrial firms just prior to their board appointment, there is no particular industry concentration among this group.

Thirty of the thirty-nine FASB members over the sample period held the certified public accountant (CPA) designation at one point in their careers, consistent with the idea that accounting rule-making—even under the FASB—remains largely the domain of professional accountants. All the FASB members who have served over the sample period had undergraduate degrees; about 60 percent of members also had graduate degrees. There is no particular university that is overrepresented in this group. Finally, the average age of FASB members on first appointment to the board is in the midfifties, a number that appears to have held steady over time.

The Evidence

The evidence on the impact of FASB members on accounting rule-making is inferred from numerous multivariate regressions. The dependent variables in these regressions are variously the Big N auditors' and the research associates' assessments of EDs' increased relevance and decreased reliability. The primary explanatory variables are the average background characteristics of the FASB members in office at the time a given ED was issued.[24] Additional explanatory variables include the background characteristics of SEC commissioners, similarly calculated. There is a high observed correlation between the variables capturing the professional backgrounds of the regulators and the variables capturing their political leanings. These correlations have been observed in studies on regulators from other industries as well, but there is no general theory to explain them.[25] To explore the impact of all explanatory variables, we run several sets of regressions: those using only FASB members' and SEC commissioners' tenure and professional backgrounds as explanatory variables, those using only FASB members' and SEC commissioners' political leanings as explanatory variables, and those using all explanatory variables together.

In the discussion that follows, I focus mainly on results from regressions where Big N auditors' assessments of the EDs are used as dependent variables. Regressions using the research associates' assessments yield qualitatively similar inferences with respect to FASB members (the full details of these regressions are available in the published paper). The regressions on Big N auditors' assessments of EDs include numerous control variables, including those for prevailing macroeconomic conditions, as well as controls for any effects that might be idiosyncratic to each of the Big N audit firms.[26]

When the regulators' tenure and professional backgrounds are the explanatory variables, we find a positive association between FASB members' and SEC commissioners' tenure and EDs perceived as decreasing accounting reliability. We find no relation between FASB and SEC tenures and EDs perceived as increasing relevance. The evidence suggests that longer regulatory tenures facilitate decreased reliability in GAAP, which—assuming such decreased reliability delivers private benefits to certain financial-statement preparers and financial intermediaries at the expense of the general interest—is consistent with regulatory capture of the FASB and the economic theory of regulation first expounded by Professor Stigler. In these regressions, we find no association between the proportion of FASB members with prior employment in the auditing industry and EDs perceived as increasing relevance/decreasing reliability. This is inconsistent with our expectations and with our findings in chapter 4. But we do find that the proportion of FASB members with prior employment in the financial-services industry is positively associated both with EDs perceived as increasing relevance and with decreasing reliability. These results are consistent with our expectations that, all else equal, FASB members from the financial-services industry are more focused on preserving and augmenting accounting relevance (at the potential expense of reliability), consistent with their interest in fair-value accounting. There is also evidence of a positive and statistically significant association between SEC commissioners with prior employment in the financial-services industry and EDs perceived as decreasing reliability.

In additional regressions that use the research associates' assessments of EDs as the dependent variable, we are able to corroborate the inference about the impact of FASB members' prior employment in financial services on increased relevance and decreased reliability. Note that the research associates evaluate EDs as increasing relevance based in part on the use of fair-value methods in the EDs. Thus the results using the research associates' measures provide direct evidence of a positive association between EDs that use more fair-value methods and the proportion of FASB members' with prior employment in the financial-services industry.

When FASB members' political leanings are the explanatory variables, we find a negative association between the proportion of FASB members leaning Democratic and EDs perceived as decreasing reliability/increasing relevance. The implication of this finding is that Democratic-leaning FASB members are associated with accounting rules that promote reliability over relevance.

If such rules are less popular with companies because they constrain accounting choice, then this result is consistent with Democratic-leaning FASB members being less business friendly. However, we also find a negative association between the proportion of FASB members leaning Republican and EDs perceived as increasing relevance. This latter finding calls into question the interpretation of the preceding result. There is no evidence of an association between SEC commissioners' political leanings and EDs perceived as decreasing reliability/increasing relevance.

When FASB members' and SEC commissioners' tenure, professional backgrounds, and political leanings are all included as the explanatory variables, one result stands out as statistically robust: the proportion of FASB members with prior employment in the financial-services industry (investment banking and investment management) is positively associated both with EDs perceived as increasing relevance and with decreasing reliability. Put differently, across the full battery of controls in the multivariate regression, the data are consistent with the proposition that a prior career in financial services predisposes FASB members to favor accounting relevance over reliability. Given the increase in the proportion of FASB members from the financial-services industry from zero in the first half of the sample period to just under 30 percent toward the end of the sample period, this result could be especially germane to understanding the growth of fair-value accounting. I discuss this proposition further in the following section.

Discussion and Conclusions

Broadly, the evidence across thirty-four years of FASB rule-making presented in this chapter suggests that the background characteristics of individual FASB members explain in part the nature of accounting rules they propose. While these accounting proposals are subject to considerable constituent lobbying before they become final rules (as has been seen from preceding chapters), the evidence herein affirms the notion that FASB members also matter in the determination of GAAP.

At first blush, this summary interpretation might appear as a victory or at least a vindication for the model of the FASB—the idea of an independent rule-making body separated de jure from the interests it regulates. In this sense, the interpretation could be seen as inconsistent with Professor Stigler's "theory of capture," which holds that constituent lobbying predominantly determines regulatory outcomes because regulators are captured by their special-interest constituents. Rather, the evidence could be seen as more consistent with the alternative economic theory of regulation: the theory of ideology. This theory holds that constituent lobbying is only one input to regulation, which is eventually determined by regulators' own ideologies.[27] Under the ideology theory, constituent lobbying is less a *direct* instrument of policy influence (as under the capture theory) and more a signal to regulators of the preferences and alliances of constituents. The evidence that there is a systematic association between FASB members' backgrounds and the nature of FASB EDs, if interpreted plainly, suggests that the ideology theory—rather than the capture theory—is a better explanation for accounting rule-making under the FASB. The implication is therefore at least a partial endorsement of the FASB model.

A closer read of the evidence in this chapter, however, yields a more nuanced interpretation. First, recall that FASB members should, according to their own stated commitments, be guided by the board's conceptual framework in their rule-making; the notion that the members' individual characteristics matter suggests that the conceptual framework may not be so fundamental to the process. This interpretation, in turn, opens the possibility for special-interest capture because it suggests that board members are not strictly bound by their framework for financial reporting. Second, note that the evidence suggests that longer regulatory tenures are associated with accounting proposals that likely decrease reliability in GAAP, with attendant social-welfare implications—a result more consistent with the regulatory "coziness" predicted under the capture theory. Third, while there is evidence to suggest that FASB members' political leanings affect the accounting rules they propose, the result is seen across both major political parties—a finding for which there is no straightforward explanation under either the capture or the ideology theories. Finally, and perhaps most important, is the result associating the proportion of FASB members from the financial-services sector to accounting proposals that promote relevance over reliability, a phenomenon associated with fair-value accounting. This result has particularly significant implications for the question of FASB capture. I expand on this proposition below.

Fair-value accounting is one of the most important issues in financial-reporting policy today—it affects the very basis of accounting and, therefore, accounting's role in performance measurement, corporate stewardship, and valuation. The general argument for fair-value accounting is that it increases the direct association between accounting numbers and contemporaneous equity values.[28] By incorporating managerial estimates of future firm performance, a fair-value-based accounting system becomes a timelier metric of current firm value and thus more "valuation relevant." The argument against fair values is that it can erode accounting's core competence: the emphasis on matching, verifiability, and conservatism.[29]

Fair-value accounting is not a recent innovation. Various forms of fair-value accounting existed in the GAAP of the 1920s, prior to SEC regulation of listed-company financial-reporting practices.[30] But such fair-value practices were seen as contributing to the misinformation that preceded the stock-market crash of 1929, and fair-value accounting was effectively banned by the SEC from the 1930s through the period of the advent of the FASB.[31]

Starting in the late 1970s, the proportion of FASB EDs that employed fair-value methods increased. In the 1980s, the use of fair values was sporadic. By the 1990s, a substantial proportion (about one-half) of FASB EDs was employing fair-value methods. A number of academic studies were published in that decade showing that the use of fair-value accounting increased the direct correlation between corporations' accounting reports and stock prices. At first, the studies were influential in both academia and policy making. By the 2000s, however, concerns over the mechanical nature of such studies were raised in the academic literature (the use of such studies to justify further fair-value rules constitutes a form of circular reasoning).[32] But such studies continue to be cited from time to time in policy making.

Just as fair-value accounting started to gain currency in GAAP during the 1990s, there came in 2001 an ominous signal of its potential cost: the spectacular unraveling of Enron. In its emerging trading business, Enron had aggressively deployed fair-value accounting to recognize revenue from projects well before such revenues were verifiably "earned" and "realizable"—the traditional criteria for revenue recognition. For example, upon signing a contract in July 2000 with the film-distribution company Blockbuster to supply video on demand to certain American markets, Enron recognized a profit of over $110 million. This profit number was based on estimating the revenues and expenses from providing the video-on-demand service over the deal's twenty-year horizon. These "fair value" revenue and expense estimates were highly subjective given the uncertainties associated with the contract's long time frame, including "serious questions about technical viability and market demand." At the time it booked the $110 million profit, Enron had tested its video-on-demand service in only a "few dozen apartments" in three American cities.[33] The result was an overstatement of Enron's income that misled investors as to the company's performance. When the excesses of Enron's use of fair values were uncovered about a year later, they contributed to a coordinated loss of confidence in the company and its eventual dramatic downfall.

Notwithstanding the lessons of Enron and the academic writings about the potential dangers of fair values, the proportion of FASB EDs—and eventual standards—using fair-value methods continued to increase through the 2000s. In many cases, the fair-value estimates being used in GAAP financial

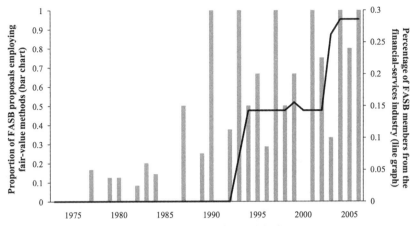

FIGURE 5.4. Graph representing the shift to fair-value methods by the FASB
Source: Adapted from Karthik Ramanna, "Why 'Fair Value' Is the Rule: How a Controversial Accounting Approach Gained Support," *Harvard Business Review* 91, no. 3 (2013): 99–101.

reports were based not on observable prices in liquid markets but rather on managerial conjectures about the future.

The increase in the use of fair values over the 1990s and 2000s corresponded with the increase in the proportion of FASB members from the financial-services industry. As noted earlier, the proportion of FASB members with prior employment in financial services rose from zero in the early 1990s to just under 30 percent by 2006. These concurrent trends are likely behind the dominant result of this chapter's empirical analysis. (See figure 5.4 for a graph representing the shift to fair-value methods by the FASB.)

There are numerous reasons for the financial-services industry to support fair-value accounting. Some are more benign than others. First, investment banks and asset managers are accustomed to using fair values in their day-to-day operations, particularly to prepare in-house balance sheets for risk-management purposes. Their familiarity with fair-value use in internal controls may have shaped their preferences (or "ideology") for fair values in GAAP rules.

Second, GAAP profits defined on a fair-value basis—relative to the traditional historical-cost approach—accelerate the recognition of gains particularly in periods of rising asset prices. (Fair-value based GAAP profits are also higher because they exclude depreciation and amortization charges.) This means bigger payouts for executives whose bonuses are based on GAAP profits. Notably, in the period of rising asset prices that led to the stock-market crash of 2008, fair-value gains on certain securitized financial assets retained on the books of financial institutions were recognized in net income.[34] The result was more favorable accounting-based performance metrics used in evaluating some financial-sector managers and thus higher bonuses for those managers. In fact, such bonuses likely incented further securitizations.[35] Ironically, after asset prices began falling, many financial executives blamed fair-value markdowns for accelerating the crisis. Despite these complaints, an academic review of the role of fair-value accounting during the 2008 Financial Crisis found "little evidence that banks' reported fair values [suffered] from excessive write-downs." The study concluded, "If anything, the evidence points in the opposite direction, suggesting that banks used the discretion in the accounting rules to keep asset values high relative to concurrent market prices and expectations."[36]

Third, as discussed extensively in chapter 3, the use of fair values in accounting for goodwill acquired in M&A—that is, to determine goodwill impairment in lieu of the historical-cost approach of goodwill amortization— reduces, on average, the "drag" on an acquiring firm's earnings, thus potentially increasing M&A activity. Investment banks, which earn their revenue from M&A activity, can therefore be better off under the fair-value approach to goodwill. Beyond this broad benefit to investment banks, there is specific evidence to suggest that financial institutions themselves benefited from the flexibility in goodwill impairment rules during the 2008 Financial Crisis. A study in 2009 examined the goodwill impairment decisions of the fifty largest banks trading in the United States as of December 31, 2008. Forty-eight of these banks had goodwill recorded on their books based on acquisitions made during the period leading up to the crisis. The aggregate goodwill of these banks exceeded $270 billion. Despite substantial declines in their market values in the last quarter of 2008 (in fact, thirty-six of the banks had market values below their book values), only fifteen banks recorded goodwill impairment. Of the banks that did not record goodwill impairment despite having goodwill on their books—there were thirty-three such banks— twenty were trading at market prices below their book values. The aggregate book value of goodwill of these twenty banks—which included some of the country's largest financial institutions, such as Bank of America, JP Morgan Chase, and Wells Fargo—exceeded $190 billion.[37]

To put it all together, a key takeaway from this chapter is that there is robust evidence of a relation between the growth of financial-services representation on the FASB and the fair-value rules that, while potentially beneficial to the financial-services industry, potentially impose welfare costs on the economy by compromising accounting's role in performance measurement and corporate control. A natural follow-up question is then: What explains the growth of financial-services representation on the FASB?

One likely explanation is the growth of finance itself.[38] Put differently, the growing representation of financial-services interests on the FASB has accompanied the growth of the financial-services sector in the U.S. economy more broadly. In the early 1970s, when the FASB was starting off, the financial-services sector represented about 4 percent of U.S. gross domestic product (GDP). By 1980, the sector had grown to about 4.9 percent of U.S. GDP. Between 1980 and 2006, the sector's annual growth rate was nearly double that from the similar period that preceded. By 1990, the financial-services sector represented about 6 percent of GDP, and by 2006 it had grown to an all-time high of 8.3 percent of GDP.[39] Over the course of the FASB's first thirty-four years, finance came to represent a significant part of the U.S. economy. Thus one plausible explanation for the main takeaway from this chapter is that the selection process for FASB members has come under the influence of special interests from finance that have progressively become more powerful with the financialization of the U.S. economy.

It is difficult to verify this explanation through statistical tests because the selection of FASB members is a relatively opaque process managed by the trustees of the FASB's governing board, the Financial Accounting Foundation (FAF), and influenced by the SEC.[40] For example, as of 2013, the FAF's public descriptions on its website of its roles and responsibilities include little detail on the process underlying the appointment of FASB members. In addition, there have been important changes to the composition of the FASB over time that have been effected without much public consideration. For example, in 2008, the FASB's membership was reduced to five members from seven members "to enhance the [FASB's] efficiency, effectiveness, and independence."[41] Then in 2010, the FASB's membership was restored to seven members to address "the unprecedented challenges facing the American capital markets in the months and years ahead."[42] Similarly, the FAF has from time to time emphasized the need for representing various constituencies on the FASB; however, such structural changes have been governed by ad hoc criteria, and there is no general conceptual understanding of the FASB's composition. Thus it is plausible that as the financial sector has grown, the FAF may have come to view the sector as a core constituent of the FASB whose interests need to be advanced, including by inducting more members from this sector to the FASB.[43]

In this narrative on the political evolution of fair-value accounting, it is also important to consider the role of the SEC. The FASB receives its mandate to determine U.S. GAAP accounting rules from the SEC and—as seen from the discussion in chapter 3 of the evolution of M&A accounting rules in SFAS 141 and 142—the SEC has an important role to play in the rule-making process. Indeed, the growth of fair-value accounting would not have been possible without the support (both implicit and explicit) of the SEC. As noted earlier, the SEC was from its inception through the 1970s strongly opposed to fair-value rules, perhaps a relic of the bad experiences with fair values in the crash of 1929. But as the memory of those experiences faded, so too did the SEC's mistrust of fair-value accounting, particularly when applied to financial instruments. Starting in the 1970s, the SEC's accounting leadership gradually began to express a new openness to fair-value accounting—the notion was no longer anathema.[44] By the early 1990s, two key offices at the SEC—those of chairman and chief accountant—were occupied by individuals enthusiastic for fair-value accounting.[45] And since the early 1990s, the SEC has remained generally sympathetic to the use of fair values for financial instruments.[46] Of course, the SEC's own openness to fair-value accounting is likely to be driven at least in part by changing political dynamics, including the rising influence of the financial-services industry in the political process. The SEC is, after all, beholden to Congress for its budget and oversight, and the interests of the financial-services industry are well represented in Congress.[47]

The proposition that interests of the financial-services sector have shaped important changes in GAAP around fair-value accounting does not rule out the potential for "ideology" also manifesting in the accounting rule-making process. As noted earlier, the financial-services sector likely enjoys both a commercial interest in and an ideological preference for fair-value accounting (the latter due to the sector's use of fair values in day-to-day operations). Moreover, the chapter's core result—that background characteristics of individual FASB members explain, in part, the nature of accounting rules they propose—is consistent with a role for regulatory ideology in GAAP rulemaking. Along these lines, a recent long-run study of dissenting votes by FASB members on GAAP rules found a decrease in such dissents over time, particularly on votes concerning fair-value proposals. This result is consistent with greater "ideological homogenization" of the FASB around fair-value accounting.[48]

To this point, I conducted an analysis of the five academics who have served on the FASB over the thirty-four years studied in this chapter. (For this analysis, an "academic" is defined as an individual appointed from a professorial position at a university.) During most of this period, there has been one academic at a time serving on the FASB. Over the sample period, the voting positions of these academics on GAAP rules that increase the use of fair-value accounting have tended toward support of those rules. The first academic to serve on the FASB (from 1973 to 1985) voted on seven fair-value-increasing GAAP rules during his tenure, assenting to four and dissenting on three.[49] Two of those three dissents were driven by his disapproval of fair-value use. Remarkably, these two dissents marked the only times an academic serving on the FASB has disapproved of fair-value use in votes on GAAP rules. Each of the four academics to have since served on the FASB (through the end of 2006) either has assented to the fair-value-increasing GAAP rules or has dissented to such rules because the academic believed the rules did not go far enough in embracing fair values.

This near-complete embrace of fair-value accounting among academics serving on the FASB is especially noteworthy given that fair-value accounting, particularly in the absence of liquid market prices, is not universally embraced in the academic literature. Indeed, as the discussion in chapter 2 suggests, an economics-based approach to accounting rules, which is not uncommon in accounting academia, raises serious concerns with fair-value accounting in certain cases. The voting pattern of academics serving on the FASB suggests that these members have been drawn not to represent the cross section of scholarly arguments in accounting academia but rather to reinforce the shift toward fair-value accounting.

Together, the data suggest that the rise of fair-value accounting can be attributed to demands of the increasingly significant financial-services industry and that this rise has been reinforced conceptually by select academics who are ideologically predisposed to the use of fair values in financial reporting. And although one would expect the Big N auditors to be concerned about this growth in fair values (particularly, fair values that are unverifiable) and therefore to resist that growth, the data from the previous chapter suggest that these auditors have not opposed fair value's rise. This is partly because the auditors' liability under such rules may be limited in several circumstances.

Thus one narrative on the rise of fair-value accounting is as follows. The financial-services sector—empowered by its growing size and presence in the U.S. economy and driven by its own incentives and preferences to promote fair-value accounting—has both secured greater representation on the FASB and co-opted other FASB members ideologically predisposed to fair-value accounting to promulgate more such standards in GAAP. If true, the implication is a kind of ideology-enabled capture of the accounting rule-making process.[50] This conception of "ideological capture" may be especially salient to understanding one of the most important developments in U.S. GAAP over the past twenty-five years: fair-value accounting. Rather than as in the pure theory of capture, where the regulated (in this case, the financial-services industry) simply control their regulators, the political process underlying fair-value accounting can be more appropriately described as one where the relevant special-interest group allied with (seemingly) independent third-party experts (in this case, auditors and academics) to gradually advance their agenda. These independent experts appear to have provided the technical and conceptual arguments (or ideologies) that have facilitated the rise of fair-value accounting.

In fact, the changes to the FASB's conceptual framework (described in chapter 2)—in particular, the reduced emphasis on "reliability" in the new conceptual framework—can be viewed in the context of this narrative of ideological capture on fair-value accounting. As discussed in chapter 2, fair-value accounting, especially in cases involving assets with nonliquid markets, is difficult to reconcile with "verifiability," which was a key component of "reliability" in the FASB's original conceptual framework. As the proportion of fair-value rules in GAAP grew, the FASB itself acknowledged the tension this growth posed to "reliability" in the original conceptual framework.[51] The issue was resolved by the new conceptual framework, which replaced "reliability" with "representational faithfulness." If capture theory alone could describe the political process underlying the growth of fair-value accounting, this significant change in the conceptual framework would not have been necessary. That the conceptual framework was revised alongside the growth of fair-value accounting suggests that this framework (and ideologies therein) play a meaningful role in the political process at the FASB.

This narrative of the growth of fair-value accounting suggests that the political process in accounting is not so simple that special interests—even powerful ones such as financial-services industry—can get whatever it is they want just by lobbying for it. Rather, to secure their preferences, it appears that special interests must co-opt allies and present their arguments in ways that are consistent with acceptable ideologies. Thus the nature of capture in accounting rule-making is perhaps more appropriately described as requiring an element of ideological grounding—ostensibly that of the conceptual framework—even if that grounding can itself be gradually changed over time.

6

Local Interests in Global Games: The Cases of China and India

The evidence in the chapters thus far pertains predominantly to accounting's political process in the United States. Indeed, the major thrust of this book is an evaluation of the rule-making infrastructure that surrounds the FASB. But accounting rule-making is a worldwide phenomenon and, moreover, like the business world in general, it has been globalizing. In fact, one of the most important developments in financial regulation over the last fifteen years has been the establishment of the International Accounting Standards Board (IASB) and the growing acceptance across numerous jurisdictions of the standards it promulgates, International Financial Reporting Standards (IFRS).[1]

In this chapter, I present some international evidence on the political process in accounting rule-making. The objective is to show that the case of the United States, on which I have focused thus far, is not unique. Indeed, special-interest groups appear to play an important role in determining the nature of accounting rules in other jurisdictions as well.[2] Here I focus on two countries: China and India. The case of China illustrates the role of especially powerful local special interests in determining the *global* accounting rules that are promulgated by the IASB. The case of India illustrates what happens when local special interests lack such global reach — in such situations, local accounting rules tend to develop limited exceptions to the global standards. Both cases are rooted in the globalization of accounting rule-making through the development and proliferation of IFRS. Thus I begin this chapter with a brief introduction to the IASB and IFRS.

Since the IASB was formed in 2001, more than one hundred countries, including several of the world's major economies, either have adopted IFRS, or have initiated an IFRS harmonization program, or have in place some national strategy to respond to IFRS. The rapid growth of IFRS is an ironic twist

to accounting's staid reputation in popular culture. Particularly when compared with other related business areas such as product quality standards,
occupational safety standards, environmental standards, securities law, and
immigration reform, accounting has been at the forefront of globalization.

The IASB was established in 2001 as an international equivalent to the
FASB.[3] The organizational architecture and the due process of the IASB—
for example, the independence of board members, their accountability to
a private foundation, the procedures through which new accounting rules
would be created—closely paralleled those of the FASB. Indeed, from the
very beginning, the IASB was structured to make U.S. adoption of IFRS pal-
atable to regulators, investors, auditors, bankers, and industrial companies in
America.[4] In fact, as noted earlier in chapter 2, following the developments
in U.S. GAAP over the 1990s, the nascent IASB adopted fair-value accounting as an important element of its rule-making agenda. And throughout the
first decade of its existence, the IASB maintained a close working relationship
with the FASB, and American interests enjoyed substantial influence in IASB
matters.[5]

An episode to this latter point occurred early in the history of the IASB,
in 2001, when the fledgling new body was seeking funding for its ambitious
agenda. The then chairman of the board of trustees overseeing the IASB, Paul
Volker (who had previously led the U.S. Federal Reserve System), had approached Kenneth Lay, the chairman of Enron, for a donation to the IASB
fund corpus.[6] The request was not unreasonable given that Enron was at the
time one of the largest and most admired companies in the world. The request
must have made its way to Enron's chief accounting officer, Rick Causey, who
in turn directed Enron's auditor, Arthur Andersen, to handle the details—
Arthur Andersen, as one of the Big Five audit firms, was an important player
in worldwide accounting rule-making issues. David Duncan, the lead Andersen partner on the Enron account, took charge of Mr. Causey's request.
Writing to his Andersen colleagues on February 23, 2001, shortly before both
his client firm and his own firm would unravel, Mr. Duncan was blunt about
what Enron expected in return for a donation to the IASB: "While I think
that Rick [Causey] is inclined to do this given Enron's desire to increase their
exposure and influence in rule-making broadly, he is interested in knowing
whether these types of commitments will add any formal or informal access
to this process (i.e., would these types of commitments present opportunities
to meet with the trustees of these groups or other benefits)."[7]

Mr. Duncan's candid note, which was revealed in a subsequent U.S. Senate investigation of the Enron collapse, is a perhaps an extreme characterization of the role of self-interest in lobbying. Nevertheless, the note does

provide a cautionary reminder of the sharp incentives at play in the political process underlying accounting rule-making at both the FASB and the IASB.

While U.S.-based interests have played an important role in shaping the nature of IFRS, they were not the only force behind the establishment and initial development of the IASB. The European Union (EU) is arguably more central to the IASB's story.[8] By the late 1990s, the European Commission (EC) was becoming increasingly serious about a single set of accounting rules for its "common market." At the same time, the EC saw an opportunity to play an important role in the worldwide harmonization of accounting rules and thus avoid U.S. dominance of this process.[9] In 2000, the EC designated the as-yet-unborn IASB its de facto accounting rule-maker. Not surprisingly, when the IASB was established, it was decided to physically locate board members and their staff within the EU, in London. Also, the IASB's first chairman was Britain's then-chief accounting rule-maker, David Tweedie. In 2002, the European Parliament required all EU-listed companies to report under IFRS effective 2005.[10,11]

Just as EU interests were central to the IASB's foundation, these interests continued to shape the IASB's development through its first decade. A palpable example of the EU's centrality to the IASB came during the Financial Crisis of 2008. The issue at hand was the extant international rules on measurement, recognition, and disclosure of financial instruments. The rules did not provide companies the flexibility to reclassify financial instruments that were being recorded on a fair-value basis to a historical-cost basis. This situation put several major European banks in a tenuous position at the height of the financial crisis when the fair values of many asset classes were depressed. These banks argued that they expected to hold several of the assets being recorded at fair values—including mortgage-based assets—for very long periods. So, the banks reasoned, transitory depressions in fair values should not affect their balance sheets. The banks thus sought a reclassification of these assets to a cost basis.[12]

The timing of the banks' demand seemed opportunistic: the banks had recognized fair-value gains as the asset prices were rising but were objecting to fair-value losses as asset prices fell. But the European banks could point to a similar reclassification that had just been afforded to their U.S. counterparts by the FASB.[13] Arguing for a "level playing field" with the Americans, the EC's Economic and Financial Affairs Council, under pressure from major players in the European banking industry, called on the IASB on October 7, 2008, to address the issue.[14] On October 8, the EC president threatened legislation to create a European carve-out from IFRS on reclassification, a move that could have subverted the IASB's legitimacy in the midst of the financial crisis. On

October 13, the IASB rushed through amendments that gave the banks the ability to reclassify previously fair-valued assets to a historical-cost basis, a decision backdated to July 1 of that year.[15,16]

While the EC's influence over the IASB in this matter was not unequivocal, it is pertinent to note that the IASB—at some damage to its own emerging reputation for due process—hurriedly caved to the EC's threat of subverting IFRS on the subject.[17] Evidence on the EU's centrality to the IASB can also be seen in more formal statistical tests. For example, a study I conducted with Professor Ewa Sletten of Boston College on the diffusion of IFRS across nearly ninety jurisdictions worldwide found "network effects" in the decisions of particularly smaller countries to adopt IFRS—that is, smaller countries were more likely to adopt IFRS because other countries were doing so. Importantly, the study found such "network effects being largely driven by" the embrace of IFRS among EU member states.[18]

Over the 2001–10 period, countries have varied in the degree and timing of their commitment to IFRS. In this chapter, I discuss the evidence of special-interest politics in explaining some of this variation, particularly in the cases of China and India. In making this pointed tour of accounting rule-making incentives in these countries, it is important to acknowledge the substantial differences in the institutions and culture of their capital markets versus those in the United States. The differences are likely to shape the nature of accounting rules in these jurisdictions in important ways, so that the conceptually "correct" answer for U.S. GAAP is not always similar to that for the GAAPs of China and India. Put differently, there are a number of hypotheses for why, how, and to what extent countries converge with IFRS that have also been explored in the scholarly literature in accounting. These hypotheses include cultural differences, differences in corporate-governance environments, technological differences, and differences in countries' natural resources.[19] What is relevant to note here is that special-interest politics likely plays a role in countries' IFRS adoption decisions even after controlling for these other factors. With that recognition, here I focus on two limited cases where special interests dilute core accounting principles in potentially costly ways.

One final introductory note on the IASB, relevant to what follows in this chapter: Although the IASB was established with the view of eventual U.S. adoption of IFRS, more than a decade on, that situation has not come to pass. In 2013, an SEC staff report on U.S. adoption of IFRS effectively delayed indefinitely any conclusive decision on the matter.[20] The IASB's long courtship of the FASB, it appears, will have to continue. The continued noncommittal stance of the United States to IFRS has irritated some of the core interests at the IASB, including EU member states.[21] The situation, together with the fall-out of the 2008 Financial Crisis and the weaknesses it revealed in the American financial system, has encouraged the IASB to look to the East, which is where I now turn.[22]

Global Politics: The Case of China

Through a series of liberalizing reforms starting in the late 1970s, the Chinese central government has transformed that country from a centrally planned agrarian economy into an export-driven industrial powerhouse. Between 1978 and 2012, China grew by an average annual rate exceeding 12 percent.[23] By 2010, China had overtaken Japan to become the world's second-largest economy. In March 2013, the Organisation for Economic Co-operation and Development was forecasting that China would overtake the United States to become the world's largest economy by 2016.[24] Chinese manufacturing exports were at the center of this spectacular growth. From 1978 through 2012, exports grew from under $10 billion to over $2 trillion. In 2009, China became the world's largest exporter, a record it has continued to hold since.[25]

While exports have played a central role in the thirty-five-year story of China's spectacular growth, China's domestic capital markets have remained a relative sideshow. This is partly due to the fact that shareholding has a relatively short history in modern China, having only reemerged in the mid-1980s as part of government efforts to create greater operating efficiencies among state-controlled enterprises. In mid-2009, China's two major stock exchanges, located in Shanghai and Shenzhen, had a total market capitalization of less than $3 trillion, only about 30 percent of the equivalent value at the New York Stock Exchange (NYSE). The number of listed companies and the monthly trading volume on the NYSE were 2,354 and $1.4 trillion, respectively, in mid-2009. The equivalent totals for the Shanghai and Shenzhen Stock Exchanges were 1,603 and $674 billion, respectively.[26]

Through the first decade of the 2000s, large and visible Chinese companies preferred to list or to have a second listing on overseas stock markets, such as those in New York, or on the stock market in Hong Kong, which through its legacy as a British colony has a relatively well-developed capital-market infrastructure. In June 2009, the market capitalization of the sixty-five mainland Chinese firms listed on the NYSE was $1.1 trillion, or more than half the total market capitalization of China's domestic stock exchanges.[27] The ten largest of these alone—including Petrochina and China Mobile, with NYSE market capitalizations of $369 billion and $192 billion, respectively—had a total market value of over $965 billion.[28]

In part to address the deficiencies of its domestic capital markets, China, in 2005, announced plans to converge its accounting standards with IFRS. There had been numerous studies tying concerns with China's weak accounting institutions and questionable corporate reporting to the stunted development of its capital markets.[29] IFRS adoption was expected to improve accounting quality in China. In 2006, China introduced new accounting standards that, with a few important exceptions, were based on IFRS.[30] By 2008, listed companies on China's two major stock exchanges as well as most of the country's largest state-controlled enterprises had already begun using the new standards. By 2011, all Chinese companies were expected to adopt them.

The capital-market benefits expected to accrue from IFRS adoption are a common theme behind most countries' decisions to embrace the standards.[31] The remarkable pace of Chinese adoption of IFRS-based standards suggests, however, that China had additional motives when it accepted international accounting standards. One such motive, unique but critically important to export-driven China, is the country's bedevilment in international antidumping lawsuits, which I discuss below.

Much of China's spectacular economic expansion to date has been driven by government and private spending on infrastructure and manufacturing facilities and, importantly, by rising exports. Beginning in 1992, economic liberalization accelerated and the country started integrating more fully into the global economy. In 2001, China was accepted into the World Trade Organization (WTO), a sign of its emergence from economic isolationism into one of the world's foremost traders. Around this time, China became notably more dependent on imported inputs, particularly to meet its growing energy needs. Nevertheless, China enjoyed a persistent and growing trade surplus: by 2007 China exported over $1.3 trillion, or nearly 30 percent more than it imported.[32] This led critics to question whether China conducted its trade fairly.

China's overseas trade competitors increasingly resorted to litigation and other measures to counter what they saw as unfair trading advantages such as the "dumping" of Chinese manufactured products in their home markets. ("Dumping" occurs when merchandise is sold in a foreign market at less than its normal value, determined by the price of the merchandise in its home market or by the cost of production.) These antidumping lawsuits, usually brought by governments and other groups in destination markets, generally allege that a Chinese exporter is selling its products in the destination market at below cost (to establish a presence in that market). From 1995 to 2008, over 20 percent of all antidumping measures worldwide were targeted at China.[33]

To contest an antidumping lawsuit, a defendant must show evidence of its "true" costs. Such evidence is particularly difficult for Chinese manufacturers to provide because, per China's WTO accession protocols, the country is classified as a "nonmarket economy"—as such, cost data from Chinese companies is considered unreliable in international litigation.[34] Under these circumstances, antidumping lawsuits may be adjudicated using cost data from "surrogate" manufacturers in another country: common surrogates are companies from India, Indonesia, and even the United States,[35] countries that are generally not as competitive vis-à-vis China in the worldwide manufacturing exports. As a result of these conventions, the success of Chinese manufacturers in contesting antidumping lawsuits is unimpressive.[36]

However, China's WTO accession protocol allows for exceptions to the surrogate rule in antidumping litigation if the litigated exporter can show that "market economy conditions" apply in manufacturing.[37] As part of establishing market economy conditions, the litigated exporter is generally required to provide audited financial statements prepared in line with "international accounting standards," which are understood to include IFRS.[38] Thus compliance with IFRS can provide a significant advantage to Chinese exporters and, in turn, the Chinese economy. In fact, since China has adopted IFRS-based standards, there have been several successful cases of Chinese companies qualifying for market economy treatment on the basis of providing internationally compliant financials: in one case involving transport equipment, the winning exporter was able to reduce import tariffs by nearly 40 percent.[39,40]

The considerable antidumping benefits from IFRS adoption that can accrue to China's export-driven economy suggest that harmonizing local accounting standards with IFRS was a major priority for the country, in particular, its Ministry of Finance (MOF), which oversees accounting matters. The process of harmonizing local accounting rules in a country with IFRS usually involves creating numerous local carve-outs and exceptions to accommodate domestic interests, as will be seen from the case on India that follows. But for IFRS as applied by Chinese manufacturers to carry weight in international litigation, it can only differ minimally from IFRS as issued by the IASB. In fact, the notable differences between the IASB's IFRS and its Chinese equivalent have created, in some circumstances, difficulties for China's exporters in antidumping litigation. For example, in a 2010 case involving a Chinese fine-paper manufacturer litigated in the EU, the EC ruled against the company despite it having demonstrated on paper "market economy conditions," including providing audited financials in accordance with Chinese the version of IFRS. As part of its justification for the ruling, the EC noted differences between the IASB's and China's versions of IFRS.[41]

This particular feature of IFRS compliance resulted in the MOF's harmonization process with the IASB generating changes in the worldwide standards themselves. Put differently, instead of tailoring the local application of IFRS to its domestic interests, as many countries do and as China has done in some cases, the MOF in China was successful, in at least one major instance, in tailoring worldwide IFRS to satisfy Chinese interests. I describe this process below.

When China signed on to IFRS harmonization in 2005, a key issue for the MOF in Beijing was the IFRS standards on disclosure of related-party transactions, particularly as they applied to state-controlled enterprises. The disclosure of related-party transactions is an elemental feature of accounting, central to maintaining the integrity of the "entity concept"—the fundamental idea in accounting that an enterprise's financials are its own. In fact, so basic is the entity concept to financial reporting that it is usually discussed in the first or second day of the required first-year introductory accounting course at Harvard Business School (and, I expect, at most other institutions). If related-party transactions are unknown to users of financial statements, those users will be unable to sensibly interpret even the most basic measures of performance. For example, without knowledge of related-party transactions, users cannot rule out the possibility that a firm's reported revenues and income were generated simply by transferring inventory to another firm in a non–arm's length transaction. Thus in the absence of adequate related-party disclosures, the entire premise of financial reporting can come apart.

Several of China's largest companies are state controlled, and, as such, state-controlled enterprises are an important part of the country's economy. In 2009, all thirty-four Chinese companies in the Global Fortune 500 list were state controlled, including Sinopec, China National Petroleum, State Grid, and the Industrial and Commercial Bank of China, the four Chinese companies that ranked among the Fortune 100.[42] According to a strict interpretation of the IASB standard on related-party transactions in existence during 2005 (called IAS 24), many state-controlled enterprises, due to their common government control, would have been considered "related parties" and accordingly subject to exhaustive related-party disclosure requirements.

The nature and extent of these disclosures were daunting for the state-controlled enterprises and therefore for the MOF. For a state-controlled company to disclose all its related-party transactions "would require thousands of pages," remarked one Chinese regulator.[43] Prior to 2003, state-controlled entities were exempt from IAS 24's related-party disclosure requirements. That exemption was removed in a 2003 revision, which specified that profit-oriented state-controlled entities that use IFRS must disclose transactions with other state-controlled entities. Most of the largest Chinese state-controlled enterprises qualified as "profit oriented." The argument was that such profit-oriented state-controlled entities were in practice operating as and competing with private (nongovernmental) companies and thus should be subject to the same capital-market rules. Thus pursuant to "market economy conditions," profit-oriented state-controlled entities had to meet the related-party disclosure requirements of IAS 24.

In 2006, even as the MOF and IASB announced plans to converge Chinese accounting standards with IFRS, the two bodies began consultations on "clarifying" IAS 24 requirements for transactions between entities with significant state control. The objective was to find a way for Chinese state-controlled entities to report under IFRS rules without having to provide exhaustive related-party disclosures. For the Chinese state-controlled entities, such an accommodation was important because it would avoid costly (and potentially damaging) disclosures about their dealings with each other. For the IASB, the accommodation was a way to ease China's accession to IFRS: bringing one of the world's largest and fastest growing countries under the IFRS tent would be a major victory for the board, which had embraced the objective of proliferating IFRS as rapidly and as widely as possible. China's embrace of IFRS was expected to provide momentum ("network benefits") for other emerging markets and Asian economies to adopt IFRS. "There is going to be a chain reaction as a result of this," predicted then IASB chairman Mr. Tweedie as China's decision on IFRS was announced.[44]

In February 2007, the IASB released a draft of proposed amendments to IAS 24, which would exempt some state-controlled entities from related-party disclosures based, in part, on the independence of the entities' boards of directors. The IASB offered a comment period limited to ninety days in the hopes that the amendment could be in place before the end of the 2007 financial year. But from October 2007 through January 2008, the IASB discussions became increasingly complicated. They ended, as the board later noted, "in a degree of confusion," after the board determined that "in some jurisdictions, including China, the State often nominates one or more board members." That meant, the IASB noted, "that the State would normally 'participate in the operating and financial decisions' of state-controlled entities and thus [that the entities] would always fail the exemption criteria [for related-party disclosures]."[45]

In response to this development, from September to November 2008, the IASB formulated a new approach whereby related-party transactions of state-controlled entities would not need to be disclosed, but instead general disclosures about the types and extent of significant transactions would be required. In July 2009, the IASB tentatively approved changes to IAS 24 to be made effective January 1, 2011. This revised, formal version was finally issued in November 2009. It provides a worldwide "partial exemption for government-related entities" on disclosures normally required of related parties.[46] In announcing its decision, the IASB wrote:

> The IASB has revised IAS 24 in response to concerns that the previous disclosure requirements and the definition of a "related party" were too complex and difficult to apply in practice, especially in environments where government control is pervasive. The revised standard addresses these concerns by . . . providing a partial exemption for government-related entities. Until now, if a government controlled, or significantly influenced, an entity, the entity was required to disclose information about all transactions with other entities controlled, or significantly influenced by the same government. The revised standard still requires disclosures that are important to users of financial statements but eliminates requirements to disclose information that is costly to gather and of less value to users.[47]

Under the IASB's revised version of IAS 24, state-controlled entities enjoyed discretion to determine which related-party transactions were "costly to gather" or "of less value to users" and thus unnecessary to disclose. How they would use that discretion was beyond the scope and jurisdiction of the IASB. (See figure 6.1 for a timeline of the events leading up to the IASB's modified position on related-party disclosures.)

The narrative on IAS 24 and Chinese state-controlled entities is significant for at least two reasons. First, the substantive impact of the IAS 24 change cannot be overstated. As noted earlier, the disclosure of related-party transactions is a central principle in accounting. That a country with significant state ownership of industry was able to redefine worldwide accounting standards on an issue that is so central to accounting is indicative of the power of special-interest politics even in international accounting rule-making. The compromise on IAS 24 that brought China into the IFRS fold also introduced a potentially costly dilution of the integrity of the entity concept in accounting. Users of financial statements now have less information about related-party transactions in state-controlled entities. On the one hand, this situation could save investors in such entities the costs of unnecessary voluminous related-party disclosures. But more worryingly, this situation could also enable state-controlled entities to mislead investors, customers, suppliers, and competitors by overstating their profitability or understating their losses, resulting in costly misallocation of resources in the world economy. In the extreme, the current related-party disclosure rules could incubate an Enron-like situation in a state-controlled entity. Enron was able to hide

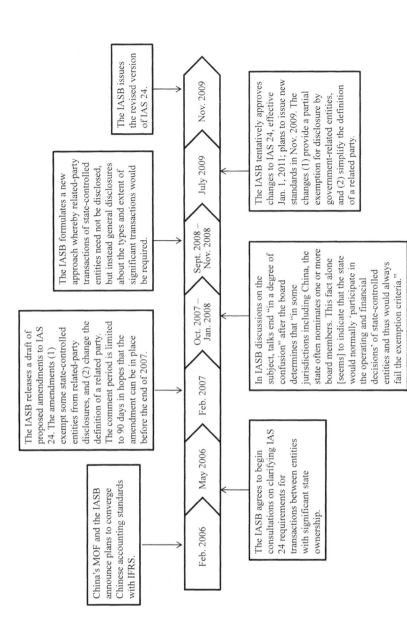

FIGURE 6.1. Timeline of events leading up to the IASB's modified position on related-party disclosures

Source: Adapted from IAS Plus, "IASB Agenda Project," Deloitte Touche, accessed November 2009, http://www.iasplus.com.

important truths about its performance through the use of fair-value-based income reporting, acquiring sound competitors along the way. Similarly, an unscrupulous state-controlled entity (motivated by a managerial proclivity toward empire building or by some sense of national pride) could overstate its profitability, driving private (nongovernmental) competitors out of business and creating a distortionary monopoly in its product market.

Second, the Chinese state-controlled entities' role in the changes to IAS 24 can be an indication of the role of special-interests more generally in determining IFRS. Just as the experience of the FASB shows that a narrowly focused interest group can from time to time shape the nature of accounting rules in a self-serving manner, IFRS rule-making can become captured on certain issues by special-interest groups. Indeed, the episodes with Enron's proposed donation to the IASB in 2001 and with the European banks' opportunistic carve-out on fair-value accounting at the height of the 2008 Financial Crisis, both described earlier, are consistent with this proposition. The incident with China and IAS 24 can also be a harbinger of a growing role for international power politics in IFRS standard setting. On this point, note that China's strong central government allowed special interests within the country (i.e., state-controlled enterprises) to speak with one voice when advocating at the IASB. Special interests from other emerging-market countries such as India have been less successful in such international power politics, as the following section discusses.

Local Politics: The Case of India

This section describes a critical accounting challenge faced by Tata Steel, one of India's largest and most respected companies, as it embarked on an ambitious phase of globalization. The Tata Steel experience provides an example of the complexities that can emerge as business operations, accounting rules, and national economic policy globalize at different paces. The role of special-interest politics in resolving these disparities is particularly salient in this case study.

Tata Steel is one of India's oldest, largest, and most visible conglomerates. Its history, dating to the 1800s, is tied to the history of the industrialization of India itself, and, as such, the company and its parent, the Tata Group, enjoy high prestige in the subcontinent. Over the past twenty years, as the Indian economy has liberalized and opened itself up to international competition, the company has embraced a more global outlook. Its aggressive globalization strategy has been driven partly by the need to maintain its competitive position at home. As part of this strategy, in 2007, Tata Steel acquired U.K.-based Corus Steel for $12.1 billion, in what was then the largest overseas acquisition by an Indian company. The deal attracted considerable media attention for Tata both in India and abroad. The Corus deal catapulted Tata Steel from ranking as the world's fifty-sixth largest steelmaker to a place among the top ten.[48]

Tata Steel funded the Corus acquisition in part through loans totaling to the equivalent of $6.2 billion drawn by a European subsidiary. Tata Steel planned to service the debt through the cash flows of its European operations, including Corus' sales to manufacturers in the EU, which transacted largely in euros.[49] A key concern with the debt was the risk of fluctuating foreign-currency exchange rates; prudent companies prefer to avoid situations where the revenues from investing borrowed capital and the interest payments on those borrowings are in different currencies. To hedge against this currency risk, Tata Steel denominated the bulk of the Corus debt in euros, a practice known as an "operational hedge."[50] In its fiscal-year 2008 annual report, the company described the debt-funded deal and the operational hedge it proposed to use to protect cash flows from currency risk:

> Despite very volatile credit markets globally, the company raised around U.S. $6.2 billion of term debt with an average life of around 5 years at very competitive terms. This debt being nonrecourse in nature was determined based on the cash flow servicing capability of our European operations and will be serviced by the Tata Steel U.K. (Corus) cash flows. The syndication of the above debt was completed during the year with more than 25 banks and institutions participating in the process . . .
>
> Tata Steel Netherlands, the entity in whose books the nonrecourse debt has been taken, was successful in encouraging a high proportion of investors to voluntarily convert their debt to euro via the re-denomination route. The majority of the balance debt was then swapped to euro from GBP so that foreign currency risk could be minimized. Tata Steel Netherlands also hedged the majority of its euro interest rate risk.[51]

However, Tata Steel's consolidated financials, prepared under a version of Indian Generally Accepted Accounting Principles (IGAAP) that was harmonizing with IFRS, could not recognize the operational hedge. IGAAP, following IFRS, mandated that foreign currency loans be "translated" into an entity's functional (home) currency for reporting purposes.[52] Tata Steel's functional currency is the Indian rupee.

Translation is the process of expressing amounts denominated in various currencies in terms of a single home currency by using the spot exchange rates between the relevant currencies on the reporting date. Translation is generally used to consolidate the financial statements of an entity's foreign subsidiaries into a single set of parent financial statements. Translation is also used in cases where an entity had direct foreign assets and liabilities—that is, the entity is not operating overseas via a subsidiary. Any change in exchange rates over a reporting period could lead to a translation gain or loss in the consolidated financial statements. These gains or losses are reported either directly in the income statement or in a "foreign-currency translation" account on the balance sheet. Conceptually, translation allows financial-statement users to obtain an all-inclusive picture of a company's financial position and performance. Additionally, translation provides equity investors whose claims are settled in the home currency a comprehensive understanding of the claims against their assets.

Pursuant to IGAAP, the Corus loan was expressed in Indian rupees in Tata Steel's consolidated financial statements starting 2008. With the onset of the financial crisis in 2008–9 and the subsequent appreciation of the euro against the rupee, this accounting treatment led to the loan amount increasing by $630 million on Tata Steel's balance sheet over that period. $630 million represented about 6.4 percent of Tata Steel's net debt for the fiscal year ending 2009 and about 64 percent of its net income. Koushik Chatterjee, chief financial officer for Tata Steel, summarized: "While the cash flow impact of currency movements is being protected by our [operational] hedging strategy, the income statement and balance sheet are open to the impact of currency translations, making these statements very volatile. Translation changes the capital structure, and it could, at times, make the company look more leveraged than it actually is, thus materially impacting the company's ability to use the balance sheet for further financing."[53] Companies facing this problem can purchase derivative securities that would nullify the financial-reporting effect of foreign currency fluctuations. But such derivative securities can be costly and they serve no *real* purpose—they only overcome the effect of the foreign-currency translation rule. Mr. Chatterjee explained, "Our view has been that we need to protect our [real] cash flow rather than only our financial reports from foreign currency risk."[54]

The IFRS requirement to translate foreign liabilities into a reporting entity's functional currency (usually, the home currency) is less troubling to U.S. and European companies that can effectively avoid the requirement by raising home-currency-denominated debt on world markets. It is also less troubling to companies domiciled in jurisdictions with relatively fixed exchange rates such as China and Hong Kong. But Tata Steel, as an Indian multinational, finds it difficult to raise rupee-denominated debt abroad because the Indian rupee, due to capital controls imposed by the Indian government, is not freely available overseas and because the rupee remains a volatile, floating currency.

The translation requirement—and the volatility it induced in Tata Steel's financial statements—presented the company with difficult options. It could (1) switch the entire company's functional currency to euros, a move that would expose the company's Indian operations to currency fluctuations; (2) ignore the translation impact and hope equity and debt investors did the same, but this approach did not address covenants that could be triggered by the impact of currency fluctuations; (3) engage in relatively costly lobbying with the IASB to seek an exception to the translation rule for companies from countries such as India; or (4) lobby Indian standard setters to create an IFRS exception in IGAAP for situations such as this.

Mr. Chatterjee expounded, "What are the options an [Indian] multinational can look at? We can look at changing our functional currency to euro, in which case our Indian business gets [exposed] in terms of euro ... [so that] does not protect our balance sheet from a capital structure perspective," he noted, ruling out option 1.[55] Option 2 was unviable as well: "I [am] sure that there are many [Indian] companies [that] have to bear this volatility, which in turn is confusing to . . . an investor or a rating agency that is looking at what the underlying fundamentals of the company are about."[56] Considering option 3, he pointed out, "The translation issue will continue to be a challenge not only for Tata Steel, but also for any Indian corporate with global ambitions." "[But negotiating with the IASB] requires country leadership in a more institutional form rather than one big group going and talking about it," he noted.[57] This left the company with option 4.

Through its 142-year history, the Tata Group has been at the forefront of developing industries in India, opening the country's first luxury hotel in 1903, its first private steel company in 1907, its first airline in 1932, and its first software firm in 1968. By 2009, it was India's largest conglomerate, with revenues of $70.8 billion, contributing over 5 percent of the country's GDP.[58] Its ninety-eight group companies, operating in more than eighty countries, employed 357,000 people. The group's twenty-seven publicly listed companies had a combined market capitalization of about $60 billion, the highest among Indian business houses, and a shareholder base of 3.2 million individuals.[59] The group also received recognition for its focus on innovation: in 2010, Tata had been ranked seventeenth on *Bloomberg BusinessWeek*'s "50 Most Innovative Companies" list.[60] Additionally, political leaders in India had acknowledged the group's contribution toward nation building over the years. Jawaharlal Nehru, the first prime minister of India, described the group's first leader J. N. Tata as "one of the big founders of modern India."[61] Manmohan Singh, India's prime minister from 2004 to 2014, described the group as "the unique temple of modern India," crediting it for creating "wealth, employment, new capabilities and new possibilities" for all Indians.[62]

With this background, not surprisingly, Tata Steel had a history of leadership in shaping corporate policy, including accounting policy, within India. To this effect, Mr. Chatterjee recalled an instance in the 1990s when IGAAP rules failed to reflect what the company saw as the economic reality of a transaction. In that case, Tata Steel had successfully negotiated alternative reporting rules with Indian accounting rule-makers. Facing an increasingly global competitive landscape, Tata Steel, in the mid-1990s, had decided to restructure. The restructuring plan envisioned nearly halving the company's workforce. India had no social security system at the time, so Tata Steel, a company recognized for its responsible labor practices, devised a series of generous early retirement schemes. The schemes allowed employees to receive their base salary until original retirement age: the company saved on retirement benefits, pay increases, bonuses, and overtime, which amounted to about 50 percent of the total employee compensation. IGAAP rules at the time required that the entire severance amount (the present value of a retiring employee's future basic salary until retirement age) be written off in the quarter in which it was undertaken.

This accounting approach was consistent with the principle of conservatism, which dictates that expected costs be recognized at once in financial statements, although expected benefits are deferred until they are verifiable. Conservatism is a key element of the economic theory of financial reporting. But the conservative approach to accounting for Tata Steel's severance package would have resulted in a substantial hit to the company's bottom line. The company saw this as distortionary because it expected to make the payments over an average of about twelve years. It preferred an approach that would "smooth" the hit to its earnings by recognizing only a part of the expense each year. Mr. Chatterjee recalled:

> The accounting regulation required that all severance amounts had to be written off . . . This would create a skew because the payment would happen over the next 15 years, whereas the liability and cost would be recognized at inception. We argued with the ASBI [Accounting Standards Board of India] that this rule would work in a company where only a minimum severance amount was paid. However, in India, [Tata] is actually replacing what a social security system would have done and therefore you need to allow us to amortize this over a longer period on a deferred basis. I calculated the average unexpired

service life at 12 years. The ASBI extended the amortization principle for five years or the financial year ending 2010, whichever was earlier.[63]

To Mr. Chatterjee, the compromise with the ASBI over early retirement accounting was an example of business successfully working with regulators to shape corporate accounting policy. Although the accounting treatment was not conservative and was inconsistent with basic accounting theory, Tata Steel was able to leverage its respectability in India to secure the treatment. The outcome put the company's financials in a better light. Given this experience, in the case of foreign currency translations related to the Corus acquisition, option 4—securing an IFRS exception in IGAAP—seemed reasonable. Importantly, the company found support for this option from powerful technocratic allies. For example, as Tata Steel was dealing with the problem of foreign-currency translations, Y. H. Malegam, chairman of India's National Advisory Committee on Accounting Standards and one of the country's most respected names in accounting and auditing, made the case for the company: "If [a] U.S. [company] borrows money abroad, often it will denominate that borrowing in dollars, therefore eliminating the translation impact. However, if [an] India[n company] borrows money abroad they have to denominate it in sterling, [in] dollars, or in euros, leading to a translation impact and creating unnecessary volatility . . . [An Indian] company [that] has dollar borrowings and dollar earnings can repay the loan from its dollar earnings; the exchange rate during the period of the loan is irrelevant," he declared.[64]

So it was in 2009 that the relevant accounting authorities in India issued an amendment to the IGAAP foreign-currency translation rule. The amendment—called "paragraph 46," referring to its placement in the original rule, Indian Accounting Standard No. 11. Paragraph 46—gave companies the option to capitalize any foreign-currency translation differences from certain long-term debt to a special reserve account with an especially wordy and abstruse name, the "Foreign Currency Monetary Item Translation Difference Account." Companies were permitted to gradually amortize foreign-currency translation losses accumulated in this reserve account over the life of the underlying debt or March 31, 2011, whichever was earlier.[65] The impact of paragraph 46, given the substantial depreciation of the Indian rupee in 2009, was a substantial improvement in the income statements of Indian companies with foreign debt. As with the case of the revised accounting treatment for severance expenses, the revised treatment in paragraph 46 was non-conservative and contributed to a "smoothing" of earnings.

Paragraph 46 was unusual in at least two aspects. First, it established a departure of IGAAP from IFRS even as the country was promising that it would adopt all IFRS rules within two years. (India subsequently twice delayed its IFRS adoption date and, as of January 2014, had not adopted IFRS.) Second, it was retrospective by over two years—specifically, it applied fully to all transactions arising after December 7, 2006. This latter provision was particularly beneficial to Tata Steel since it meant that any debt arising from the Corus acquisition would qualify for paragraph 46 treatment. Not surprisingly, Tata Steel elected to apply paragraph 46 in its financial statements. The impact on its year 2009 income statement was an increase in profit before taxes of about U.S. $180 million or about 11 percent of pretax income.[66]

Paragraph 46's departure from conservative accounting principles—the rule effectively delays the income-statement recognition of certain foreign-currency translation losses—was not lost on certain critical minds. Writing in the local press, one accountant observed sarcastically, "One wonders whether accounting prescriptions . . . keep changing every year to address the reporting needs at the end of the year."[67]

Paragraph 46, when originally issued, was intended to expire on March 31, 2011. But accounting rules that delay the recognition of losses are often difficult to reverse given the impact such a reversal would have on powerful corporate interests. As the March 2011 deadline approached, the Indian accounting authorities announced that the rule would be in place for another year. Then, in December 2011, the authorities issued "paragraph 46A," which effectively extended the rule's life through 2020.[68]

Tata Steel's efforts to shape accounting policy in India highlight the impact of special interests on accounting rules in a non-U.S. context. Indeed, there is some conceptual merit to Tata Steel's argument that the translation rules uniquely hurt certain emerging-market-based multinational companies. But the earnings-smoothing solution that was obtained in this case, while beneficial to Tata Steel and other companies in its position, is inconsistent with the core accounting principle of conservatism—it yields a distorted picture of financial performance.[69] Two wrongs do not make a right. The lesson from this case study is simple: the political forces that underlie the determination of accounting rules in the United States are likely to manifest in other market-capitalist jurisdictions as well.

I conclude this chapter with a brief coda on the Tata Steel–Corus deal. In May 2013, about six years after it acquired the British steelmaker, Tata Steel announced that it was taking a $1.6 billion goodwill impairment charge mostly related to the Corus deal. *The Economist* magazine, in reporting on the write-down, called the acquisition a "financial disaster," arguing that a write-off had been due for at least four years. The magazine argued that the timing of the write-off was significant: Ratan Tata, the group's longtime chief executive, who had championed Corus as his "biggest deal" had recently stepped down. For the incoming chief executive, the magazine argued, this was a good time to address the accumulated financial impact of an "underperforming business."[70] The parallels of the Corus write-down's timing to the evidence and discussion in chapter 3 on the timing of goodwill write-downs in the United States are germane.

My Own Private Company Council:
How a New Accounting Rule-Maker Is Born

On May 23, 2012, in their suite on the top floor of an inconspicuous office building in a suburban office park in Norwalk, Connecticut, the trustees of the Financial Accounting Foundation (FAF) approved the establishment of America's first major corporate accounting rule-maker with substantial independence from the FASB: the Private Company Council (PCC). The PCC is charged with producing GAAP accounting rules for private (i.e., unlisted) companies, which make up about one-half of U.S. gross domestic product.[1]

Until the creation of the PCC, GAAP in the United States for both public and private companies had been established by the FASB under the oversight of the trustees of the FAF. The creation of the PCC represented the culmination of more than three years of active lobbying of the FAF by advocates for a separate private-company accounting rule-maker. These advocates were a complex but powerful coalition of the U.S. Chamber of Commerce, executives from several large private companies, the American Institute of Certified Public Accountants (AICPA), and the smaller (i.e., non–Big Four) audit firms. The advocates argued that GAAP determined by the FASB was largely aimed at meeting the needs of publicly listed companies and their dispersed stockowners, emphasizing the need for "fairness" in disclosure as mandated by the SEC. They lobbied for a rule-maker fully independent of the FASB and vested with the authority to set accounting rules for private companies. They argued that private companies had different financial reporting needs that could only be met by a separate body.

There was some opposition to the idea of the PCC as well—including from academia, elements of the Big Four audit firms, and some members of the FASB itself. These groups argued that there were no conceptual differences between public and private company accounting and that the demand for a new, independent private-company rule-maker was focused on the wrong issues. The FASB was likely additionally concerned because the creation of the PCC would significantly narrow its mandate. But the FASB was still reeling from charges that the fair-value rules it had put in place over the last few years had contributed in some way to the Financial Crisis of 2008 (see chapter 5). In addition, the FASB had a relatively new chair after its previous head quit abruptly in part over these issues.[2] So as with several other cases discussed in the previous chapters, the opponents to the PCC were not nearly as forceful, organized, and incented as the advocates for it, and the new private-company accounting rule-maker was brought into being.

The decision to create the PCC was not easy for the then-chairman of the FAF. John J. "Jack" Brennan had come to assume the top job in the nation's accounting rule-making infrastructure after a long career at the asset-management firm Vanguard. He described his role as "a fiduciary for the market system."[3]

Brennan acknowledged the position of those lobbying for the establishment of the PCC: "The cost to private companies from complexities in U.S. GAAP is the number one issue driving demand for a PCC. . . . My own sense is that there can be different disclosure standards [for private companies]."[4] But he worried that some of the PCC advocates, particularly those pushing for the PCC to be independent of the FASB, "wanted the brand value of GAAP without the burdens of compliance."[5] Mulling over the creation of the PCC, he wondered, "Is the integrity of U.S. GAAP being compromised?"[6]

Economic Arguments for Separate Private-Company GAAP

Publicly listed companies in the United States are required to prepare financial reports in accordance with U.S. GAAP. This requirement dates back to the Securities Acts of 1933 and 1934, which were passed in the wake of the stock market crash of 1929 and in the shadow of the Great Depression. A stated purpose for regulating the accounting standards of public companies is the safeguarding of the integrity of U.S. capital markets and the protection of investors—particularly small, unsophisticated investors—who might be misled by false profits and return metrics.[7] Private companies, on the other hand, do not have a legal requirement to prepare financials according to U.S. GAAP. Their adherence to GAAP is de facto, not de jure, often stemming from their need to have their financials audited to secure bank or trade credit.

Three important trends had shaped the nature of U.S. GAAP in the years leading up to the FAF's consideration of a PCC. First, as discussed earlier, the FASB had been increasingly incorporating fair-value methods for measur-

ing assets and liabilities in U.S. GAAP. Fair-value accounting requires periodic valuation estimates, which in many cases are provided by specialist
appraisers, adding to the compliance costs of GAAP. Second, the accounting scandals of the early 2000s, such as those at Enron and WorldCom, had
been followed by numerous new requirements—including those required
by Congress in the Sarbanes-Oxley Act (SOX) of 2002—aimed at promoting
increased disclosure and more comprehensive recognition of assets and liabilities in financial statements. These changes to GAAP had resulted in what
was sometimes described as an overload of "rules" that impaired the role for
management judgment in the accounting process. Post-SOX, listed companies also faced increased regulatory and litigation risks over nondisclosure
or misinformation in financial reports. These risks had further contributed
to the trend of increased disclosure and recognition in GAAP financial statements. Third, for more than a decade, the FASB had been engaged in a process
to "converge" U.S. GAAP with International Financial Reporting Standards
(IFRS). This convergence process, which was both technically challenging
and politically charged, had resulted in U.S. GAAP being tugged in directions
developed by the International Accounting Standards Board.

Together, the three trends described above had contributed to a phenomenon sometimes referred to as the increasing "complexity" of U.S. GAAP.
Some experts argued that GAAP was "complex" because it codified numerous standards and requirements from a myriad of agencies serving multiple
objectives, such as IFRS convergence, SOX compliance, and increasing stock-
price valuation relevance. Others pointed out that GAAP complexity was the
result of the increasing complexity of business practices: Advances in production, information, and financial technologies, together with the globalization of business relationships, meant that even small businesses deployed
relatively sophisticated supply chains, compensation methods, and financial
instruments as part of a basic operating strategy to remain competitive. For
example, while entering into interest-rate swap agreements or overseas sub-
contracting was uncommon among industrial companies in the early 1990s,
by 2012 such practices were widely utilized. In this increasingly complex business environment, if financial statements were to continue to be useful in
evaluating firm performance and risk, GAAP had to develop more complex
procedures, the argument went.

Regardless of its source, complexity increases the cost of GAAP compliance because it requires more accountants, auditors, and sophisticated controls and information systems. By the time the proposal for a PCC was being
considered at the FAF, the issue of GAAP complexity had become widely acknowledged. In 2006, an SEC commissioner herself, Cynthia Glassman, said

mockingly: "The financial reporting landscape is littered with pronouncements from the FASB, the AICPA, EITF, the APB, the SEC and the PCAOB.
We have pronouncements, rules, regulations, guidelines, bulletins, audit
standards, interpretations and practice aids in the form of SOPs, FAQs, SABs,
Q&As and FSPs. This has been going on for decades. The result is that today,
U.S. GAAP is made up of over 2,000 pronouncements. That's a lot of ABCs,
even for a CEO or CFO with a CPA."[8]

The costs of GAAP complexity are acutely felt among private companies,
which argue that many requirements in GAAP—particularly those aimed
at capital-market fairness and stock-price valuation—are irrelevant to their
investors. Steve Feilmeier, the chief financial officer of Koch Industries, one
of the largest private companies in the United States, noted, "The elephant in
the room is the SEC, who responds to clamoring from Congress . . . that they
want more information in financial disclosures."[9] Mark Bielstein, a partner at
KPMG, agreed that complexity was a major concern among private companies. But he added that "complexity in accounting standards and disclosure
requirements is a significant issue for all companies, including private companies, public companies, and not-for-profit organizations."[10]

Mr. Feilmeier also considered fair-value accounting and the related cost
of compliance one of the most arduous and taxing requirements for private
companies. "The value of all these new rules [on fair value accounting] is
next to nothing," he explained.[11] "When banks are recording income because
their debt is trading down, that makes no sense," Feilmeier said, referring to
recently adopted U.S. GAAP rules that allow banks to record their liabilities
at fair value.[12] "It's hard enough to make sense of whether the accounting
works; now we have to untangle the effects of fair value, now we have to hire
lawyers and appraisers."[13] Feilmeier illustrated:

> Georgia-Pacific, a Koch Industries subsidiary, acquired three OSB [oriented
> strand board] plants for about one-third of original construction cost shortly
> after the 2008 housing crisis. The previous owners had reportedly built the
> plants for in excess of $1 billion. Ernst & Young [Koch Industries' auditor]
> said because you have a "bargain purchase," you have to recognize the differ-
> ence as "income." But we were the only ones at the auction. Who is to say we
> didn't overpay? Our accountants are making us show income that our bankers
> had to back out. We had to spend $200,000 on the appraisal! These types of
> standards are a waste of time and money for private companies. . . . Suppose
> I don't want to use fair-value accounting in my acquisition, should that deny
> me [an unqualified] audit opinion?[14]

Users of private-company financial statements include equity owners and
creditors. Both groups are usually sophisticated investors with access to in-

sider information beyond what is reported in financial statements. Speaking of his relationship with his bankers, Mr. Feilmeier observed, "They don't care what your fair value is. . . . They want to look you in the eye and get your private assessment of the facts."[15] Summarizing his thoughts on a separate GAAP for private companies, Feilmeier concluded, "It is not illogical to conclude that the needs of private companies' users differ from those of public companies' users."[16]

The arguments around GAAP compliance costs for private companies resonate particularly with smaller companies. Most private companies are relatively small and therefore lack the financial means to comply with the accounting, auditing, and control procedures necessitated by GAAP financial reporting. As an illustration of the rising costs of compliance, some experts noted that following the passage of SOX, the United States experienced a reduction in companies going public. Between 1980 and 2000, the annual average number of initial public offerings was 311. That number dropped to 102 for the period 2001–11.[17] Furthermore, one estimate following SOX revealed that 70 percent of small public companies considered reprivatizing, while 77 percent of small foreign firms considered abandoning U.S. listings.[18] In 2008, the SEC reported that the cost of compliance stemming from certain control requirements in SOX averaged $2.3 million per company, a figure that weighed on smaller companies.[19] Another study showed that some companies, in an attempt to avoid SOX regulations, chose to "go dark," or voluntarily delist from public exchanges.[20]

The compliance-costs arguments suggest that the differences in GAAP requirements between private and public companies are really differences in requirements between small and large companies. Mr. Bielstein of KPMG explained, "Many of the issues raised about [private-company] GAAP need to be addressed on a broader scale than just private companies."[21] Daryl Buck, a FASB board member with a private-company background, agreed: "There are some similarities between small public companies and small private companies. On the same token there are similarities between very large and sophisticated private and public companies."[22] Leslie Seidman, chairman of the FASB, put it more succinctly: "We can solve this problem without creating a whole new GAAP for private companies."[23]

Moreover, some defenders of extant FASB rules (e.g., some within the Big Four audit firms) argue that the compliance costs of U.S. GAAP represent the price of having high-quality financial reporting. They argue that small companies concerned about GAAP complexity should explore alternative non-GAAP accounting bases. Mr. Bielstein of KPMG explained, "In some cases, private companies may not need GAAP financial statements. In those instances, their users might accept tax basis or cash basis financial statements or financial information on some other basis of accounting."[24]

The Politics of Separate GAAP for Private Companies

Between 1971 and 2009, eleven reports commissioned by Congress and various accounting bodies examined the financial reporting issues of private and nonprofit entities.[25] In January 2007, responding to concerns that private-company interests were being sidelined at the FASB, the Board established the Private Company Financial Reporting Committee (PCFRC). This body was charged with providing the FASB ongoing support on issues of private-company interest.[26] The PCFRC was composed of thirteen members: four users of private-company financial statements (e.g., bank lenders and venture capitalists), four financial executives from private companies, four practicing auditors, and a chairman who was a FASB employee. The PCFRC met four to five times a year, and FASB board members attended meetings on a rotating basis.

In practice, the PCFRC had a limited impact on GAAP. Recommendations made by the PCFRC were nonbinding and subject to FASB approval.[27] The FASB and PCFRC did not develop and agree on a common framework for considering private-company exceptions and modifications to GAAP.[28] The president and chief executive of FAF, Terri Polley, conjectured that the limited impact of the PCFRC on standard setting might have been the result of a view widely held within the FASB that there were no conceptual differences between private and public companies that justified significantly different accounting rules.[29] That "combined with the growing complexity of [FASB] standards led to a lot of frustration [among private companies]," she added.[30] "Not to mention you had an economy that was going downhill fast, putting additional pressure on companies' resources," she noted, referring to the macroeconomic situation in 2009.[31]

In December 2009, under pressure from the AICPA and the U.S. Chamber of Commerce, which had begun to champion the interests of private companies on this issue, the FAF convened a "blue ribbon panel" (BRP) to make a recommendation on accounting standard setting for private companies. Earlier that year, also at the AICPA's and chamber's behest, the FAF had undertaken a nationwide "listening tour," where it was exposed to demands for a separate private-company accounting body.[32]

The AICPA, which traditionally represented the smaller audit firms, had a strong interest in the issue because most private companies were audited by small auditors.[33] Moreover, until the passage of SOX, the AICPA was also responsible for the development of the nation's standards for auditing. SOX created a new agency, the Public Company Accounting Oversight Board (PCAOB), that assumed responsibility for auditing standards for public companies, leaving the AICPA in charge of only private-company auditing standards. A separate private-company accounting rule-maker would give the AICPA the opportunity to extend its impact.

Terri Polley of the FAF commented on the AICPA's role in the establishment of the BRP: "The leadership of the AICPA pushed very hard on this. Their message to [FAF chair] Jack [Brennan] and me was that something had to be done about private companies. They wanted to set up a blue ribbon panel and they wanted the outcome to be a separate standard-setting body. They clearly had a specific end goal in mind. The AICPA was conducting a public campaign about the need for a BRP and a separate standard setter for private companies."[34] Polley added, "We [had] heard concerns [about private-company standard setting] during our listening tour, through our meetings with advisory groups, etc. As a result of those concerns, the FAF and FASB had started to make some significant improvements to engage with private-company stakeholders. But we hadn't been very effective in communicating those changes; we didn't have the access to stakeholders the way the AICPA's [public relations] capabilities could send a message to 300,000 accountants. So, we were losing ground even as we were taking steps to address the problem."[35]

Barry Melancon, the president of the AICPA, was clear about his priorities: "For the past thirty-plus years FAF and FASB have been influenced by the demands of public companies. For much of recent history, FASB members have overwhelmingly come from public companies. However, public companies constitute less than half the economy."[36] He argued that FASB standard setting was biased to public company issues and demanded structural reforms.[37]

In addition to the AICPA, the FAF invited the National Association of State Boards of Accountancy (NASBA) to assume the role of cosponsor of the BRP.[38] NASBA is a confederation of the nation's state accounting boards, which has the authority to charter, accredit, supervise, and discipline accountants and auditors. NASBA serves as a forum for standardizing procedures across the various state accounting regulators. Hitherto, NASBA had been relatively inactive in accounting standards issues, so its inclusion by the FAF as a BRP sponsor was likely a maneuver to balance the AICPA's ambitions.

Among the members of the BRP were Mr. Feilmeier of Koch, Mr. Melancon of the AICPA, Ms. Polley of the FAF, and Billy Atkinson, chair of the NASBA. (See table 7.1 for a full list of BRP members and their professional affiliations.)

In January 2011, the BRP, citing GAAP standards that did not adequately

TABLE 7.1. List of BRP members and their professional affiliations

Name	Professional affiliation
Rick Anderson (chair)	Chairman and CEO, Mass Adams, LLP
Billy Atkinson	Chairman, National Association of State Boards of Accountancy
Daryl Buck*	Senior vice president and CFO, Reasor's Holding Company, Inc.
Steve Feilmeier	CFO, Koch Industries
Hubert Glover	President and cofounder, REDE, Inc.
David Hirschmann	President and CEO, Center for Capital Markets Competitiveness, U.S. Chamber of Commerce
William Knese	Vice president, finance and administration, Angus Industries
Kewsong Lee	Managing director, Warburg Pincus
Paul Limbert	President and CEO, WesBanco, Inc.
Krista McMasters	CEO, Clifton Gunderson
Barry Melancon	President and CEO, American Institute of Certified Public Accountants
Jason Mendelson	Managing director and cofounder, Foundry Group
Michael Menzies	President and CEO, Easton Bank and Trust Company
David Morgan	Co-managing partner, Lattimore, Black, Morgan, and Cain, PC
Terri Polley**	President and CEO, Financial Accounting Foundation
Dev Strischek	Senior vice president and senior credit policy officer, corporate risk management, SunTrust Banks, Inc.
Mark Vonnahme	Clinical professor, University of Illinois
Teri Yohn	Associate professor, Indiana University

* Mr. Buck resigned from the BRP prior to the vote on its final report because he was appointed to the FASB.

** Nonvoting member.

Source: Adapted from American Institute of Certified Public Accountants, Report to the Board of Trustees of the Financial Accounting Foundation, Blue Ribbon Panel on Standard Setting for Private Companies, January 2011, accessed April 2012, http://www.aicpa.org/interestareas/frc/accountingfinancialreporting/pcfr/downloadabledocuments/blue_ribbon_panel_report.pdf.

address the needs of private companies, issued the following recommendation: "The BRP recommends a U.S. GAAP model with exceptions and modifications for private companies, with process enhancements. A supermajority of BRP members further recommends that a separate private company standard-setting board under the FAF be established to ensure that those enhancements are made and result in appropriate and sufficient exceptions and modifications for private companies."[39]

There was a lone dissent on the BRP. The dissent came from the panel's only research professor, Teri Yohn of Indiana University:

There has . . . been no compelling evidence or framework presented to the Panel to suggest that the objectives of financial reporting differ between private companies and public companies. The Panel has merely been presented with a list of standards that accountants associated with private companies do not find desirable. . . .

Proponents of differential standards for private companies focus on the costs and benefits of applying standards from the company's perspective. The proponents have considered only the cost of providing financial information and having the information audited. This is a narrow view of the costs and benefits associated with financial reporting. It is important to note that not providing relevant information to financial statement users can also be costly. . . .

Proponents of differential standards for private companies raise a concern over the number of qualified opinions that have been issued for private companies. However, given that there is no regulatory requirement to file audited financial statements for most private companies, these companies can choose to not prepare financial statements under U.S. GAAP if it is not beneficial. . . . There is no reason to modify the standards so that companies can get unqualified opinions. This is like writing an exam so that every student gets 100 percent.[40]

This dissent notwithstanding, the overwhelming support on the BRP for a separate private-company accounting body left the FAF with limited options. It could accept the BRP's recommendations to create an autonomous and authoritative rule-making board for private companies, or it could try to find a middle ground, such as a new body that worked within the FASB's infrastructure to determine which GAAP principles could be modified or exempted for private companies. Despite Professor Yohn's dissent, the option to continue with the status quo, where the FASB remained the primary body to determine all GAAP, seemed off the table.

While the FAF considered the BRP recommendations, the AICPA initiated a public campaign for the FAF to adopt those recommendations, particularly the creation of a separate private-company standard-setting board. The campaign utilized the AICPA's vast membership network of hundreds of thousands of accountants and auditors, and the FAF was inundated with more than ten thousand letters supporting the AICPA's position (the overwhelming majority of these letters were "form letters" in which members affixed their personal details to a template provided by the AICPA).[41] Mr. Melancon was unambiguous about his position: "The issues for private companies should not be resolved within the framework of the FASB."[42] He pointed out that state and local governments had their own accounting standard setter within the FAF, the Governmental Accounting Standards Board (GASB), so a separate body for private-company GAAP was not unprecedented: "Why should governments have the GASB? Why not let the FASB do government accounting standards? We don't have FASB do government accounting and we have GASB because of special needs. Similarly, why not let private companies have their own standard setter?"[43]

In the meantime, to clarify its position, the FAF held a series of private meetings with small public accounting firms, preparers and users of private-company financial statements, and a group of academics who had done research on private-company issues, but the FAF was criticized for the private nature of the meetings.[44]

In October 2011, the FAF issued a request for comment on a proposal to establish a Private Company Standards Improvement Council (later shortened to Private Company Council; see figure 7.1 for a timeline of events in the creation of the PCC). The FAF proposal differed from the BRP report in that it did not embrace the idea of the PCC being an independent body under the FAF, equal to the FASB; instead, the PCC would work with the FASB and have its decisions subject to FASB approval. As envisioned by the FAF, the proposed PCC would serve two functions: (1) to recommend suggested modifications and exceptions in GAAP to the FASB for ratification and (2) to act as the FASB's primary advisory body on private-company issues. The PCC would consist of a chairperson, a FASB member appointed by the FAF with substantial private-company professional experience, and eleven to fifteen other members.[45] Members would serve an initial three-year term, staggered to ensure continuity, and be eligible for two one-year extensions. The group would meet four to six times per year. The PCC would rely on the FASB's full-time staff and financial resources to conduct its research. The PCC would report to the FAF trustees through a special review committee. Reporting would include occasional in-person reports and quarterly written reports.[46]

The AICPA was unsupportive of the FAF's proposal. Mr. Melancon criticized what he saw as the excessive influence of the largest audit firms at the FASB: "Not everyone in the largest firms understands the mom and pop accounting issues [of private companies]."[47] He sought to limit their presence on the PCC: "If we have to live with the PCC [as proposed by the FAF], then we need to make sure that it is interacting with small business and smaller audit firms."[48] Tom Quaadman, vice president of the U.S. Chamber of Commerce's Center for Capital Markets Competitiveness, saw the FAF's proposal as a victory for the traditionally powerful interests in GAAP standard setting: "The Big Four, the SEC, and the FASB are all resistant to the idea [of a separate private-company standard setter]; hence we ended up with [the proposal]."[49] David Morgan, an accountant who served on the BRP and who had previously chaired the AICPA's Private Companies Practice Section, saw little real reform in the FAF's proposal: "The recent FAF proposal largely retains

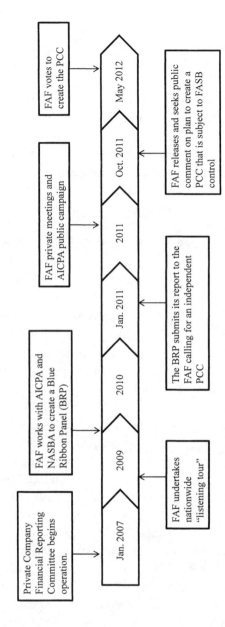

FIGURE 7.1. Timeline of events in the creation of the PCC

Source. Adapted from Karthik Ramanna and Luis Viceira, *The Private Company Council* (HBS No. 113-045) (Boston: Harvard Business School Publishing, 2013).

the status quo, and the status quo is not working. It proposes to create a new Private Company Council, which really is just an enhancement of the existing Private Company Financial Reporting Committee, which has met with only limited success, having not seen its major recommendations approved by [the] FASB during its five-year existence. There is no reason to think that the new council would fare any better."[50]

Members of the Big Four largely supported the FAF's October 2011 proposal. KPMG's Mark Bielstein agreed with the proposal, noting that the proposed structure for the PCC was "a way to gain additional and more useful information for [the] FASB from private company constituents."[51] A view within the Big Four was that something needed to be done to get the issues between the FASB and the AICPA resolved and that the FAF proposal helped achieve that resolution. A policy position released by PricewaterhouseCoopers noted, "We are sympathetic to concerns over complexity, cost and relevancy. And steps other than separate [private-company] standards can be taken."[52]

For members of the FAF, the compromise of a PCC that worked within the FASB infrastructure was a way to contain the potential of a runaway PCC that developed a version of GAAP substantially different from that produced by the FASB. Defending the FAF's proposal, Mr. Brennan of the FAF applauded the openness of the deliberations: "One of the criticisms of standard setters is that they listen but don't hear. To me the creation of the PCC is a manifestation of listening and hearing."[53] Ms. Seidman, the FASB chair, agreed: "This process demonstrates our commitment to better serving the needs of all private company stakeholders . . . without sacrificing the quality and fundamental level of comparability that are the touchstones of the U.S. accounting system and U.S. capital markets."[54]

Mr. Brennan, however, understood how some could be skeptical of the FAF's proposed solution. "Ten years ago, there was a level of insularity in Norwalk," he said, referring to charges that the FASB was unresponsive to opposition, particularly over fair-value accounting.[55] He also acknowledged challenges in the process thus far; in particular, a lack of clarity in the expected outcomes of the BRP, whose proposal for a separate private-company standard setter, he felt, had polarized the issue. "Never delegate—even implicitly—the most important parts of your strategic plan," he reflected. "Own the issues that are most critical to your organization."[56]

The FAF initiated a series of public meetings to solicit constituent input on its October 2011 proposal. Four meetings were organized: in Atlanta, Georgia, in Fort Worth, Texas, in Palo Alto, California, and in Boston, Massachusetts. Most of the attendees at the four meetings were somehow affiliated with private companies—as either private-company executives, investors, auditors, or lawyers. Quickly, the FAF learned that pressure for a separate private-company accounting body ran deep. At the Atlanta meeting, participants emphasized their opposition to the FASB's "ratification" power over the PCC. At the Fort Worth meeting, participants complained about the lack of autonomy for the PCC under the FAF proposal. At the Palo Alto meeting, focus fell on the "disclosure overload" in GAAP affecting private companies. And at the Boston meeting, participants objected to the FAF proposal that a FASB member chair the PCC.[57]

Mr. Melancon of the AICPA continued his criticism of the FAF's October 2011 proposal: "The FASB system with SEC oversight does not allow changes that would benefit private companies."[58] Raising concerns about the FAF's proposal to have the PCC's chair be a FASB member, he said, "People on the PCC should be people who believe in private-company standards, not doubters."[59] Mr. Melancon also cited a financial conflict of interest from having the FAF fund the PCC through fees collected from public companies: "When you have a standard-setting board paid for by public companies, how will you get private company views addressed?"[60] The funding issue was complicated by differences between the FAF's proposal and the AICPA's view on the employment status of PCC members. The FAF envisioned the PCC members serving as part-time volunteers (as did members of other FASB groups, such as the Emerging Issues Task Force), a relatively low-cost arrangement. The AICPA's preference was for the PCC to comprise a full-time chair and part-time paid professionals, with its own technical staff, an arrangement that was expected to cost several million dollars. Responding to the FAF's observation that this latter structure would require a separate source of funding, as it could not be supported from fees assessed on public companies, Mr. Melancon asked rhetorically, "Can we please not have a discussion on what is the right accounting for half of the U.S. economy based on a question of funding of a few million dollars?"[61]

Mr. Morgan of the BRP and AICPA scoffed at the FAF's proposal that PCC decisions be under FASB review: "[The] FASB would retain complete authority over any recommendations to modify GAAP for private companies. In fact, all FASB members would participate in every PCC meeting; even its chair would be a FASB member. The dominance of [the] FASB over any decision made by the new PCC would mean that private-company constituents would lack sufficient power in determining accounting standards relevant to private companies."[62] Mr. Quaadman of the Chamber of Commerce pushed for PCC independence: "How the FASB is represented in the PCC is a big issue. If the PCC is a wholly owned subsidiary of the FASB, it is going to fail. The PCC needs to be seen as the driver of private-company standards."[63]

Experts close to the situation warned that the FAF risked losing its authority over GAAP if it misread constituent sentiments, noting that if the PCC didn't have independence from the FASB, the larger interests among private companies could push for an outright takeover of private-company accounting from the FAF.

Discussion and Conclusion

The FAF's final decision on the PCC came in May 2012, just under three months after its last public hearing on the issue in Boston. The final structure of the PCC differed in at least four important ways from the October 2011 proposal. First, decisions by the PCC were no longer to be subject to "ratification" by the FASB. Instead, the FASB would "endorse" PCC decisions— the endorsement was nonbinding. Second, the requirement that the PCC be chaired by a FASB member was dropped—the PCC would have its own non-FASB chairman. Third, the PCC would have its own dedicated, full-time research staff drawn from the ranks of FASB employees. Finally, the PCC would have effective independence on agenda-setting issues—although the FASB was provided with an input role on this matter, its reach was advisory. The FAF suggested that it would revisit the structure of the PCC after three years of operation to assess its performance.[64]

AICPA president Barry Melancon expressed satisfaction with the outcome, saying that the FAF had "taken solid steps in the right direction" with this decision. He added, "We look forward to continuing to work together to effect meaningful changes in U.S. GAAP for private companies and the users of their financial statements."[65]

On September 19, 2012, the FAF announced the inaugural membership of the PCC. Billy Atkinson, a member of the BRP and the chairman of NASBA, was appointed the first PCC chairman.[66] (See table 7.2 for the initial list of PCC members and their professional affiliations.)

The potential implications for the macroeconomy of separate private-company accounting rules are substantial. For example, one of the first decisions of the PCC, announced in late 2013, was related to accounting for acquired goodwill (discussed extensively in chapter 3). The PCC provided private firms with an alternative to the FASB's fair-value-based impairment-only approach to goodwill, first introduced in SFAS 142. The PCC reversed the FASB's decision in SFAS 142 by reintroducing the principle of goodwill amortization. Private companies were given the option of amortizing goodwill over a period not exceeding ten years.[67] This reversal is particularly salient given the controversial political economy of SFAS 142 and the evidence on its misuse in the years since (see chapter 3).

TABLE 7.2. Initial list of PCC members and their professional affiliations

Name	Professional affiliation	Nominated to the PCC by
Billy Atkinson (chair)	Chairman, National Association of State Boards of Accountancy	National Association of State Boards of Accountancy
George Beckwith	Vice president and CFO, National Gypsum Company	
Steve Brown	Vice president, U.S. Bank	American Bankers Association
Jeffery Bryan	Partner, Professional Standards Group, Dixon Hughes Goodman LLP	
Mark Ellis	CFO, PetCareRx, Inc.	American Institute of Certified Public Accountants
Thomas Groskopf	Director and owner, Barnes, Dennig & Company	
Neville Grusd	President, Merchant Financial Corporation	
Carleton Olmanson	Managing principal, GMB Mezzanine Capital	
Diane Rubin	Partner, Novogradac & Company LLP	
Lawrence Weinstock	Vice president, finance, Mana Products, Inc.	National Association of State Boards of Accountancy

Source: Adapted from Financial Accounting Foundation, "Financial Accounting Foundation Appoints Members to Newly Created Private Company Council," press release, September 19, 2012, accessed December 2013, http://www.fasb.org/cs/ContentServer?c=FAFContent_C&pagename=Foundation/FAFContent_C/FAFNewsPage&cid=1176160336308.

On the one hand, the PCC's early decision to reintroduce goodwill amortization is promising for reasons relating to the deficiencies of fair-value-based goodwill impairment. In this sense, the PCC could provide competition of sorts to the FASB (and vice versa), potentially limiting the impact of special-interest politics in GAAP. Indeed, the emergence of the PCC could be viewed as an institutional response, rooted in market forces, to potential capture of the FASB by certain special interests. An alternative scenario, however, is one where the PCC and the FASB continue to take different routes on fair-value issues and other accounting rules, each driven by the pressures of its respective special-interest constituencies—that is, the notion of separate private-company GAAP could be misused by a select few with the expertise and concentrated interests to do so, to create self-serving exceptions in the rules that determine performance of private companies. After all, if the process of establishing the PCC was itself largely outside the public eye, the process of determining accounting rules within the PCC is unlikely to be subject to the kinds of checks and balances we imagine of healthy political processes. With the bifurcation of the political process of determining accounting rules into private and public company rule-making, relevant special-interest groups may enjoy more concentrated influence and thus even greater opportunities to advance their private agendas.

In this case, the usefulness and comparability of financial statements across private and public companies can become significantly impaired. This, in turn, can have an impact on performance evaluation and capital allocation across private and public companies, with attendant real economic consequences. As FAF chairman Jack Brennan remarked about the creation of the PCC, "What goes on in Norwalk affects every single American."[68]

Despite these potentially significant implications, much of the political process that determined the eventual shape of the PCC occurred outside the public eye, among finance and accounting specialists acting in the interests of the groups they represented. Mr. Brennan himself recognized the relative obscurity of the accounting standards establishment he headed: "When they called me twelve years ago [to serve on the FAF], even I asked, 'What is the FAF?'"[69]

As the preceding narrative on the creation of the PCC suggests, there were many complex factors that interconnected in the process to establish a new accounting rule-maker for private companies. First, there were the private companies themselves, concerned about the rising costs of compliance with GAAP—such GAAP compliance, although not mandatory, was critical to securing public credit. Second, there was the U.S. Chamber of Commerce that was concerned about the SEC's growing disclosure mandate—for some within the chamber, this was a core ideological battle. Third, there were the smaller audit firms, concerned about the clout of the Big Four at the FASB—to this group, the PCC represented an opportunity to obtain some control over accounting rule-making issues. Fourth, there was the AICPA, which was seeking to reassert itself in the regulatory sphere after SOX stripped it of powers over setting public-company auditing standards.

In addition to the above factors, the FASB—which stood to lose significantly from the creation of the PCC—was weakened at the time of the debate, chiefly from the aftermath of the 2008 Financial Crisis. The FASB had taken criticism over the potential role of fair-value accounting in that crisis. Finally, there was the FAF, the core decision-making authority in this process. This body, although nominally at the apex of the accounting standards establishment, had been relatively unassertive for much of its history, particularly on the substantive issues of accounting rule-making. The debate over the creation of the PCC saw the relatively unknown FAF drawn into a political process with powerful voices and determined interests. The eventual outcome saw the FAF having to abandon its quest for a middle ground on the issue of the PCC's relation to the FASB.

It is too early to tell what material impact, if any, the PCC will have on economic activity. The conceptual arguments for separate private-company accounting rules are sparse, as Professor Yohn noted. (Relatedly, a committee of academics from the American Accounting Association charged with evaluating the establishment of the PCC was split six to five, with the majority arguing against separate private-company standards.[70]) And although there is some legitimacy to the claim about the high compliance costs of GAAP, this argument applies to all companies, not just private companies. Eventually, the narrative of the PCC's establishment largely hangs on the description of a political process, not on conceptual reasons for separate private-company accounting rules. It is this result that raises the most concern about the venture.

Political Standards:
Lobbying in Thin Political Markets

Thus far, this book has been chiefly concerned with providing evidence on the nature and outcomes of the political process underlying accounting rule-making. Below, I briefly summarize the key takeaways from chapters 3 through 7, where this focus is particularly evident.

Chapters 3–5 discuss evidence on the use of the political process in accounting to structure U.S. GAAP rules in ways that can opportunistically serve various special-interest groups. In each of these cases, the rule-making outcomes deviate in important ways from both the economic conceptual framework for accounting and the FASB's own original conceptual framework for what accounting rules should look like. Specifically, chapter 3 shows that, at least since 2001, U.S. GAAP accounting rules for goodwill acquired in M&A have been structured in a way that can decrease the accountability of corporate merger activity. The genesis of these rules can be traced to lobbying by firms with the ability to manipulate the rules. There is also evidence that these firms co-opted their allies in Congress as a way to increase pressure on the FASB to effect the compromised rules. Given the multitrillion-dollar M&A industry in the United States, the compromised goodwill rules can impose large costs on the market economy. And indeed, there is evidence to suggest that firms with the ability to manipulate the rules delay the recognition of goodwill that is likely impaired by at least eight quarters. Moreover, as would be expected under a regime that compromises the accountability for purchase premiums in M&A, there is evidence to suggest overpayment in corporate mergers has increased since these rules were put in place.

Whereas chapter 3 is focused on the potential social costs generated by a single, major accounting rule (for acquired goodwill), chapters 4 and 5 look at the political process that has accompanied the spectacular growth of fair-value accounting in U.S. GAAP. Although there are some cases where fair-value rules can be part of an economically efficient accounting system, the widespread use of fair-value rules even in areas where they are entirely subjective raises concerns about the potential for large-scale abuse. And indeed, the role of fair-value accounting in major accounting scandals related to the collapse of Enron and the 2008 Financial Crisis is consistent with these concerns. Chapter 5 documents that the growth of fair-value accounting can be traced to the growing proportion of FASB regulators from the financial-services industry. This industry, which has itself grown in economic and political power over the past twenty-five years, has strong commercial interests in the rise of fair-value accounting. Chapter 4 documents that while the Big N audit firms have lobbied the FASB in a self-serving manner (largely to protect themselves from liability), they have not resisted the rise of fair-value accounting. This is perhaps at least partly because their liability for fair-value estimates appears to be limited, ironically more so in those cases where the estimates are particularly unverifiable (e.g., goodwill). Collectively, chapters 4 and 5 suggest a powerful political wind behind the rise of fair-value rules, which, while enriching to the financial-services industry, can from time to time impose large costs on the market system.

Chapter 6 presents evidence that the self-serving use of the political process in accounting is not limited to U.S. GAAP. The case of the Chinese government's role in rewriting worldwide disclosure rules for related-party transactions in a manner that could obfuscate the profitability of Chinese state-controlled enterprises raises serious concerns about the integrity of these firms' financial statements. With obfuscated financials that overstate their profitability, these firms could distort the allocation of capital and the efficiency of markets in their respective industries, with attendant costs to the worldwide economy. A similar potential exists on a smaller regional scale with the accounting distortions created through lobbying by an influential Indian multinational.

Chapter 7 discusses the potential for a different form of special-interest politics: rather than attempt to redefine specific accounting rules, private companies and associated groups have successfully created their own accounting rule-maker. And although it is too soon to evaluate whether this rule-maker, the Private Company Council (PCC), will in fact become captured, the absence of strong conceptual arguments for why private companies need separate accounting rules does not bode well for the new body.

What, if any, are the commonalities across the various studies presented in the preceding chapters? In this chapter, I distill the evidence into a conceptual description of the accounting rule-making process. I argue that the process embodies a peculiar phenomenon of our capitalist system: that of a "thin political market."

The accounting rule-making process is an esoteric world, ensconced in a shell of specialist knowledge and removed from the eyes of the unschooled public. In this sense, it is largely immune from the dangers of populist policy making (although populism has from time to time been effectively wielded as a weapon in shaping rule-making outcomes, most notably in the case of determining accounting rules for employee stock options[1]). But this technical world is not immune to political dynamics, as the preceding chapters have shown. Put differently, in the United States and beyond, across industrial companies, financial institutions, and audit firms, and over both substantive issues and the design of relevant institutions, the corporate accounting rule-making process is at once deeply technical and political.

Those with the knowledge to shape accounting rules—corporate managers, defined to include auditors, bankers, and other financial intermediaries—accumulate such knowledge because of their experience and their concentrated economic interests in the outcome of the rule-making process. Conversely, those with dispersed interests—ordinary savers and the average citizen—rarely enjoy the expertise necessary to engage productively in rule-making; acquiring such expertise is economically unviable given their limited interests. Accordingly, the political process of accounting rule-making is largely attended by a handful of keen special interests and largely ignored by the general interest. And, not surprisingly, the outcomes of this process, in several instances, skew toward the special interests and away from conceptual expectations of what accounting rules should look like.

In their efforts to shape accounting rules, the special interests have been aided from time to time by seemingly independent experts, including academics. For example, chapter 5 introduces evidence that academics who have served on the FASB since the mid-1980s have been unequivocally supportive of fair-value accounting. The overwhelming support for fair values among academics serving on the FASB is in contrast to the more contentious status of fair-value accounting in the wider academic community.[2] The data suggest that academics on the FASB may have been selected for their predisposition to fair-value accounting—to provide conceptual validation to the special-interest groups advancing fair values. This explanation, if true, suggests that the regulatory model of the determination of GAAP is more nuanced than that derived from a straightforward application of capture theory.[3] Rather, the regulatory model can be described as one of "ideological capture," where prevailing special-interest groups co-opt certain conceptual arguments and associated experts to advance their agendas in the political process.[4]

Furthermore, while a certain special interest might capture the political process in a given instance, there is little evidence of comprehensive capture. On a given issue, those with the strongest incentives and the deepest expertise have the loudest voice and an important say in the outcome. But the portfolio of accounting rules to be determined is broad—spanning all sectors of the economy—and the expertise necessary in each instance is considerable. Thus a special interest on one issue can be part of the general interest on another. Special-interest capture in accounting rule-making appears to be localized; the system itself is not beholden to any one group.

The behavioral model emerging from this description of corporate accounting rule-making is the pursuit of self-interest by participants during the political process. This is true of the corporations and investment banks lobbying on M&A and goodwill accounting in chapter 3, the Big N audit firms protecting themselves from liability in chapter 4, the investment banking and investment management professionals serving on the FASB seeking fair-value accounting rules in chapter 5; the Chinese state-controlled enterprises and the Indian multinational carving out self-serving protections in chapter 6, and the private-company interests pushing for their own regulator in chapter 7. Participants from across the spectrum seek to increase their own profits as they engage in the accounting rule-making game. This behavior is entirely consistent with the competitive spirit that underlies capitalism. Indeed, it embodies the moral imperative of competitive strategy, as Milton Friedman and many others have pointed out.[5]

But capitalism encourages self-interest on the premise of competition; and competition—particularly competition from groups representing ordinary savers and citizens—is uncharacteristic of the accounting rule-making process. Thus the pursuit of profit, which otherwise engineers markets away from iniquitous amassment of wealth and power toward aggregate prosperity, produces a quilt of special-interest concessions in accounting rule-making. This outcome is what I characterize as "political standards."

There are substantive implications of political standards for the future of GAAP accounting in particular and for market capitalism more broadly. If, as the evidence in the preceding chapters suggests, the political process in accounting yields GAAP rules that benefit a handful of special-interest players at the expense of the general interest, then GAAP in the long run can lose its legitimacy as the primary basis for communicating financial information to markets. In fact, one of the major findings in accounting research over the past decade is the increasing volatility and decreasing persistence of GAAP earnings, particularly since the 1990s.[6] One study of the properties of earnings of the thousand largest U.S. firms over the last forty years found that the volatility of earnings has increased by about 50 percent between 1990 and 2003 while the persistence of earnings has declined by over a third during that period. The evidence suggests that these findings are not driven by changes in the fundamental economics of firms that underlie earnings. Rather, the study attributes its findings to U.S. GAAP's declining emphasis on matching and increasing shift to fair-value accounting over that period.[7]

One consequence of the changes to earnings described above is the declining informativeness of GAAP earnings to stock-market valuation, again particularly since the early 1990s. This decline is somewhat ironic given that the FASB's concurrent shift toward more fair-value accounting was made under a broad aspiration of creating more "valuation relevant" GAAP rules.[8] The research in this area has shown that over time managers have been increasingly emphasizing their own "pro forma" summary metrics of financial performance and deemphasizing GAAP earnings. Moreover, the magnitude of the difference between the non-GAAP and GAAP earnings metrics has been increasing. And starting in about 1992, listed companies' stock prices have increasingly become more highly associated with non-GAAP earnings than with GAAP earnings.[9] Interestingly, this shift away from GAAP relevance coincides with the time period over which the proportions of both FASB members from the financial-services industry and fair-value-based GAAP rules began to increase (see chapter 5).

The associated academic literature offers two primary hypotheses for these findings: First, GAAP earnings are increasingly less informative to equity pricing because of the decreasing quality of GAAP rules. Second, equity investors have increasingly become more "fixated" on non-GAAP earnings, as managers opportunistically structure these pro forma metrics to provide more favorable signals of their performance. The hypotheses are not mutually exclusive and, indeed, several recent assessments of this literature conclude that the evidence is consistent with both hypotheses.[10]

Moreover, both hypotheses, when considered in light of the findings on "political standards," do not bode well for the future of GAAP accounting. The narrative that emerges from the joint interpretation of these findings is as follows. Over time, and particularly since the early 1990s, as the political process in GAAP rule-making has become increasingly captured by special interests— especially those from the financial-services industry who have advanced fair-value accounting for self-serving and idiosyncratic reasons—the relative informativeness to equity prices of GAAP earnings versus pro forma non-GAAP earnings has declined. And pursuant to the growing valuation relevance of non-GAAP earnings, some managers have structured their pro forma earnings numbers in opportunistic ways that may have misled the market.

Beyond evidence of the declining informativeness of GAAP earnings to stock-market valuation, there is evidence of declining use of GAAP balance-sheet values in the covenants embedded in corporate debt contracts. As discussed in chapter 2 and elsewhere, the use of accounting information in explicit contracting between the firm and its stakeholders is one of the primary economic determinants of accounting rules. One relevant study found that whereas 80 percent of unlisted corporate debt contracts were based on balance sheet values in 1996, that number declined to only 32 percent in 2007. That study attributes the decline to "the long-term shift in standard setting" toward fair-value accounting.[11] My own interpretation is that "political standards"—including those on fair values—have shifted U.S. GAAP in directions that have decreased the usefulness of GAAP numbers in explicit contracts.

There are costly implications of the above findings and conclusions for the future of both GAAP accounting and capital markets. If the capture of GAAP rules is sustained, it could further delegitimize GAAP accounting until eventually GAAP rules become altogether irrelevant or the rule-making process is fundamentally restructured in the wake of political upheaval (as happened in the early 1970s when the Accounting Principles Board was replaced with the FASB; see chapter 3). In fact, the recent emergence of the PCC—as a substitute GAAP rule-making body to the FASB, at least for private companies (see chapter 7)—is consistent with this latter eventuality. But in the interim, before institutional mechanisms can develop to respond to the capture of GAAP rule-making, society bears the costs from distortionary performance-evaluation metrics and consequently from distortionary resource-allocation decisions in capital markets.

Prices or Politics?

Given the evidence on capture of the political process of accounting rule-making and on the potential costs of that capture, one might credibly ask why must accounting rules be "political" at all? In other words, should accounting rules be regulated? Is the existence of a governmentally sanctioned accounting rule-maker, such as the FASB, necessary to the functioning of market capitalism? Might the issue of capture be avoided altogether if accounting rules were organically determined through economic or "price-based" markets rather than through "political markets"?

Answering these questions requires a framework for what it takes for price-based markets and for market capitalism, more broadly, to function. A rich history of economic research in this area has identified at least six conditions as essential to the functioning of market capitalism and of market prices therein.[12] These conditions are described below. Together they provide a framework that yields insights to the issue of whether prices or politics are the more appropriate way to determine accounting rules. To facilitate exposition, with each condition, I offer examples of how the condition is approximated in practice in the case of U.S. capital markets, which are generally considered well developed.

Well-defined property rights: Property rights enable private ownership of assets, which is central to the ability of individuals to engage in voluntary exchange. Such voluntary exchange is at the heart of price-based markets since it allows individuals to allocate their resources in ways that suit their preferences. In a prospective transaction, if a seller's property rights in the underlying good or service is unclear, the buyer is unlikely to engage in a sale or is likely to demand a significant discount. In the limit, the absence of property rights precludes all market activity.[13] In U.S. capital markets, for example, property rights in financial instruments are usually well defined. They are chiefly established through public institutions such as corporate and securities laws and enforced through federal and state law enforcement agencies as well as private intermediary institutions such as asset-custodial and security firms. Capital markets in several emerging-market nations do not enjoy the level of clarity and enforcement provided under U.S. law, compromising underlying asset prices and, eventually, the price-based markets' effectiveness in allocating investments across competing ventures.[14]

Complete knowledge: For a price-based market to function in a theoretically pure sense, the parties to a voluntary exchange must be acting with full knowledge of the good or service that is being transacted.[15] This means that both the buyer and seller are aware of all humanly known properties of the unit being exchanged, particularly as those properties are relevant to the unit's value-in-exchange. As a practical matter, this condition is rarely, if ever, likely to be met; but it implies that asymmetry of knowledge between buyers and sellers introduces frictions in markets.[16] The greater the degree of knowledge asymmetry, the less likely the price-based market will function as intended. Numerous institutions in U.S. capital markets mitigate the asymmetry of knowledge between suppliers of capital (investors) and users of capital (firms). These include the accounting and auditing industries, financial analysts and ratings agencies, and the financial press.[17]

Enforceable contracts: The voluntary exchanges that underlie price-based markets are generally premised on "contracts" that purport to deliver some good or service of value in return for monetary or equivalent consideration. Without these contracts, the exchanges are unlikely to be consummated, particularly if the deliverables-in-exchange are to be made at or over some period of time in the future. Thus the existence and enforceability of contracts are central to the functioning of most price-based markets.[18] In U.S. capital markets, the legal and accounting industries, together with enforcement through the judicial system, provide the basis for enforceable contracts. Beyond these institutions, numerous other private intermediaries, such as financial insurance providers, are involved in supporting the contracts that underlie capital markets.[19]

No agency problem: In a complex society, transactions in price-based markets are executed on behalf of buyers and sellers by their agents. In theory, these agents act in the interests of their principals. In practice, the agents' own incentives can cloud their actions so that the exchange price or volume may not reflect the interests of the underlying principals.[20] The more severe the agency problem, the less effectively the price-based markets will function. In U.S. capital markets, corporate governance institutions play an important role in mitigating the agency problem between suppliers and users of capital—that is, between investors and corporate managers. These corporate governance institutions include boards of directors, investor protection laws such as the law on fiduciary duties, the practice of financial reporting, and the auditing of financial reports.[21]

Noncollusion: Related to the condition of "no agency problem" is the condition that the transacting parties in a market exchange are not in collusion with each other. In other words, if a market price is to serve as a reliable indicator of the value-in-exchange of a particular good or service, the exchange must be between two parties at arm's length of each other. Mitigating collusion in U.S. capital markets is the business of a number of prominent institutions. These include the SEC, federal prosecutors, short sellers, financial analysts, and auditors, all whom rely in some measure on accounting reports—particularly accounting rules on related-party transactions—to conduct their business.[22]

Free entry and exit: Also embedded in the idea of a market is the assumption that players in the market are free to enter and exit as desired. To function, price-based markets rely on the continuous emergence of new ventures and the dissolution of old ones. This notion is otherwise popularly referred to as "creative destruction" or "economic Darwinism."[23] In practice, "entry and exit" in U.S. capital markets manifests through numerous well-known institutions such as (1) "going public," where new ventures are launched into public securities markets; (2) mergers, acquisitions, and divestitures, where publicly listed companies reorganize their ownership base to realize and unleash synergies; and (3) hostile takeovers, delistings, and bankruptcy, where poorly performing ventures are eliminated from the pool of publicly traded investment options.[24] Corporate accounting reports play a critical role in the functioning of all these institutions.

Two themes are apparent from the discussion above. First, many of the institutions fulfilling the conditions necessary to the functioning of price-based markets and market capitalism are for-profit organizations. In other words, organizations operating in price-based markets are themselves functioning as institutions that support the conditions of price-based markets. This is a key strength of the capitalist system—it is self-reinforcing. For example, in U.S. capital markets, a host of intermediary financial institutions—such as accountants, analysts, auditors, commercial and investment bankers, custodial firms, investment managers, lawyers, and ratings agencies—motivated by profit, contribute to the conditions that ensure the functioning of the price-based market between investors and corporations.

Second, corporate accounting is an important institutional mechanism fulfilling several of the conditions necessary to the functioning of price-based markets and market capitalism. In capital markets alone, corporate accounting reports facilitate the establishment of and contracting on property rights on financial securities; the mitigation of information asymmetries between corporate managers and investors (and relatedly the agency problems and threats of collusion); and the operation of institutions ensuring the entry and exit of publicly listed companies.[25] The standards that govern the production of corporate accounting reports enable the comparability, consistency, materiality, reliability, and understandability of those reports. Accounting rules are thus central to capital markets.

Beyond capital markets, other markets within a capitalist system are also critically dependent on accounting reports and the rules that govern their production. For example, contracting relationships between a firm and its suppliers and between a firm and its customers are often defined using accounting reports, particularly, if those relationships are intended to be long-lasting or if they span distant geographies or multiple jurisdictions (e.g., see the related discussion in chapter 6 on International Financial Reporting Standards).[26] Furthermore, in several countries (although not in the United States), tax collection by governments from corporations are based on publicly reported accounting statements, so the rules that govern those statements are essential to public revenue.[27]

But even if accounting rules are central to capitalism and price-based markets therein, the question still remains whether accounting rules should be regulated—that is, produced through a political process by an organization such as the FASB, which, albeit private, has a monopoly charter from the SEC. After all, as noted above, a particularly attractive feature of capitalism is that the profit motive, in many instances, is itself responsible for institutions that sustain the conditions for price-based markets. Can accounting rule-making be similarly generated through the profit motive and subject to competition in price-based markets?

The brief answer is that a fully private price-based market for accounting rule-making is likely infeasible. A number of conditions necessary to sustain such a market cannot be met in practice. In particular, accounting rules are both nonrival and nonexcludable in nature. Here, nonrival means that any one group's use of accounting rules does not preclude use by another. Nonexcludable means it is difficult to exclude corporations, accountants, and auditors from using accounting rules once produced.[28] Together, the conditions imply that property rights over accounting rules cannot be reasonably established and that production of these rules cannot be contracted upon in a price-based setting.[29] Thus accounting rule-making, like several other critical market institutions such as law making, is a "public good." As such, public goods are more feasibly produced in political markets.[30]

This is not to say that absent government regulation, accounting rules would not exist. Indeed, prior to the establishment of the SEC in the 1930s, companies and their auditors developed rules for preparation of accounting reports on an ad hoc basis. Such rules emerged out of commonalities in accounting practice across several companies.[31] And to this day, companies are known to innovate with accounting practice in ways that eventually result in new GAAP rules. For example, in chapter 4, I described how when Apple first launched the iPhone, it was dissatisfied with the state of extant accounting rules for such products and so decided to adopt different rules on a pro forma basis. Eventually, the company was able to successfully lobby to introduce those pro forma rules into U.S. GAAP.[32] More systematically, there is growing evidence that certain companies continued to emphasize conservative accounting practices in the period leading up to the 2008 Financial Crisis, despite GAAP rule changes to the contrary. In the wake of the crisis, such companies, benefiting from the decreased information asymmetry accorded to greater accounting conservatism, suffered less severe declines in investment activity, debt-raising capacity, and stock prices relative to all other firms.[33]

Notwithstanding the evidence on private innovation in accounting practice giving rise to broader rules in certain instances, such a process alone is likely to undersupply the full complement of accounting rules necessary for a modern complex capital-market economy. This is due to the public-goods nature of accounting rules discussed earlier. Moreover, rules emerging from practice are not generally comparable or consistent, at least until they are widely applied, which, absent fiat, might not happen. This was the case with the rules in place in the 1920s and 1930s prior to regulated accounting rule-making. Writing in 1937, prior to the establishment of the first formal accounting rule-making body in the United States, the then-chief accountant of the SEC lamented, "I am very much afraid it is difficult to name many [accounting] principles that are generally accepted."[34]

Although accounting rule-making is unlikely to be sustainable in a competitive profit-making context, rule-making bodies themselves can be subject to competition. In this regard, as noted earlier, the emergence of the PCC as a potential substitute for the FASB could be viewed as an interesting development. Of course, the PCC is limited in its scope of authority to private companies and is responsible to the Financial Accounting Foundation—the FASB's parent organization. Thus the PCC is unlikely to be independent of the FASB, and its status as a competitor to the FASB is questionable. Moreover, the PCC is likely to be subject to similar political pressures as the FASB—from special-interest groups eager to create self-serving rules—so it is not clear that the emergence of the PCC per se will mitigate capture at the FASB.

The FASB could also be exposed to competition from other jurisdictions' accounting rule-making bodies. For example, differences in corporate securities laws across U.S. states serve as a basis for competition between states for the incorporation of business entities, and several legal scholars view this system as generally satisfactory.[35] Similarly, differences in accounting rules across jurisdictions could serve as a competitive basis for accounting rule-making bodies worldwide.[36] Such competition would at least provide an external validity check on a given jurisdiction's accounting rules, potentially mitigating the extent of special-interest capture. However, as a practical matter, such competition has not materialized, particularly since accounting rule-makers across several jurisdictions spent the better part of the last decade harmonizing their activities with each other and with the International Accounting Standards Board (IASB; see chapter 6).[37] The internationalization of accounting set in place more cooperation, rather than competition, in accounting rule-making. Furthermore, as with the case of the PCC and the FASB, accounting rule-makers outside the United States are also subject to political pressure from asymmetrically powerful interests, so competition in this context could have the perverse effect of rule-makers "racing to the bottom" to cater to special-interest groups.

If we accept the conceptual arguments for—and the practical reality of—accounting rule-making as a public good, the best-case scenario would be a benevolent and omniscient regulator who set rules in the broadest public interest: in this case, to facilitate the functioning of price-based markets and market capitalism.[38] While such a scenario might seem imaginary, economic and political theorists have long postulated it as a solution to the problem of certain public goods.[39] For example, the enormous (undemocratic) power of central banks—particularly the U.S. Federal Reserve—is sometimes justified on this basis.[40] As a practical matter, however, the idea that central banks or other regulators are above political pressures and unsusceptible to special-interest capture is questionable.[41] Moreover, in the case of accounting rule-making, as noted earlier, the necessary substantive expertise for regulation rests with corporate managers and accountants and their auditors and bankers, so the idea of an "independent" regulator is infeasible.

Thus we are left with the condition of accounting rules produced through a political process. There remains, then, the issue of how to interpret the evidence on the capture of this process that has been presented thus far.[42] Is the evidence unique? Are there commonalities across other market institutions generated through political processes? The following section addresses these questions.

The State of Political Markets

Beyond accounting rule-making, a number of institutions that support the conditions for price-based markets and market capitalism are produced through political processes. In the United States, some of these institutions—such as incorporation laws, bankruptcy laws, securities laws, and corporate disclosure rules—are determined by Congress, its agencies (such as the SEC), or state legislatures and are thus purely public. Others—such as standards for auditing and for the conduct of lawyers, bankers, and actuaries—are determined in part by professional bodies. Institutions in this latter class, including the FASB, would not exist in their current form without some government support or charter and are thus somewhere in between public and private.

How do corporate interests—broadly defined to include industrial, financial, and professional organizations—engage in the political process that creates and sustains at least some of the identifiable conditions for capitalism? A large number of academic studies across numerous disciplines, functions, and geographies have generally yielded a common answer to this question. When contributing to the political process of market-supporting institutions, corporate managers lobby in their own interests, consistent with their profit motive. This usually means lobbying to create conditions that sustain their competitive advantage in markets, even if it is at the expense of the long-term stability and legitimacy of market capitalism.

The bulk of the evidence on this issue comes from studies of the political process of various institutions in the United States, where data on political contributions and lobbying expenditures by managers and corporations are, in a relative sense, widely available. A number of studies have shown a link between corporate political spending and their demands for legislation both from the U.S. Congress and from state legislatures.[43] One study examined the relation between campaign contributions from three specialized financial sectors—commercial banking, investment banking, and insurance—and congressional legislation in the 1980s and 1990s to eliminate barriers to operating in the three sectors. The setting allowed for the clear identification of competing interests across the three financial sectors. The study found stable long-term relations between campaign contributions and the profit interests of the financial institutions in proposed legislation.[44]

Similar results have been obtained in studies of the motives behind corporations when lobbying U.S. regulatory agencies. For example, a study of corporate lobbying of the Federal Communications Commission in 1998 showed that large firms, in particular, are sensitive both to free riding by industry peers and to the risk of disclosing proprietary information when crafting their lobbying strategies. The evidence suggests firms, motivated by their own interests, employ sophisticated lobbying strategies that dynamically shift between cooperation and individual lobbying as necessary.[45] Another study of how audit firms lobby in the determination of auditing standards found systematic relations between the firms' internal technological capacities and the types of standards they favored. In particular, those firms that relied more on the professional judgment of their staff in conducting audits (and less on formal statistical audit methodologies) were less supportive of attempts to standardize procedures across the auditing profession. Such standardization would likely lessen their advantage in exercising professional judgment.[46]

Studies of corporate political engagement outside the United States also suggest opportunism as the dominant corporate motive, although inferences from these studies are less persuasive since the international data are coarser. One study looked at over twenty thousand firms across nearly fifty countries and found "widespread" evidence that controlling shareholders and top officers have connections with national parliaments and governments. In this study, politically connected firms represented 7.72 percent of the world's stock market capitalization. The announcement of a corporate manager or large shareholder entering politics generated, on average, a statistically significant increase in the firm's stock price, particularly for firms in countries perceived as corrupt.[47]

Beyond the direct political engagement of corporate managers in the political process, there are also studies of their opportunistic shaping of information in political discourse. As discussed earlier, equal access to information is a foundational assumption in the theory of efficient functioning of markets and capitalism. The opportunistic use of information, through strategic disclosure, strategic omission, and spin, can create distortions in the political process, ultimately affecting the functioning of markets. For example, one study found that corporations standing to benefit from proposed import tariffs against competitors opportunistically lower reported accounting profits just prior to political deliberation on those proposals, as if to appear more in need of the tariffs.[48]

Another study, which I coauthored with Professor Sugata Roychowdhury of Boston College, found evidence of corporations managing the information environment around U.S. congressional elections in ways that appear to benefit political candidates with whom they have relationships. Specifically, during the 2004 U.S. general election where corporate offshoring was a major campaign issue, firms engaged in offshoring opportunistically lowered reported accounting profits when political candidates with whom they had relationships were in close races. Higher levels of reported profits usually bring greater media scrutiny; thus the firms, by understating profits, were likely attempting to deflect media attention from themselves and their preferred candidates.[49]

The basic tendency of corporate managers to use their wealth and knowledge advantage to lobby for institutions in their own interest is thus widely documented. Indeed, this insight was the basis of the economic theory of regulation and the theory of capture first expounded by Professor George Stigler of the University of Chicago (for which he was awarded a Nobel Prize).[50] The idea that profit maximizing individuals will seek to subvert the conditions for markets was even identified by Adam Smith as he developed his theory of capitalism in the *Wealth of Nations*: "People of the same trade seldom meet together, even for merriment and diversion, but the conversation ends in a conspiracy against the public, or in some contrivance to raise prices."[51]

It is with this insight that Professor Stigler and others have warned against regulation.[52] In fact, one view within economics is that regulation of the provision of public goods and the attendant burdens of regulatory capture are more costly to society than simple distortions in the supply of the public goods that might arise should they remain unregulated. For example, Professor Milton Friedman argued that in cases where the production of a good was a "natural monopoly"—rendering it a public good since price-based markets would be inefficient—it would be less desirable to society to seek regulation than to live with a profit-seeking monopolist.[53] In this spirit, it is likely wise public policy to continue to promote some innovation in accounting practice among companies and auditors, as with the examples described earlier of Apple accounting for the iPhone and of companies being more conservative than GAAP rules demanded in the period leading up to the 2008 Financial Crisis. These arguments notwithstanding, as a practical matter, at least in most democratic societies, there is a consensus for regulation of numerous public goods, including accounting rule-making. The democratic consensus renders moot the theoretical nirvana of no regulation imagined by Professors Friedman and Stigler and others.

Moreover, self-serving corporate political engagement resulting from attempts to capture a regulatory process need not in itself be a cause for concern. After all, profit-seeking behavior is the engine of capitalism. But the condition that makes this statement valid is "competition." In other words, if the political process is sufficiently "thick"—in that diverse interests are well represented and these interests have access to substantive knowledge to shape political outcomes—then a self-serving political engagement strategy by all individuals involved can at least sometimes result in outcomes that advance social welfare. And even if the outcomes are not welfare increasing, a thick political process is unlikely to be captured by a small set of special-interest groups. Here, the logical analogy to the functioning of price-based markets is germane. Political competition in this sense refers not just to competing corporate interests—as in the case of the study on commercial banks, investment banks, and insurance firms mentioned earlier—but also to active engagement by labor unions, pensioners, environmental groups, and ideological forums that represent certain normative viewpoints such as organized religion or libertarianism.

And even in cases of regulation where the interests of smaller players such as consumers, retail investors, or common citizens are not directly represented in the political process, the media can play an important intermediating role in "thickening" the political process. Competition among media organizations to sell stories ("scoops") about regulatory capture could help drive down the influence of special-interest groups such as corporations and labor unions.[54]

For example, the political market for patent regulation in the United States is one that is generally well represented by diverse, powerful, and (importantly) competing interests, including the pharmaceutical industry lobby, the software industry lobby, lobbies for patients and their families, consumer lobbies, labor-union lobbies, and even church lobbies, together with widespread media coverage.[55] Outcomes of this process are unlikely to be driven by any one interest group. Moreover, such outcomes, although controversial and potentially undesirable to any single group, could in fact at times represent aggregate social interests. Similarly, the political markets for Social Security policy and universal health care in the United States are both well publicized and well attended by numerous competing interest groups, likely mitigating capture by any one group.[56] In the case of such thick political markets, the ideal model for engagement might in fact be self-interested profit-increasing behavior.

In fact, the general consensus from much of the literature on corporate political engagement of the U.S. Congress on broad policy issues is that such engagement is more consistent with "informing" congresspersons about proposed policy than with the "capture" of the policy-making process. The evidence suggests that corporations develop long-term relationships with members of Congress in attempts to influence policy; the evidence does not suggest that policy from Congress can simply be "bought" through large campaign contributions or lavish lobbying expenditures.[57]

How do we reconcile the neutral evidence on corporate political engagement—particularly on widely understood and actively attended policy issues—with the evidence on special-interest capture of the accounting rule-making process presented in this book? The answer lies in appreciating that not all political markets are equally liquid and deep. When the policy product is esoteric and the costs to the general interest to remain informed about policy options are high, there is a greater likelihood for special-interest capture. The following section focuses on defining a class of "thin political markets" where this is likely the case.[58]

By rigorously defining the notion of thin political markets, we can understand a key logical and ethical limit to the unrestrained deployment of the profit motive by corporations. The result can be an improved understanding of the functioning of markets and an improved ability to sustain the legitimacy of market capitalism.

Thin Political Markets

Why is the process of determining accounting rules a "thin political market"? And how might we be able to identify other thin political markets? In this section, I propose a definition for thin political markets. The definition arises inductively from the evidence and understanding of the phenomenon in accounting rule-making. Like all inductive definitions, it is a first iteration at conceptualizing an issue. I conclude the section with some examples of other potential thin political markets, with the view that additional research and scholarship into this question will eventually lead us to a sharper description of the notion.

A thin political market is characterized by three distinct but interrelated conditions. First, there is a group or constituency with concentrated economic interests in the outcome of the political process. Second, this special-interest group also commands experience-based subject-matter expertise necessary for crafting the relevant rules or regulation being determined through the political process. And third, there is little political opposition from the general interest on the issue, particularly from those representing the interests of individual savers and ordinary citizens. Below I expand on each of these conditions.

The first condition is that one group, more than any other, experiences concentrated economic opportunity from the outcome of the political process. In other words, there is a particularly concentrated special-interest group—a "primary" special-interest group—among the various constituents to the process. This primary special-interest group can be a company, an industry, a profession, or coalitions or subgroups thereof. The notion of a "primary special interest" in the context of accounting rule-making is already implicit in the numerous cases discussed in the preceding chapters. For example, in the case of accounting for M&A, investment banks and certain high-technology firms vested in an acquisitions strategy constitute the primary special interest with concentrated economic opportunity. Similarly, in the case of determining the liability that can arise from the application of judgment in accounting rules, the audit firms constitute the primary special interests. And in the case of introducing the fair-value methodology as an alternative accounting basis, the investment management and investment banking firms are the primary special-interest group.

A corollary to the existence of this primary special-interest group in thin political markets is the notion that there is also a "general interest" and potentially secondary special interests in the outcome of the political process. Members of the general-interest group have little individual economic interest in the outcome, although the collective economic stake of the general interest can be substantial. The general interest thus suffers from a form of the collective-action problem.[59] In the case of accounting rule-making, the general interest usually includes the individual saver and the common citizen in whose benefit the capital-market system is deployed. Additionally, companies and industries not part of the primary special interest on any given issue could also be part of the general interest on that issue. Alternatively, they may be organized as a secondary special-interest group on the issue, facilitated by preexisting political organizational ties that lower their collective-action costs. In this case, the individual economic interest in the political process' outcome among members of the secondary special interest is, by definition, less intense than that among members of the primary special interest.

The second condition that characterizes thin political markets is that resolution of the issue being adjudicated through the political process relies (in part) on the substantive *experiential* expertise of the primary special-interest group. That is, the primary special-interest group enjoys a significant experience-based knowledge advantage over the general interest and, if applicable, other secondary special interests. This experiential knowledge is generated in the course of business activities that are the source of the group's interest in the political process. In other words, the group has a "special interest" in the outcome of the political process because of certain business activities, and the pursuit of those activities gives rise to a body of expertise relevant to the political process. Note that this second condition is not simply about a knowledge gap between the primary special interest and everyone else, one that could (in theory) be unraveled through rigorous conceptual analyses by independent experts (e.g., academics). It is the recognition that such knowledge cannot, by definition, exist outside the primary special interest because the primary special interest acquires this knowledge through its operations—the same operations that are the source of its interest in the outcomes of the political process. Thus in thin political markets, a component of the relevant knowledge for regulation is tacit or a posteriori in nature and is generated within the primary special interest. (The notion of experiential knowledge discussed here has been explored in a rich management-science literature on organizational learning.[60])

As with the first condition, this second condition is apparent in several of the cases already discussed in the book. Consider, for example, the case of crafting accounting rules for M&A. As seen from the process described in chapter 3, determining these rules requires know-how on the practice of M&A—such as how acquisitions are funded, how assets and liabilities are valued, and how purchase premiums are calculated—and on the accounting for such practice. This knowledge is acquired by investment banks and companies regularly engaged in M&A—the primary special interests—in the course of their operations. This knowledge is not readily known to an outside accounting expert (such as an accounting professor) who is not involved in the practice of M&A. (And if this expert is involved in the practice of M&A, then she or he is no longer an "outsider" but rather likely an agent of the primary special interest.)

To those familiar with the nature of accounting, the existence of such experiential knowledge is well known. But to those unfamiliar with accounting practice, the notion that (at least some) accounting expertise can be experiential is potentially, at first blush, surprising. But the political process in accounting, which has been the subject of this book, itself betrays the experiential nature of accounting knowledge—after all, accounting rule-making is largely delegated by the government (SEC) to those with practical experience (FASB members), who in turn, on specific issues, largely rely on the input (via private meetings, testimonials, and comment letters) of those with deeper subject-matter experience (industrial mangers, financial-services executives, and auditors). That is, rather than simply dictate accounting rules from above, the government—and, in turn, the FASB—rely considerably on field expertise in rule-making, recognizing the tacit or a posteriori nature of relevant knowledge.

To be clear, the existence and role of experiential knowledge in thin political markets does not preclude a role for a priori knowledge as well. For example, in the case of accounting rule-making, the economic conceptual framework or the FASB conceptual frameworks discussed in chapter 2 can constitute the relevant a priori knowledge. Moreover, a priori knowledge can be applied ex post facto to test regulations for evidence of capture, as in the case of this book. But the point to emphasize in setting out this second condition for thin political markets is that some of the information that is meaningful to crafting a regulatory solution rests within the primary special interest, by virtue of expertise acquired from its operations.

The first two conditions defining thin political markets together suggest that concentrated interest and expertise are comingled in regulatory issues that can be classified as thin political markets. The implication is that that an "independent" regulatory body is conceptually infeasible in such markets because such a regulator would by definition lack the full expertise necessary to determine regulation. Thus the philosophy behind the creation of the FASB—an independent regulator free from direct intervention of the interests it regulates—is irreconcilable with the nature of the FASB's tasks in accounting rule-making. Given these two conditions, one might reasonably conclude that regulatory capture by the primary special interest is inevitable, obviating the need for any further conditions in characterizing thin political markets. But such a conclusion ignores the potential of focused public accountability on the regulator to at least mitigate the extent or frequency of such capture. That is, the regulator might still be driven to effect regulation in the general interest if the general interest is actively engaged in the political process—a dose of "sunlight" could "disinfect" against the threat of capture.[61] This is where the third condition becomes relevant.

The third condition of a thin political market is that there is little opposition to the primary special interest from the general interest. This could be for a variety of reasons, but these reasons largely boil down to the salience of the issue at hand—that is, the substantive issue in a thin political market does not secure the attention of the general interest, largely because it is esoteric or abstruse or simply boring. Of course, the general interest in a political process is usually represented via intermediaries (e.g., for-profit groups, not-for-profit advocacy groups, the media, and elected politicians).[62] But as a literature in political science has argued, the effectiveness of such intermediaries is tied to the salience of the issue at hand.[63] And in thin political markets, low issue salience hinders the effectiveness of intermediaries.

For example, consider in turn the various intermediaries that might be involved in the thin political market that is accounting rule-making: for-profit groups, not-for-profit advocacy groups, the media, and elected politicians. Here, the key for-profit intermediary for the general interest (particularly ordinary savers) is investment management firms. In theory, the investment management firms should routinely be involved in the GAAP political process on behalf of savers. And should they lack the experiential expertise on any given issue (condition two), they would, again in theory, acquire the relevant primary special interest with such expertise—many investment management firms certainly have the scale to do so. But in practice, these firms are only involved in the political process on certain issues, and when involved, they largely represent their *own* interests rather than the interests of individual savers. For example, chapter 5 provides evidence that the investment management sector is associated with potentially distortionary accounting rules that could make the sector's own performance appear more favorable than it actually is, resulting in overcompensation of executives in the sector at the expense of returns for ordinary savers. This evidence is consistent with an unresolved agency problem between investment managers and the savers they represent, a thesis recently expounded on by my colleague Professor Mihir Desai.[64] The agency problem is unresolved in part because of the esoteric nature of the subject matter: investment managers can game their own accountability and performance metrics because ordinary savers seem to be unable to detect such gaming, at least in the intermediate run. Ostensibly, it is more profitable for investment managers to engage in such gaming of their own metrics than to represent the general interest (savers) in determining accounting metrics for the economy as a whole.

In a related vein, the not-for-profit advocacy groups otherwise involved in representing ordinary savers in a thin political market are largely absent from the accounting rule-making process because the issues at stake are largely inaccessible to them—that is, the issues are generally so complex that these not-for-profit groups cannot on their own understand them (the second condition). Of course, as with the for-profit intermediaries, the not-for-profits could, in theory, acquire the special-interest group with substantive experiential expertise on a given issue. For example, in the case of M&A accounting, one could imagine, in theory, a not-for-profit intermediary acquiring an investment bank so as to effectively participate in the political process. But to do this, the not-for-profit would have to raise funds from the general interest, which would again require that the issue of M&A accounting was sufficiently salient to the general interest to make such fund-raising efforts feasible. Effectively, the barriers to the not-for-profit intermediaries (and therefore the general interest) in acquiring the expertise necessary to overcome the knowledge gap described above is insurmountable in thin political markets due to low issue salience.

The media, another potentially vocal intermediary for individual savers and the common citizen, are also relatively silent in accounting rule-making debates because the issues at stake are not "exciting" enough to sell newspapers, television shows, online posts, or the like. Put differently, the substance of the issue being determined in the political process—in this case, accounting rules—affects the role the media will play in intermediating for the general interest. After all, the media are driven by their own profit motives, and the capture of accounting rule-making does not make for captivating headlines.

Relatedly, elected politicians in the executive and legislature, who might be expected to intervene for the public interest as they do on some issues, also lack the incentive to do so. The substantive issues in thin political markets—such as accounting rule-making—do not capture the public imagination and do not serve as a basis on which to run successful election campaigns. In fact, in the cases where politicians do become involved in the political process—for example, accounting for M&A or stock options (see chapter 3)—they generally do so *in favor of* special-interest groups, likely because politicians face little public accountability on their actions related to accounting rule-making. It appears to take extraordinary events, such as the accounting frauds at Enron and WorldCom and attendant public concern about the integrity of the market system, for members of Congress to represent the general interest in thin political markets. This was the case with congressional intervention on stock options, where (as discussed in chapter 3) most members of Congress opposed real expensing of stock options when the issue was first considered by the FASB in the 1990s. It was in the early to mid-2000s, after a series of very visible corporate accounting frauds, that the congressional tide turned toward stock-option expensing. Thus account-ability of special interests to the general public that is sometimes introduced through the democratic process is generally absent in thin political markets.[65]

Even if all intermediaries fail to act for the general interest in thin politi-cal markets, individual members of the general interest might still attempt to engage in the political process (perhaps due to an idiosyncratic affinity for the subject matter at hand). Indeed, from time to time, individual savers and or-dinary citizens do write comment letters on accounting rule-making issues. But these comment letters appear to be largely ineffective in swaying eventual outcomes. A key reason for this ineffectiveness is that individual members of the general interest lack the credibility to engage in the technocratic process of thin political markets. This can be either because they lack the substantive knowledge (condition two) or because of (perceived) barriers associated with the professionalization of thin political markets—that is, in thin political markets the political process is implicitly or explicitly "professionalized"—organized within the auspices of an exclusive community perceived as being open only to experts.[66] For example, until the creation of the FASB, account-ing rule-making was organized under the American Institute of Certified Public Accountants (AICPA), the professional society for accountants. Even under the FASB, where there is no requirement for board members to be pro-fessional accountants, a large majority of board members have been certified public accountants (CPAs; see chapter 5). Moreover, FASB public hearings on accounting issues are rarely, if ever, attended by nonaccountants or those not closely associated with accounting such as corporate managers, bankers, and business lawyers. This creates a sense of exclusiveness to the process that dissuades or discredits general-interest participation.

To summarize, thus far I have argued that there are three conditions that characterize a thin political market: (1) there exists a group or constituency with concentrated economic interests in the regulatory outcome, (2) this primary special-interest group enjoys necessary experience-based subject-matter expertise, and (3) this group experiences little political opposition from the general interest and its intermediaries on the issue, largely due to low issue salience of the subject matter.

Each of these conditions is alone unlikely to precipitate regulatory cap-ture. For example, the problem of concentrated economic interests (on its own) can be mitigated through collective action organized via intermediaries such as not-for-profits or the media, as discussed earlier. Similarly, a special-interest group's knowledge advantage (on its own) could be overcome if op-posing interests are sufficiently concentrated so as to be incented to acquire the special-interest group and thus acquire its knowledge base. Finally, a political process that is poorly attended by general interests (e.g., because it is professionalized) could still mitigate special-interest capture if the relevant expertise is sufficiently heterogeneously distributed. A thin political market is the result of the confluence of all three conditions described above. In fact, I use the term "thin political *market*" (rather than "thin political *process*") because the three conditions that characterize it—the conditions that lead to special-interest capture—are analogous, in this sense, to the conditions underlying the definition of price-based markets.

Although already implicit in the discussion above, it is worth reiterating how the problem of thin political markets differs from the classic collective-action problem that political scientists have been studying for at least the past fifty years.[67] At the most basic level, the collective-action problem arises in political processes where a few special interests dominate the general interest because members of the latter group have little individual incentive to organize themselves. The problem of thin political markets is distinct from the simple collective-action problem in at least two ways. First, in a thin political market, special interest and expertise are comingled, and the source of the special interest's expertise is experience based. This means that the classical solution to the collective-action problem—to bring in "independent" experts to act for the general interest—will not work in thin political markets, because such experts do not exist. Second, thin political markets occur in areas of low salience with the general public. Thus the other traditional solution to the collective-action problem—to encourage intermediaries such as the media and politicians to act for the general interest—is also infeasible in thin political markets.

In describing what a thin political market is, it is also worth considering the dynamic nature of this concept. Political processes that are generally "thin" could, under some circumstances, become "thick" and vice versa. The most likely cause for such thickening is a change in the issue salience (the third condition that defines a thin political market). For example, from time to time, crises or large-scale scandals can bring an otherwise obscure or esoteric process into wider public attention. In these cases, intermediaries such media-persons or politicians, who in usual times have little incentive to represent the general interest, can assume a countervailing position against the primary special interest. The result could be a decreased likelihood of capture in regulatory outcomes. The previously discussed case of congressional intervention in stock-options accounting following the Enron and WorldCom scandals, where Congress reversed its earlier support for firms resisting the real expensing of stock options, is an example of a political process thickening in the wake of increased public salience. But notwithstanding the conceptual feasibility of thin political markets thickening, I expect such cases to be generally uncommon in practice.

Even with the characterization of thin political markets above, there remains the question of clarifying how these markets lack legitimacy. To be sure, thin political markets can create the conditions for special-interest capture, as several preceding chapters have suggested. But it is important to recognize that at least in the case of the institutions of accounting rule-making, particularly the FASB in the United States and the IASB globally, there is no obvious circumvention of existing due process on the road to capture. Put differently, the concern over compromised legitimacy in thin political markets in accounting does not stem from a systematic misapplication of current rules of procedure.

Since its inception, the FASB has been committed to a rigorous process for determining accounting rules. This process includes deliberating with experts on the items for its agenda, continued consultation with experts before drafting its proposals, openly soliciting comment letters on those proposals from its constituents in a transparent manner, and public votes on final standards by board members.[68] Moreover, since the proliferation of the Internet, the FASB has on numerous occasions made its board meetings and other hearings widely accessible.[69] Its financials are also available for scrutiny, and it is overseen by trustees encouraged to act in the public interest. The IASB, which from its beginnings has been modeled after the FASB, has similar traditions of due process, transparency, and accountability; although, as seen in chapter 6, the global nature of its mission complicates these goals from time to time. In fact, were it not for the meticulous due process and the generous transparency of the FASB and the IASB, the data for the empirical and case studies of accounting's political process described in this book would not have been available.

The findings in this book suggest that despite all these safeguards and traditions, the political process in accounting rule-making is subject to capture. In particular, the outcomes of the political process in accounting rule-making are, as shown in the various preceding chapters, sometimes removed from what would be considered optimal or desirable for the functioning of market capitalism. These findings suggest that the due process applied in thin political markets, at least in the case of accounting rule-making, is insufficient or incomplete—thus such thin political markets can generate substantial costs to society at large. In the following chapter, which concludes this book, I consider what can be done about this problem, suggesting alternative approaches for the conduct of thin political markets.

Before transitioning, here I offer some additional candidates for politically derived market institutions that might qualify as thin political markets. I caution that this list is preliminary; I have not studied these institutions in the depth that I have examined accounting rule-making.

> *Standards for banking regulation and supervision:* These include the processes that define key banking metrics such as "Tier 1 capital," "risk-weighted assets," and the "capital adequacy ratio," which are essential timely indicators of the health of banks and the banking sector. These also include the processes that determine disclosure rules for banks, including qualitative public and governmental disclosure on banks' credit risks, liquidity risks, and operating risks. Standards for banking regulation and supervision in the United States are determined by the Treasury Department and the Board of Governors of the Federal Reserve System. Internationally, the standards are negotiated through the Bank for International Settlements in Basel, Switzerland.[70]
>
> *Standards for auditing:* The rules under which auditors certify the financial statements of companies in the United States are called Generally Accepted Auditing Standards (GAAS). Until the passage of the Sarbanes-Oxley Act in 2002, GAAS were produced by the Auditing Standards Board, a committee of the AICPA. The act created a new body—the Public Company Accounting Oversight Board—to produce standards for auditing of publicly listed companies.[71] Standards for audits of private companies continue to be produced by the AICPA committee.[72]
>
> *Standards for governmental accounting:* Accounting rules for state and local governments in the United States are produced by the Governmental Accounting Standards Board.[73] In many cases, these rules are different from FASB rules, in part because governments do not use accruals as extensively as corporations. Several studies have provided evidence of local governments manipulating these rules, particularly around elections.[74]

Note that not all instances of rule-making in these contexts are necessarily "thin." There are cases in accounting rule-making, for instance, where competition between special interests or relatively high issue salience among the general interest prevents any one group from dominating outcomes. The same can be true in these contexts as well. Comprehensive research programs on the nature of regulation in each of these areas can help shed more light on the extensiveness of thin political markets beyond accounting rule-making.

9

Managers and Market Capitalism

On a cool, crisp fall day in late November 2011, over three dozen distinguished leaders from across corporate America gathered in a classroom in Hawes Hall on the campus of Harvard Business School. The business leaders were joined by luminaries from the U.S. government and not-for-profit institutions to discuss the problem of declining U.S. competitiveness. The conference was hosted by Harvard Business School professors Michael Porter and Jan Rivkin, who had just concluded an extensive survey of the school's alumni. The survey had revealed that the alumni—many of whom occupied senior corporate management positions worldwide—were concerned about deteriorating market and public institutions in the United States. At least 50 percent of survey respondents had said that America was "falling behind" other countries on eight of seventeen critical infrastructure issues identified by Professors Porter and Rivkin. These eight issues were effectiveness of the political system, the K–12 education system, complexity of the tax code, logistics infrastructure, macroeconomic policy, regulation, availability of skilled labor, and efficiency of legal framework.[1]

In the concluding sessions of the conference, Professors Porter and Rivkin shared data from the survey and invited the corporate leaders present to offer reactions and solutions. A vigorous discussion ensued. As one of a handful of Harvard Business School faculty invited to observe the conversations, I hurriedly scribbled notes as the participants reacted to the data. At the time, the thesis for this book and the notion of thin political markets had not yet become fully apparent to me. A few days later, I typed up my notes and left them to gestate. In the fall of 2013, nearly two years later, as I was organizing the outline for this book, I serendipitously came across my notes. Their relevance to this chapter was striking. In my assessment from that afternoon in November 2011, three themes had emerged from the discussion.

1. *The problem of declining U.S. competitiveness is a problem of the commons.* The participants, when presented with the survey results by Professors Porter and Rivkin, had pointed out that many of the institutions underlying the areas where the United States was falling behind were supplied by the government or the not-for-profit sector. These were problems where value creation was not easily captured by private interests and thus the problems were not solvable through the pursuit of profit—the traditional realm of business. In other words, these were "problems of the commons."

2. *There is a failure of leadership among politicians and regulators.* Several participants expressed frustration with the deep divisions in the U.S. Congress that were crippling governmental response in many cases. They also criticized regulators for failing to stand up to outside pressure groups such as labor unions, environmental lobbies, political ideologies, and certain firms.

3. *The business of business is business.* Many participants did not see a responsibility or opportunity for business to engage in matters of national institution building, partly because they saw such engagement as being outside their mandate from shareholders and partly because they saw themselves as global firms with no allegiance to any one country.

Why are some of the most distinguished business leaders in corporate America reluctant to engage in solving problems of the commons? Is it because they feel doing so is outside their legitimate mandate? Or is it because they lack the incentives to act in the public interest? The answers to these questions are also relevant to the issue of what can be done about the problem of thin political markets, which is the focus of this chapter. Because capture in thin political markets—and the compromised efficiency of the capitalist system that can arise as a result—is also a problem of the commons. No single firm might have a compelling profit motive to work toward a solution, but collectively, a society deploying capitalism can lose from a situation where its thin political markets are captured.

In defense of the business leaders, there is, in fact, strong precedence and intellectual heft behind their reluctance to engage in problems of the commons. The academic perhaps most closely identified with this argument, at least in popular culture, is Milton Friedman, who famously argued in a brief but comprehensive *New York Times Magazine* article in 1970 that "the social responsibility of business is to increase its profits."[2]

Professor Friedman eschewed the notion that corporate managers have responsibilities to customers, suppliers, employees, or the commons, beyond those already implicit in their charge to increase corporate profits. To be clear, he affirmed that profit-increasing behavior was always subject to limits imposed by the law—but once that constraint had been satisfied, the primary goal of business was earning returns for shareholders. This did not preclude product safety, employee perquisites, and charitable or political activities, as long as the connection to corporate profit was apparent—for example, charitable activities that built the firm's brand, increasing product visibility or the ability to raise prices, were permissible and, indeed, encouraged.

Professor Friedman went further to argue that any deviation from this dictum was eventually destructive to the prosperity expected to accrue from a capitalist system. He argued that the single-minded pursuit of profits drove firms toward the kind of competition that eventually allowed the "invisible hand" to manifest itself and deliver aggregate wealth.[3] Attempts to distract managers from profit-increasing behavior, such as the corporate social responsibility movement, were misguided at best.

These arguments are rooted in sound theory that is well known and understood among academic economists today. Perhaps the most important reason behind these arguments is the problem of agency, described earlier in chapter 8.[4] The agency argument essentially recognizes that managers are agents for shareholders. They have been entrusted with stewarding and investing shareholders' capital with the objective of generating returns. This is generally understood as the singular moral imperative for corporate managers within the context of a capitalist system. Giving managers the license to focus on priorities that compete with increasing shareholder returns opens the door to squandering shareholders' wealth, at best, on do-good projects or, worse still, on the managers' own comforts. If managers are permitted to go down this path, shareholders will eventually withhold their capital from financial markets and the whole system will come apart.[5]

These arguments have resonated in academia and in practice.[6] In fact, some of the most successful attempts at getting managers to focus on constituencies other than shareholders have structured the case around increasing (at least eventually) corporate profits. For example, Professor Porter's recent work on "creating shared value" makes the case for focusing managerial attention on problems of U.S. competitiveness by explicitly linking it to long-run corporate profitability.[7] Thus any suggestion on how corporate managers (defined to include auditors, bankers, and other financial intermediaries) might engage in the problem of thin political markets must take into consideration these arguments.

To be sure, one potential solution to the problem of thin political markets is to encourage greater innovation in practice with the expectation that at least some of these innovations will eventually come to shape the nature of regulations. For example, in the context of accounting rule-making, innovation in accounting practice around greater conservatism (in the light of increasing fair-value rules in GAAP) can eventually come to reshape GAAP accounting rules toward conservatism, if in fact such conservatism is economically beneficial. And indeed, there is evidence of firms and their lenders adjusting GAAP rules for the purposes of writing accounting-based covenants, when they find such GAAP rules to be unsuitable.[8] But as discussed in chapter 8, while this practice may hold some promise in the long run, in the intermediate term it is at best a partial solution. It may solve the problem of captured GAAP rules in the context of a private arrangement, but it does not provide a broader societal solution unless the private innovations in accounting practice are eventually adopted in GAAP. Put differently, given the regulated nature of the product markets in question, the problem is one that requires a *political* solution as much as a price-based solution.

Before proceeding, it is worth reiterating explicitly why the political solution to thin political markets must involve managers. Recall that thin political markets are defined as areas of regulation where managers, by virtue of their experience, have the substantive knowledge necessary to structure the rules of the game. The conditions that define a thin political market—including low issue salience among the general interest for the subject matter at hand—make it difficult for a third party to acquire this knowledge. This implies that solving the problem of thin political markets cannot simply involve creating new regulation or even a new "independent" regulator—as has been the case in the past when, in 1959, the Accounting Principles Board (APB) replaced the Committee on Accounting Procedure (CAP) and when, in 1973, the FASB replaced the APB. In thin political markets, the reliance on managerial expertise remains regardless of the regulatory structure. The implication is that the solution to the problem of thin political markets cannot simply involve regulatory reform; such a solution must involve changing managerial lobbying *behavior* in these areas. In other words, addressing special-interest capture in thin political markets will require shifting the established and accepted managerial ethic in this context.

At this point, I expect my readers to be a little jarred. The book thus far has been chiefly focused on offering an assessment of the political process in accounting rule-making and on developing inductively the notion of thin political markets. It has remained largely in the realm of mainstream economics and positive research methodologies. In this chapter, as I consider potential solutions to the problem of thin political markets, I make a shift from economics to ethics and from positive to normative research methodologies. While I acknowledge that my proposals here are by no means dispositive, I argue that normative ethics is a strong starting point for any solution to a problem as structural and fundamental as capture in thin political markets.

Arguments from ethics have the tendency to draw jeers or smirks from seasoned minds, weathered to be skeptical of human behavior. But nonetheless, ethics is at the heart of *legitimizing* managerial behavior in the context of capitalism.[9] In the following section, I explain how Professor Friedman's contentions are, at their core, ethical arguments, how capitalism is fundamentally an ethical system, and how profit-increasing behavior is socially legitimated because it is ethical. Then, in the next section, I develop the ethics of thin political markets. I make the case for why managers are ethically necessitated to engage in the public interest on the problem of thin political markets, addressing the concerns raised by Professor Friedman and others around managerial agency to shareholders.

Of course, simply asserting that managers have an ethical responsibility to the public interest in thin political markets is hardly in itself likely to change their behavior. As the evidence from the preceding chapters of this book demonstrate, managers act in their own interest absent governance mechanisms to the contrary. So the task of bringing managers to act on this ethical responsibility to the public interest is one that will require a substantial governance architecture, analogous to the governance architecture that sustains managers' responsibility to shareholders. This architecture includes both formal institutions, such as auditing and the law, and informal institutions, such as the norms and practices that govern the behavior of auditors and lawyers. In the final section of this chapter, I offer some suggestions on how we might begin to build such a governance architecture in the context of managerial lobbying in thin political markets, providing examples of emerging innovations in this regard. Finally, I consider how a system where managers assume a responsibility to the public interest could mitigate special-interest capture in thin political markets.

Capitalism as an Ethic

Although markets in some form have been a part of civilized society since very ancient times, the establishment of markets as an organizing force for society—under the rubric of "market capitalism"—is a relatively recent phenomenon.[10] Adam Smith's tome on the "wealth of nations," published in 1776, was a defining intellectual event in the development of market ideology.[11] In the two centuries since, the technical and philosophical arguments for markets have been substantially refined.[12] In the wake of the Cold War that emerged from the conclusion of World War II, "capitalism" developed in Western democracies as an ideological and practical counterpoint to "communism" and "socialism."[13]

Capitalism has an impressive track record in its postwar history. Its deployment across numerous societies has been accompanied by rising aggregate prosperity and eventually rising standards of human development and happiness.[14] Over the last thirty years, several formerly communist and socialist countries across the world—including China and India—have adopted some form of market capitalism with impressive economic results.[15] For example, since China enacted market-based reforms in 1978, its gross domestic product has grown nearly fortyfold, an annualized rate of 12.2 percent.[16]

At the core of capitalism is the deployment of self-interested profit-seeking behavior. Mr. Smith famously remarked: "Give me that which I want, and you shall have this which you want . . . It is not from the benevolence of the butcher, the brewer, or the baker that we expect our dinner, but from their regard to their own interest. We address ourselves, not to their humanity, but to their self-love, and never talk to them of our own necessities, but of their advantages."[17] In many religious and cultural traditions, such sentiments could be classified as "greed," "avarice," "covetousness," or "materialism" and accordingly considered immoral or at least undesirable.[18] But within the framework of market capitalism, self-interest is legitimate, even encouraged, because it is expected to deliver on certain higher normative goals. Indeed, the ethical logic that underlies capitalism is sufficiently rigorous and universal that it has been able to overcome and withstand centuries of religious teachings on altruism and benevolence.

The ethical case for markets has a long history in political philosophy, but the case for market capitalism, as it is generally understood today, can be traced to a handful of twentieth-century economists and philosophers. The ethics of capitalism can broadly be rooted in two normative ideals. The first is the consequentialist argument that capitalism is the most practicable way to *efficiently* allocate scarce resources across the diversity of human preferences in a modern, complex society. The second is the argument that capitalism enables *freedom* for individuals in an otherwise hierarchical society. Such freedoms might be desirable for their own sake or they may be instruments to a better life.

The efficiency argument for capitalism is well articulated in the scholarly literature in economics and is, perhaps, the more widely accepted of the two arguments among academics. The core of the efficiency argument is established through what is known in economics as the "welfare theorems." The welfare theorems demonstrate that any allocation of scarce resources across diverse preferences that is accomplished through a competitive market is efficient.[19] Here, both "competitive market" and "efficient" have specific meanings. A competitive market is one that achieves all the primitive conditions specified in chapter 8 (i.e., well-defined property rights, complete knowledge, enforceable contracts, no agency problem, noncollusion, and free entry and exit). Of course, as noted in chapter 8, none of these conditions are ever expected to be fully met in practice; so, pragmatically, a competitive market is one that enjoys institutions that closely approximate these conditions.

Efficiency, in the statement of welfare theorems, refers to an allocation outcome where no individual can be made better off without making another worse off. This definition of efficiency has the advantage guaranteeing that there is "no money left on the table"—that is, if an individual's lot can be improved without damaging that of others, an efficient allocation will accomplish it. Beyond this guarantee, "efficiency" embeds strong protection for the lot of every individual: no one can be expropriated in the name of efficiency.[20]

Efficiency, as a justification for capitalism, has its limitations. The welfare theorems are indifferent on the distribution of wealth and income in market outcomes. For example, an outcome that results in the significant concentration of wealth among corporate CEOs could meet the technical definition of efficient, although such an outcome is unlikely to pass broad muster. Thus, in practice, many "efficient" market outcomes are likely to be adjusted after the fact by political institutions to satisfy certain normative social preferences on the distribution of wealth and income.

The "freedom" argument for capitalism is, arguably, more widely appreciated than the argument on efficiency. There are at least two conceptions of freedom within this ethical tradition. The first is a libertarian conception— that is, freedom for its own sake—and is a deontological argument. The second, like the efficiency argument, is a consequentialist conception—that is, freedom is seen as an enabler of other normative goals.

The libertarian, deontological conception of freedom has roots in the Enlightenment and the political documents it spurred, including the American Declaration of Independence and the French Declaration of the Rights of Man and Citizen. Under this view, the ability of individuals to be *free*—to make decisions about how to use their resources to satisfy their preferences—is one of the highest normative goals in society.[21] The post–World War II writings of two well-known economists Friedrich Hayek and Milton Friedman perhaps most clearly embody the libertarian conception of freedom as the ethical logic for capitalism. Professors Hayek and Friedman were responding in part to the growth of communism when they championed freedom as the logic for capitalism. They noted that markets are predicated on individuals acting voluntarily in their own interest and thus that markets promote individual freedom. Moreover, they argued, the self-reinforcing nature of market capitalism means that markets, when unleashed unfettered, will grow to continually empower more individuals to be "free to choose."[22]

The consequentialist conception of freedom argues that the aggregate prosperity ushered in through capitalism raises the ability of individuals to focus beyond primitive needs, such as survival, to higher-level preferences. In this sense, capitalism enables freedom from hunger and effects freedom to indulge in tertiary desires such as the arts, vacations, and sport. With the prosperity of capitalism also come (over the long run) higher-order political freedoms such as freedom from discrimination and the uninhibited freedom to marry.[23]

Beyond these arguments around efficiency and freedom, there are other cases to be made for capitalism,[24] but they bring us to the same conclusion: that capitalism is explicitly and implicitly legitimized by certain normative principles. The logic for capitalism is, at its core, ethical in nature. The pursuit of self-interested, profit-increasing behaviors, when deployed within the framework of market capitalism, is an *ethical* pursuit. This is not to say that individuals would not exhibit self-interested behavior absent ethical grant; indeed, as Mr. Smith pointed out, self-interest appears to be innate to human behavior. But the social acceptability of profit-seeking—its glorification and promotion in the face of centuries of religious and cultural traditions to the contrary—is anchored in ethical arguments, both consequentialist and deontological. We encourage it, and perhaps see greater degrees of it, because it is virtuous. The ethical legitimacy of self-interested profit seeking in the context of competitive capitalism is a powerful force for its unabashed existence in capitalist societies.

Similarly, I argue, an awareness of ethical *illegitimacy* of self-interested profit-seeking behavior in thin political markets can be a potent force for incenting and perhaps eventually reshaping corporate managerial behavior in this context. It is to this task that I now turn.

The Ethics of Thin Political Markets

Here I make the case for why self-interested profit-seeking behavior by corporate managers is illegitimate in thin political markets and why, instead, the legitimate model for managerial behavior is a public-interest stewardship of the thin political market. The arguments here are based on joint work with Professor Rebecca Henderson of Harvard Business School.

The nature of thin political markets is such that there is a breakdown in the core capitalist logic of competing self-interested behavior equilibrating to advance the collective good. In this context, the impressive corpus of ethical arguments for self-interested, profit-seeking behavior just described might seem less pertinent. But this is not so. In fact, the roots of an ethical argument for legitimate corporate managerial behavior in thin political markets can be found in Professor Friedman's own work on the moral foundations of capitalism and managerial behavior therein.

Professor Friedman makes two key arguments. First, capitalism is ethically virtuous because it delivers freedom—an elemental normative ideal at least since the Enlightenment. Second, managers have a "social responsibility" to act on this ideal, which, in the context of competitive markets, involves increasing corporate profits. From these two arguments, we can develop the foundations of an ethical framework for thin political markets. This requires two observations.

The first observation is that the ethical ideals that underlie capitalism—predominantly freedom, in Professor Friedman's assessment—continue to be relevant in the context of thin political markets. This is because thin political markets create and sustain institutions that fulfill the conditions for capitalism. Put differently, for capitalism to deliver on its legitimizing ideals, market institutions must approximate certain basic conditions such as well-defined property rights, enforceable contracts, complete knowledge, no agency, noncollusion, and free entry and exit. At least some of the market institutions that estimate these conditions function as thin political markets (e.g., the accounting rule-making process). Thus without a resolution of the problem of thin political markets, the ethical ideals that underlie capitalism cannot be realized.[25]

The second observation is the following: Just as corporate managers have a "social responsibility" to deliver on the ideals of capitalism through the generation of corporate profits, corporate managers must have a "social responsibility" to address the problem of thin political markets. After all, delivering on the first social responsibility is unlikely to yield the desired normative goals unless the problem of thin political markets is also addressed. In other words, if we accept the notion of and evidence on thin political markets, and we accept the arguments in Professor Friedman's own exposition of the ethics of market capitalism and managerial conduct therein, then the ethics of managerial conduct in thin political markets is self-evident. Managers have a social responsibility to assume public stewardship of the commons problems in thin political markets because failing to do so obviates the ethical objectives of capitalism and the moral imperative to increase corporate profits.

A similar conclusion on the ethics of thin political markets may be reached without explicitly relying on Professor Friedman's arguments. As noted in the previous section, there are numerous potent ethical arguments for capitalism on grounds of efficiency, prosperity, or the ability to transcend basic survival needs and embrace higher-order ideals such as human intellectual development. From any one of these reasons, one can construct a case for preserving capitalism. This then includes addressing the problem of thin political markets, particularly in areas that supply critical structural institutions of capitalism such as accounting rule-making. For corporate managers who see virtue in their pursuit of profit within a capitalist system, there is a compelling logic to preserve that virtue when stewarding a thin political market.

As a principle, the ethical obligation of corporate managers to increase corporate profits is established through managerial agency to shareholders. This is the singular moral imperative—the "social responsibility"—in Professor Friedman's seminal work on the ethics of capitalism. By extension, I argue, the ethical obligation of corporate managers to address problems of thin political markets requires the establishment of managerial agency to the capitalist system.[26] The idea that managers have an agency responsibility to the capitalist system might seem, at first, difficult to swallow—after all, "the capitalist system" is an impersonal, abstract notion, unlike "shareholders," who are real individuals. But, of course, here the system represents the individuals in whose interest market capitalism is deployed. Moreover, the idea that certain agents might be responsible to the system as a whole is not altogether novel. For example, public prosecutors in the United States, given their tremendous power to effect decisions in the public good, are expected to serve as stewards for the justice system as a whole, while also serving in an adversarial (competitive) role against defense attorneys at specific trials.[27]

To be clear, the managerial agency to the capitalist system that I argue for is limited to the context of thin political markets. The evidence on "thick" political markets (i.e., competitive political processes with dispersed competencies), discussed in chapter 8, suggests that the extant logic of managers focusing on corporate profits holds water in those contexts. Moreover, as Professor Friedman warned, giving managers unrestricted agency to the capitalist system could open the door for value-destructive activities—ranging from do-good decisions that are economically unviable to outright managerial theft—that could, eventually, unravel capitalism itself.

In practice, the agency of managers to shareholders is enforced by numerous formal and informal institutions.[28] Among these is the law, which makes managers fiduciaries for shareholders in many jurisdictions and corporate organizational forms.[29] If a similar managerial agency to the capitalist system is to be effective, considerable effort must be expended to make it practicable. The following section addresses this issue in greater detail. But, for now, it is useful to point out that the law of fiduciaries, at least as it currently stands in the United States, is consistent with a managerial agency to the capitalist system. Specifically, while the law certainly does impose on managers a fiduciary duty to shareholders, it makes no stipulation that this duty singularly involves increasing corporate profits.[30] As Professor Einer Elhauge of Harvard Law School has argued, "The law has consistently been willing to recognize an explicit power to sacrifice corporate profits in the public interest. Indeed, that is exactly what the law did in the 1980s when hostile takeover bids required such a choice by offering stock premiums that made manager claims of long run profitability implausible, and state courts and legislatures responded by making managers' discretion to sacrifice profits more explicit."[31]

Moreover, beyond creating a duty to shareholders, the law also makes managers fiduciaries for the corporation as a whole.[32] And corporations may not be able to compete and survive on a long-run sustainable basis absent certain capitalist institutions determined through thin political markets. Thus a managerial fiduciary duty to corporations could be interpreted as sanctioning managers to address the problem of thin political markets in the interest of preserving the capitalist system.

Furthermore, the corporate charter itself provides some basis for a corporate responsibility to the interests of the system. After all, corporations are not naturally occurring; rather, they are creations of society organized through a state.[33] The earliest charters for corporations of the modern form were granted in explicit recognition that the corporations would create public value—for example, the East India Company was created in the United Kingdom to provide increased revenue for the British Crown.[34] And the rights inherent in the modern American corporate charter—limited liability to shareholders, survival beyond founders, corporate personhood, and engagement in the electoral process—imply expectation of value-creation in the general interest. Of course, this expectation is generally fulfilled through the pursuit of profit, as Professor Friedman and others have postulated, but in the case of thin political markets, I argue that serving the general interests involves a more explicit managerial agency for the capitalist system.

Indeed, a recent regulatory ruling in Britain concerning the nonaudit work (the tax and management consulting practice) of Big Four auditing firm Deloitte is consistent with this argument. Under rules in place in England and Wales, practicing accountants are required to consider the "public interest" in the conduct of their business activities. In a dispute involving consulting work Deloitte did for carmaker MG Rover, Deloitte argued that the "public interest" rules did not apply to its nonaudit work. The British regulatory tribunal hearing the case disagreed. Furthermore, Deloitte argued that since MG Rover was a private (unlisted) company, the "public interest" did not apply. Again the regulatory tribunal differed, recognizing the externalities to society from all corporate activity, whether listed or unlisted.[35] Of course, the position of this regulatory tribunal is hardly the last word on the question at hand—the tribunal itself could be subject to regulatory capture—but it does indicate that there is some traction in practice for the idea that managers have an agency responsibility to the system as whole.

The proposition of managerial agency for the capitalist system in thin political markets raises another important issue: How might managers balance this agency for the system with their preexisting agency for shareholders? Could they possibly be expected to serve two masters? Of course, in practice, this line of questioning is a red herring—corporate managers routinely serve as fiduciaries for multiple parties, even parties with competing interests. For example, senior executive officers of large corporations routinely serve as nonexecutive directors of other large corporations. Both positions entail agency responsibilities. Consider Eric Schmidt, who served from 2006 to 2009 on the board of Apple while he was also CEO of Google. During this period, when Mr. Schmidt had a fiduciary duty to both companies, Apple launched the iPhone while Google acquired a start-up called Android from which it developed its own operating system for Internet-enabled mobile phones.[36]

Similarly, partners and other senior executives at venture-capital firms routinely serve on the boards of public companies—and both positions generate fiduciary duties. Consider the celebrated venture capitalist John Doer, a senior executive at (and fiduciary for investors in) the early-stage investment firm Kleiner Perkins Caufield & Byers. At the same time during which this firm had an investment in the online start-up Groupon, Mr. Doer served on the board of potential competitor Google, which even tried (unsuccessfully) to acquire Groupon.[37] These examples demonstrate that managers often assume and fulfill multiple (competing) agency responsibilities, so, at least as a matter of feasibility, the proposition that in thin political markets managers hold agency responsibilities both to their host corporations and to the system as a whole is not inconceivable.

Thus far, I have focused on building the case for what constitutes legitimate corporate managerial engagement in thin political markets. The case is based on the ethics of capitalism and the expectations of managerial conduct therein. Beyond this purely normative case, there is a utilitarian case to be made for managerial agency of the capitalist system in thin political markets. This is what follows.

If the result of profit-seeking managerial behavior in thin political markets is special-interest capture of critical institutions of capitalism, then the resulting market system will not be competitive. New entrants will not be able to break into markets and existing firms will find it difficult to diversify into new industries. Monopolies, collusion, and corruption can emerge, and public faith in the capitalist system is likely to be eroded. Several recent studies have explored a related form of this argument in the context of market institutions that are structured through political processes. A notable example is *Saving Capitalism from the Capitalists*, where Professors Raghuram Rajan and Luigi Zingales of the University of Chicago focus in particular on the potential for capture during bad economic times. They argue: "In an economic downturn, the capitalist is more likely to focus on costs of the competition emanating from free markets than on the opportunities they create . . . Using the cover and the political organization provided by the distressed, the capitalist captures the political agenda."[38]

In these situations, overall economic activity will decline, as the nature of the economy is reoriented from growing the pie to simply slicing it up in different ways. The very scenario Professor Friedman imagined if managers did not pursue corporate profits in a competitive context could emerge if they do not assume public stewardship of thin political markets.

Under this scenario, political ideologies hostile to market capitalism can take root. There are numerous examples in the history of the twentieth century of radical ideologies emerging in the wake of market crises: for instance, the rise of fascism, socialism, and communism in Europe in the depression-economy years between the two world wars.[39] More recently, in the United States, the emergence and growth since the Financial Crisis of 2008 of anti-establishment movements such as Occupy Wall Street and the Tea Party are reminders that the legitimacy of capitalism is always under social scrutiny.[40]

A situation such as the one described above is not in the long-term interest of corporations, managers, and others who see virtue in the capitalist system. At best, it will result in a kind of crony capitalism where incumbents benefit but only to the extent that they enjoy the favor of mercurial political bosses. Freedom—both libertarian and instrumental—will be eroded, together with prosperity and efficiency. Corporate managers with an interest in the higher ideals that legitimize capitalism thus have a strong utilitarian reason to assume stewardship of thin political markets, particularly those political processes that determine critical market institutions such as accounting rules. Of course, the public goods nature of these institutions means the incentive for any one manager to free ride is high. This brings us back to the normative argument for managerial stewardship of thin political markets.

The idea that managers have a responsibility to the institutions of capitalism has been accumulating greater authority through the research of numerous business scholars (although this research has not generally limited its argument to the context of thin political markets). The work by Professors Porter and Rivkin on the problem of declining U.S. competitiveness, mentioned earlier, is one prominent example of such research. Another noteworthy instance is the study of market institutions by Professors Joseph Bower, Dutch Leonard, and Lynn Paine of Harvard Business School in the book *Capitalism at Risk*. These authors argue "that business must begin taking a more active role in assuring the market system's ongoing health and sustainability. Much as we might wish to believe that the system will take care of itself through the magic of the invisible hand, we cannot in good conscience claim that narrow self-interest and competitive forces alone will ensure the system's performance for society."[41]

To summarize, here I argue that managers have, in Professor Friedman's words, a "social responsibility" to assume the public's interest when engaging in thin political markets. The logic underlying this responsibility closely mirrors the logic underlying managers' social responsibility to profit seeking in competitive markets. The responsibility in thin political markets can be characterized as managerial agency for the capitalist system. In the concluding section, which follows, I outline some suggestions on how we might move from the status quo to this proposed ethic.

Building the New Ethic

This book is primarily an empirical and analytical exercise. I present evidence on the nature and outcomes of the political process in accounting and inductively develop a theory of thin political markets. The irony of the problem of thin political markets is this: the model of managerial behavior that characterizes thin political markets—self-interested profit seeking—is that of the capitalist spirit; but in the absence of competitive forces, self-interested profit-seeking behavior results in special-interest capture, ultimately potentially compromising the legitimacy of capitalism. This book is chiefly aimed at raising this general point, to rally for ideas and action.

In that sense, this chapter is an anomaly, an indulgence. It is the beginning of what I see as the solution to the problem of thin political markets. But I also add that the proposals here are intended to be not the final word but rather provocative and catalytic.

As noted earlier, self-interested profit-seeking behavior is moral in the context of competitive markets. It is moral because of the ethical framework that legitimizes capitalism. But what is moral in the context of competitive markets is not moral in a thin political market—due to the very nature of that political process. The ethics of thin political markets are distinct from the ethics of capitalism, as argued in the preceding sections. If we assume at a minimum that the desire to be perceived as moral motivates human behavior, at least in part, then the notion that self-interested profit-seeking behavior is no longer moral in thin political markets should resonate with some of the individuals involved in this context, including certain corporate managers. Moreover, at least some of these managers might be persuaded to reconsider their objective function when lobbying in thin political markets—away from focusing solely on self-interested profit seeking toward assuming an agency responsibility for the capitalist system. This is a start.

It is worth clarifying at this point that this proposition—getting managers to act on their agency responsibility to the system in thin political markets—is not expected to always generate the "right" outcome (i.e., one that maximizes aggregate welfare). It is probable that even when the most informed experts act in the public interest, they have at best incomplete knowledge of the relevant subject matter, resulting in some policy errors. But what the proposition can accomplish is mitigating the likelihood of obtaining the "wrong" outcome (i.e., one that caters exclusively to a special-interest group). This is in itself an improvement over the status quo.

The prevailing approach to lobbying in thin political markets—that of self-interest—persists under the mistaken assumption that such self-interested behavior eventually generates aggregate welfare. For example, investment bankers advancing fair-value accounting rules do so because it is in their own interest; but they may take some comfort that such self-interested lobbying is acceptable because it eventually yields outcomes in the public interest. Getting managers to explicitly recognize and embrace their agency responsibility to the system in thin political markets at least removes any veneer of legitimacy that managers might seek for self-interested lobbying strategies. Moreover, with their responsibility to the system now explicit, perhaps some managers can be expected to alter their lobbying strategies in ways that preserve and advance the interests of the market system as a whole.

But simply wanting to do the "right thing" is likely not enough. As behavioral ethicists Professors Max Bazerman of Harvard Business School and Ann Tenbrunsel of the University of Notre Dame point out, often the desire to do the right thing can be obfuscated by moral "blind spots."[42] Furthermore, converting moral intent into action can be a Sisyphean task. The preceding chapters provide numerous examples of corporate managers acting in self-serving ways absent governance mechanisms to the contrary. So any attempt to bring managers to act on their agency responsibility to the capitalist system in thin political markets will require a well-coordinated architecture of governance mechanisms. Here, I offer what can be the beginnings of such an architecture.

Leveraging my background in economics, I focus on effecting this shift in the objective function of managers through a shift in their incentives. Incentives can be changed through either formal or informal institutions or both. As discussed earlier, the nature of thin political markets is such that formal institutional solutions alone, at least those pertaining to regulatory reform, are unlikely to succeed—after all, the development of the FASB itself was an institutional solution to conflict-of-interest issues arising from its predecessor body, the APB. So, I argue, this leaves us with also considering informal institutional solutions that change behavioral norms in the context of lobbying in thin political markets.

Norms can be powerful motivators of human behavior.[43] Some common examples of norms include not staring at each other in a crowded elevator; surrendering one's seat in a crowded public bus or train to the elderly or infirm; holding the door to a public space open for someone approaching; and even dressing appropriately for an occasion, whether a casual barbeque, a Christmas party, or a wedding.

Norms can be defined as unwritten rules, understood by group members, carried out without need for legal enforcement.[44] Norms are also characterized by their ability to express some resistance to change over time.[45] They are distinct from laws or formal rules. For example, the rules established by the FASB or the rules that govern the due process of the FASB are more akin to laws; norms are the informal codes of conduct under which such rules are developed and executed (such as norms about civility and courtesy in FASB meetings).[46]

A large literature explores the evolutionary basis of norms. In this view, norms are seen a means to an end, albeit with some "stickiness." Behaviors that help group members satisfy shared preferences—either primitive preferences such as shelter, security, and food or higher-order preferences such as friendship—survive and are passed on to subsequent members of the group. Over time, such behaviors become sticky or resistant to change and can be considered "norms." Indeed, such stickiness—that is, the ability of individuals to adhere to certain behaviors regardless of their functional purpose—is what characterizes norms.[47]

It is in this evolutionary or instrumental sense that I propose the use of norms as the first step in shaping managerial lobbying conduct in thin political markets—that is, creating norms that highlight managers' agency of the system when lobbying in thin political markets. The evolutionary basis for such norms is the intrinsic desire of managers to be perceived as "good" (in the context of competition, such goodness is achieved through profit-seeking activities). Furthermore, such norms could also be sustained through managerial interest in the continued legitimacy of capitalism. Capitalism is itself desirable for a number of normative reasons as discussed earlier, and, moreover, the continued legitimacy of capitalism allows for managers to continue earning profits in competitive markets.

Effective norms, by definition, must be generally robust to defection— that is, they must provide sufficient motive to forgo noncompliance. But to be effective, norms must be continually reinforced.[48] Consider, for example, the following study of norms on littering. Researchers randomly assigned participants into two groups: one exposed to an individual picking up litter and the other exposed to an individual walking past litter. The study found that the former group was less likely to litter because the visual cue they were exposed to "focuses the great majority of observers 'on the extent to which other people approve or disapprove of littering.'"[49]

A key implication of this study (and the broader literature on enforcement of norms) is the role of leadership in defining and reinforcing norms. An additional implication is that norms are not static. They can change because they are ignored or because of active attempts to do so. For example, over the past decade, norms around nondiscrimination against transgendered employees, particularly in the United States, have changed. As recently as the year 2002, only 3 percent of U.S. Fortune 500 companies included a policy on nondiscrimination over their employees' gender identities. By the year 2014, that proportion had risen to 61 percent.[50] This increase is despite the lack of any comprehensive U.S. federal law encouraging or affirming the rights of transgendered employees and only a patchwork of state and municipal laws on the subject. And while economic considerations could have contributed to companies' decisions to adopt such nondiscrimination policies, economic logic alone cannot account for the policy change. After all, transgendered individuals are estimated to be a very small fraction of the U.S. population (about 0.3 percent),[51] and transgendered civil rights have received relatively scarce media attention (particularly relative to civil-rights coverage for gay and lesbian individuals).[52] A nontrivial part of this change in attitudes toward transgendered employees can be attributed to changing norms among senior business leaders in U.S. corporations on their responsibilities to employees and what is considered unacceptable grounds for discrimination.

Analogously, the task I propose here is finding ways to change the status quo norms around lobbying in thin political markets—from self-interested profit-seeking behavior to norms that recognize managerial agency of the system. Since I first became aware of the problem of thin political markets, I have been studying numerous ways to do so. Below, I discuss three efforts in this regard that have struck me as salient.[53]

First is the role of ethics in graduate business and management education, particularly leading MBA programs in the United States. While ethics has been a part of several major MBA program curriculums for at least two decades, it has assumed a new urgency and distinction since the Financial Crisis of 2008. One likely cause for this change is evidence of the paucity of ethical imperatives beyond self-interested profit-seeking behavior among financial-services managers in the period leading up to the crisis, even among managers holding explicit stewardship roles. For example, a common practice during this period was bond-ratings agencies' collaborating with mortgage-securities underwriters to structure financial products so that they would earn high ratings; a plausible analogy is that of a judge working with a defendant on legal strategy to ensure an acquittal.[54] Beyond bond rating, there is evidence that some managers in banking and auditing, even upon recognizing the underlying weakness of financial securities they were organizing or evaluating, were not compelled to act in ways consistent with their stewardship responsibilities. Of particular note in these examples is the impact on individual behavior of culture and institutions of the modern financial-services industry— culture and institutions that are largely focused on profit making.[55]

The stories from this period have encouraged deeper introspection on how situation affects character and how personal values and aspirations can come to be overwhelmed by formal institutions (particularly monetary incentives) and the informal culture of the workplace. Two courses at Harvard Business School that have been exploring these issues are among the school's most popular elective courses: they are "Authentic Leadership Development" and "Reimagining Capitalism." Authentic Leadership Development is focused on encouraging students to develop a personal leadership vision through an understanding and acknowledgement of their experiences to date. The course also enables students to recognize what truly motivates them, both extrinsically and intrinsically, so that they are better prepared to handle the complexities and trade-offs they will encounter as business leaders. Students develop an appreciation of why leaders fail themselves—that is, what factors drive leaders off the path of their leadership vision. This aspect of the course aspires to build greater self-awareness among future leaders who will face competing responsibilities and will have to make difficult compromises in the process.[56]

Where Authentic Leadership Development is focused on introspection, Reimagining Capitalism is focused on intellectualization. The course is premised on the observation that free-market capitalism is the greatest known organizing force for prosperity and development in complex societies. Students are led to discover the conditions that underlie the effective functioning of capitalism (using a framework similar to that introduced in chapter 8), so that they have a sense of the opportunities available to business leaders when market institutions are incomplete. This knowledge is then applied to examine what role, if any, businesses can play in addressing numerous pressing social problems such as the decline of the commons, regulatory and political capture, corruption, and inequality.[57]

The broader point to discussing these courses is to highlight that there is demand for and supply of pedagogical materials in major business-leadership training academies on ethics beyond profit-increasing behavior and on the building of new norms to sustain such ethics in practice. The innovation in MBA programs to this effect is a promising development and can have an impact on the way the next generation of business leaders view their responsibilities in thin political markets.

But these young leaders are incubated and promoted by the existing elite, and, moreover, the problem of thin political markets is current. So we must look at initiatives among existing business leadership as well, which is the focus of the second of the three efforts on norm building I discuss here. In this realm, of note is the attempt to inductively define a "higher-ambition" leadership among corporate chief executives. This concept refers to business leaders who identify their role as both delivering economic returns to shareholders and adding value to the societies in which they operate. Of course, under certain conditions described by Professor Friedman and others, the former results in the latter. But as discussed earlier, those conditions are unlikely to be approximated in many situations in practice, including in thin political markets. Recognizing these voids, higher-ambition business leaders assume a joint mandate, making decisions that are consistent with creating value to both shareholders and society.[58]

What is particularly interesting about this phenomenon is that is has emerged organically in practice: the formal characterization of such business leaders as "higher ambition" is an after-the-fact exercise by business scholars seeking to understand the phenomenon. What the formal characterization of higher-ambition leadership accomplishes is a sense of community: a community in which norms for ethical leadership conduct can be built. Senior corporate managers identified as higher-ambition leaders gather once a year in Boston to exchange ideas, share experiences, and develop best practices in a two-day summit.[59] The summit also serves as an opportunity to reinforce emerging behaviors around the dual mandate to shareholders and society.

Exercises such as these can play a major role in changing norms around corporate engagement in problems of the commons, including lobbying in thin political markets. But while the higher-ambition program is promising, the jury is still out on whether higher-ambition business leadership will in fact survive the test of time and the harsh realities of the competitive marketplace. It is an innovation to watch.

Both the curricular innovations discussed and higher-ambition leadership are focused on addressing leadership challenges and opportunities emerging from market failures more generally. In this sense, they are broader than the problem of thin political markets. But this breadth can come at the expense of focus, and the nebulous nature of broad market failures, such as those emerging from human technological limitations, can detract from the immediacy of ethical managerial action needed in the narrow and well-defined cases of thin political markets. The third of the three efforts on norm building that I discuss is especially relevant because it appears to be specifically focused on the problem of thin political markets.

At the center of this effort is a private, for-profit organization called Tapestry Networks.[60] This company is in the business of organizing networks in which leaders in business and government work together to find new approaches to regulation, particularly regulation in highly specialized and technical areas of the market economy. Some examples of Tapestry's project spaces include bank and insurance governance standards and pharmaceutical drug-approval procedures. The networks are sponsored by carefully selected "client" members, who have interests in the outcome of the regulations.

At first blush, Tapestry might appear as a hybrid between a business-focused think tank and a lobbying shop. On one level this might be true, but what makes the Tapestry model interesting is the number of steps it has taken to distinguish itself from the traditional business-government facilitation industry. First, Tapestry is selective about the kind of problems it tackles. It is careful to avoid policy deliberations around broad "market failure" areas such as health care or systematic financial risk. Rather, Tapestry focuses on more targeted problems that have identifiable boundaries and outcomes. For example, one of Tapestry's major efforts has been in developing clinical-trials standards in the European Union for drug development related to type 2 diabetes.[61]

Second, Tapestry is selective about who it includes in its network. Company executives, members of corporate boards, regulators, and other relevant experts such as academics are only included to the extent that they "appreciate the interdependent systems in which they operate," recognize the collective-action nature of the problems being addressed, and are willing to recognize unrepresented or underrepresented interests in the process.[62] In this sense, Tapestry emphasizes that members of the network are recruited as individuals acting in their own agency, as leaders in society, rather than as agents of the organizations they serve.

But important questions still remain about the Tapestry model. For example, finding and developing facilitators to run the conversations is a challenge for the organization. As one Tapestry participant notes, the reason "Tapestry is not imitated is that the business model is one they won't get rich on. They [have] found this marriage with [client firms] and are living off of that. Look, if you're into altruism and making a modest living, this is a good model."[63] Furthermore, there are questions about Tapestry's legitimacy. In order to be effective, Tapestry must be exclusionary, keeping network meetings small and omitting unsophisticated (and potentially underrepresented) participants. With such low visibility comes the threat of decreased accountability.

These issues suggest that the eventual success of Tapestry and the other innovations discussed earlier remains an empirical question. Here I have discussed three different innovations in the area of norm shifting around corporate managerial responsibility to society, particularly as they might apply to the problem of thin political markets. These innovations are promising, but I emphasize that they are only a start—and they could yet sputter to a stop. Using norms to shift lobbying incentives, particularly in the face of strong countervailing economic interests is, realistically, only a first step. As the literature in behavioral ethics argues, emerging norms have to be continually reinforced, through formal and informal governance mechanisms, to have a meaningful impact on behavior. The more focused and forceful the mechanisms to emphasize managers' agency responsibility to the capitalist system in thin political markets, the more plausibly managerial lobbying behavior in these contexts will likely change. In this spirit, below I outline four practicable mechanisms that can be introduced in thin political markets such as accounting rule-making.

First, managers lobbying in these markets should be encouraged to publicly recognize their agency responsibility to the system. Managers should be encouraged to assert under penalty of liability that they are representing the public interest in their lobbying. This might seem like a trivial and inconsequential step, but getting managers to explicitly recognize that they are expected to act in the general interest—rather than in the interest of their shareholders alone—can have a significant impact on their behavior. Results from experimental studies on issue framing offer support for this argument: for example, these studies have found that the simple act of declaring that a form will be completed truthfully reduces an individual's opportunism when completing the form.[64] As a thought experiment on this proposal, one can ask whether managers lobbying against an accounting rule mandating the expensing of employee stock options would continue to hold such a position if they were required to assert under penalty of liability that such nonexpensing was in the greater interest of mitigating capital-market information asymmetries. My expectation is that forcing such an assertion of managers would at least moderate the stand of some. Of course, realistically, this proposal is unlikely to effect a dramatic change in lobbying behavior. But the proposal, if implemented, could mitigate the levels of self-interested behavior now observed (and considered legitimate) when lobbying in thin political markets.

Second, a group of subject-matter experts (e.g., academics, retired corporate executives, and retired regulators) should be invited to evaluate managerial lobbying positions after the fact. Given the nature of the knowledge gap in thin political markets, such evaluations are likely to be feasible only several years after the actual lobbying, when evidence on how the rules are being used becomes available. But delays notwithstanding, such evaluations—the kind in this book—should be regularly commissioned by regulatory bodies and widely disseminated. For example, in the context of the FASB, its parent body (the Financial Accounting Foundation [FAF]) could commission every ten years a decennial report on potential capture in accounting rule-making. The results of this report would then be made widely available for discussion in civil society. Such evaluations can serve as a follow-up accountability mechanism for managerial lobbying, with managers and rule-makers subject to reputational penalties in cases of evident capture. In the most egregious cases of self-serving lobbying, such evaluations could even provide the basis for legal action against those involved, although such instances are likely to be very rare because it is difficult for plaintiffs to prevail in legal actions of this nature.

Third, as much as there is a role for penalties and accountability for harmful behaviors in thin political markets, there must also be opportunities to celebrate those managers who have shown leadership in these contexts. Public-spirited behavior in thin political markets is unlikely to yield direct monetary rewards to any agent, so we must develop alternative mechanisms to reward such behavior. Social recognition plays an important role in stimulating competitive individuals such as business managers to achieve their best. This is particularly the case beyond a certain threshold of wealth and income, where the marginal benefit of another dollar earned is likely outweighed by the marginal benefits of social recognition. Business schools and the media can play important roles in generating such recognition for leaders in thin political markets. These institutions often profile managers for their commercial acumen, and such profiles go a long way in shaping public perception of what constitutes successful conduct for business leaders. In a similar vein, business schools and the media can leverage their positions of influence to highlight individuals who have acted in the public interest when afforded unique and unchallenged opportunities to shape outcomes in thin political markets.

The final proposed mechanism focuses not on effecting managerial lobbying behavior per se but on the selection of members of the FASB itself. As seen in chapter 5, FASB members have an important role in shaping the nature of GAAP, and they tend to advance rules that favor the industries from which they hail. The process of selecting FASB members is currently quite opaque, with little public input from even the academic accounting community. I propose the FAF introduce greater accountability in this process by inviting academic members of the American Accounting Association to issue fairness and competence ratings on proposed FASB members. This would be similar to the input from the American Bar Association on U.S. judicial nominees. Furthermore, as noted in chapter 5, the number of (and consequently the voting rules for) FASB members has fluctuated from time to time in a seemingly ad hoc manner. In the long run, such arbitrary changes can undermine the legitimacy of GAAP. I propose that the FAF commit to adopting a more transparent due process before enacting such fundamental changes to the nature of the FASB. Such a process can involve consulting a wide range of academics, business journalists, and (retired) managers—and making public the results of such a consultation—before introducing major changes to the structure of the FASB.

Collectively, these mechanisms could over time raise awareness of and compliance with the managerial agency responsibility to the capitalist system in thin political markets.

To summarize, the key takeaway from this chapter is the proposition that thin political markets constitute a distinct problem in the maintenance of capitalist institutions. The problem is distinct because corporate managers' "social responsibility" (in Professor Friedman's words) in the context of thin political markets—a responsibility to the capitalist system—is distinct from that in "thick" political markets and in capitalism more broadly—a responsibility to self-interested profit seeking. Much in the tradition of over thirty-five years of scholarship and practice in addressing managerial agency to shareholders, the problem of thin political markets—given its centrality to the outcomes of the capitalist system—behooves us to address the agency of managers to the capitalist system. Professor Friedman, I hope, would agree.

Afterword

For nearly a decade, I have been engaged in conceptual and empirical research into the political process of accounting rule-making. When, in early 2004, I started this research agenda as a first-year doctoral student, I had little idea of the path my research would take, of the results the research would yield, and of the notion of thin political markets that would eventually emerge from my studies. By late 2012, I had conceived the idea for this book, but some of the conceptual and empirical studies that underlie the book's thesis were still works in progress. Indeed, even as I complete the draft for this book, my research into the process is ongoing. I expect that to continue.

The nature of academic research is the careful exploration of phenomena, the discovery of relationships, and the development of theories. Then the cycle continues, as emerging theories are tested on new data or phenomena, so that they may be affirmed, refined, or rejected. Such, I expect, is the course for the notion of thin political markets, which this book has introduced. Indeed, a key objective in writing this book is to stimulate additional research and examination into thin political markets. My hope is that this book is the first word—rather than the last word—on the subject.

My other objective in writing this book is to consolidate and interpret my findings on the political process of accounting—to make, as it were, a wide-ranging assessment of the state of accounting rule-making. Here too, I anticipate the conclusions to be subject to ongoing testing. As new rule-making institutions such as the Private Company Council emerge, as new individuals come to the FASB, and as the technology and culture in industrial and financial companies develop, we can expect new findings to surface from studies of accounting's political process. The book's takeaway on special-interest capture should be subject to continual reexamination. Indeed, pursuing the reversal of this result is a worthy quest.

Bibliographic Note

I offer below a short bibliographic note and comment on the research methods employed in this book.

There are two types of chapters in the book: those that discuss evidence and those that inductively build theory. Chapters 3–7 are of the former type, and chapters 2, 8, and 9 are of the latter.

The evidence in Chapters 3–7 is drawn from academic articles and Harvard Business School (HBS) case studies that I have authored or coauthored over the past several years. Chapter 3 is based in part on (1) my HBS case study "The Politics and Economics of Accounting for Goodwill at Cisco Systems," (2) my article "The Implications of Unverifiable Fair-Value Accounting: Evidence from the Political Economy of Goodwill Accounting" published in the *Journal of Accounting and Economics*, and (3) my article "Evidence on the Use of Unverifiable Estimates in Required Goodwill Impairment" coauthored with Professor Ross Watts of the Massachusetts Institute of Technology and published in the *Review of Accounting Studies*.

Chapter 4 is based on my article "The Auditing Oligopoly and Lobbying on Accounting Standards" coauthored with Professor Abigail Allen of HBS and Professor Sugata Roychowdhury of Boston College. Chapter 5 is based on my articles "Towards an Understanding of the Role of Standard Setters in Standard Setting" published in the *Journal of Accounting and Economics* and "Why 'Fair Value' Is the Rule: How a Controversial Accounting Approach Gained Support" published in the *Harvard Business Review*. The former is coauthored with Professor Allen. Chapter 6 is based on my article "The International Politics of IFRS Harmonization" published in the journal *Accounting, Economics, and Law* and on my HBS case studies "IFRS in China" and "Leadership in Corporate Reporting Policy at Tata Steel." Chapter 7 is based on my case study "The Private Company Council" coauthored with Professor Luis Viceira of HBS.

The theoretical framework in chapter 2 is drawn from two articles: "Implications for GAAP from an Analysis of Positive Research in Accounting" published in the *Journal of Accounting and Economics* and coauthored with Professor S. P. Kothari of the Massachusetts Institute of Technology and Professor Doug Skinner of the University of Chicago and "A Framework for Research on Corporate Accountability Reporting" published in the journal *Accounting Horizons.*

The primary method for inferences in each of these articles is the application of economic theory and theory from political science. The studies underlying chapters 3–5 use formal statistical tests on archival data. The studies underlying chapters 6 and 7 are field-based projects that combine original interviews with other primary and secondary sources.

Each of these articles and cases, on its own, has a specific objective in advancing the understanding of accounting phenomena that is unrelated to the central objective of this book. In fact, when I started work on most of these articles and cases, the idea of this book had not yet crystalized. It was only as I undertook a retrospective look for commonalities across my work (as part of a personnel review process at Harvard Business School in 2011) that I first saw the seeds of this book.

Chapters 8 and 9 are distinct from the other chapters. They are based on an ongoing project with Professor Rebecca Henderson of HBS called "Managers and Market Capitalism." The project aims to understand the role of corporate managers in those cases where (individual) profit seeking and (social) problem solving do not align (such as in thin political markets). I had the good fortune to meet Professor Henderson and initiate the project just as I was formulating the idea for this book. It was through my collaboration with her that the core of chapters 8 and 9 emerged.

Collectively, this book is an aggregation of many parts, with the hope that the "whole" that emerges is greater than the sum of those parts. I owe a heavy debt to all my coauthors listed above (and to many others identified in the acknowledgments). Without their partnership, the evidence and ideas that eventually led to this illustration of the problem of thin political markets would not have been possible.

Acknowledgments

Academia is at once a collaborative and a lonely profession—one characterized by alternating periods of vibrant engagement with fellow scholars and deep private reflection. Writing this book involved many hours of time alone, cloistered in my offices at Morgan Hall on the Harvard Business School (HBS) campus and at home in Cambridge, Massachusetts. But the book could not have been conceived and would not have been completed were it not for the generous collaboration, guidance, criticism, and support of a number of individuals, whom I acknowledge below.

My first debt is to my coauthors on the various studies that have constituted elements of this book. I have identified these individuals within various chapters and in a brief bibliographic note that precedes these acknowledgments, but their contribution is so substantial that it certainly bears repeating here. A special thanks to Abigail Allen, Rebecca Henderson, S. P. Kothari, Sugata Roychowdhury, Doug Skinner, Luis Viceira, and Ross Watts. As coauthors, these individuals unreservedly invested their time in joint projects with me; this book is indelibly tied to those investments.

One's productivity is a function of one's ability to leverage time, and, for an academic, much of such leverage comes from quality research assistance. In this regard, I have been very fortunate. Thanks to Matt Shaffer, who served as my research associate over three years during which the idea for this book was being developed, and to Alexa Rahman and Alastair Su, who diligently cross-checked and formatted the references in the manuscript and who proofed many drafts. In addition, several other research associates were involved in the various articles and cases from which this book draws: thanks to Daniela Beyersdorfer, Beiting Cheng, Nancy Dai, G. A. Donovan, Michael Kregar, Karol Misztal, Scott Renner, John Sheridan, and Rachna Tahilyani.

I also owe acknowledgments to my administrative assistants whose clerical and technical support over the years has made the journey of getting to this book considerably easier: Elizabeth Connolly, Alyssa Konopka, Maria Maxell, Katherine Talbot, and Mary Wozniak.

From time to time, I have been fortunate to be able to sit down with individuals from the Financial Accounting Foundation, the Financial Accounting Standards Board, and the International Accounting Standards Board—some of the regulatory institutions discussed in the book. These conversations have helped me get a better perspective on the functioning of these organizations. Here, I particularly thank Jack Brennan, Prabhakar Kalavacherla, Terri Polley, Tom Seidenstein, and Wei-Guo Zhang. Relatedly, I want to acknowledge Charry Boris, Ron Guerrette, and Stacey Sutay, all professional staff at the Financial Accounting Foundation, whose dedication to that organization's mission of transparency enabled access to the data upon which substantial parts of this book are based.

Writing a book is highly unusual in accounting academia and is generally considered the purview of very senior scholars or those attempting to reach only practitioners. But the cumulative nature of my research in accounting's political economy made writing a book especially appropriate, and I thank, in particular, Paul Healy and Krishna Palepu for encouraging me to take on this wide-ranging project. My colleagues at HBS and elsewhere, even if not directly involved in my research as coauthors, provided an extraordinary intellectual climate, which allowed me to develop the ideas in this book. For helpful conversations over several years, I owe thanks to Joe Badaracco, Dennis Campbell, Srikant Datar, Mihir Desai, David Hawkins, Nien-hê Hsieh, Bob Kaplan, Rob Kaplan, Tarun Khanna, Rakesh Khurana, Dutch Leonard, Joshua Margolis, David Moss, V. G. Narayanan, Lynn Paine, Clayton Rose, Bob Simons, Ewa Sletten, Eugene Soltes, Suraj Srinivasan, Sandra Sucher, and Joe Weber, among many others.

At HBS, research and teaching are closely intertwined. Faculty developing new ideas are encouraged to find ways to introduce and test these ideas in the classroom, where the commonsense perspective of MBA students and executive-education participants can refine and augment abstract theories into practical concepts. Taking advantage of this opportunity, over the past several years I have taught materials related to the arguments in this book in my various classes. Thus I owe thanks to my many students over the years (about one thousand as of this writing) for their implicit feedback on my scholarship. On this note, I also owe thanks to my colleagues from the various teaching groups on which I have served, for their patience and encouragement in allowing me to introduce new teaching materials. Thanks in particular to the faculty chairs of these teaching groups: Joe Badaracco, Rohit Deshpande, David Hawkins, Krishna Palepu, and Sandra Sucher. Finally, I want to acknowledge HBS Dean Nitin Nohria for encouraging and enabling my switch from teaching accounting to teaching leadership and ethics as the plan for this book started to emerge. It is through this latter teaching assignment that I was able to refine the ideas in chapters 8 and 9.

I turn next to the community of individuals that has been directly involved in the development of this manuscript. First, thanks to my subject editor at the University of Chicago Press, Joe Jackson, whose careful stewardship guided this book to completion, and to his assistant, Jillian Tsui, who helped me prepare the manuscript for publication. Thanks also to my production editor, Jenni Fry; my copyeditor, Kyriaki Tsaganis; and my indexer, Steve Csipke. Next, a special thanks to the many experts from fields as diverse as accounting, ethics, political economy, and sociology who read all or part of the manuscript and gave me excellent and timely feedback: Abigail Allen, Jim Alt, Joe Badaracco, Mary Barth, Rob Bloomfield, Dan Carpenter, Srikant Datar, Frank Dobbin, Paul Healy, Rebecca Henderson, Prabhakar Kalavacherla, Peter Katzenstein, S. P. Kothari, Krishna Palepu, Sugata Roychowdhury, Bob Simons, Shyam Sunder, Ross Watts, Joseph Weber, Stephen Zeff, and Wei-Guo Zhang. Many of these individuals read multiple drafts of the book, patiently offering suggestions for improvement as I iterated through different approaches to present the core materials.

This book represents nearly a decade of work initiated during my graduate studies and completed over seven years into my faculty appointment at HBS. Over the course of this period, a number of individuals, including many of those already mentioned, have contributed to my professional development by offering insightful feedback. Here I acknowledge five individuals in particular, who have at various periods given extraordinary amounts of their time to help improve my scholarship. Ross Watts, who served as my dissertation chair at the Massachusetts Institute of Technology, was the first to encourage me to pursue my interests in accounting's political process, despite this field being considered a "dangerous" area for new scholars. S. P. Kothari, also at the Massachusetts Institute of Technology, has served from those early days as a sounding board for new ideas, meeting with me sometimes almost biweekly as I explored new avenues. Krishna Palepu, who first recruited me to Harvard, introduced me to the art of marrying traditional research methods with case writing and teaching and has since consistently encouraged me to apply this powerful combination to take on big problems. Paul Healy, through careful counsel, eased my transition from accounting to leadership and ethics, a journey he pioneered several years prior. And Rebecca Henderson, whom I serendipitously met as I was first sketching out the notion of thin political markets, has provided me with both the courage and the intellectual companionship to take on this fundamental reexamination of the institutions of capitalism.

I close, of course, with a note of thanks to my family and friends, who every day give me so much fulfilment. And Jon, thank you for being so patient!

Notes

Chapter One

1. Milton Friedman, "The Social Responsibility of Business Is to Increase Its Profits," *New York Times Magazine*, September 13, 1970.

2. For arguments in political science related to thin political markets, see the criticism of classical "group theory" by Schattschneider (1960) and the exposition of "quiet politics" by Culpepper (2011). Elmer E. Schattschneider, *The Semi-Sovereign People: A Realist's View of Democracy in America* (New York: Holt, Rinehart and Winston, 1960); Pepper D. Culpepper, *Quiet Politics and Business Power: Corporate Control in Europe and Japan* (Cambridge, UK: Cambridge University Press, 2011).

3. See, for example, Adam Smith, *An Inquiry into the Nature and Causes of the Wealth of Nations* (1776; repr., Pennsylvania State College: Pennsylvania State Electronic Classics Series Publication, 2005); Friedrich A. Hayek, "The Use of Knowledge in Society," *American Economic Review* 35, no. 4 (1945): 519–30; Paul Samuelson, *Foundations of Economic Analysis* (Cambridge, MA: Harvard University Press, 1947); Kenneth Arrow, "An Extension of the Basic Theorems of Classical Welfare Economics," in *Proceedings of the Second Berkeley Symposium on Mathematical Statistics and Probability*, ed. Jerzy Neyman (Berkeley, CA: University of California Press, 1951), 507–32; Amartya Sen, "Markets and Freedom: Achievements and Limitations of the Market Mechanism in Promoting Individual Freedoms," *Oxford Economic Papers* 45, no. 4 (1993): 519–41.

4. SDC Platinum, "M&A Activity 1980–2012," accessed September 2013, http://thomson reuters.com/sdc-platinum; Bureau of Economic Analysis, "Gross Domestic Product," accessed September 2013, http://www.bea.gov.

5. See, for example, Gregor Andrade, Mark Mitchell, and Erik Stafford, "New Evidence and Perspectives on Mergers," *Journal of Economic Perspectives* 15, no. 2 (2001): 103–20.

6. See, for example, P. Raghavendra Rau and Theo Vermaelen, "Glamour, Value and the Post-Acquisition Performance of Acquiring Firms," *Journal of Financial Economics* 49, no. 2 (1998): 223–53.

7. See, for example, Brenda Masters-Stout, Michael L. Costigan, and Linda M. Lovata, "Goodwill Impairments and Chief Executive Officer Tenure," *Critical Perspectives on Accounting* 19, no. 8 (2008): 1370–83.

8. For evidence on this point as it applies to goodwill accounting, see Kevin K. Li and Rich-

ard G. Sloan, "Has Goodwill Accounting Gone Bad?" (working paper, University of Toronto, Toronto, Canada, 2009). For an examination of market inefficiency as it relates to accounting numbers, see Charles M. C. Lee, "Market Efficiency and Accounting Research: A Discussion of 'Capital Market Research in Accounting' by S. P. Kothari," *Journal of Accounting and Economics* 31, nos. 1−3 (2001): 233−53.

9. For evidence on this point as it applies to goodwill accounting, see chapter 3. For more general evidence and arguments on the contracting uses of accounting numbers, see Ross L. Watts and Jerold L. Zimmerman, *Positive Accounting Theory* (Englewood Cliffs, NJ: Prentice Hall, 1986).

10. Securities Act of 1933, 15 U.S.C. §77a (1933); Securities and Exchange Act of 1934, 15 U.S.C. §78a (1934); Sarbanes-Oxley Act of 2002, Pub. L. No. 107−204, 116 Stat. 745 (2002).

11. See, for example, Stephen Zeff, "The Evolution of U.S. GAAP: The Political Forces behind Professional Standards," *CPA Journal* 75, no. 2 (2005): 18−27.

12. American Institute of Certified Public Accountants, *Report of the Study on Establishment of Accounting Principles: Establishing Financial Accounting Standards, March 1972* (New York: American Institute of Certified Public Accountants, 1972), 3.

13. See, for example, The Securities and Exchange Commission Historical Society, "The Richard C. Adkerson Gallery on the SEC Role in Accounting Standards Setting: Accounting Principles Board (1959−1973)," accessed September 2013, http://www.sechistorical.org/museum/galleries/rca/rca04b-fasb-organization.php; The Securities and Exchange Commission Historical Society, "The Richard C. Adkerson Gallery on the SEC Role in Accounting Standards Setting: Financial Accounting Standards Board (1973−Present)," accessed September 2013, http://www.sechistorical.org/museum/galleries/rca/rca04d-fasb-organization.php.

14. American Institute of Certified Public Accountants, *Report of the Study on Establishment of Accounting Principles*, 83.

15. Chapter 2 is based in part on my articles, "Implications for GAAP from an Analysis of Positive Research in Accounting," *Journal of Accounting and Economics* 50, nos. 2−3 (2010): 246−86; and "A Framework for Research on Corporate Accountability Reporting," *Accounting Horizons* 26, no. 2 (2013): 409−32. The former is coauthored with Professors S. P. Kothari of MIT and Doug Skinner of the University of Chicago.

16. There is an active debate in academic accounting literature on the objectives of financial reporting. Chapter 2 discusses elements of this debate.

17. See, in particular, Financial Accounting Standards Board, "Statement of Financial Accounting Concepts No. 2, May 1980," accessed November 2013, http://www.fasb.org/pdf/con2.pdf.

18. Specifically, in 2010, the FASB introduced the Statement of Financial Accounting Concepts No. 8, which replaced the Statement of Financial Accounting Concepts Nos. 1 and 2, which had been introduced in 1978 and 1980, respectively.

19. Financial Accounting Standards Board, "Conceptual Framework: Statement of Financial Accounting Concepts No. 8 September 2010," accessed November 2013, http://www.fasb.org/jsp/FASB/Page/PreCodSectionPage&cid=1176156317989.

20. Chapter 3 is partly based on my HBS case study, *The Politics and Economics of Accounting for Goodwill at Cisco Systems (A)* (HBS No. 109-002) (Boston: Harvard Business School Publishing, 2008) and on my articles, "The Implications of Unverifiable Fair-Value Accounting: Evidence from the Political Economy of Goodwill Accounting," *Journal of Accounting and Economics* 45, nos. 2−3 (2008): 253−81; and "Evidence on the Use of Unverifiable Estimates in

Required Goodwill Impairment," *Review of Accounting Studies* 17, no. 4 (2012): 749–80. The latter is coauthored with Professor Ross Watts of MIT.

21. Prepared statement of Dennis Powell, in *Pooling Accounting: Hearing before the Committee on Banking, Housing, and Urban Affairs, United States Senate*, 106th Cong., 2d session (Washington, DC: Government Printing Office, 2000), 62.

22. Financial Accounting for Intangibles Reexamination Act, H.R. 5365, 106th Cong. (2000).

23. George Alexandridis, Christos F. Mavrovitis, and Nickolaos G. Travlos, "How have M&As Changed? Evidence from the Sixth Merger Wave," *European Journal of Finance* 18, no. 8 (2012): 663–88.

24. See, for example, Paula Dwyer, "The Big Four: Too Few to Fail," *BusinessWeek*, August 31, 2003, accessed September 2013, http://www.businessweek.com/stories/2003-08-31/commentary-the-big-four-too-few-to-fail; Joseph Nocera, "Auditors: Too Few to Fail," *New York Times*, June 25, 2005, accessed September 2013, http://www.nytimes.com/2005/06/25/business/25nocera.html?pagewanted=all&_r=0.

25. Chapter 4 is partly based on my article, "The Auditing Oligopoly and Lobbying on Accounting Standards" (working paper 13-054, Harvard Business School, Boston, MA, 2013), coauthored with Professor Abigail Allen of HBS and Professor Sugata Roychowdhury of Boston College.

26. For example, in 2007, the SEC organized a committee on "improvements to financial reporting" that was charged with addressing the issue, but the committee's report was not implemented partly because it was issued in the midst of the commotion that was the 2008 Financial Crisis. Securities and Exchange Commission, *Final Report of the Advisory Committee on Improvements to Financial Reporting to the United States Securities and Exchange Commission*, accessed September 2013, http://www.sec.gov/about/offices/oca/acifr/acifr-finalreport.pdf.

27. Chapter 5 is partly based on my articles, "Towards an Understanding of the Role of Standard Setters in Standard Setting," *Journal of Accounting and Economics* 55, no. 1 (2013): 66–90; and "Why 'Fair Value' Is the Rule: How a Controversial Accounting Approach Gained Support," *Harvard Business Review* 91, no. 3 (2013): 99–101. The former is coauthored with Professor Abigail Allen of HBS.

28. See, for example, Stephen Zeff, "The SEC Rules Historical Cost Accounting: 1934 to the 1970s," *Accounting and Business Research* 37, no. 1 (2007): 49–62.

29. See, for example, Paul M. Healy and Krishna G. Palepu, "The Fall of Enron," *Journal of Economic Perspectives* 17, no. 2 (2003): 3–26.

30. See, for example, Krishna G. Palepu, Suraj Srinivasan, and Aldo Sesia, *New Century Financial Corporation* (HBS No. 109-034) (Boston: Harvard Business School Publishing, 2009).

31. See, for example, the ruling in Fait v. Regions Financial Corp., 655 F.3d 105 (2d Cir. 2011). The implications of this ruling and other elements of auditor liability for fair-value estimates are discussed in chapter 5.

32. See, for example, Robert W. Holthausen and Ross L. Watts, "The Relevance of the Value-Relevance Literature for Financial Accounting Standard Setting," *Journal of Accounting and Economics* 31, nos. 1–3 (2001): 3–75; Mary E. Barth, William H. Beaver, and Wayne R. Landsman, "The Relevance of the Value Relevance Literature for Financial Accounting Standard Setting: Another View," *Journal of Accounting and Economics* 31, nos. 1–3 (2001): 77–104.

33. Elements of the notion of ideological capture can be found in numerous works on regulation in market societies, including Marion Fourcade, *Economists and Societies: Discipline and Profession in the United States, Britain, & France, 1890s to 1990s* (Princeton, NJ: Princeton

University Press, 2009) and Nolan McCarty, Keith T. Poole, and Howard Rosenthal, *Political Bubbles: Financial Crises and the Failure of American Democracy* (Princeton, NJ: Princeton University Press, 2013).

34. See, for example, Ray Ball, "International Financial Reporting Standards (IFRS): Pros and Cons for Investors," *Accounting and Business Research* 36, no. 1 (2006): 5−27.

35. Chapter 6 is partly based on my article, "The International Politics of IFRS Harmonization," *Accounting, Economics, and Law* 3, no. 2 (2013): 1−46, and on my HBS case studies, *IFRS in China* (HBS No. 110-037) (Boston: Harvard Business School Publishing, 2009) and *Leadership in Corporate Reporting Policy at Tata Steel* (HBS No. 111-028) (Boston: Harvard Business School Publishing, 2010).

36. Chapter 7 is partly based on my HBS case study, *The Private Company Council* (HBS No. 113-045) (Boston: Harvard Business School Publishing, 2013) coauthored with Professor Luis Viceira of HBS.

37. American Institute of Certified Public Accountants, *Report to the Board of Trustees of the Financial Accounting Foundation,* Blue Ribbon Panel on Standard Setting for Private Companies, January 2011, accessed April 2012, http://www.aicpa.org/interestareas/frc/accounting financialreporting/pcfr/downloadabledocuments/blue_ribbon_panel_report.pdf, 22.

38. Chapters 8 and 9 are partly based on my article, "Managers and Market Capitalism" (working paper 13-075, Harvard Business School, Boston, MA, 2013) coauthored with Professor Rebecca Henderson of HBS.

39. See, for example, Ilia D. Dichev and Vicki W. Tang, "Matching and the Changing Properties of Accounting Earnings over the Last 40 Years," *Accounting Review* 83, no. 6 (2008): 1425−60.

40. See, for example, Mark T. Bradshaw and Richard G. Sloan, "GAAP versus the Street: An Empirical Assessment of Two Alternative Definitions of Earnings," *Journal of Accounting Research* 40, no. 1 (2002): 41−66.

41. See, for example, Peter R. Demerjian, "Accounting Standards and Debt Covenants: Has the 'Balance Sheet Approach' Led to a Decline in the Use of Balance Sheet Covenants?" *Journal of Accounting and Economics* 52, no. 2 (2011): 178−202.

42. See, for example, Karthik Balakrishnan, Ross L. Watts, and Luo Zuo, "Accounting Conservatism and Firm Investment: Evidence from the Global Financial Crisis" (working paper, University of Pennsylvania, Philadelphia, PA, 2013).

43. An example of a rules-based approach to address captured decision making in political processes is found in McCarty et al., *Political Bubbles.*

Chapter Two

1. The economic theory of financial reporting is derived from a large number of studies published in scholarly journals in accounting over the past four decades. Some key works include the following: Nicholas J. Gonedes and Nicholas Dopuch, "Capital Market Equilibrium, Information Production, and Selecting Accounting Techniques: Theoretical Framework and Review of Empirical Work," *Journal of Accounting Research* 12 (1974): 48−129; Ross L. Watts, "Corporate Financial Statements: A Product of the Market and Political Processes," *Australian Journal of Management* 2, no. 1 (1977): 53−75; Robert W. Holthausen and Richard W. Leftwich, "The Economic Consequences of Accounting Choice: Implications of Costly Contracting and Monitoring," *Journal of Accounting and Economics* 5 (1983): 77−117; Paul M. Healy, "The Effect of

Bonus Schemes on Accounting Decisions," *Journal of Accounting and Economics* 7, no. 1 (1985): 85–107; Ross L. Watts and Jerold Zimmerman, *Positive Accounting Theory* (Englewood Cliffs, NJ: Prentice Hall, 1986); Ray Ball, "Infrastructure Requirements for an Economically Efficient System of Public Financial Reporting and Disclosure," *Brookings-Wharton Papers on Financial Services* (2001): 127–69; Paul M. Healy and Krishna G. Palepu, "Information Asymmetry, Corporate Disclosure, and the Capital Markets: A Review of the Empirical Disclosure Literature," *Journal of Accounting and Economics* 31, nos. 1–3 (2001): 405–40; Robert W. Holthausen and Ross L. Watts, "The Relevance of the Value-Relevance Literature for Financial Accounting Standard Setting," *Journal of Accounting and Economics* 31, nos. 1–3 (2001): 3–75; Mary E. Barth, William H. Beaver, and Wayne R. Landsman, "The Relevance of the Value Relevance Literature for Financial Accounting Standard Setting: Another View," *Journal of Accounting and Economics* 31, nos. 1–3 (2001): 77–104; Ross L. Watts, "Conservatism in Accounting Part I: Explanations and Implications," *Accounting Horizons* 17, no. 3 (2003): 207–21.

2. Financial Accounting Standards Board, "Statement of Financial Accounting Concepts No. 1, November 1978," accessed September 2014, http://www.fasb.org/pdf/con1.pdf, 6.

3. See, for example, Watts, "Corporate Financial Statements"; Healy and Palepu, "Information Asymmetry."

4. See, for example, Ross L. Watts and Jerold L. Zimmerman, "Towards a Positive Theory of the Determination of Accounting Standards," *Accounting Review* 53, no. 1 (1978): 112–34.

5. See, for example, William H. Beaver, *Financial Reporting: An Accounting Revolution*, 2nd ed. (Englewood Cliffs, NJ: Prentice Hall, 1989).

6. See, for example, Adolf Berle and Gardiner Means, *The Modern Corporation and Private Property* (New York: Harcourt, Brace, 1932); Michael C. Jensen and William H. Meckling, "Theory of the Firm: Managerial Behavior, Agency Costs and Ownership Structure," *Journal of Financial Economics* 3, no. 4 (1976): 305–60; Eugene F. Fama and Michael C. Jensen, "Separation of Ownership and Control," *Journal of Law and Economics* 26, no. 2 (1983): 301–25.

7. See, for example, Patricia M. Dechow, "Accounting Earnings and Cash Flows as Measures of Firm Performance: The Role of Accounting Accruals," *Journal of Accounting and Economics* 18, no. 1 (1994): 3–42.

8. Financial economists refer to this phenomenon as the problem of "asset substitution." See, for example, Stewart C. Myers, "Determinants of Corporate Borrowing," *Journal of Financial Economics* 5, no. 2 (1977): 147–75; Clifford W. Smith and Jerold B. Warner, "On Financial Contracting: An Analysis of Bond Covenants," *Journal of Financial Economics* 7, no. 2 (1979): 117–61.

9. See, for example, Holthausen and Watts, "The Relevance of the Value-Relevance Literature."

10. Financial economists refer to this phenomenon as the problem of "underinvestment." See, for example, Myers, "Determinants of Corporate Borrowing"; Smith and Warner, "On Financial Contracting."

11. See, for example, Richard A. Lambert and David F. Larcker, "An Analysis of the Use of Accounting and Market Measures of Performance in Executive Compensation Contracts," *Journal of Accounting Research* 25 (1987): 85–125; Richard G. Sloan, "Accounting Earnings and Top Executive Compensation," *Journal of Accounting and Economics* 16, nos. 1–3 (1993): 55–100.

12. See, for example, Dechow, "Accounting Earnings and Cash Flows."

13. This phenomenon is referred to in accounting theory as "dirty-surplus accounting." For a discussion of dirty-surplus accounting's role in the economic theory of financial report-

ing, see, for example, Holthausen and Watts, "The Relevance of the Value-Relevance Literature," Sec. 4.3; S. P. Kothari, Karthik Ramanna, and Douglas J. Skinner, "Implications for GAAP from an Analysis of Positive Research in Accounting," *Journal of Accounting and Economics* 50, nos. 2–3 (2010): 260.

14. See, for example, Watts and Zimmerman, "Towards a Positive Theory."

15. See, for example, Douglas J. Skinner, "Why Firms Voluntarily Disclose Bad News," *Journal of Accounting Research* 32, no. 1 (1994): 38–60; Sudipta Basu, "The Conservatism Principle and the Asymmetric Timeliness of Earnings," *Journal of Accounting and Economics* 24, no. 1 (1997): 3–37; S. P. Kothari, Susan Shu, and Peter D. Wysocki, "Do Managers Withhold Bad News?" *Journal of Accounting Research* 47, no. 1 (2009): 241–76.

16. See, for example, Healy, "The Effect of Bonus Schemes."

17. Ollman v. Evans, 750 F.2d 970 (DC Cir. 1984).

18. See, for example, Ross L. Watts and Jerold L. Zimmerman, "Auditors and the Determination of Accounting Standards" (working paper GPB 78-06, University of Rochester, Rochester, NY, 1982).

19. See, for example, Ross L. Watts and Jerold L. Zimmerman, "Agency Problems, Auditing and the Theory of the Firm: Some Evidence," *Journal of Law and Economics* 26, no. 3 (1983): 613–33.

20. See, for example, Basu, "The Conservatism Principle"; Watts, "Conservatism in Accounting Part I"; Ryan LaFond and Ross L. Watts, "The Information Role of Conservative Financial Statements," *Accounting Review* 83, no. 2 (2008): 447–78.

21. On this point, see the discussion of moral hazard in Bengt Holmstrom, "Moral Hazard and Observability," *Bell Journal of Economics* 10, no. 1 (1979): 74–91.

22. See, for example, Douglas J. Skinner, "Accounting for Intangibles—A Critical Review of Policy Recommendations," *Accounting and Business Research* 38, no. 3 (2008): 191–204.

23. See, for example, Basu, "The Conservatism Principle"; Stephen G. Ryan, "Identifying Conditional Conservatism," *European Accounting Review* 15, no. 4 (2006): 511–25.

24. See, for example, Holthausen and Watts, "The Relevance of the Value-Relevance Literature."

25. See, for example, Jensen and Meckling, "Theory of the Firm"; Smith and Warner, "On Financial Contracting."

26. For a recent review of research on the agency problem between shareholders and creditors and its implications for accounting, see, for example, Christopher S. Armstrong, Wayne R. Guay, and Joseph P. Weber, "The Role of Information and Financial Reporting in Corporate Governance and Debt Contracting," *Journal of Accounting and Economics* 50, no. 2 (2010): 179–234.

27. For evidence on this argument as it applies to creditors, see, for example, Jieying Zhang, "The Contracting Benefits of Accounting Conservatism to Lenders and Borrowers," *Journal of Accounting and Economics* 45, no. 1 (2008): 27–54.

28. For a recent review of the literature on this topic, see, for example, Healy and Palepu, "Information Asymmetry."

29. See, for example, Mary E. Barth, "Research, Standard Setting, and Global Financial Reporting," *Foundations and Trends in Accounting* 1, no. 2 (2006): 71–165.

30. See, for example, Holthausen and Watts, "The Relevance of the Value-Relevance Literature"; Healy and Palepu, "Information Asymmetry."

31. Professor Katherine Schipper, a FASB member from 2001 to 2006, was perhaps most explicit on this point. See, for example, Katherine Schipper, "Fair Values in Financial Reporting"

(presentation, American Accounting Association Annual Meetings, San Francisco, CA, August 2005).

32. See, for example, Holthausen and Watts, "The Relevance of the Value-Relevance Literature."

33. Financial Accounting Standards Board, "Conceptual Framework: Statement of Financial Accounting Concepts No. 8, September 2010," accessed November 2013, http://www.fasb.org/jsp/FASB/Page/PreCodSectionPage&cid=1176156317989, 9.

34. Ibid., 17.

35. Ibid., 17–18.

36. Ibid., 19–21.

37. Ibid., 20.

38. On this point, FASB senior project manager L. Todd Johnson notes, "the Board does not accept the view that reliability should outweigh relevance for financial statement measures." L. Todd Johnson, "Relevance and Reliability," *FASB Report*, February 28, 2005, accessed November 2013, http://www.fasb.org/articles&reports/relevance_and_reliability_tfr_feb_2005.pdf.

39. See, for example, Holthausen and Watts, "The Relevance of the Value-Relevance Literature"; Barth, Beaver, and Landsman, "The Relevance of the Value Relevance Literature."

40. See, for example, Ilia D. Dichev and Vicki W. Tang, "Matching and the Changing Properties of Accounting Earnings over the Last 40 Years," *Accounting Review* 83, no. 6 (2008): 1425–60.

41. See, for example, Watts, "Conservatism in Accounting Part I."

42. FASB, "Conceptual Framework," 28.

43. See, for example, Holthausen and Watts, "The Relevance of the Value-Relevance Literature."

44. See, for example, Karthik Ramanna and Ross L. Watts, "Evidence on the Use of Unverifiable Estimates in Required Goodwill Impairment," *Review of Accounting Studies* 17, no. 4 (2012): 749–80.

45. For some reviews of the evidence, see, for example, Paul M. Healy and James M. Wahlen, "A Review of the Earnings Management Literature and Its Implications for Standard Setting," *Accounting Horizons* 13, no. 4 (1999): 365–83; Thomas D. Fields, Thomas Z. Lys, and Linda Vincent, "Empirical Research on Accounting Choice," *Journal of Accounting and Economics* 31, no. 1 (2001): 255–307; Anne Beyer et al., "The Financial Reporting Environment: Review of the Recent Literature," *Journal of Accounting and Economics* 50, no. 2 (2010): 296–343.

46. Financial Accounting Standards Board, "Statement of Financial Accounting Concepts No. 2, May 1980," accessed November 2013, http://www.fasb.org/pdf/con2.pdf.

47. Ibid., 5.

48. Ibid., 23–24.

49. Ibid., 28–35.

50. Ibid., 35.

51. See, in particular, Financial Accounting Standards Board, "Statement of Financial Accounting Concepts No. 6, December 1985," accessed January 2014, http://www.fasb.org/pdf/con6.pdf.

52. On this point, see, for example, the discussion by FASB senior project manager L. Todd Johnson, "Relevance and Reliability."

53. Jivas Chakravarthy, "The Ideological Homogenization of the FASB" (working paper, Emory University, Atlanta, GA, 2014).

54. Financial Accounting Standards Board, "Statement of Financial Accounting Concepts No. 7, February 2000," accessed October 2014, http://www.fasb.org/pdf/con7.pdf, 10.

55. Financial Accounting Standards Board, "The Norwalk Agreement," accessed November 2013, http://www.fasb.org/news/memorandum.pdf.

56. For instance, five of the original fourteen members of the IASB were from the United States. See, for example, Kees Camfferman and Stephen A. Zeff, *Financial Reporting and Global Capital Markets: A History of the International Accounting Standards Committee, 1973–2000* (New York: Oxford University Press, 2007).

57. Barth, "Research, Standard Setting," 98.

58. See, for example, Schipper, "Fair Values."

59. FASB, "Conceptual Framework," 23.

60. Ibid., 26–27.

61. See, for example, the commentary on the issuance of Statement of Financial Accounting Standards Nos. 2 and 5 in Stephen Zeff, "The Evolution of U.S. GAAP: The Political Forces Behind Professional Standards," *CPA Journal* 75, no. 2 (2005): 20.

62. The problems of information asymmetry and uncertainty have occupied a central place in modern economic theory from its very beginnings. Some seminal works in this area include Friedrich A. Hayek, "The Use of Knowledge in Society," *American Economic Review* 35, no. 4 (1945): 519–30; George A. Akerlof, "The Market for 'Lemons': Quality Uncertainty and the Market Mechanism," *Quarterly Journal of Economics* 84, no. 3 (1970): 488–500; Michael Spence, "Job Market Signaling," *Quarterly Journal of Economics* 87, no. 3 (1973): 355–74.

Chapter Three

1. Prepared statement of Dennis Powell, in *Pooling Accounting: Hearing before the Committee on Banking, Housing, and Urban Affairs, United States Senate*, 106th Cong., 2d session (Washington, DC: Government Printing Office, 2000), 62–66.

2. See *Pooling Accounting*.

3. Powell statement, in *Pooling Accounting*, 62–66.

4. Dennis Powell, "Dennis Powell to Financial Accounting Standards Board," Letter of Comment No. 25A, file ref. 1033-201 (Norwalk, CT: FASB, 1999), 2.

5. For the original guidance on the use of the pooling and purchase methods, see Accounting Principles Board, "Opinions of the Accounting Principles Board No. 16, Business Combinations" (New York: American Institute of Certified Public Accountants, 1970).

6. Financial Accounting Standards Board, "Statement of Financial Accounting Concepts No. 6, December 1985," accessed January 2014, http://www.fasb.org/pdf/con6.pdf.

7. Powell, "Dennis Powell to Financial Accounting Standards Board," 2.

8. Ibid., 3.

9. See, for example, Steven C. Wheelwright et al., *Cisco Systems, Inc.: Acquisition Integration for Manufacturing (A)* (HBS No. 600-015) (Boston: Harvard Business School Publishing, 2000).

10. Powell statement, in *Pooling Accounting*, 62–66.

11. Powell, "Dennis Powell to Financial Accounting Standards Board," 4–5.

12. Ibid., 5.

13. Dennis Powell, "Business Combination Purchase Accounting: Goodwill Impairment Test" (appendix to minutes of Financial Accounting Standards Board meeting, FASB, Norwalk, CT, September 29, 2000).

14. See Financial Accounting Standards Board, "Exposure Draft 201-R: Business Combinations and Intangible Assets—Accounting for Goodwill" (Norwalk, CT: FASB, 2001).

15. See Financial Accounting Standards Board, "Statement of Financial Accounting Standards No. 141: Business Combinations June 2001," accessed January 2014, http://www.fasb.org/pdf/fas141.pdf; Financial Accounting Standards Board, "Statement of Financial Accounting Standards No. 142: Goodwill and Other Intangible Assets June 2001," accessed January 2014, http://www.fasb.org/pdf/fas142.pdf.

16. Cisco Systems, "Form 10-K for the Fiscal Year Ended July 27, 2013," accessed January 2014, http://www.sec.gov/Archives/edgar/data/858877/000085887713000049/csco-2013727x10k.htm.

17. See, for example, Frank R. Rayburn and Ollie S. Powers, "A History of Pooling of Interests Accounting for Business Combinations in the United States," *Accounting Historians Journal* 18, no. 2 (1991): 155–92.

18. Stephen A. Zeff, "The Evolution of U.S. GAAP: The Political Forces behind Professional Standards Part 1," *CPA Journal* 75 (2005): 22–23.

19. The Securities and Exchange Commission Historical Society, "The Richard C. Adkerson Gallery on the SEC Role in Accounting Standards Setting: Accounting Principles Board (1959–1973)," accessed September 2013, http://www.sechistorical.org/museum/galleries/rca/rca04b-fasb-organization.php.

20. See, for example, Zeff, "The Evolution of U.S. GAAP," 18–27.

21. See, for example, Kenneth Nelson and Robert H. Strawser, "A Note on APB Opinion No. 16," *Journal of Accounting Research* 8, no. 2 (1970): 284–89; Rayburn and Powers, "A History of Pooling."

22. See, for example, Rayburn and Powers, "A History of Pooling."

23. See, for example, Nelson and Strawser, "A Note on APB Opinion No. 16."

24. See, for example, Zeff, "The Evolution of U.S. GAAP."

25. See, for example, Nelson and Strawser, "A Note on APB Opinion No. 16."

26. See Accounting Principles Board, "Opinions of the Accounting Principles Board No. 16, Business Combinations"; Accounting Principles Board, "Opinions of the Accounting Principles Board No. 17, Intangible Assets" (New York: American Institute of Certified Public Accountants, 1970).

27. See, for example, Zeff, "The Evolution of U.S. GAAP."

28. The Securities and Exchange Commission Historical Society, "The Richard C. Adkerson Gallery."

29. See, for example, Rayburn and Powers, "A History of Pooling."

30. See, for example, Richard W. Leftwich, "The Agenda of the Financial Accounting Standards Board" (working paper, University of Chicago, Chicago, IL, 1995).

31. Thomas Lys and Linda Vincent, "An Analysis of Value Destruction in AT&T's Acquisition of NCR," *Journal of Financial Economics* 39, no. 2 (1995): 353–78.

32. Lynn E. Turner, "Initiatives for Improving the Quality of Financial Reporting" (speech, New York Society of Security Analysts, New York, February 10, 1999).

33. Jane Adams, "Current Accounting Projects" (speech, Twenty-Fifth Annual National Conference on Current SEC Developments, Washington, DC, 1997), accessed March 2015, http://www.sec.gov/news/speech/speecharchive/1997/spch194.txt.

34. Financial Accounting Standards Board, "Exposure Draft 201-A: Business Combinations and Intangible Assets" (Norwalk, CT: FASB, 1999), 34.

35. Financial Accounting Standards Board, "Invitation to Comment 192-A: Methods of Accounting for Business Combinations: Recommendations of the G4+1 for Achieving Convergence" (Norwalk, CT: FASB, 1998).

36. Financial Accounting Standards Board, "Invitation to Comment 174: Issues Associated with FASB Project on Business Combinations" (Norwalk, CT: FASB, 1997).

37. FASB, "Invitation to Comment 192-A."

38. See, for example, Financial Accounting Standards Board, "Invitation to Comment 192-A: Methods of Accounting for Business Combinations: Recommendations of the G4+1 for Achieving Convergence, Analysis of Comment Letters, March 24" (Norwalk, CT: FASB, 1999).

39. FASB, "Exposure Draft 201-A," 34.

40. Alain J. Hanover, "Alain J. Hanover to Financial Accounting Standards Board," Letter of Comment No. 33, file ref. 1033-201 (Norwalk, CT: FASB, 1999), 2.

41. Cynthia L. Lucchese, "Cynthia L. Lucchese to Financial Accounting Standards Board," Letter of Comment No. 32A, file ref. 1033-201 (Norwalk, CT: FASB, 1999), 1.

42. Robert R. B. Dykes, "Robert R. B. Dykes to Financial Accounting Standards Board," Letter of Comment No. 31A, file ref. 1033-201 (Norwalk, CT: FASB, 1999), 1, 3.

43. See *Pooling Accounting; Accounting for Business Combinations: Should Pooling Be Eliminated? Subcommittee on Finance and Hazardous Materials of the Committee on Commerce,* United States House of Representatives, 106th Cong., 2d session (Washington, DC: Government Printing Office, 2000).

44. *Pooling Accounting,* 47.

45. *Accounting for Business Combinations,* 53.

46. Ibid., 57.

47. *Pooling Accounting,* 9.

48. Financial Accounting for Intangibles Reexamination Act, H.R. 5365, 106th Cong. (2000), 1.

49. Spencer Abraham, "Spencer Abraham to Financial Accounting Standards Board," Letter of Comment No. 208, file ref. 1033-201 (Norwalk, CT: FASB, 2000), 1–2.

50. Dennis R. Beresford, "Congress Looks at Accounting for Business Combinations," *Accounting Horizons* 15, no. 1 (2001): 74.

51. Congressional intervention in accounting rule-making appears to be limited to a few key issue areas, including M&A accounting, accounting for leases, and accounting for stock options, suggesting that special interests on these issues are particularly well connected with politicians.

52. Beresford, "Congress Looks at Accounting," 73–86.

53. The PAC data were obtained in part from the Center for Responsive Politics, accessed September 2005, http://www.opensecrets.org.

54. See, for example, Stephen Ansolabehere, James M. Snyder, and Micky Tripathi, "Are PAC Contributions and Lobbying Linked? New Evidence from the 1995 Lobby Disclosure Act," *Business and Politics* 4, no. 2 (2002): 131–55. Further, as Snyder (1992) points out, virtually all scholarly work relating corporations with congressional decisions focuses on PAC contributions. James M. Snyder Jr., "Long-Term Investing in Politicians: Or, Give Early, Give Often," *Journal of Law and Economics* 35, no. 1 (1992): 15–43.

55. More details on the regression design, control variables, alternative explanations, and robustness tests are found in my paper, "The Implications of Unverifiable Fair-Value Accounting: Evidence from the Political Economy of Goodwill Accounting," *Journal of Accounting and Economics* 45, nos. 2–3 (2008): 253–81.

56. For a fuller description of these ideology variables, see Keith T. Poole, "Recovering a Basic Space from a Set of Issue Scales," *American Journal of Political Science* 42 (1998): 954–93.

57. For empirical work, see, for example, Snyder, "Long-Term Investing in Politicians"; Randall S. Kroszner and Thomas Stratmann, "Corporate Campaign Contributions, Repeat Giving, and the Rewards to Legislator Reputation," *Journal of Law and Economics* 48, no. 1 (2005): 41–71; Thomas Stratmann, "Some Talk: Money in Politics; A (Partial) Review of the Literature," *Public Choice* 124, nos. 1–2 (2005): 135–56. For theoretical work, see, for example, David Austen-Smith, "Campaign Contributions and Access," *American Political Science Review* 89, no. 3 (1995): 566–81; Gene M. Grossman and Elhanan Helpman, *Special Interest Politics* (Cambridge, MA: MIT Press, 2001).

58. See, for example, Kroszner and Stratmann, "Corporate Campaign Contributions."

59. From January 1998 to June 2001 (the duration of the FASB's M&A accounting project), the firm-average value of M&A deals completed using the pooling method was $11.9 billion among propooling firms. The corresponding figure for firms supporting the FASB's position to mandate goodwill amortization under the purchase method was $5.4 billion.

60. Reflecting in 2002 on the intervention of his colleagues in the pooling versus purchase issue, Senator Chris Dodd of Connecticut (who is not classified as a propooling congressperson) remarked, "[We] have been involved in the past when there have been efforts by people who wanted to have us vote on some of these matters. I recall three or four years ago [sic] the debate was over pooling and purchasing [sic] accounting standards . . . the idea that the Senate might vote 51 to 49 to pick one accounting standard over another is just ludicrous on its face. We do not want to set a precedent, in my view, of the Congress of the United States deciding what accounting practices ought to be." 107th Cong. Rec. S6773 (July 15, 2002).

61. See, for example, Snyder, "Long-Term Investing in Politicians."

62. Financial Accounting Standards Board, "FASB Board Meeting" (minutes, FASB, May 31, 2000).

63. Financial Accounting Standards Board, "FASB Board Meeting" (minutes, FASB, September 29, 2000).

64. FASB, "Exposure Draft 201-R."

65. In 2009, the FASB introduced the Accounting Standards Codification project to simplify how users reference various U.S. GAAP rules. The codification provides a new taxonomy to identify accounting rules, including those previously identified by "SFAS" numbers (e.g., SFAS 141). Because much of this book refers to FASB rules prior to 2009, I continue to use the precodification terminology.

66. FASB, "Statement of Financial Accounting Standards No. 141."

67. FASB, "Statement of Financial Accounting Standards No. 142."

68. In explaining the reason for this difference between ED 201-R and SFAS 142, the FASB cited "costs related to estimating the fair value" of nongoodwill net assets. See FASB, "Statement of Financial Accounting Standards No. 141," paragraph B127, 61.

69. George W. Harrington, "George W. Harrington to Financial Accounting Standards Board," Letter of Comment No. 139, file ref. 1033-201R (Norwalk, CT: FASB, 2001), 2, 4.

70. Michael R. Spychala, "Michael R. Spychala to Financial Accounting Standards Board," Letter of Comment No. 85, file ref. 1033-201R (Norwalk, CT: FASB, 2001), 3.

71. See, for example, Ross L. Watts, "Conservatism in Accounting Part I: Explanations and Implications," *Accounting Horizons* 17, no. 3 (2003): 207–21; Sugata Roychowdhury and Ross L. Watts, "Asymmetric Timeliness of Earnings, Market-to-Book, and Conservatism in Financial Reporting," *Journal of Accounting and Economics* 44, no. 1 (2007): 2–31.

72. See, in particular, Financial Accounting Standards Board, "Statement of Financial Ac-

counting Standards No. 131: Disclosures about Segments of an Enterprise and Related Information June 1997," accessed January 2014, http://www.fasb.org/pdf/fas131.pdf.

73. More details on the regression design, control variables, alternative explanations, and robustness tests are found in my paper, "The Implications of Unverifiable Fair-Value Accounting."

74. See, for example, Ross L. Watts and Jerold L. Zimmerman, "Towards a Positive Theory
of the Determination of Accounting Standards," *Accounting Review* 53, no. 1 (1978): 112–34;
Jere R. Francis, "Lobbying against Proposed Accounting Standards: The Case of Employer's
Pension Accounting," *Journal of Accounting and Public Policy* 6, no. 1 (1987): 35–57; Edward B.
Deakin, "Rational Economic Behavior and Lobbying on Accounting Issues: Evidence from the
Oil and Gas Industry," *Accounting Review* 64, no. 1 (1989): 137–51.

75. See Douglas J. Skinner, "Discussion of 'the Implications of Unverifiable Fair-Value Accounting: Evidence from the Political Economy of Goodwill Accounting,'" *Journal of Accounting
and Economics* 45, nos. 2–3 (2008): 282–88.

76. FASB, "Statement of Financial Accounting Standards No. 142," 7.

77. Ibid.

78. For a review of this literature, see Thomas D. Fields, Thomas Z. Lys, and Linda Vincent, "Empirical Research on Accounting Choice," *Journal of Accounting and Economics* 31, no. 1
(2001): 255–307.

79. See, for example, Ross L. Watts and Jerold Zimmerman, *Positive Accounting Theory* (Englewood Cliffs, NJ: Prentice Hall, 1986); Jennifer Francis, J. Douglas Hanna, and Linda Vincent,
"Causes and Effects of Discretionary Asset Write-Offs," *Journal of Accounting Research* 34, sup.
(1996): 117–34; Fields, Lys, and Vincent, "Empirical Research on Accounting Choice"; Anne
Beatty and Joseph P. Weber, "Accounting Discretion in Fair Value Estimates: An Examination
of SFAS 142 Goodwill Impairments," *Journal of Accounting Research* 44, no. 2 (2006): 257–88.

80. More details on the regression design, control variables, alternative explanations, and
robustness tests are found in my paper, "Evidence on the Use of Unverifiable Estimates in Required Goodwill Impairment" coauthored with Professor Watts and published in the *Review of
Accounting Studies* 17, no. 4 (2012): 749–80.

81. George Alexandridis, Christos F. Mavrovitis, and Nickolaos G. Travlos, "How Have
M&As Changed? Evidence from the Sixth Merger Wave," *European Journal of Finance* 18, no. 8
(2012): 663–88.

82. It is important to clarify that this evidence on announcement-period returns is not
dispositive on the question of the effects of SFAS 142—the decrease in announcement-period
returns might be attributable to other changes that have occurred in the economy over the
1999–2002 period.

83. See, for example, Solomon Fabricant, "Revaluations of Fixed Assets, 1925–1934," *National Bureau of Economic Research* 62 (1936): 1–12; Kristin Ely and Gregory Waymire, "Intangible Assets and Stock Prices in the Pre-SEC Era," *Journal of Accounting Research* 37, sup. (1999):
17–44; Jan Barton and Gregory Waymire, "Investor Protection under Unregulated Financial
Reporting," *Journal of Accounting and Economics* 38 (2004): 65–116.

84. This premise is adapted from evolutionary biology, where it is sometimes referred to
as the "Red Queen Hypothesis." The term—borrowed from an observation by the Queen of
Hearts in *Alice in Wonderland*—refers to the argument that a species (firm) has to continually
evolve to survive. A species (firm)—even if it is the best adapted to its environment at any given
time—that stops evolving will eventually be outcompeted by other species (firms). See Leigh
Van Valen, "A New Evolutionary Law," *Evolutionary Theory* 1 (1973): 1–30.

85. Another approach to goodwill accounting is provided by the economic value added (EVA) method. EVA is a private alternative to GAAP accounting used by about ten percent of the Fortune 500 companies to evaluate management performance. EVA takes neither the amortization nor the impairment-only approach to goodwill accounting. Under EVA accounting, accumulated goodwill is treated as part of a firm's capital stock that must earn the firm's cost of capital. This goodwill-inclusive capital charge is subtracted from the firm's operating income (which excludes goodwill amortization) to calculate the bottom-line income number. The net effect of the EVA treatment can be a lower drag on bottom-line income than that imposed by amortizing goodwill, but the EVA treatment still imposes greater accountability for acquired goodwill than an impairment-only approach. See, for example, G. Bennett Stewart III, *The Quest for Value: The EVA Management Guide* (New York: Harper Collins, 1991).

86. See, for example, Watts and Zimmerman, "Towards a Positive Theory"; Dan S. Dhaliwal, "Some Economic Determinants of Management Lobbying for Alternative Methods of Accounting: Evidence from the Accounting for Interest Cost Issue," *Journal of Business Finance and Accounting* 9, no. 2 (1982): 255–65; Lauren Kelly, "Corporate Management Lobbying on FAS No. 8: Some Further Evidence," *Journal of Accounting Research* 23, no. 2 (1985): 619–32; Francis, "Lobbying against Proposed Accounting Standards"; Deakin, "Rational Economic Behavior"; Patricia M. Dechow, Amy P. Hutton, and Richard G. Sloan, "Economic Consequences of Accounting for Stock-Based Compensation," *Journal of Accounting Research* 34, sup. (1996): 1–20.

87. Of course, Mr. Churchill intended this comment, made in August 1940, as a compliment to the pilots of the Royal Air Force who were, at the time, engaged in a fierce air battle to defend the United Kingdom from Nazi Germany. Here, I use the quote somewhat pejoratively. See Winston Churchill, "The Few" (speech, House of Commons, London, UK, August 1940), accessed February 2014, http://www.winstonchurchill.org/learn/speeches/speeches-of-winston-churchill/1940-finest-hour/113-the-few.

88. Accounting Principles Board, "Opinions of the Accounting Principles Board No. 25, Accounting for Stock Issued to Employees" (New York: American Institute of Certified Public Accountants, 1972).

89. Financial Accounting Standards Board, "Exposure Draft: Accounting for Stock-Based Compensation" (Stamford, CT: FASB, 1993).

90. Accounting Standards Reform Act, S. 2525, 103rd Cong. (1994).

91. For an overview of the events leading up to the FASB's issuance of SFAS 123, see, for example, D. Scott Lee et al., "Political Costs and the Fate of the FASB Proposal to Recognize the Costs of Employee Stock Options," *Journal of Financial Statement Analysis* 3 (1998): 67–79.

92. Financial Accounting Standards Board, "Statement of Financial Accounting Standards No. 123," accessed February 2014, http://www.fasb.org/pdf/fas123.pdf.

93. See, for example, Michael P. Coyne, "History Repeating Itself: The Debate over Accounting for Stock Options," *Pennsylvania Journal of Business and Economics* 10, no. 1 (2004): 1–14.

94. Financial Accounting Standards Board, "Statement of Financial Accounting Standards No. 123R," accessed February 2014, http://www.fasb.org/pdf/fas123r.pdf.

95. Financial Accounting Standards Board, "Accounting for Goodwill for Public Business Entities and Not-for-Profits," February 18, 2014, accessed February 2014, http://www.fasb.org/cs/ContentServer?c=FASBContent_C&pagename=FASB%2FFASBContent_C%2FProjectUpdatePage&cid=1176163679475.

Chapter Four

1. See, for example, Paul M. Healy and James M. Wahlen, "A Review of the Earnings Management Literature and Its Implications for Standard Setting," *Accounting Horizons* 13, no. 4 (1999): 365–83.

2. See, for example, William Z. Ripley, *Main Street and Wall Street* (Boston: Little, Brown, 1927); David F. Hawkins, "The Development of Modern Financial Reporting Practices among American Manufacturing Corporations," *Business History Review* 37, no. 3 (1963): 135–68; Joel Seligman, *The Transformation of Wall Street*, 3rd ed. (New York: Aspen Publishers, 2003). For a general history of the crash of 1929, see, for example, John K. Galbraith, *The Great Crash of 1929* (1929; repr. New York: Houghton Mifflin Harcourt, 2009).

3. Ollman v. Evans, 750 F.2d 970 (DC Cir. 1984).

4. See, for example, Ross L. Watts, "What Has the Invisible Hand Achieved?," *Accounting and Business Research* 36, sup. (2006): 51–61.

5. See, for example, Ross L. Watts and Jerold L. Zimmerman, "Agency Problems, Auditing and the Theory of the Firm: Some Evidence," *Journal of Law and Economics* 26, no. 3 (1983): 613–33.

6. See, for example, Paul M. Healy and Krishna G. Palepu, "The Fall of Enron," *Journal of Economic Perspectives* 17, no. 2 (2003): 3–26.

7. Sarbanes-Oxley Act of 2002, Pub. L. No. 107–204, 116 Stat. 745 (2002).

8. The academic literature in accounting generally recognizes the scale economies in auditing. See, for example, George J. Benston, "The Market for Public Accounting Services: Demand, Supply and Regulation," *Journal of Accounting and Public Policy* 4, no. 1 (1985): 33–79; Linda E. DeAngelo, "Auditor Size and Audit Quality," *Journal of Accounting and Economics* 3, no. 3 (1981): 183–99.

9. Government Accountability Office, "Public Accounting Firms: Mandated Study on Consolidation and Competition: July 2003," accessed January 2014, http://www.gao.gov/new.items/d03864.pdf.

10. Ibid.

11. Ibid.; Government Accountability Office, "Audits of Public Companies: Continued Concentration in Audit Market for Large Public Companies Does Not Call for Immediate Action: January 2008," accessed January 2014, http://www.gao.gov/new.items/d08163.pdf.

12. See, for example, Lawrence A. Cunningham, "Too Big to Fail: Moral Hazard in Auditing and the Need to Restructure the Industry before It Unravels," *Columbia Law Review* 106 (2006): 1698–1748; Paula Dwyer, "The Big Four: Too Few to Fail," *BusinessWeek*, August 31, 2003, accessed September 2013, http://www.businessweek.com/stories/2003-08-31/commentary-the-big-four-too-few-to-fail; Joseph Nocera, "Auditors: Too Few to Fail," *New York Times*, June 25, 2005, accessed September 2013, http://www.nytimes.com/2005/06/25/business/25nocera.html?pagewanted=all&_r=0.

13. Nocera, "Auditors."

14. See, for example, The Securities and Exchange Commission Historical Society, "In the Midst of Revolution: The SEC (1973–1981)," accessed January 2014, http://www.sechistorical.org/museum/galleries/rev/rev04e.php.

15. Ibid.

16. See John R. Haring Jr., "Accounting Rules and 'the Accounting Establishment,'" *Journal of Business* 52 (1979): 507–19; Paul R. Brown, "A Descriptive Analysis of Select Input Bases of the Financial Accounting Standards Board," *Journal of Accounting Research* 19, no. 1 (1981): 232–46.

17. See Ross L. Watts and Jerold L. Zimmerman, "Auditors and the Determination of Accounting Standards" (working paper GPB 78-06, University of Rochester, Rochester, NY, 1982); Marsha Puro, "Audit Firm Lobbying before the Financial Accounting Standards Board: An Empirical Study," *Journal of Accounting Research* 22, no. 2 (1984): 624–46. Also see Brandon Gipper, Brett Lombardi, and Douglas J. Skinner, "The Politics of Accounting Standard-Setting: A Review of Empirical Research," *Australian Journal of Management* 38, no. 3 (2013): 523–51.

18. Since the early 1980s, at least one empirical study has examined auditor lobbying at the Auditing Standards Board. See William R. Kinney, "Audit Technology and Preferences for Auditing Standards," *Journal of Accounting and Economics* 8 (1986): 73–89.

19. See, for example, Kent St. Pierre and James A. Anderson, "An Analysis of the Factors Associated with Lawsuits against Public Accountants," *Accounting Review* 59 (1984): 242–63; Thomas Lys and Ross L. Watts, "Lawsuits against Auditors," *Journal of Accounting Research* 32 (1994): 65–93; Ross L. Watts, "Conservatism in Accounting Part I: Explanations and Implications," *Accounting Horizons* 17, no. 3 (2003): 207–21.

20. See, for example, Thomas D. Fields, Thomas Z. Lys, and Linda Vincent, "Empirical Research on Accounting Choice," *Journal of Accounting and Economics* 31, no. 1 (2001): 255–307; Ross L. Watts and Jerold L. Zimmerman, *Positive Accounting Theory* (Englewood Cliffs, NJ: Prentice Hall, 1986).

21. See, for example, Francois Brochet, Krishna Palepu, and Lauren Barley, *Accounting for the iPhone at Apple, Inc.* (HBS No. 111-003) (Boston: Harvard Business School Publishing, 2011).

22. For a recent review of the incentives of auditors, as explored in empirical accounting research, see Mark L. DeFond and Jieying Zhang, "A Review of Archival Auditing Research" (working paper, University of Southern California, Los Angeles, CA, 2013).

23. On this point, also see Watts and Zimmerman, "Auditors and the Determination of Accounting Standards."

24. See Financial Accounting Standards Board, "Statement of Financial Accounting Concepts No. 2, May 1980," accessed November 2013, http://www.fasb.org/pdf/con2.pdf.

25. See, for example, Jay M. Feinman, "Liability of Accountants for Negligent Auditing: Doctrine, Policy, and Ideology," *Florida State Law Review* 31 (2003): 17–65; S. P. Kothari et al., "Auditor Liability and Information Disclosure," *Journal of Accounting, Auditing and Finance* 3 (1988): 307–39.

26. See, for example, Lys and Watts, "Lawsuits against Auditors."

27. Basic Inc. v. Levinson, 485 U.S. 224, 108 S. Ct. 978, 99 L. Ed. 2d 194 (1988).

28. See, for example, Feinman, "Liability of Accountants."

29. See, for example, Jong-Hag Choi, Rajib K. Doogar, and Ananda R. Ganguly, "The Riskiness of Large Audit Firm Client Portfolios and Changes in Audit Liability Regimes: Evidence from the U.S. Audit Market," *Contemporary Accounting Research* 21, no. 4 (2004): 747–85.

30. See, for example, Ashiq Ali and Sanjay Kallapur, "Securities Price Consequences of the Private Securities Litigation Reform Act of 1995 and Related Events," *Accounting Review* 76, no. 3 (2001): 431–60.

31. See, for example, Steven F. Cahan and Wei Zhang, "After Enron: Auditor Conservatism and Ex-Andersen Clients," *Accounting Review* 81, no. 1 (2006): 49–82.

32. This argument is an extension of the "deep pocket" theory of litigation and the "political costs" hypothesis in accounting. For more on the deep pocket theory, see, for example, Guido Calabresi, *The Cost of Accidents: A Legal and Economic Analysis* (New Haven, CT: Yale University Press, 1970); Zoe-Vonna Palmrose, "An Analysis of Auditor Litigation and Audit Service Quality," *Accounting Review* 63 (1988): 55–73. For more on the political costs hypothesis, see, for

example, Ross L. Watts and Jerold L. Zimmerman, "Towards a Positive Theory of the Determination of Accounting Standards," *Accounting Review* 53, no. 1 (1978): 112–34.

33. More details on the regression design, control variables, alternative explanations, and robustness tests are found in my paper, "The Auditing Oligopoly and Lobbying on Accounting Standards" (working paper 13-054, Harvard Business School, Boston, MA, 2013), coauthored with Professor Abigail Allen of HBS and Professor Sugata Roychowdhury of Boston College.

34. Table 4.2 excludes data for the year 1987 because no Big N auditor assessments of FASB exposure drafts were available for that year at the time we initiated the study.

35. The period begins in 1977 rather than 1973 because the year 1976 saw an important court case (Ernst & Ernst v. Hochfelder) that reduced auditor liability. Thus the 1973–76 period is strictly distinct from the 1977–83 period. Ernst & Ernst v. Hochfelder, 425 U.S. 185, 96 S. Ct. 1375, 47 L. Ed. 2d 668 (1976).

36. For a description of some factors that could have precipitated audit industry consolidation, see Government Accountability Office, "Public Accounting Firms."

37. See, for example, S. P. Kothari, Karthik Ramanna, and Douglas J. Skinner, "Implications for GAAP from an Analysis of Positive Research in Accounting," *Journal of Accounting and Economics* 50, nos. 2–3 (2010): 246–86.

38. See Securities and Exchange Commission, "SEC Establishes Advisory Committee to Make U.S. Financial Reporting System More User-Friendly for Investors," news release, June 27, 2007, accessed January 2014, http://www.sec.gov/news/press/2007/2007-123.htm. For the final report of the committee, see Securities and Exchange Commission, *Final Report of the Advisory Committee on Improvements to Financial Reporting to the United States Securities and Exchange Commission*, August 1, 2008, accessed September 2013, http://www.sec.gov/about/offices/oca/acifr/acifr-finalreport.pdf.

39. For a description of constituent responses to the SEC committee on the future of financial reporting, see, for example, Karthik Ramanna, *The Future of Financial Reporting* (HBS video case No. 110-701) (Boston: Harvard Business School Publishing, January 2010).

40. Financial Accounting Standards Board, "Summary of Statement No. 159," accessed January 2014, http://www.fasb.org/summary/stsum159.shtml.

41. KPMG, "KPMG to Financial Accounting Standards Board," Letter of Comment No. 58, file ref. 1250-001 (Norwalk, CT: FASB, 2006), 1.

42. Ernst & Young, "Ernst & Young to Financial Accounting Standards Board," Letter of Comment No. 67, file ref. 1250-001 (Norwalk, CT: FASB, 2006), 1.

43. Deloitte & Touche, "Deloitte & Touche to Financial Accounting Standards Board," Letter of Comment No. 47, file ref. 1250-001 (Norwalk, CT: FASB, 2006), 1.

44. Public Company Accounting Oversight Board, "SAS No. 101: Auditing Fair-Value Measurement and Disclosures," accessed January 2014, http://pcaobus.org/Standards/Auditing/Pages/AU328.aspx.

45. Fait v. Regions Financial Corp., 655 F.3d 105 (2d Cir. 2011).

46. See, for example, Paul Dutka, "Defending 1993 ACT Claims: Rewriting the Playbook after Fait v. Regions Fin. Corp," *Bloomberg Law*, August 27, 2013, accessed January 2014, http://about.bloomberglaw.com/practitioner-contributions/defending-1933-act-claims-rewriting-the-playbook-after-fait-v-regions-fin-corp; Brad S. Karp and Paul Weiss, "Second Circuit Clarifies Materiality Requirement in Securities Fraud Cases," *Harvard Law School Forum on Corporate Governance and Financial Regulation* (blog), September 10, 2011, accessed January 2014, https://blogs.law.harvard.edu/corpgov/tag/fait-v-regions-financial.

Chapter Five

1. The Securities and Exchange Commission Historical Society, "The Richard C. Adkerson Gallery on the SEC Role in Accounting Standards Setting: Financial Accounting Standards Board (1973–Present)," accessed September 2013, http://www.sechistorical.org/museum/galleries/rca/rca04d-fasb-organization.php.

2. The Securities and Exchange Commission Historical Society, "The Richard C. Adkerson Gallery on the SEC Role in Accounting Standards Setting: Accounting Principles Board (1959–1973)," accessed September 2013, http://www.sechistorical.org/museum/galleries/rca/rca04b-fasb-organization.php.

3. The precise compensation levels for members of the FASB are unknown, but annual compensation is expected to exceed U.S. $500,000, based on data released by the FASB in 2006. See, for example, David M. Katz, "Hot Times for Accounting Officials," CFO, March 11, 2008, accessed December 2013, http://ww2.cfo.com/accounting-tax/2008/03/hot-times-for-accounting-officials.

4. American Institute of Certified Public Accountants, *Report of the Study on Establishment of Accounting Principles: Establishing Financial Accounting Standards, March 1972* (New York: American Institute of Certified Public Accountants, 1972).

5. See, for example, Joseph P. Kalt and Mark A. Zupan, "Capture and Ideology in the Economic Theory of Politics," *American Economic Review* 74, no. 3 (1984): 279–300.

6. See, for example, Marianne Bertrand and Antoinette Schoar, "Managing with Style: The Effect of Managers on Firm Policies," *Quarterly Journal of Economics* 118, no. 4 (2003): 1169–1208; Linda S. Bamber, John Jiang, and Isabel Y. Wang, "What's My Style? The Influence of Top Managers on Voluntary Corporate Financial Disclosure," *Accounting Review* 85, no. 4 (2010): 1131–62; Scott D. Dyreng, Michelle Hanlon, and Edward L. Maydew, "The Effects of Executives on Corporate Tax Avoidance," *Accounting Review* 85, no. 4 (2010): 1163–89; Weili Ge, Dawn Matsumoto, and Jenny L. Zhang, "Do CFOs Have Style? An Empirical Investigation of the Effect of Individual CFOs on Accounting Practices," *Contemporary Accounting Research* 28, no. 4 (2011): 1141–79.

7. For some of the first evidence on the role of constituent lobbying in accounting rule-making, see, for example, Marsha Puro, "Audit Firm Lobbying before the Financial Accounting Standards Board: An Empirical Study," *Journal of Accounting Research* 22, no. 2 (1984): 624–46; Ross L. Watts and Jerold L. Zimmerman, "Towards a Positive Theory of the Determination of Accounting Standards," *Accounting Review* 53, no. 1 (1978): 112–34.

8. Financial Accounting Standards Board, "Statement of Financial Accounting Concepts No. 2, May 1980," accessed November 2013, http://www.fasb.org/pdf/con2.pdf.

9. Financial Accounting Standards Board, "Conceptual Framework: Statement of Financial Accounting Concepts No. 8 September 2010," accessed November 2013, http://www.fasb.org/jsp/FASB/Page/PreCodSectionPage&cid=1176156317989.

10. See, for example, Thomas Dyckman, Robert P. Magee, and Glenn Pfeiffer, *Financial Accounting*, 3rd ed. (Westmont, IL: Cambridge Business Publishers, 2011); Clyde P. Stickney et al., *Financial Accounting*, 13th ed. (Mason, OH: South-Western Cengage Learning, 2010).

11. These data were made available thanks to the generous cooperation of the Financial Accounting Foundation.

12. On the role of macroeconomic conditions on accounting policy making, see, for example, Jeremy Bertomeu and Robert P. Magee, "From Low-Quality Reporting to Financial Crises:

Politics of Disclosure Regulation along the Economic Cycle," *Journal of Accounting and Economics* 52, no. 2 (2011): 209–27.

13. Financial Accounting Standards Board, "FASB Standard Establishes Fair Value Option for Financial Assets and Liabilities," news release, February 15, 2007, accessed January 2014, http://www.fasb.org/news/nr021507.shtml.

14. Financial Accounting Standards Board, "Summary of Statement No. 157," accessed January 2014, http://www.fasb.org/summary/stsum157.shtml.

15. See, for example, William T. Gormley Jr., "A Test of the Revolving Door Hypothesis at the FCC," *American Journal of Political Science* 23 (1979): 665–83; Jeffrey E. Cohen, "The Dynamics of the 'Revolving Door' on the FCC," *American Journal of Political Science* 30 (1986): 689–708; Clare Leaver, "Bureaucratic Minimal Squawk Behavior: Theory and Evidence from Regulatory Agencies," *American Economic Review* 99 (2009): 572–607. For a recent review, see Ernesto Dal Bo, "Regulatory Capture: A Review," *Oxford Review of Economic Policy* 22, no. 2 (2006): 203–25.

16. George J. Stigler, "The Theory of Economic Regulation," *Bell Journal of Economics and Management Science* 2 (1971): 3–21.

17. See, for example, Cohen, "The Dynamics of the 'Revolving Door.'"

18. On this point, also see Robert L. Kellogg, "Accounting Activities, Security Prices, and Class Action Lawsuits," *Journal of Accounting and Economics* 6, no. 3 (1984): 185–204; Ross L. Watts, "Conservatism in Accounting Part I: Explanations and Implications," *Accounting Horizons* 17 (2003): 207–21. Further, for some survey-based evidence on auditors' incentives, see Mark W. Nelson, John A. Elliott, and Robin L. Tarpley, "Evidence from Auditors about Managers' and Auditors' Earnings Management Decisions," *Accounting Review* 77, no. s-1 (2002): 175–202.

19. On this point, see, for example, the comment letter by the Investment Company Institute, the U.S. industry association for investment management firms, filed during the financial crisis in 2008. The letter strongly supported the use of fair-value accounting. Also see the discussions concerning the three major investment banks and fair-value rules for acquired goodwill in chapter 3. Investment Company Institute, "Comment Letter by CEO Paul S. Stevens on the SEC's Request for Comment on Mark-to-Market Accounting," accessed April 2011, http://www.ici.org/pdf/23068.pdf.

20. See, for example, Gormley, "A Test of the Revolving Door."

21. Figures 5.1–5.3 exclude data for the year 1987 because this year was not part of our study. No Big N auditor assessments of FASB exposure drafts were available for 1987 at the time we initiated the study; thus the year 1987 could not be included in regression analyses.

22. Because the "financial services" category is limited to FASB members from investment banking and investment management, one FASB member, Frank E. Block, a financial analyst, is not included in this category. Mr. Block served on the FASB from 1979 to 1985.

23. The president of the United States appoints the SEC commissioners, but no more than three of the five commissioners at any time can belong to the same political party. Note that the proportion of SEC commissioners from a political party *can* sometimes exceed three-fifths because of vacancies between appointments.

24. In supplemental tests, we recompute the explanatory variables using the average background characteristics of only those FASB members who assented to the ED when it was finally approved in GAAP—that is, we eliminate the background characteristics of dissenting FASB members from the regressions. The results under this alternative specification are substantively similar to those discussed here.

25. On this point, see, for example, the discussion in Dal Bo, "Regulatory Capture."

26. More details on the regression design, control variables, alternative explanations, and robustness tests are found in my paper, "Towards an Understanding of the Role of Standard Setters in Standard Setting," coauthored with Professor Abigail Allen and published in the *Journal of Accounting and Economics* 55, no. 1 (2013): 66–90.

27. For an overview of the theory of ideology, see, for example, Kalt and Zupan, "Capture and Ideology"; Torsten Persson and Guido E. Tabellini, *Political Economics: Explaining Economic Policy* (Cambridge, MA: MIT Press, 2002); Gene M. Grossman and Elhanan Helpman, *Special Interest Politics* (Cambridge, MA: MIT Press, 2001).

28. See, for example, Mary E. Barth, William H. Beaver, and Wayne R. Landsman, "The Relevance of the Value Relevance Literature for Financial Accounting Standard Setting: Another View," *Journal of Accounting and Economics* 31, nos. 1–3 (2001): 77–104.

29. See, for example, Watts, "Conservatism in Accounting Part I."

30. See, for example, Solomon Fabricant, "Revaluations of Fixed Assets, 1925–1934," *National Bureau of Economic Research* 62 (1936): 1–12; Kristin Ely and Gregory Waymire, "Intangible Assets and Stock Prices in the Pre-SEC Era," *Journal of Accounting Research* 37, sup. (1999): 17–44; Jan Barton and Gregory Waymire, "Investor Protection under Unregulated Financial Reporting," *Journal of Accounting and Economics* 38 (2004): 65–116.

31. See, for example, Stephen A. Zeff, "The SEC Rules Historical Cost Accounting: 1934 to the 1970s," *Accounting and Business Research* 37, sup-1 (2007): 49–62.

32. For a critical review of the market-association studies on fair-value accounting, see Robert W. Holthausen and Ross L. Watts, "The Relevance of the Value-Relevance Literature for Financial Accounting Standard Setting," *Journal of Accounting and Economics* 31, nos. 1–3 (2001): 3–75. For an alternative view, see Barth, Beaver, and Landsman, "The Relevance of the Value Relevance."

33. Paul M. Healy and Krishna G. Palepu, "The Fall of Enron," *Journal of Economic Perspectives* 17, no. 2 (2003): 10.

34. See, for example, Stephen G. Ryan, "Accounting in and for the Subprime Crisis," *Accounting Review* 83, no. 6 (2008): 1605–38.

35. See, for example, S. P. Kothari and Rebecca Lester, "The Role of Accounting in the Financial Crisis: Lessons for the Future," *Accounting Horizons* 26, no. 2 (2012): 335–51.

36. See, for example, Christian Laux and Christian Leuz, "Did Fair-Value Accounting Contribute to the Financial Crisis?" *Journal of Economic Perspectives* 24, no. 1 (2010): 113, and the citations therein.

37. Disclosure Insight, "Bank Goodwill Impairment Study," March 2009, accessed March 2015, https://www.sec.gov/comments/4-573/4573-230.pdf.

38. See, for example, Robin Greenwood and David Scharfstein, "The Growth of Finance," *Journal of Economic Perspectives* 27, no. 2 (2013): 3–28.

39. Data are from Greenwood and Scharfstein, "The Growth of Finance."

40. For example, as of 2013, the FAF's public descriptions on its website of its roles and responsibilities include little detail on the process underlying the appointment of FASB members.

41. Financial Accounting Foundation, "The Financial Accounting Foundation Board of Trustees Approves Changes to Oversight, Structure and Operations of FAF, FASB and GASB," news release, February 26, 2008, accessed February 2014, http://www.fasb.org/jsp/FASB/Page/nr022608.pdf.

42. Financial Accounting Standards Board, "Financial Accounting Foundation to Increase

Size of FASB: FASB Chairman Herz to Retire after More than Eight Successful Years," news release, August 24, 2010, accessed January 2014, http://www.fasb.org/cs/ContentServer?pagename
=FASB/FASBContent_C/NewsPage&cid=1176157228010.

43. On this point, see the discussion in Joni J. Young, "Making up Users," *Accounting, Organizations and Society* 31, no. 6 (2006): 579–600.

44. See, in particular, Zeff, "The SEC Rules Historical Cost Accounting."

45. The chairman was Richard Breeden, who served from 1989 to 1993; the chief accountant
was Walter Schuetze, who served from 1992 to 1995.

46. The SEC's position on fair value for property, plant, and equipment is unclear. I thank
Professor Steve Zeff for bringing this to my attention.

47. See, for example, Randall S. Kroszner and Thomas Stratmann, "Interest-Group Competition and the Organization of Congress: Theory and Evidence from Financial Services' Political
Action Committees," *American Economic Review* 88, no. 5 (1998): 1163–87.

48. Jivas Chakravarthy, "The Ideological Homogenization of the FASB" (working paper,
Emory University, Atlanta, GA, 2014).

49. For this analysis, "fair-value-increasing GAAP rules" are those identified as such based
on data supplied by the two seasoned research associates who evaluated FASB EDs for their impact on accounting relevance and reliability (see the earlier discussion in this chapter).

50. There is a rich exploration of the notion of ideological capture, particularly as it relates
to the technology of market capitalism, in sociology literature. See, for example, Marion Fourcade, *Economists and Societies: Discipline and Profession in the United States, Britain, & France,
1890s to 1990s* (Princeton, NJ: Princeton University Press, 2009). A precursor to the notion of
ideological capture in accounting can be found in Michael Power, "The Politics of Brand Accounting in the United Kingdom," *European Accounting Review* 1, no. 1 (1992): 39–68. For an
economics-based discussion of ideological capture, see, for example, Luigi Zingales, "Preventing Economists' Capture," in *Preventing Regulatory Capture*, eds. Daniel Carpenter and David A. Moss (New York: Cambridge University Press, 2014), 124–51. The role of ideology in
facilitating capture is also a theme in the creation of "political bubbles" as described by Nolan
McCarty, Keith T. Poole, and Howard Rosenthal, *Political Bubbles: Financial Crises and the Failure of American Democracy* (Princeton, NJ: Princeton University Press, 2013).

51. See, for example, L. Todd Johnson, "Relevance and Reliability," *FASB Report*, February 28, 2005, accessed November 2013, http://www.fasb.org/articles&reports/relevance_and
_reliability_tfr_feb_2005.pdf.

Chapter Six

1. For an overview of the IFRS phenomenon, see, for example, Ray Ball, "International
Financial Reporting Standards (IFRS): Pros and Cons for Investors," *Accounting and Business
Research* 36, no. 1 (2006): 5–27.

2. For an overview of the political process in accounting in the European Union, see, for
example, Chapters 5 and 6 of Christian Leuz, Dieter Pfaff, and Anthony Hopwood, eds., *The
Economics and Politics of Accounting: International Perspectives on Research Trends, Policy, and
Practice* (New York: Oxford University Press, 2004).

3. International Financial Reporting Standards, "About the IFRS Foundation and the IASB,"
accessed November 2013, http://www.ifrs.org/The-organisation/Pages/IFRS-Foundation-and
-the-IASB.aspx; Financial Accounting Standards Board, "International Convergence of Ac-

counting Standards—A Brief History," accessed November 2013, http://www.fasb.org/jsp/FASB/Page/SectionPage&cid=1176156304264.

4. George J. Benston et al., *Worldwide Financial Reporting: The Development and Future of Accounting Standards* (New York: Oxford University Press, 2006), 230.

5. For evidence on the central role for U.S. interests in IFRS standard setting, see, for example, Tim Büthe and Walter Mattli, *The New Global Rulers: The Privatization of Regulation in the World Economy* (Princeton, NJ: Princeton University Press, 2011).

6. Greg Hitt and Michael Schroeder, "Enron Hoped to Extend Influence to International Accounting Group," *Wall Street Journal*, February 14, 2002, accessed January 2014, http://online.wsj.com/news/articles/SB101364132635637280.

7. 107th Cong. Rec. S736, daily ed., February 13, 2002.

8. See, in particular, chapters 12 and 13 of Kees Camfferman and Stephen A. Zeff, *Financial Reporting and Global Capital Markets: A History of the International Accounting Standards Committee, 1973–2000* (New York: Oxford University Press, 2007).

9. Ibid., 17.

10. Strictly speaking, the EU maintains an independent process to evaluate each IFRS. Due to modifications that can emerge in this process, the EU's version of IFRS is not identical to that issued by the IASB.

11. European Parliament, "Proposal for a European Parliament and Council Regulation on the Application of International Accounting Standards," accessed November 2013, http://www.europarl.europa.eu/sides/getDoc.do?type=REPORT&reference=A5-2002-0070&language=EN.

12. See, for example, Norris (2010) and the discussion and citations in Laux and Leuz (2009). Floyd Norris, "New Cast Enters Fight in Accounting," *New York Times*, October 22, 2010; Christian Laux and Christian Leuz, "The Crisis of Fair-Value Accounting: Making Sense of the Recent Debate," *Accounting, Organizations and Society* 34, no. 6 (2009): 826–34.

13. See, for example, John Christoffersen, "Board Approves New Guidance for Accounting Rules That Could Help Ease Financial Crisis," *Associated Press Newswires*, October 10, 2008.

14. Council of the European Union, "Immediate Responses to Financial Turmoil, Council Conclusions—Ecofin Council of 7 October 2008," accessed November 2013, http://www.consilium.europa.eu/uedocs/cms_Data/docs/pressdata/en/misc/103202.pdf.

15. Reclassifying entities were required to disclose in footnotes results absent reclassification.

16. International Financial Reporting Standards, "Reclassification of Financial Assets, Amendments to IAS 39 Financial Instruments: Recognition and Measurement and IFRS 7 Financial Instruments; Disclosures, October 2008," accessed November 2013, http://www.ifrs.org/News/Press-Releases/Documents/AmdmentsIAS39andIFRS7.pdf.

17. This turn of events led at least one British parliamentarian to refer to the board as "spineless." Marie Leone, "'Spineless?' UK Pressure Targets Fair Value Weakening," *CFO*, November 11, 2008, accessed November 2013, http://www.cfo.com/article.cfm/12586836?f=related.

18. Karthik Ramanna and Ewa Sletten, "Network Effects in Countries' Adoption of IFRS," *Accounting Review* 89, no. 4 (2014): 1517–43.

19. On the complementarities of accounting standards with local institutions, see, for example, Ball, Kothari, and Robin (2000), Ball (2006), and Leuz (2010). Ramanna and Sletten (2009) discuss hypotheses on the degree and timing of countries' IFRS harmonization. Ray Ball, S. P. Kothari, and Ashok Robin, "The Effect of International Institutional Factors on Properties of Accounting Earnings," *Journal of Accounting and Economics* 29, no. 1 (2000): 1–51; Ball,

"International Financial Reporting Standards (IFRS)"; Christian Leuz, "Different Approaches to Corporate Reporting Regulation: How Jurisdictions Differ and Why," *Accounting and Business Research* 40, no. 3 (2010): 229−56; Karthik Ramanna and Ewa Sletten, "Why Do Countries Adopt International Financial Reporting Standards?" (working paper 09-102, Harvard Business School, Boston, MA, 2009).

20. Securities and Exchange Commission, "SEC Staff Publishes Final Report on Work Plan for Global Accounting Standards," press release, July 13, 2012, accessed November 2013, http://www.sec.gov/news/press/2012/2012-135.htm; Securities and Exchange Commission, *Work Plan for the Consideration of Incorporating International Financial Reporting Standards into the Financial Reporting System for U.S. Issuers: Final Staff Report*, accessed November 2013, http://www.sec.gov/spotlight/globalaccountingstandards/ifrs-work-plan-final-report.pdf.

21. See, for example, Floyd Norris, "Accounting Détente Delayed," *New York Times*, July 19, 2012.

22. See, for example, Karthik Ramanna, Karol Misztal, and Daniela Beyersdorfer, *The IASB at a Crossroads: The Future of International Financial Reporting Standards (B)* (HBS No. 113-089) (Boston: Harvard Business School Publishing, 2013).

23. The World Bank Group, "World Development Indicators," accessed November 2013, http://data.worldbank.org/data-catalog/world-development-indicators.

24. Organisation for Economic Co-operation and Development, "Economic Survey of China 2013," accessed November 2013, http://www.oecd.org/economy/china-2013.

25. The World Bank Group, "World Development Indicators," accessed September 2009, http://data.worldbank.org/data-catalog/world-development-indicators.

26. World Federation of Exchanges, "Statistics," accessed October 2012, http://www.world-exchanges.org/statistics.

27. Data compiled from various sources by Karthik Ramanna, G. A. Donovan, and Nancy Dai, *IFRS in China* (HBS No. 110-037) (Boston: Harvard Business School Publishing, 2009).

28. New York Stock Exchange, "NYSE Euronext and Greater China," accessed September 2009, http://www.nyse.com/pdfs/NYSEEuronext_China_factsheet-CN.pdf.

29. See, for example, Mark L. DeFond, T. J. Wong, and Shuhua Li, "The Impact of Improved Auditor Independence on Audit Market Concentration in China," *Journal of Accounting and Economics* 28, no. 3 (1999): 269−305; Yunwei Tang, "Bumpy Road Leading to Internationalization: A Review of Accounting Development in China," *Accounting Horizons* 14, no. 1 (2000): 93−102.

30. Deloitte Touche Tohmatsu Limited, "China Adopts 38 New Accounting Standards," *IASPlus*, February 16, 2006, accessed November 2013, http://www.iasplus.com/en/news/2006/February/news2654; Ministry of Finance, "British 'Financial Times': China Will Be Part of the Adoption of International Accounting Standards," February 16, 2006, accessed November 2013, http://www.mof.gov.cn/zhuantihuigu/kjsjzzfbh/mtbd/200805/t20080519_23014.html; Ministry of Finance, "Wang: Chinese Language Has Been with the International Accounting Standards Convergence," February 28, 2007, accessed November 2013, http://www.mof.gov.cn/zhengwuxinxi/caijingshidian/xinhuanet/200805/t20080519_25808.html.

31. For evidence on such benefits, see, for example, Christopher S. Armstrong et al., "Market Reaction to the Adoption of IFRS in Europe," *Accounting Review* 85, no. 1 (2010): 31−61.

32. The World Bank Group, "World Development Indicators," accessed September 2009, http://data.worldbank.org/data-catalog/world-development-indicators.

33. European Commission, "Council Regulation No. 1174/2005," accessed November 2013, http://eur-lex.europa.eu/LexUriServ/LexUriServ.do?uri=OJ:L:2005:189:0001:0014:EN:PDF, 7.

34. World Trade Organization, "Accession of the People's Republic of China," November 10, 2001, accessed June 2011, http://www.wto.org/english/thewto_e/acc_e/protocols_acc_membership_e.htm, 8–9.

35. Ibid., 9.

36. See, for example, the World Trade Organization's statistics on antidumping initiations at World Trade Organization, "Anti-Dumping," accessed November 2013, http://www.wto.org/english/tratop_e/adp_e/adp_e.htm#statistics.

37. World Trade Organization, "Accession of the People's Republic of China," 9.

38. See, for example, European Commission, "Council Regulation No. 1225/2009," accessed November 2013, http://trade.ec.europa.eu/doclib/docs/2010/april/tradoc_146035.pdf, 55.

39. See, for example, European Commission, "Council Regulation No. 1174/2005," 7.

40. The United States generally does not allow individual companies from nonmarket economies to qualify for market economy treatment. A recent attempt by the U.S. government to permit such treatment for Chinese companies met with resistance from U.S. businesses and was unsuccessful. See Department of Commerce, "Antidumping Methodologies in Proceedings Involving Certain Non-Market Economies: Market-Oriented Enterprise," *Federal Register* 72, no. 101 (2007): 29302–4; International Trade Administration, "Public Comments Received on Antidumping Methodologies in Proceedings Involving Certain Non-Market Economies: Market-Oriented Enterprise (72 FR 29302)," June 25, 2007, accessed November 2013, http://ia.ita.doc.gov/download/nme-moe/nme-moe-cmt-20070625-index.html.

41. European Commission, "Council Regulation No. 1042/2010," accessed November 2013, http://eur-lex.europa.eu/LexUriServ/LexUriServ.do?uri=OJ:L:2010:299:0007:0028:EN:PDF, 12.

42. "Global 500: China," *Fortune*, accessed October 2009, http://money.cnn.com/magazines/fortune/global500/2009/countries/China.html.

43. Quote from an official at the Shenzhen Stock Exchange, identity withheld. Ramanna, Donovan, and Dai, *IFRS in China*, 6.

44. Richard McGregor, "China Adopts New Accounting Standards," *Financial Times*, February 16, 2006, accessed January 2014, http://www.ft.com/cms/s/0/c69ba44a-9e07-11da-b641-0000779e2340.html#axzz2sr2B0Mv2.

45. Deloitte Touche Tohmatsu Limited, "Amendments to IAS 24 Related Party Disclosures," *IASPlus: IASB Agenda Project*, accessed October 2009, http://www.iasplus.com/agenda/relatedparty.htm.

46. International Accounting Standard Board, "IASB Simplifies Requirements for Disclosure of Related-Party Transactions," press release, accessed February 2015, http://www.ifrs.org/News/Press-Releases/Documents/IASBsimplifiesrequirementsfordisclosureofrelatedpartytransactions2.pdf.

47. IASB, "IASB Simplifies Requirements."

48. See, for example, "Tata Corus Taking Big Steps to Streamline Ops," *Moneycontrol*, October 13, 2007, accessed November 2013, http://www.moneycontrol.com/video/business/tata-corus-taking-big-steps-to-streamline-ops-_307914.html.

49. Koushik Chatterjee, interview by Karthik Ramanna, via telephone, February 22, 2010.

50. Hedging in corporations refers to the practice of lowering firm exposure to uncertain market events such as fluctuations in exchange rates, interest rates, and commodity prices. Hedging strategies can broadly be thought of as "operational" or "financial." Operational hedges lower risks by restructuring real transactions (such as in the Tata Steel case where the loan was restructured as a euro-denominated loan). Financial hedges do not alter real transactions; they usually involve the purchase and sale of derivative instruments as offsets to the real risks.

51. Tata Steel, *2007–2008 Annual Report*, accessed May 2010, http://www.tatasteel.com/investors/annual-report-07-08/annual-report-07-08.pdf, 28.

52. See, for example, PricewaterhouseCoopers, "Similarities and Differences: A Comparison of IFRS, US GAAP, and Indian GAAP," accessed November 2013, http://www.pwc.in/assets/pdfs/india-publications-similarities-differences.pdf, 87.

53. Tata Steel, *2007–2008 Annual Report*, 28.

54. Chatterjee, interview.

55. Ibid.

56. Ibid.

57. Ibid.

58. Kalai N. Selvan, *Tata's Business and Growth Strategy* (Hyderabad, India: Icfai University Press, 2008).

59. See, for example, Tarun Khanna, Krishna G. Palepu, and Richard J. Bullock, *House of Tata: Acquiring a Global Footprint* (HBS No. 708-446) (Boston: Harvard Business School Publishing, 2009).

60. "Innovation: Tata Ahead of BMW, Nokia, Dell!" *Rediff Business News*, April 16, 2010, accessed April 2010, http://business.rediff.com/slide-show/2010/apr/16/slide-show-1-innovation-tata-ahead-of-bmw-nokia-dell.htm.

61. Tata Group, "The Quotable Jamsetji Tata," March 2008, accessed April 2010, http://www.tata.com/aboutus/articles/inside.aspx?artid=1U2QamAhqtA=.

62. Press Information Bureau, "Prime Minister Addresses the Tata Centenary Celebrations," press release, April 22, 2008, accessed April 2010, http://www.pib.nic.in/release/release.asp?relid=37731.

63. Chatterjee, interview.

64. Y. H. Malegam, interview by Karthik Ramanna, Mumbai, India, January 8, 2010.

65. See, for example, KPMG, "Additional Relief on Foreign Exchange Capitalization," 2012, accessed December 2013, http://www.moneycontrol.com/news_html_files/news_attachment/2012/Flash%20News%20-%20Additional%20relief%20on%20foreign%20exchange%20capitalisation%20Final.pdf.

66. Tata Steel, *2008–2009 Annual Report*, accessed December 2013, http://www.tatasteel.com/media/pdf/annual-report-2008-09.pdf, 172.

67. S. D. Bala, "The effects of changes in AS 11 rules," *Hindu Business Line*, April 16, 2009.

68. See, for example, KPMG, "Additional Relief."

69. A more appropriate solution to this problem likely involves relaxing capital controls on the functional currency (in this case, the Indian rupee) so that multinational companies can raise functional-currency debt in overseas markets.

70. "Goodwill Hunting: What the Corus Write-Off Reveals," *Economist*, May 18, 2013, accessed November 2013, http://www.economist.com/news/business/21578082-what-corus-write-reveals-goodwill-hunting.

Chapter Seven

1. Bureau of Economic Analysis, "Gross Domestic Product by Industry," accessed October 2013, http://www.bea.gov.

2. See, for example, David Reilly and Michael Rapoport, "Early Exit of FASB Chairman Raises Anxiety," *Wall Street Journal*, August 25, 2010, accessed October 2013, http://online.wsj.com/news/articles/SB10001424052748704125604575450073232699814.

3. John J. Brennan, interview by Karthik Ramanna and Luis Viceira, Cambridge, MA, July 6, 2012.

4. Ibid.

5. Ibid.

6. Ibid.

7. Securities and Exchange Commission, "The Laws That Govern the Securities Industry," accessed October 2012, http://www.sec.gov/about/laws.shtml.

8. Cynthia Glassman, "Complexity in Financial Reporting and Disclosure Regulation" (speech, Twenty-fifth Annual USC Leventhal School of Accounting SEC and Financial Reporting Institute Conference, Pasadena, CA, June 8, 2006).

9. Steve Feilmeier, interview by Karthik Ramanna, New York, July 30, 2012.

10. Mark Bielstein, interview by Karthik Ramanna and Luis Viceira, Norwalk, CT, July 27, 2012.

11. Feilmeier, interview.

12. When a bank's credit rating falls, the fair value of its liabilities also falls (because interest rates rise); the resulting change in fair values is recognized as income in the bank's financial statements. For example, in Q1 of 2009, Citigroup added $30 million to its bottom line from a credit rating downgrade of its own bond debt. Citigroup, "Form 10-Q," March 31, 2009, accessed January 2014, http://www.sec.gov/Archives/edgar/data/831001/000104746909005290/a2192899z10-q.htm.

13. Feilmeier, interview.

14. Ibid.

15. Ibid.

16. Ibid.

17. Jay R. Ritter, Xiaohui Gao, and Zhongyan Zhu, "Where Have All the IPOs Gone?" (working paper, University of Florida, Gainesville, FL, 2012).

18. "Whatever Happened to IPOs?" *Wall Street Journal*, March 22, 2011, accessed April 2012, http://online.wsj.com/article/SB10001424052748704662604576203002012714150.html?mod=googlenews_wsj.

19. James Freeman, "The Supreme Case against Sarbanes-Oxley," *Wall Street Journal*, December 15, 2009, accessed September 2012, http://online.wsj.com/article/SB10001424052748704431804574539921864252380.html.

20. Christian Leuz, Alexander J. Triantis, and Tracy Yue Wang, "Why Do Firms Go Dark? Causes and Economic Consequences of Voluntary SEC Deregistration," *Journal of Accounting and Economics* 45, nos. 2–3 (2008): 181–208.

21. Bielstein, interview.

22. Daryl Buck, interview by Karthik Ramanna and Luis Viceira, Norwalk, CT, July 27, 2012.

23. Leslie Seidman, interview by Karthik Ramanna and Luis Viceira, Norwalk, CT, July 27, 2012.

24. Bielstein, interview.

25. Financial Accounting Foundation, "Request for Comment: Plan to Establish the Private Company Standards Improvement Council, October 4, 2011," accessed April 2012, http://www.accountingfoundation.org/cs/ContentServer?site=Foundation&c=Document_C&pagename=Foundation%2FDocument_C%2FFAFDocumentPage&cid=1176158991959.

26. Judith Kamnikar, Edward Kamnikar, and Ashley Burrowes, "One Size Does Not Fit All," *Journal of Accountancy* 213, no. 1 (2012): 46.

27. American Institute of Certified Public Accountants, *Report to the Board of Trust-*

ees of the Financial Accounting Foundation, Blue Ribbon Panel on Standard Setting for Private Companies, January 2011, accessed April 2012, http://www.aicpa.org/interestareas/frc/accountingfinancialreporting/pcfr/downloadabledocuments/blue_ribbon_panel_report.pdf.

28. Financial Accounting Foundation, "Request for Comment."

29. Terri Polley, interview by Karthik Ramanna and Luis Viceira, Norwalk, CT, July 27, 2012.

30. Ibid.

31. Ibid.

32. Ibid.

33. Barry Melancon, interview by Karthik Ramanna and Luis Viceira, Norwalk, CT, July 27, 2012.

34. Polley, interview, July 27, 2012.

35. Terri Polley, telephone interview by Karthik Ramanna and Luis Viceira, November 30, 2012.

36. Melancon, interview.

37. Melancon, interview.

38. Polley, interview, July 27, 2012.

39. American Institute of Certified Public Accountants, *Report to the Board of Trustees*.

40. Ibid., 22.

41. Polley, interview, July 27, 2012.

42. Melancon, interview.

43. Ibid.

44. Polley, interview, July 27, 2012.

45. Financial Accounting Foundation, "Request for Comment."

46. Ibid.

47. Melancon, interview.

48. Ibid.

49. Thomas Quaadman, interview by Karthik Ramanna and Luis Viceira, Norwalk, CT, July 27, 2012.

50. David Morgan, "Private Company Reporting Needs and Independent Board," *Accounting Today* 26, no. 1 (2012): 11.

51. Bielstein, interview.

52. PricewaterhouseCoopers, "Point of View: Financial Reporting for Private Companies," October 2010, accessed April 2012, http://www.pwc.com/us/en/point-of-view/private-companies-reporting.jhtml.

53. Brennan, interview.

54. "Private Companies: The Path to a Different Standard-Setting Framework," *FASB In Focus*, July 11, 2011, accessed April 2012, http://www.fasb.org/cs/ContentServer?site=FASB&c=Document_C&pagename=FASB%2FDocument_C%2FDocumentPage&cid=1176158732399.

55. Brennan, interview.

56. Ibid.

57. Financial Accounting Foundation, "Private Company Council (PCC)," audio recording, accessed October 2013, http://www.accountingfoundation.org/jsp/Foundation/Page/FAFSectionPage&cid=1176158985794.

58. Melancon, interview.

59. Ibid.

60. Ibid.

61. Ibid.

62. Morgan, "Private Company Reporting."

63. Quaadman, interview.

64. Financial Accounting Foundation, "Financial Accounting Foundation Board of Trustees: Establishment of the Private Company Council Final Report," May 30, 2012, accessed October 2013, http://www.accountingfoundation.org/cs/ContentServer?site=Foundation&c=Document_C&pagename=Foundation%2FDocument_C%2FFAFDocumentPage&cid=1176160066778.

65. Ken Tysiac, "FAF Creates Private Company Council," *Journal of Accountancy*, July 1, 2012, accessed October 2013, http://www.journalofaccountancy.com/Issues/2012/Jul/FAF-creates-Private-Company-Council.htm.

66. Financial Accounting Foundation, "Financial Accounting Foundation Appoints Members to Newly Created Private Company Council," press release, September 19, 2012, accessed October 2013, http://www.accountingfoundation.org/cs/ContentServer?site=Foundation&c=FAFContent_C&pagename=Foundation%2FFAFContent_C%2FFAFNewsPage&cid=1176160336308.

67. Other important differences between the PCC's new goodwill rules and the FASB's goodwill rules are as follows. If a private company elects to amortize goodwill, then that goodwill can be subject to impairment testing at the entity level, rather than at the reporting-unit level. Further, the impairment test will involve comparing the entity's fair value to its book value; the fair-value of the entity's nongoodwill net assets need not be estimated. See Private Company Council, "Overview of Decisions Reached on PCC Issue No. 13-01 A, 'Accounting for Identifiable Intangible Assets in a Business Combination,' and PCC Issue No. 13-01B, 'Accounting for Goodwill,'" accessed October 2013, http://www.fasb.org/cs/BlobServer?blobkey=id&blobnocache=true&blobwhere=1175827727994&blobheader=application%2Fpdf&blobcol=urldata&blobtable=MungoBlobs.

68. Brennan, interview.

69. Ibid.

70. Mark Bradshaw et al., "Financial Reporting Policy Committee of the American Accounting Association's Financial Accounting and Reporting Section: Accounting Standard Setting for Private Companies," *Accounting Horizons* 28, no. 1 (2014): 175–92.

Chapter Eight

1. Populism colored the accounting rule-making debates in the 1990s and 2000s on whether corporate stock-option grants to employees should be treated as an expense in corporate income statements. See, for example, the related discussion in chapter 5 and Floyd Norris, "Accounting Board Wants Options to Be Reported as an Expense," *New York Times*, April 1, 2004, accessed September 2013, http://www.nytimes.com/2004/04/01/business/01options.html.

2. Chapter 2 provides citations to numerous studies that discuss and critique the role of fair-value accounting in financial reporting.

3. Capture theory, generally attributed to Professor George Stigler, is introduced and discussed in chapter 5.

4. On the notion of ideological capture in accounting, see, for example, Michael Power, "The Politics of Brand Accounting in the United Kingdom," *European Accounting Review* 1, no. 1 (1992): 39–68. On the notion of ideological capture in market economies more broadly, see,

for example, Marion Fourcade, *Economists and Societies: Discipline and Profession in the United States, Britain, & France, 1890s to 1990s* (Princeton, NJ: Princeton University Press, 2009); Nolan McCarty, Keith T. Poole, and Howard Rosenthal, *Political Bubbles: Financial Crises and the Failure of American Democracy* (Princeton, NJ: Princeton University Press, 2013); Luigi Zingales, "Preventing Economists' Capture," in *Preventing Regulatory Capture*, eds. Daniel Carpenter and David A. Moss (New York: Cambridge University Press, 2014), 124–51.

5. The formal economic logic for this statement flows from the welfare theorems. See, for example, Kenneth J. Arrow, "An Extension of the Basic Theorems of Classical Welfare Economics," in *Proceedings of the Second Berkeley Symposium on Mathematical Statistics and Probability*, ed. Jerzy Neyman (Berkeley, CA: University of California Press, 1951), 507–32; Gerard Debreu, "The Coefficient of Resource Utilization," *Econometrica* 19, no. 3 (1951): 273–92. Also see Milton Friedman, "The Social Responsibility of Business is to Increase its Profits," *New York Times Magazine*, September 13, 1970.

6. See, for example, Ilia D. Dichev, "On the Balance Sheet-Based Model of Financial Reporting," *Accounting Horizons* 22, no. 4 (2008): 453–70.

7. Ilia D. Dichev and Vicki W. Tang, "Matching and the Changing Properties of Accounting Earnings over the Last 40 Years," *Accounting Review* 83, no. 6 (2008): 1425–60.

8. For a recent review of this literature, see, for example, Anne Beyer et al., "The Financial Reporting Environment: Review of the Recent Literature," *Journal of Accounting and Economics* 50, no. 2 (2010): 296–343.

9. See, in particular, Mark T. Bradshaw and Richard G. Sloan, "GAAP versus the Street: An Empirical Assessment of Two Alternative Definitions of Earnings," *Journal of Accounting Research* 40, no. 1 (2002): 41–66; Lawrence D. Brown and Kumar Sivakumar, "Comparing the Value Relevance of Two Operating Income Measures," *Review of Accounting Studies* 8, no. 4 (2003): 561–72.

10. See, for example, Beyer et al., "The Financial Reporting Environment"; Jeffery S. Abarbanell and Reuven Lehavy, "Letting the 'Tail Wag the Dog': The Debate over GAAP versus Street Earnings Revisited," *Contemporary Accounting Research* 24, no. 3 (2007): 675–723.

11. Peter R. Demerjian, "Accounting Standards and Debt Covenants: Has the 'Balance Sheet Approach' Led to a Decline in the Use of Balance Sheet Covenants?" *Journal of Accounting and Economics* 52, no. 2 (2011): 178–202.

12. The basics of this literature were established in the economic theory of prices. For an excellent and accessible overview of the theory of price, see George J. Stigler, *The Theory of Price* (London: Macmillan, 1946). See also Milton Friedman, *Price Theory* (New Brunswick, NJ: Transaction Publishers, 1962).

13. For an overview on the role of property rights in market development, see, for example, Suzanne Scotchmer, *Innovation and Incentives* (Cambridge, MA: MIT Press, 2006).

14. See, for example, Rafael LaPorta et al., "Investor Protection and Corporate Valuation," *Journal of Finance* 57, no. 3 (2002): 1147–70; Andrei Shleifer and Daniel Wolfenzon, "Investor Protection and Equity Markets," *Journal of Financial Economics* 66, no. 1 (2002): 3–27.

15. See, for example, Stigler, *Theory of Price*.

16. See, for example, George A. Akerlof, "The Market for 'Lemons': Quality Uncertainty and the Market Mechanism," *Quarterly Journal of Economics* 84, no. 3 (1970): 488–500.

17. See, for example, Paul M. Healy and Krishna G. Palepu, "Information Asymmetry, Corporate Disclosure, And The Capital Markets: A Review Of The Empirical Disclosure Literature," *Journal of Accounting and Economics* 31, no. 1 (2001): 405–40.

18. For studies on the role of contracts in facilitating intertemporal exchange, see, for example, Harold Demsetz, "Toward a Theory of Property Rights," *American Economic Review* 57, no. 2 (1967): 347–59; Clifford W. Smith and Jerold B. Warner, "On Financial Contracting: An Analysis of Bond Covenants," *Journal of Financial Economics* 7, no. 2 (1979): 117–61.

19. For the role of the insurance industry, see, for example, Franklin Allen and Anthony M. Santomero, "The Theory of Financial Intermediation," *Journal of Banking and Finance* 21, no. 11 (1997): 1461–85.

20. See, for example, Stephen A. Ross, "The Economic Theory of Agency: The Principal's Problem," *American Economic Review* 63, no. 2 (1973): 134–39; Michael C. Jensen and William H. Meckling, "Theory of the Firm: Managerial Behavior, Agency Costs and Ownership Structure," *Journal of Financial Economics* 3, no. 4 (1976): 305–60.

21. There is a vast literature in accounting, economics, and finance on institutions that mitigate the agency problem in firms, particularly agency problems between managers and shareholders and between shareholders and bondholders. For a recent review, see Christopher S. Armstrong, Wayne R. Guay, and Joseph P. Weber, "The Role of Information and Financial Reporting in Corporate Governance and Debt Contracting," *Journal of Accounting and Economics* 50, no. 2 (2010): 179–234.

22. For some studies discussing the importance of mitigating collusion in the context of insider trading in capital markets, see, for example, Hayne E. Leland, "Insider Trading: Should It Be Prohibited?" *Journal of Political Economy* 100, no. 4 (1992): 859–87; Lisa K. Meulbroek, "An Empirical Analysis of Illegal Insider Trading," *Journal of Finance* 47, no. 5 (1992): 1661–99.

23. On "creative destruction," see Joseph A. Schumpeter, *Capitalism, Socialism and Democracy* (New York: Harper & Row, 1942).

24. On the importance of entry and exit in U.S. capital markets, see, for example, Michael C. Jensen and Richard S. Ruback, "The Market for Corporate Control: The Scientific Evidence," *Journal of Financial Economics* 11, nos. 1–4 (1983): 5–50; Michael C. Jensen, "The Agency Costs of Free Cash Flow: Corporate Finance and Takeovers," *American Economic Review* 76 (1986): 323–29.

25. See, for example, Beyer et al., "The Financial Reporting Environment."

26. See, for example, Anna M. Costello, "Mitigating Incentive Conflicts in Inter-Firm Relationships: Evidence from Long-Term Supply Contracts," *Journal of Accounting and Economics* 56, no. 1 (2013): 19–39.

27. See, for example, Myron S. Scholes et al., *Taxes and Business Strategy: A Planning Approach* (Upper Saddle River, NJ: Pearson Prentice Hall, 2005).

28. In theory, such exclusion could be effected via very stringent patent enforcement by rule-making bodies of their rules. In practice, such enforcement is likely to be technically infeasible or prohibitively costly.

29. See, for example, Mary E. Barth, "Research, Standard Setting, and Global Financial Reporting," *Foundations and Trends in Accounting* 1, no. 5 (2006): 71–165.

30. See, for example, Paul A. Samuelson, "The Pure Theory of Public Expenditure," *Review of Economics and Statistics* (1954): 387–89.

31. The Securities and Exchange Commission Historical Society, "Accounting and Auditing in the 1930s," accessed September 2013, http://www.sechistorical.org/museum/galleries/rca/rca02a-profession.php.

32. See, for example, Francois Brochet, Krishna Palepu, and Lauren Barley, *Accounting for the iPhone at Apple, Inc.* (HBS No. 111-003) (Boston: Harvard Business School Publishing, 2011).

33. See Karthik Balakrishnan, Ross L. Watts, and Luo Zuo, "Accounting Conservatism and Firm Investment: Evidence from the Global Financial Crisis" (working paper, University of Pennsylvania, Philadelphia, PA, 2013).

34. Carmen Blough, "Some Accounting Problems of the Securities and Exchange Commission" (speech, New York State Society of Certified Public Accountants, January 11, 1937), accessed March 2015, http://www.sechistorical.org/collection/papers/1930/1937_0111_Blough NewYorkCPAT.pdf.

35. See, for example, Roberta Romano, "The States as a Laboratory: Legal Innovation and State Competition for Corporate Charters," *Yale Journal on Regulation* 23, no. 2 (2006): 209–47. For a less favorable view, see Lucian A. Bebchuk, "Federalism and the Corporation: The Desirable Limits on State Competition in Corporate Law," *Harvard Law Review* 105, no. 7 (1992): 1435–1510.

36. See, for example, Ronald A. Dye and Shyam Sunder, "Why Not Allow the FASB and IASB Standards to Compete in the U.S.?," *Accounting Horizons* 15, no. 3 (2001): 257–71.

37. See, for example, Karthik Ramanna and Ewa Sletten, "Network Effects in Countries' Adoption of IFRS," *Accounting Review* 89, no. 4 (2014): 1517–43.

38. For a discussion of alternative mechanisms for the determination of accounting standards, see, for example, Shyam Sunder, "Political Economy of Accounting Standards," *Journal of Accounting Literature* 7 (1988): 31–41.

39. See, for example, Arthur C. Pigou, *The Economics of Welfare*, rev. ed. (1920; repr., London: Macmillan, 1938).

40. See, for example, Kenneth Rogoff, "The Optimal Degree of Commitment to an Intermediate Monetary Target," *Quarterly Journal of Economics* 100, no. 4 (1985): 1169–89.

41. See, for example, Daron Acemoglu et al., "When Does Policy Reform Work? The Case of Central Bank Independence," *Brookings Papers on Economic Activity* 39, no. 1 (2008): 351–429.

42. For a discussion of the challenges associated with monitoring the production of public goods, see, for example, Shyam Sunder, "Structure for Organizations of Public and Private Goods" (working paper, Carnegie Mellon University, Pittsburg, PA, 1999).

43. See, for example, Thomas Stratmann, "Some Talk: Money in Politics; A (Partial) Review of the Literature," *Public Choice* 124, nos. 1–2 (2005): 135–56; Amy J. Hillman, Gerald D. Keim, and Douglas Schuler, "Corporate Political Activity: A Review and Research Agenda," *Journal of Management* 30, no. 6 (2004): 837–57.

44. Randall S. Kroszner and Thomas Stratmann, "Interest-Group Competition and the Organization of Congress: Theory and Evidence from Financial Services' Political Action Committees," *American Economic Review* 88, no. 5 (1998): 1163–87.

45. John M. Figueiredo and Emerson H. Tiller, "The Structure and Conduct of Corporate Lobbying: How Firms Lobby the Federal Communications Commission," *Journal of Economics and Management Strategy* 10, no. 1 (2001): 91–122.

46. William R. Kinney, "Audit Technology and Preferences for Auditing Standards," *Journal of Accounting and Economics* 8, no. 1 (1986): 73–89.

47. Mara Faccio, "Politically Connected Firms," *American Economic Review* 96, no. 1 (2006): 369–86.

48. Jennifer J. Jones, "Earnings Management during Import Relief Investigations," *Journal of Accounting Research* 29, no. 2 (1991): 193–228.

49. Karthik Ramanna and Sugata Roychowdhury, "Elections and Discretionary Accruals: Evidence From 2004," *Journal of Accounting Research* 48, no. 2 (2010): 445–75.

50. George J. Stigler, "The Theory of Economic Regulation," *Bell Journal of Economics and Management Science* 2, no. 1 (1971): 3–21; Sam Peltzman, "Toward a More General Theory of Regulation," *Journal of Law and Economics* 19, no. 2 (1976): 211–40.

51. Adam Smith, *An Inquiry into the Nature and Causes of the Wealth of Nations* (1776; repr., Pennsylvania State College: Pennsylvania State Electronic Classics Series Publication, 2005), 111.

52. See, for example, Stigler, "The Theory of Economic Regulation"; Peltzman, "Toward a More General Theory of Regulation"; Richard A. Posner, "The Social Costs of Monopoly and Regulation," *Journal of Political Economy* 83, no. 4 (1975): 807–28; George J. Stigler, *Chicago Studies in Political Economy* (Chicago: University of Chicago Press, 1988); Andrei Shleifer and Robert W. Vishny, "Pervasive Shortages under Socialism," *Rand Journal of Economics* 23, no. 2 (1992): 237–46.

53. Milton Friedman, *Capitalism and Freedom* (Chicago: University of Chicago Press, 2002). On this point, also see Gary S. Becker, "Competition and Democracy," *Journal of Law and Economics* 1 (1958): 105–9. For a related argument in the specific context of regulating accounting rule-making, see Richard W. Leftwich, "Market Failure Fallacies and Accounting Information," *Journal of Accounting and Economics* 2, no. 3 (1980): 193–211.

54. See, for example, Timothy Besley and Robin Burgess, "The Political Economy of Government Responsiveness: Theory and Evidence from India," *Quarterly Journal of Economics* 117, no. 4 (2002): 1415–51; Alexander Dyck, David Moss, and Luigi Zingales, "Media versus Special Interests," *Journal of Law and Economics* 56, no. 3 (2013): 521–53.

55. See, for example, Scotchmer, *Innovation and Incentives.*

56. For a recent history and political economy of Social Security in the United States, see, for example, Sylvester J. Schieber and John Shoven, *The Real Deal: The History and Future of Social Security* (New Haven, CT: Yale University Press, 1999); Daniel Béland, *Social Security: History and Politics from the New Deal to the Privatization Debate* (Lawrence, KS: University Press of Kansas, 2005).

57. See, for example, James M. Snyder Jr., "Long-Term Investing in Politicians; or, Give Early, Give Often," *Journal of Law and Economics* 35, no. 1 (1992): 15–43; Stephen Ansolabehere, John M. De Figueiredo, and James M. Snyder, "Why Is There So Little Money in Politics?" *Journal of Economic Perspectives* 17, no. 1 (2003): 105–30.

58. An antecedent argument in political science on the notion of "thin political markets" can be found in Schattschneider's (1960) seminal work on Americans as a "semi-sovereign people." He noted, "The flaw in the pluralist heaven is that the heavenly chorus sings with a strong upper-class accent." Elmer E. Schattschneider, *The Semi-Sovereign People: A Realist's View of Democracy in America* (New York: Holt, Rinehart and Winston, 1960). For a more recent exposition of this idea in the context of corporate-control rules in Europe and Japan, see Pepper D. Culpepper, *Quiet Politics and Business Power: Corporate Control in Europe and Japan* (Cambridge, UK: Cambridge University Press, 2011).

59. For the original formulation of the collective action problem, see Anthony Downs, "An Economic Theory of Political Action in a Democracy," *Journal of Political Economy* 65, no. 2 (1957): 135–50; Mancur Olson, *The Logic of Collective Action: Public Goods and the Theory of Groups* (Cambridge, MA: Harvard University Press, 1965). For some work on the dynamics of collective action, see Elinor Ostrom, *Governing the Commons: The Evolution of Institutions for Collective Action* (Cambridge, UK: Cambridge University Press, 1990); Sidney G. Tarrow, *Power in Movement: Social Movements and Contentious Politics* (Cambridge, UK: Cambridge University Press, 1994).

60. For an introduction to the literature on organizational learning and its exploration of experiential knowledge, see, for example, George P. Huber, "Organizational Learning: The Contributing Processes and the Literatures," *Organization Science* 2, no. 1 (1991): 88–115.

61. The quoted words are adapted from Justice Louis D. Brandies, "What Publicity Can Do," *Harper's Weekly*, December 20, 1913. The complete quote is "Sunlight is said to be the best of disinfectants; electric light the most efficient policeman." For some literature related to the argument that participation by the general interest can mitigate capture, see, for example, Schattschneider, *The Semi-Sovereign People*; David P. Baron, "Electoral Competition with Informed and Uninformed Voters," *American Political Science Review* 88, no. 1 (1994): 33–47.

62. For an overview of the role of intermediaries in representing the general interest, see, for example, Ostrom, *Governing the Commons*.

63. On this point, see, in particular, William T. Gormley Jr., "Regulatory Issue Networks in a Federal System," *Polity* 18, no. 4 (1986): 595–620.

64. Mihir Desai, "The Incentive Bubble," *Harvard Business Review* 90, no. 3 (2012): 124–33.

65. On this point, see, for example, Schattschneider, *The Semi-Sovereign People*; Culpepper, *Quiet Politics and Business Power*.

66. On the sociology of professionalism in contemporary political economy, see, for example, Magali S. Larson, *The Rise of Professionalism: A Sociological Analysis* (Berkeley, CA: University of California Press, 1977); Steven Brint, *In an Age of Experts: The Changing Role of Professionals in Politics and Public Life* (Princeton, NJ: Princeton University Press, 1994).

67. See, for example, Downs, "An Economic Theory of Political Action in a Democracy"; Olson, *The Logic of Collective Action*; and Ostrom, *Governing the Commons*.

68. For a description of the FASB due process, see Financial Accounting Standards Board, "Standards-Setting Process," accessed September 2013, http://www.fasb.org.

69. FASB meetings can be accessed through the board's website. Financial Accounting Standards Board, "Meetings," accessed September 2013, http://www.fasb.org.

70. Office of the Comptroller of the Currency, "About the OCC," accessed October 2013, http://www.occ.gov/about/what-we-do/mission/index-about.html; Bank for International Settlements, "About the Basel Committee," accessed October 2013, http://www.bis.org/bcbs/about.htm.

71. Sarbanes-Oxley Act of 2002, Pub. L. No. 107–204, 116 Stat. 745 (2002).

72. American Institute of Certified Public Accountants, "Auditing Standards Board," accessed October 2013, http://www.aicpa.org/Research/Standards/AuditAttest/ASB/Pages/AuditingStandardsBoard.aspx.

73. Governmental Accounting Standards Board, "Facts about GASB," accessed September 2013, http://www.gasb.org.

74. See, for example, Anna M. Costello, Reining Petacchi, and Joseph P. Weber, "The Hidden Consequences of Balanced Budget Requirements" (working paper, MIT Sloan School of Management, Cambridge, MA, 2012).

Chapter Nine

1. Michael E. Porter and Jan W. Rivkin, "Prosperity at Risk: Findings of Harvard Business School's Survey on U.S. Competitiveness," accessed October 2013, http://www.hbs.edu/competitiveness/pdf/hbscompsurvey.pdf.

2. Milton Friedman, "The Social Responsibility of Business Is to Increase Its Profits," *New York Times Magazine*, September 13, 1970.

3. On this point, also see Michael C. Jensen, "Value Maximization and the Corporate Objective Function," in *Breaking the Code of Change*, eds. Michael Beer and Nitin Nohria (Boston: Harvard Business School Press, 2000), 37–58.

4. Milton Friedman, *Capitalism and Freedom* (Chicago: University of Chicago Press, 2002).

5. In prohibiting managers from focusing past the interests of shareholders, economic philosophers such as Milton Friedman have made an additional argument beyond managerial agency to shareholders. They have argued that managers lacked the *expertise* to tackle broader social problems, such as problems of the commons. While this may be true in some cases (e.g., educational reform), the evidence in this book suggests that in the thin political markets for accounting rule-making, corporate managers (including auditors and bankers) do possess the relevant expertise, at least more so than others.

6. On this point, see, for example, the economic theory of capture, first articulated by George J. Stigler, "The Theory of Economic Regulation," *Bell Journal of Economics and Management Science* 2, no. 1 (1971): 3–21; and later formalized by Sam Peltzman, "Toward a More General Theory of Regulation," *Journal of Law and Economics* 19, no. 2 (1976): 211–40.

7. Michael E. Porter and Mark R. Kramer, "Creating Shared Value," *Harvard Business Review* 89, nos. 1–2 (2011): 62–77.

8. See, for example, Richard W. Leftwich, "Accounting Information in Private Markets: Evidence from Private Lending Agreements," *Accounting Review* 58, no. 1 (1983): 23–42; Ningzhong Li, "Negotiated Measurement Rules in Debt Contracts," *Journal of Accounting Research* 48, no. 5 (2010): 1103–44.

9. Of course, beyond managerial behavior in capitalism, ethics is at the heart of legitimizing much of human behavior more generally—it gives purpose and meaning to our lives and is seemingly critical to the development of complex societies, as an emerging literature on the sociology of ethics shows. On this point, see, for example, Philip Kitcher's *The Ethical Project*, which argues that ethics represent a "pragmatic naturalism" that facilitates the formation of societies. In this view, ethics are central to human identity. Philip Kitcher, *The Ethical Project* (Cambridge, MA: Harvard University Press, 2011).

10. See, for example, Karl Polanyi, *The Great Transformation: The Political and Economic Origins of Our Time* (Boston: Beacon Press, 1957); Joyce Appleby, *Capitalism and a New Social Order* (New York: New York University Press, 1984).

11. Adam Smith, *An Inquiry into the Nature and Causes of the Wealth of Nations* (1776; repr., Pennsylvania State College: Pennsylvania State Electronic Classics Series Publication, 2005).

12. Paul Samuelson was perhaps more responsible for this development than any other economist of the twentieth century. As his Nobel Prize citation recognized, "More than any other contemporary economist, [Samuelson] has contributed to raising the general analytical and methodological level in economic science. He has in fact simply rewritten considerable parts of economic theory." Assar Lindbeck, "Award Ceremony Speech" (speech, Sveriges Riksbank Prize in Economic Sciences in Memory of Alfred Nobel, 1970), accessed November 2013, http://www .nobelprize.org/nobel_prizes/economic-sciences/laureates/1970/press.html. See also Paul A. Samuelson, *Foundations of Economic Analysis* (Cambridge, MA: Harvard University Press, 1947).

13. See, for example, Friedrich A. Hayek, *The Road to Serfdom* (London: Routledge, 1951).

14. See, for example, Friedman, *Capitalism and Freedom*.

15. For some recent descriptions on the effects of market capitalism in formerly closed economics, see, for example, Yasheng Huang, *Capitalism with Chinese Characteristics* (Cambridge, UK: Cambridge University Press, 2004); Tarun Khanna, *Billions of Entrepreneurs: How China and India are Reshaping Their Futures and Yours* (Boston: Harvard Business School Press, 2008).

16. The World Bank Group, "World Development Indicators," accessed November 2011, http://data.worldbank.org/data-catalog/world-development-indicators.

17. Smith, *Wealth of Nations*, 19.

18. See, for example, The Holy Bible (NIV) (International Bible Society, 1984; Grand Rapids, MI: Zondervan, 1989), Exodus: 20. See also *The Meaning of the Holy Qur'an*, trans. Abdullah Yusuf Ali (repr., Beltsville, MD: Amana, 2003), Surah 89 Al-Fajir: 15–20.

19. See, for example, Kenneth Arrow, "An Extension of the Basic Theorems of Classical Welfare Economics," in *Proceedings of the Second Berkeley Symposium on Mathematical Statistics and Probability*, ed. Jerzy Neyman (Berkeley, CA: University of California Press, 1951), 507–32; Gerard Debreu, "The Coefficient of Resource Utilization," *Econometrica* 19, no. 3 (1951): 273–92.

20. See, for example, Amartya Sen, "Markets and Freedom: Achievements and Limitations of the Market Mechanism in Promoting Individual Freedoms," *Oxford Economic Papers* 45, no. 4 (1993): 519–41.

21. See, for example, Jonathan I. Israel, *Radical Enlightenment: Philosophy and the Making of Modernity 1670–1750* (Oxford, UK: Oxford University Press, 2002).

22. See, for example, Hayek, *The Road to Serfdom*; Milton Friedman and Rose Friedman, *Free to Choose: A Personal Statement* (San Diego, CA: Harcourt, 1980).

23. See, for example, Benjamin M. Friedman, *The Moral Consequences of Economic Growth* (New York: Alfred A. Knopf, 2005).

24. Amartya Sen, *Development as Freedom* (Oxford, UK: Oxford University Press, 1998).

25. Rather than attempt to address the problem of thin political markets, there is also the option to deregulate them so that they are not "political" at all and instead are price based. But, as discussed in chapter 8, this solution is impractical: in modern democratic societies there is little support for the idea of replacing political processes with price-based exchanges.

26. On this point, also see Charles W. L. Hill and Thomas M. Jones, "Stakeholder-Agency Theory," *Journal of Management Studies* 29, no. 2 (1992): 131–54.

27. I thank Professor Matthew Stephenson of Harvard Law School for bringing this analogy to my attention.

28. For studies on managerial incentive alignment, see, for example, Jerold B. Warner, Ross L. Watts, and Karen H. Wruck, "Stock Prices and Top Management Changes," *Journal of Financial Economics* 20 (1988): 461–92; Michael C. Jensen and Kevin J. Murphy, "CEO Incentives: It's Not How Much You Pay, But How," *Harvard Business Review* 68, no. 3 (1990): 138–53; Michael C. Jensen and Kevin J. Murphy, "Performance Pay and Top Management Incentives," *Journal of Political Economy* 98, no. 2 (1990): 225–64; Robert Gibbons and Kevin J. Murphy, "Relative Performance Evaluation for Chief Executive Officers," *Industrial and Labor Relations Review* (1990): 30S–51S.

29. See, for example, Lynn S. Paine, *The Fiduciary Relationship: A Legal Perspective* (HBS No. 04-064) (Boston: Harvard Business School Publishing, 2009).

30. See, for example, Lynn Stout, *The Shareholder Value Myth: How Putting Shareholders First Hurts Investors* (San Francisco, CA: Berrett-Koehler, 2012). For a dissenting view, see Lucian A. Bebchuk, "The Case for Increasing Shareholder Power," *Harvard Law Review* 118, no. 3 (2005): 833–914.

31. Einer Elhauge, "Sacrificing Corporate Profits in the Public Interest," *New York University Law Review* 80, no. 3 (2005): 733–869.

32. See, for example, Paine, *The Fiduciary Relationship*.

33. See, for example, John Micklethwait and Adrian Wooldridge, *The Company: A Short History of a Revolutionary Idea* (New York: Modern Library, 2005).

34. Bruce R. Scott, *Capitalism: Its Origins and Evolution as a System of Governance* (Berlin: Springer-Verlag, 2011).

35. Floyd Norris, "When Accountants Act as Bankers," *New York Times*, September 12, 2013, accessed October 2013, http://www.nytimes.com/2013/09/13/business/when-auditors-act-as-bankers.html; Financial Reporting Council, *Tribunal Report: Deloitte & Touche and Mr. Maghsoud Einollahi*, accessed October 2013, http://www.frc.org.uk/Our-Work/Publications/Professional-Discipline/Tribunal-Report-Deloitte-Touche-and-Mr-Maghsoud-Ei.pdf.

36. See, for example, Joanna Glasner, "Icahn's eBay Claims Just Tip of Iceberg for VC-Board Conflicts," *Private Markets*, March 12, 2014, accessed March 2015, http://private1416.rssing.com/browser.php?indx=25992376&item=118.

37. Ibid.

38. Raghuram G. Rajan and Luigi Zingales, *Saving Capitalism from the Capitalists* (New York: Crown, 2003), 2.

39. See, for example, Hayek, *The Road to Serfdom*.

40. For a brief summary of Occupy Wall Street, see, for example, David C. Beckwith, "United States: Year in Review 2011," *Encyclopedia Britannica Online*, accessed October 2013, http://www.britannica.com/EBchecked/topic/1799825/United-States-Year-In-Review-2011/302905/Domestic-Policy?anchor=ref1133147. For a brief summary of the Tea Party Movement, see, for example, Michael Ray, "Tea Party Movement," *Encyclopedia Britannica Online*, accessed October 2013, http://www.britannica.com/EBchecked/topic/1673405/Tea-Party-movement.

41. Joseph L. Bower, Herman B. Leonard, and Lynn S. Paine, *Capitalism at Risk: Rethinking the Role of Business* (Boston: Harvard Business School Publishing, 2011), 4.

42. Max H. Bazerman and Ann E. Tenbrunsel, *Blind Spots: Why We Fail to Do What's Right and What to Do about It* (Princeton, NJ: Princeton University Press, 2011).

43. See, for example, Robert B. Cialdini and Noah I. Goldstein, "Social Influence: Compliance and Conformity," *Annual Review of Psychology* 55 (2004): 591–621.

44. See, for example, Robert B. Cialdini and Melanie R. Trost, "Social Influence: Social Norms, Conformity, and Compliance," in *The Handbook of Social Psychology*, eds. Daniel T. Gilbert, Susan T. Fiske, and Gardner Lindzey (Boston: Oxford University Press, 1998), 151–92; Werner Güth and Hartmut Kliemt, "The Indirect Evolutionary Approach: Bridging the Gap between Rationality and Adaptation," *Rationality and Society* 10, no. 3 (1998): 377–99; Randall Peterson and Sarah Ronson, "Group Norms," in *The Blackwell Encyclopedia of Management*, vol. 11, ed. Cary L. Cooper (Malden, MA: Blackwell Publishing, 2005), 150–51; Donna D. Bobek, Amy M. Hageman, and Charles F. Kelliher, "Analyzing the Role of Social Norms in Tax Compliance Behavior," *Journal of Business Ethics* 115, no. 3 (2013): 451–68.

45. See, for example, Güth and Kliemt, "The Indirect Evolutionary Approach"; Martha Finnemore and Kathryn Sikkink, "International Norm Dynamics and Political Change," *International Organization* 52, no. 4 (1998): 887–917; Elinor Ostrom, "Collective Action and the Evolution of Social Norms," *Journal of Economic Perspectives* 14, no. 3 (2000): 137–58.

46. For a description of the distinction between laws and norms, see, for example, Robert Sugden, "Spontaneous Order," *Journal of Economic Perspectives* 3, no. 4 (1989): 85–97; Richard A. Posner, "Social Norms and the Law: An Economic Approach," *American Economic Review* 87, no. 2 (1997): 365–69; Richard McAdams, "The Origin, Development, and Regulation of Norms," *Michigan Law Review* 96, no. 2 (1997): 338–433.

47. See, for example, Güth and Kliemt, "The Indirect Evolutionary Approach"; Finnemore and Sikkink, "International Norm Dynamics"; Ostrom, "Collective Action."

48. See, for example, Daniel C. Feldman, "The Development and Enforcement of Group Norms," *Academy of Management Review* 9, no. 1 (1984): 47–53; see also Cialdini and Goldstein, "Social Influence."

49. Raymond R. Reno, Robert B. Cialdini, and Carl A. Kallgren, "The Transsituational Influence of Social Norms," *Journal of Personality and Social Psychology* 64, no. 1 (1993): 104–12, as cited in Carl A. Kallgren, Raymond R. Reno, and Robert B. Cialdini, "A Focus Theory of Normative Conduct: When Norms Do and Do not Affect Behavior," *Personality and Social Psychology Bulletin* 26 (2000): 1006.

50. Human Rights Campaign, "Corporate Equality Index 2014," accessed June 2014, http://www.hrc.org/campaigns/corporate-equality-index.

51. Gary J. Gates, "How Many People Are Lesbian, Gay, Bisexual and Transgender?" (working paper, the Williams Institute UCLA School of Law, Los Angeles, CA, 2011).

52. In 2014, 91 percent of Fortune 500 companies prevented employment discrimination against gays and lesbians. Human Rights Campaign, "Corporate Equality Index 2014."

53. In addition to the more recent examples that I discuss in the text, consider the description of "benevolent cartels" in numerous industries—including the Japanese electronics industry—to address market failures and limitations to government action in Bower and Rhenman (1985). Joseph L. Bower and Eric A. K. Rhenman, "Benevolent Cartels," *Harvard Business Review* 63, no. 4 (1985): 124–32.

54. Aaron Lucchetti and Serena Ng, "How Rating Firms' Calls Fueled Subprime Mess," *Wall Street Journal*, August 15, 2007, accessed October 2013, http://online.wsj.com/news/articles/SB118714461352698015.

55. See, for example, John G. Taft, *Stewardship: Lessons Learned from the Lost Culture of Wall Street* (Hoboken, NJ: Wiley, 2012).

56. Jack Gabarro and Leslie Perlow, "Course Purpose," Authentic Leadership Development Course No. 2090, accessed October 2013, http://www.hbs.edu/coursecatalog/2090.html.

57. Rebecca Henderson, "Course Objectives," Reimagining Capitalism Course No. 1524, accessed October 2013, http://www.hbs.edu/coursecatalog/1524.html.

58. See, in particular, Michael Beer et al., *Higher Ambition: How Great Leaders Create Economic and Social Value* (Cambridge, MA: Harvard Business Review Press, 2011).

59. For a description of the 2013 meeting, see "How to Become a Higher-Ambition Leader," *Forbes*, January 20, 2013, accessed October 2013, http://www.forbes.com/sites/hbsworkingknowledge/2013/03/20/how-to-become-a-higher-ambition-leader.

60. See, for example, Karthik Ramanna and Matthew Shaffer, *Tapestry Networks* (HBS No. 114-051) (Boston: Harvard Business School Publishing, 2014). Also see, Tapestry Networks, "About Us," accessed October 2013, http://www.tapestrynetworks.com/about-us.

61. See, for example, Tapestry Networks, "Therapeutic Area: Type 2 Diabetes," accessed December 2013, http://www.tapestrynetworks.com/issues/healthcare/therapeutic-area-type-2-diabetes.cfm.

62. George Goldsmith, interview by Karthik Ramanna, Cambridge, Massachusetts, August 20, 2013.

63. Morten Friis, interview by Karthik Ramanna, Cambridge, Massachusetts, October 24, 2013.

64. See, for example, Nina Mazar, On Amir, and Dan Ariely, "The Dishonesty of Honest People: A Theory of Self-Concept Maintenance," *Journal of Marketing Research* 45, no. 6 (2008): 633–44; Lisa L. Shu et al., "Signing at the Beginning Makes Ethics Salient and Decreases Dishonest Self-Reports in Comparison to Signing at the End," *Proceedings of the National Academy of Sciences* 109, no. 38 (2012): 15197–200.

Bibliography

107th Cong. Rec. S736. Daily edition. February 13, 2002.

Abarbanell, Jeffery S., and Reuven Lehavy. "Letting the 'Tail Wag the Dog': The Debate over GAAP versus Street Earnings Revisited." *Contemporary Accounting Research* 24, no. 3 (2007): 675–723.

Abraham, Spencer. "Spencer Abraham to Financial Accounting Standards Board." Letter of Comment No. 208, file ref. 1033-201. Norwalk, CT: FASB, 2000.

Accounting for Business Combinations: Should Pooling Be Eliminated? Subcommittee on Finance and Hazardous Materials of the Committee on Commerce, United States House of Representatives, 106th Cong., 2d session. Washington, DC: Government Printing Office, 2000.

Accounting Principles Board. "Opinions of the Accounting Principles Board No. 16, Business Combinations." New York: American Institute of Certified Public Accountants, 1970.

———. "Opinions of the Accounting Principles Board No. 17, Intangible Assets." New York: American Institute of Certified Public Accountants, 1970.

———. "Opinions of the Accounting Principles Board No. 25, Accounting for Stock Issued to Employees." New York: American Institute of Certified Public Accountants, 1972.

Accounting Standards Reform Act of 1994. Washington, DC: Government Printing Office, 1994.

Acemoglu, Daron, Simon Johnson, Pablo Querubin, and James A. Robinson. "When Does Policy Reform Work? The Case of Central Bank Independence." *Brookings Papers on Economic Activity* 39, no. 1 (2008): 351–429.

Adams, Jane. "Current Accounting Projects." Speech given at the Twenty-Fifth Annual National Conference on Current SEC Developments, Washington, DC, December 1997. Accessed March 2015. http://www.sec.gov/news/speech/speecharchive/1997/spch194.txt.

Akerlof, George A. "The Market for 'Lemons': Quality Uncertainty and the Market Mechanism." *Quarterly Journal of Economics* 84, no. 3 (1970): 488–500.

Alexandridis, George, Christos F. Mavrovitis, and Nickolaos G. Travlos. "How Have M&As Changed? Evidence from the Sixth Merger Wave." *European Journal of Finance* 18, no. 8 (2012): 663–88.

Ali, Ashiq, and Sanjay Kallapur. "Securities Price Consequences of the Private Securities Litigation Reform Act of 1995 and Related Events." *Accounting Review* 76, no. 3 (2001): 431–60.

Allen, Abigail M., and Karthik Ramanna. "Towards an Understanding of the Role of Standard Setters in Standard Setting." *Journal of Accounting and Economics* 55, no. 1 (2013): 66–90.

Allen, Abigail M., Karthik Ramanna, and Sugata Roychowdhury. "The Auditing Oligopoly and Lobbying on Accounting Standards." Working paper 13-054, Harvard Business School, Boston, MA, 2013.

Allen, Franklin, and Anthony M. Santomero. "The Theory of Financial Intermediation." *Journal of Banking and Finance* 21, no. 11 (1997): 1461–85.

American Institute of Certified Public Accountants. "Auditing Standards Board." Accessed October 2013. http://www.aicpa.org/Research/Standards/AuditAttest/ASB/Pages/Auditing StandardsBoard.aspx.

———. *Report to the Board of Trustees of the Financial Accounting Foundation*, Blue Ribbon Panel on Standard Setting for Private Companies, January 2011. Accessed April 2012. http://www .aicpa.org/interestareas/frc/accountingfinancialreporting/pcfr/downloadabledocuments/ blue_ribbon_panel_report.pdf.

———. *Report of the Study on Establishment of Accounting Principles: Establishing Financial Accounting Standards, March 1972*. New York: American Institute of Certified Public Accountants, 1972.

Andrade, Gregor, Mark Mitchell, and Erik Stafford. "New Evidence and Perspectives on Mergers." *Journal of Economic Perspectives* 15, no. 2 (2001): 103–20.

Ansolabehere, Stephen, John M. De Figueiredo, and James M. Snyder. "Why Is There So Little Money in Politics?" *Journal of Economic Perspectives* 17, no. 1 (2003): 105–30.

Ansolabehere, Stephen, James M. Snyder, and Micky Tripathi. "Are PAC Contributions and Lobbying Linked? New Evidence from the 1995 Lobby Disclosure Act." *Business and Politics* 4, no. 2 (2002): 131–55.

Appleby, Joyce. *Capitalism and a New Social Order*. New York: New York University Press, 1984.

Armstrong, Christopher S., Mary E. Barth, Alan D. Jagolinzer, and Edward J. Riedl. "Market Reaction to the Adoption of IFRS in Europe." *Accounting Review* 85, no. 1 (2010): 31–61.

Armstrong, Christopher S., Wayne R. Guay, and Joseph P. Weber. "The Role of Information and Financial Reporting in Corporate Governance and Debt Contracting." *Journal of Accounting and Economics* 50, no. 2 (2010): 179–234.

Arrow, Kenneth. "An Extension of the Basic Theorems of Classical Welfare Economics." In *Proceedings of the Second Berkeley Symposium on Mathematical Statistics and Probability*, edited by Jerzy Neyman, 507–32. Berkeley, CA: University of California Press, 1951.

Austen-Smith, David. "Campaign Contributions and Access." *American Political Science Review* 89, no. 3 (1995): 566–81.

Bala, S. D. "The Effects of Changes in AS 11 Rules." *Hindu Business Line*, April 16, 2009.

Balakrishnan, Karthik, Ross L. Watts, and Luo Zuo. "Accounting Conservatism and Firm Investment: Evidence from the Global Financial Crisis." Working paper, University of Pennsylvania, Philadelphia, PA, 2013.

Ball, Ray. "Infrastructure Requirements for an Economically Efficient System of Public Financial Reporting and Disclosure." *Brookings-Wharton Papers on Financial Services* (2001): 127–69.

———. "International Financial Reporting Standards (IFRS): Pros and Cons for Investors." *Accounting and Business Research* 36, no. 1 (2006): 5–27.

Ball, Ray, S. P. Kothari, and Ashok Robin. "The Effect of International Institutional Factors on Properties of Accounting Earnings." *Journal of Accounting and Economics* 29, no. 1 (2000): 1–51.

Bamber, Linda S., John Jiang, and Isabel Y. Wang. "What's My Style? The Influence of Top Managers on Voluntary Corporate Financial Disclosure." *Accounting Review* 85, no. 4 (2010): 1131–62.

Bank for International Settlements. "About the Basel Committee." Accessed October 2013. http://www.bis.org/bcbs/about.htm.

Baron, David P. "Electoral Competition with Informed and Uninformed Voters." *American Political Science Review* 88, no. 1 (1994): 33–47.

Barth, Mary E. "Research, Standard Setting, and Global Financial Reporting." *Foundations and Trends in Accounting* 1, no. 2 (2006): 71–165.

Barth, Mary E., William H. Beaver, and Wayne R. Landsman. "The Relevance of the Value Relevance Literature for Financial Accounting Standard Setting: Another View." *Journal of Accounting and Economics* 31, nos. 1–3 (2001): 77–104.

Barton, Jan, and Gregory Waymire. "Investor Protection under Unregulated Financial Reporting." *Journal of Accounting and Economics* 38 (2004): 65–116.

Basic Inc. v. Levinson. 485 U.S. 224, 108 S. Ct. 978, 99 L. Ed. 2d 194 (1988).

Basu, Sudipta. "The Conservatism Principle and the Asymmetric Timeliness of Earnings." *Journal of Accounting and Economics* 24, no. 1 (1997): 3–37.

Bazerman, Max H., and Ann E. Tenbrunsel. *Blind Spots: Why We Fail to Do What's Right and What to Do about It.* Princeton, NJ: Princeton University Press, 2011.

Beatty, Anne, and Joseph P. Weber. "Accounting Discretion in Fair Value Estimates: An Examination of SFAS 142 Goodwill Impairments." *Journal of Accounting Research* 44, no. 2 (2006): 257–88.

Beaver, William H. *Financial Reporting: An Accounting Revolution.* 2nd ed. Englewood Cliffs, NJ: Prentice Hall, 1989.

Bebchuk, Lucian A. "The Case for Increasing Shareholder Power." *Harvard Law Review* 118, no. 3 (2005): 833–914.

———. "Federalism and the Corporation: The Desirable Limits on State Competition in Corporate Law." *Harvard Law Review* 105, no. 7 (1992): 1435–510.

Becker, Gary S. "Competition and Democracy." *Journal of Law and Economics* 1 (1958): 105–9.

Beckwith, David C. "United States: Year in Review 2011." *Encyclopedia Britannica Online.* Accessed October 2013. http://www.britannica.com/EBchecked/topic/1799825/United-States-Year-In-Review-2011/302905/Domestic-Policy?anchor=ref1133147.

Beer, Michael, Russell A. Eisenstat, Nathaniel Foote, and Tobias Fredberg. *Higher Ambition: How Great Leaders Create Economic and Social Value.* Cambridge, MA: Harvard Business Review Press, 2011.

Béland, Daniel. *Social Security: History and Politics from the New Deal to the Privatization Debate.* Lawrence, KS: University Press of Kansas, 2005.

Benston, George J. "The Market for Public Accounting Services: Demand, Supply and Regulation." *Journal of Accounting and Public Policy* 4, no. 1 (1985): 33–79.

Benston, George J., Michael Bromwich, Robert E. Litan, and Alfred Wagenhofer. *Worldwide Financial Reporting: The Development and Future of Accounting Standards.* New York: Oxford University Press, 2006.

Beresford, Dennis R. "Congress Looks at Accounting for Business Combinations." *Accounting Horizons* 15, no. 1 (2001): 73–86.

Berle, Adolf, and Gardiner Means. *The Modern Corporation and Private Property.* New York: Harcourt, Brace, 1932.

Bertomeu, Jeremy, and Robert P. Magee. "From Low-Quality Reporting to Financial Crises: Politics of Disclosure Regulation along the Economic Cycle." *Journal of Accounting and Economics* 52, no. 2 (2011): 209–27.

Bertrand, Marianne, and Antoinette Schoar. "Managing with Style: The Effect of Managers on Firm Policies." *Quarterly Journal of Economics* 118, no. 4 (2003): 1169–1208.

Besley, Timothy, and Robin Burgess. "The Political Economy of Government Responsiveness: Theory and Evidence from India." *Quarterly Journal of Economics* 117, no. 4 (2002): 1415–51.

Beyer, Anne, Daniel A. Cohen, Thomas Z. Lys, and Beverly R. Walther. "The Financial Reporting Environment: Review of the Recent Literature." *Journal of Accounting and Economics* 50, no. 2 (2010): 296–343.

Bielstein, Mark. Interview by Karthik Ramanna and Luis Viceira. Norwalk, CT, July 27, 2012.

Blough, Carmen. "Some Accounting Problems of the Securities and Exchange Commission." Speech given to the New York State Society of Certified Public Accountants, January 11, 1937. Accessed March 2015. http://www.sechistorical.org/collection/papers/1930/1937 _0111_BloughNewYorkCPAT.pdf.

Bobek, Donna D., Amy M. Hageman, and Charles F. Kelliher. "Analyzing the Role of Social Norms in Tax Compliance Behavior." *Journal of Business Ethics* 115, no. 3 (2013): 451–68.

Bower, Joseph L., and Eric A. K. Rhenman. "Benevolent Cartels." *Harvard Business Review* 63, no. 4 (1985): 124–32.

Bower, Joseph L., Herman B. Leonard, and Lynn S. Paine. *Capitalism at Risk: Rethinking the Role of Business.* Boston: Harvard Business School Publishing, 2011.

Bradshaw, Mark T., and Richard G. Sloan. "GAAP versus the Street: An Empirical Assessment of Two Alternative Definitions of Earnings." *Journal of Accounting Research* 40, no. 1 (2002): 41–66.

Bradshaw, Mark T., Daniel Bens, Carol Ann Frost, Elizabeth Gordon, Sarah McVay, Gregory Miller, Ray Pfeiffer, Marlene Plumlee, Catherine Shakespeare, Wayne Thomas, and Franco Wong. "Financial Reporting Policy Committee of the American Accounting Association's Financial Accounting and Reporting Section: Accounting Standard Setting for Private Companies." *Accounting Horizons* 28, no. 1 (2014): 175–92.

Brandies, Louis D. "What Publicity Can Do." *Harper's Weekly*, December 20, 1913.

Brennan, John J. Interview by Karthik Ramanna and Luis Viceira. Cambridge, MA. July 6, 2012.

Brint, Steven. *In an Age of Experts: The Changing Role of Professionals in Politics and Public Life.* Princeton, NJ: Princeton University Press, 1994.

Brochet, Francois, Krishna G. Palepu, and Lauren Barley. *Accounting for the iPhone at Apple, Inc.* (HBS No. 111-003). Boston: Harvard Business School Publishing, 2011.

Brown, Lawrence D., and Kumar Sivakumar. "Comparing the Value Relevance of Two Operating Income Measures." *Review of Accounting Studies* 8, no. 4 (2003): 561–72.

Brown, Paul R. "A Descriptive Analysis of Select Input Bases of the Financial Accounting Standards Board." *Journal of Accounting Research* 19, no. 1 (1981): 232–46.

Buck, Daryl. Interview by Karthik Ramanna and Luis Viceira. Norwalk, CT. July 27, 2012.

Bureau of Economic Analysis. "Gross Domestic Product." Accessed September 2013. http://www.bea.gov.

———. "Gross Domestic Product by Industry." Accessed October 2013. http://www.bea.gov.

Büthe, Tim, and Walter Mattli. *The New Global Rulers: The Privatization of Regulation in the World Economy.* Princeton, NJ: Princeton University Press, 2011.

Cahan, Steven F., and Wei Zhang. "After Enron: Auditor Conservatism and Ex-Andersen Clients." *Accounting Review* 81, no. 1 (2006): 49–82.

Calabresi, Guido. *The Cost of Accidents: A Legal and Economic Analysis*. New Haven, CT: Yale University Press, 1970.

Camfferman, Kees, and Stephen A. Zeff. *Financial Reporting and Global Capital Markets: A History of the International Accounting Standards Committee, 1973–2000*. New York: Oxford University Press, 2007.

Center for Responsive Politics. Accessed January 2014. http://www.opensecrets.org.

Chakravarthy, Jivas. "The Ideological Homogenization of the FASB." Working paper, Emory University, Atlanta, GA, 2014.

Chatterjee, Koushik. Interview by Karthik Ramanna. Via telephone. February 22, 2010.

Choi, Jong-Hag, Rajib K. Doogar, and Ananda R. Ganguly. "The Riskiness of Large Audit Firm Client Portfolios and Changes in Audit Liability Regimes: Evidence from the U.S. Audit Market." *Contemporary Accounting Research* 21, no. 4 (2004): 747–85.

Christoffersen, John. "Board Approves New Guidance for Accounting Rules That Could Help Ease Financial Crisis." *Associated Press Newswires*, October 10, 2008.

Churchill, Winston. "The Few." Speech given at the House of Commons, London, UK, August 1940. Accessed February 2014. http://www.winstonchurchill.org/learn/speeches/speeches-of-winston-churchill/1940-finest-hour/113-the-few.

Cialdini, Robert B., and Noah I. Goldstein. "Social Influence: Compliance and Conformity." *Annual Review of Psychology* 55 (2004): 591–621.

Cialdini, Robert B., and Melanie R. Trost. "Social Influence: Social Norms, Conformity, and Compliance." In *The Handbook of Social Psychology*, edited by Daniel T. Gilbert, Susan T. Fiske, and Gardner Lindzey, 151–92. Boston: Oxford University Press, 1998.

Cisco Systems. "Form 10-K for the Fiscal Year Ended July 27, 2013." Accessed January 2014. http://www.sec.gov/Archives/edgar/data/858877/000085887713000049/csco-2013727x10k.htm.

Cohen, Jeffrey E. "The Dynamics of the 'Revolving Door' on the FCC." *American Journal of Political Science* 30 (1986): 689–708.

Costello, Anna M. "Mitigating Incentive Conflicts in Inter-Firm Relationships: Evidence from Long-Term Supply Contracts." *Journal of Accounting and Economics* 56, no. 1 (2013): 19–39.

Costello, Anna M., Reining Petacchi, and Joseph P. Weber. "The Hidden Consequences of Balanced Budget Requirements." Working paper, MIT Sloan School of Management, Cambridge, MA, 2012.

Council of the European Union. "Immediate Responses to Financial Turmoil, Council Conclusions—Ecofin Council of 7 October 2008." Accessed November 2013, http://www.consilium.europa.eu/uedocs/cms_Data/docs/pressdata/en/misc/103202.pdf.

Coyne, Michael P. "History Repeating Itself: The Debate over Accounting for Stock Options." *Pennsylvania Journal of Business and Economics* 10, no. 1 (2004): 1–14.

Culpepper, Pepper D. *Quiet Politics and Business Power: Corporate Control in Europe and Japan*. Cambridge, UK: Cambridge University Press, 2011.

Cunningham, Lawrence A. "Too Big to Fail: Moral Hazard in Auditing and the Need to Restructure the Industry before It Unravels." *Columbia Law Review* 106 (2006): 1698–1748.

Dal Bo, Ernesto. "Regulatory Capture: A Review." *Oxford Review of Economic Policy* 22, no. 2 (2006): 203–25.

Deakin, Edward B. "Rational Economic Behavior and Lobbying on Accounting Issues: Evidence from the Oil and Gas Industry." *Accounting Review* 64, no. 1 (1989): 137–51.

DeAngelo, Linda E. "Auditor Size and Audit Quality." *Journal of Accounting and Economics* 3, no. 3 (1981): 183–99.

Debreu, Gerard. "The Coefficient of Resource Utilization." *Econometrica* 19, no. 3 (1951): 273–92.

Dechow, Patricia M. "Accounting Earnings and Cash Flows as Measures of Firm Performance: The Role of Accounting Accruals." *Journal of Accounting and Economics* 18, no. 1 (1994): 3–42.

Dechow, Patricia M., Amy P. Hutton, and Richard G. Sloan. "Economic Consequences of Accounting for Stock-Based Compensation." *Journal of Accounting Research* 34, sup. (1996): 1–20.

DeFond, Mark L., and Jieying Zhang. "A Review of Archival Auditing Research." Working paper, University of Southern California, Los Angeles, CA, 2013.

DeFond, Mark L., T. J. Wong, and Shuhua Li. "The Impact of Improved Auditor Independence on Audit Market Concentration in China." *Journal of Accounting and Economics* 28, no. 3 (1999): 269–305.

Deloitte & Touche. "Deloitte & Touche to Financial Accounting Standards Board." Letter of Comment No. 47, file ref. 1250-001. Norwalk, CT: FASB, 2006.

Deloitte Touche Tohmatsu Limited. "Amendments to IAS 24 Related Party Disclosures." *IASPlus: IASB Agenda Project.* Accessed October 2009. http://www.iasplus.com/agenda/relatedparty.htm.

———. "China Adopts 38 New Accounting Standards." *IASPlus,* February 16, 2006. Accessed November 2013. http://www.iasplus.com/en/news/2006/February/news2654.

Demerjian, Peter R. "Accounting Standards and Debt Covenants: Has the 'Balance Sheet Approach' Led to a Decline in the Use of Balance Sheet Covenants?" *Journal of Accounting and Economics* 52, no. 2 (2011): 178–202.

Demsetz, Harold. "Toward a Theory of Property Rights." *American Economic Review* 57, no. 2 (1967): 347–59.

Department of Commerce. "Antidumping Methodologies in Proceedings Involving Certain Non-Market Economies: Market-Oriented Enterprise." *Federal Register* 72, no. 101 (2007): 29302–4.

Desai, Mihir. "The Incentive Bubble." *Harvard Business Review* 90, no. 3 (2012): 124–33.

Dhaliwal, Dan S. "Some Economic Determinants of Management Lobbying for Alternative Methods of Accounting: Evidence from the Accounting for Interest Cost Issue." *Journal of Business Finance and Accounting* 9, no. 2 (1982): 255–65.

Dichev, Ilia D. "On the Balance Sheet-Based Model of Financial Reporting." *Accounting Horizons* 22, no. 4 (2008): 453–70.

Dichev, Ilia D., and Vicki W. Tang. "Matching and the Changing Properties of Accounting Earnings over the Last 40 Years." *Accounting Review* 83, no. 6 (2008): 1425–60.

Disclosure Insight. "Bank Goodwill Impairment Study." March 2009. Accessed March 2015. https://www.sec.gov/comments/4-573/4573-230.pdf.

Downs, Anthony. "An Economic Theory of Political Action in a Democracy." *Journal of Political Economy* 65, no. 2 (1957): 135–50.

Dutka, Paul. "Defending 1993 ACT Claims: Rewriting the Playbook after Fait v. Regions Fin. Corp." *Bloomberg Law,* August 27, 2013. Accessed January 2014. http://about.bloomberglaw.com/practitioner-contributions/defending-1933-act-claims-rewriting-the-playbook-after-fait-v-regions-fin-corp.

Dwyer, Paula. "The Big Four: Too Few to Fail." *BusinessWeek,* August 31, 2003. Accessed September 2013. http://www.businessweek.com/stories/2003-08-31/commentary-the-big-four-too-few-to-fail.

Dyck, Alexander, David Moss, and Luigi Zingales. "Media versus Special Interests." *Journal of Law and Economics* 56, no. 3 (2013): 521–53.

Dyckman, Thomas, Robert P. Magee, and Glenn Pfeiffer. *Financial Accounting*. 3rd ed. West-mont, IL: Cambridge Business Publishers, 2011.

Dye, Ronald A., and Shyam Sunder. "Why Not Allow the FASB and IASB Standards to Compete in the U.S.?" *Accounting Horizons* 15, no. 3 (2001): 257–71.

Dykes, Robert R. B. "Robert R. B. Dykes to Financial Accounting Standards Board." Letter of Comment No. 31A, file ref. 1033-201. Norwalk, CT: FASB, 1999.

Dyreng, Scott D., Michelle Hanlon, and Edward L. Maydew. "The Effects of Executives on Cor-porate Tax Avoidance." *Accounting Review* 85, no. 4 (2010): 1163–89.

Elhauge, Einer. "Sacrificing Corporate Profits in the Public Interest." *New York University Law Review* 80, no. 3 (2005): 733–869.

Ely, Kristin, and Gregory Waymire. "Intangible Assets and Stock Prices in the Pre-SEC Era." *Journal of Accounting Research* 37, sup. (1999): 17–44.

Ernst & Ernst v. Hochfelder. 425 U.S. 185, 96 S. Ct. 1375, 47 L. Ed. 2d 668 (1976).

Ernst & Young. "Ernst & Young to Financial Accounting Standards Board." Letter of Comment No. 67, file ref. 1250-001. Norwalk, CT: FASB, 2006.

European Commission. "Council Regulation No. 1042/2010." Accessed November 2013. http://eur-lex.europa.eu / LexUriServ/ LexUriServ.do?uri=OJ:L:2010:299:0007:0028:EN:PDF.

———. "Council Regulation No. 1174/2005." Accessed November 2013. http://eur-lex.europa .eu / LexUriServ/ LexUriServ.do?uri=OJ:L:2005:189:0001:0014:EN:PDF.

———. "Council Regulation No. 1225/2009." Accessed November 2013. http://trade.ec.europa .eu / doclib/docs/2010/april/tradoc_146035.pdf.

European Parliament. "Proposal for a European Parliament and Council Regulation on the Application of International Accounting Standards." Accessed November 2013. http://www.europarl.europa.eu /sides/getDoc.do?type=REPORT&reference=A5-2002-0070& language=EN.

Fabricant, Solomon. "Revaluations of Fixed Assets, 1925–34." *National Bureau of Economic Re-search* 62 (1936): 1–12.

Faccio, Mara. "Politically Connected Firms." *American Economic Review* 96, no. 1 (2006): 369–86.

Fait v. Regions Financial Corp. 655 F.3d 105 (2d Cir. 2011).

Fama, Eugene F., and Michael C. Jensen. "Separation of Ownership and Control." *Journal of Law and Economics* 26, no. 2 (1983): 301–25.

Feilmeier, Steve. Interview by Karthik Ramanna. New York. July 30, 2012.

Feinman, Jay M. "Liability of Accountants for Negligent Auditing: Doctrine, Policy, and Ideol-ogy." *Florida State Law Review* 31 (2003): 17–65.

Feldman, Daniel C. "The Development and Enforcement of Group Norms." *Academy of Man-agement Review* 9, no. 1 (1984): 47–53.

Fields, Thomas D., Thomas Z. Lys, and Linda Vincent. "Empirical Research on Accounting Choice." *Journal of Accounting and Economics* 31, no. 1 (2001): 255–307.

Figueiredo, John M., and Emerson H. Tiller. "The Structure and Conduct of Corporate Lob-bying: How Firms Lobby the Federal Communications Commission." *Journal of Economics and Management Strategy* 10, no. 1 (2001): 91–122.

Financial Accounting Foundation. "Financial Accounting Foundation Appoints Members to Newly Created Private Company Council." September 19, 2012. Accessed October 2013. http:// www.accountingfoundation.org/cs/ContentServer?site=Foundation&c= FAFContent_C&pagename=Foundation%2FFAFContent_C%2FFAFNewsPage&cid= 1176160336308.

———. "The Financial Accounting Foundation Board of Trustees Approves Changes to Oversight, Structure and Operations of FAF, FASB and GASB." February 26, 2008. Accessed February 2014. http://www.fasb.org/jsp/FASB/Page/nr022608.pdf.

———. *Financial Accounting Foundation Board of Trustees: Establishment of the Private Company Council Final Report.* May 30, 2012. Accessed October 2013. http://www.accountingfoundation.org/cs/ContentServer?site=Foundation&c=Document_C&pagename=Foundation%2FDocument_C%2FFAFDocumentPage&cid=1176160066778.

———. "Private Company Council (PCC)." Audio recording. Accessed October 2013. http://www.accountingfoundation.org/jsp/Foundation/Page/FAFSectionPage&cid=1176158985794.

———. "Request for Comment: Plan to Establish the Private Company Standards Improvement Council, October 4, 2011." Accessed April 2012. http://www.accountingfoundation.org/cs/ContentServer?site=Foundation&c=Document_C&pagename=Foundation%2FDocument_C%2FFAFDocumentPage&cid=1176158991959.

Financial Accounting Standards Board. "Accounting for Goodwill for Public Business Entities and Not-for-Profits." February 18, 2014. Accessed February 2014. http://www.fasb.org/cs/ContentServer?c=FASBContent_C&pagename=FASB%2FFASBContent_C%2FProjectUpdatePage&cid=1176163679475.

———. "Conceptual Framework: Statement of Financial Accounting Concepts No. 8, September 2010." Accessed November 2013. http://www.fasb.org/jsp/FASB/Page/PreCodSectionPage&cid=1176156317989.

———. "Exposure Draft: Accounting for Stock-Based Compensation." Stamford, CT: FASB, 1993.

———. "Exposure Draft 201-A: Business Combinations and Intangible Assets." Norwalk, CT: FASB, 1999.

———. "Exposure Draft 201-R: Business Combinations and Intangible Assets—Accounting for Goodwill." Norwalk, CT: FASB, 2001.

———. "FASB Board Meeting." Minutes from FASB Board Meeting, May 31, 2000.

———. "FASB Board Meeting." Minutes from FASB Board Meeting, September 29, 2000.

———. "FASB Standard Establishes Fair Value Option for Financial Assets and Liabilities." February 15, 2007. Accessed January 2014. http://www.fasb.org/news/nr021507.shtml.

———. "Financial Accounting Foundation to Increase Size of FASB: FASB Chairman Herz to Retire after More than Eight Successful Years." August 24, 2010. Accessed January 2014. http://www.fasb.org/cs/ContentServer?pagename=FASB/FASBContent_C/NewsPage&cid=1176157228010.

———. "International Convergence of Accounting Standards—a Brief History." Accessed November 2013. http://www.fasb.org/jsp/FASB/Page/SectionPage&cid=1176156304264.

———. "Invitation to Comment 174: Issues Associated with FASB Project on Business Combinations." Norwalk, CT: FASB, 1997.

———. "Invitation to Comment 192-A: Methods of Accounting for Business Combinations: Recommendations of the G4+1 for Achieving Convergence." Norwalk, CT: FASB, 1998.

———. "Invitation to Comment 192-A: Methods of Accounting for Business Combinations: Recommendations of the G4+1 for Achieving Convergence, Analysis of Comment Letters, March 24." Norwalk, CT: FASB, 1999.

———. "Meetings." Accessed September 2013. http://www.fasb.org.

———. "The Norwalk Agreement." Accessed November 2013. http://www.fasb.org/news/memorandum.pdf.

———. "Standards-Setting Process." Accessed September 2013. http://www.fasb.org.

———. "Statement of Financial Accounting Concepts No. 1, November 1978." Accessed September 2014. http://www.fasb.org/pdf/con1.pdf.

———. "Statement of Financial Accounting Concepts No. 2, May 1980." Accessed November 2013. http://www.fasb.org/pdf/con2.pdf.

———. "Statement of Financial Accounting Concepts No. 6, December 1985." Accessed January 2014. http://www.fasb.org/pdf/con6.pdf.

———. "Statement of Financial Accounting Concepts No. 7, February 2000." Accessed October 2014. http://www.fasb.org/pdf/con7.pdf.

———. "Statement of Financial Accounting Standards No. 123." Accessed February 2014. http://www.fasb.org/pdf/fas123.pdf.

———. "Statement of Financial Accounting Standards No. 123R." Accessed February 2014. http://www.fasb.org/pdf/fas123r.pdf.

———. "Statement of Financial Accounting Standards No. 131: Disclosures about Segments of an Enterprise and Related Information June 1997." Accessed January 2014. http://www.fasb.org/pdf/fas131.pdf.

———. "Statement of Financial Accounting Standards No. 141: Business Combinations June 2001." Accessed January 2014. http://www.fasb.org/pdf/fas141.pdf.

———. "Statement of Financial Accounting Standards No. 142: Goodwill and Other Intangible Assets June 2001." Accessed January 2014. http://www.fasb.org/pdf/fas142.pdf.

———. "Summary of Statement No. 157." Accessed January 2014. http://www.fasb.org/summary/stsum157.shtml.

———. "Summary of Statement No. 159." Accessed January 2014. http://www.fasb.org/summary/stsum159.shtml.

Financial Reporting Council. *Tribunal Report: Deloitte & Touche and Mr. Maghsoud Einollahi.* Accessed October 2013. http://www.frc.org.uk/Our-Work/Publications/Professional-Discipline/Tribunal-Report-Deloitte-Touche-and-Mr-Maghsoud-Ei.pdf.

Finnemore, Martha, and Kathryn Sikkink. "International Norm Dynamics and Political Change." *International Organization* 52, no. 4 (1998): 887–917.

Fourcade, Marion. *Economists and Societies: Discipline and Profession in the United States, Britain, & France, 1890s to 1990s.* Princeton, NJ: Princeton University Press, 2009.

Francis, Jennifer, J. Douglas Hanna, and Linda Vincent. "Causes and Effects of Discretionary Asset Write-Offs." *Journal of Accounting Research* 34, sup. (1996): 117–34.

Francis, Jere R. "Lobbying against Proposed Accounting Standards: The Case of Employer's Pension Accounting." *Journal of Accounting and Public Policy* 6, no. 1 (1987): 35–57.

Freeman, James. "The Supreme Case against Sarbanes-Oxley." *Wall Street Journal,* December 15, 2009. Accessed September 2012. http://online.wsj.com/article/SB10001424052748704431804574539921864252380.html.

Friedman, Benjamin M. *The Moral Consequences of Economic Growth.* New York: Alfred A. Knopf, 2005.

Friedman, Milton. *Capitalism and Freedom.* Chicago: University of Chicago Press, 2002.

———. *Price Theory.* New Brunswick, NJ: Transaction Publishers, 1962.

———. "The Social Responsibility of Business Is to Increase Its Profits." *New York Times Magazine,* September 13, 1970.

Friedman, Milton, and Rose Friedman. *Free to Choose: A Personal Statement.* San Diego, CA: Harcourt, 1980.

Friis, Morten. Interview by Karthik Ramanna. Cambridge, MA. October 24, 2013.

Gabarro, Jack, and Leslie Perlow. "Course Purpose." Authentic Leadership Development Course No. 2090. Accessed October 2013. http://www.hbs.edu/coursecatalog/2090.html.

Galbraith, John K. *The Great Crash of 1929*. 1929. Reprint, New York: Houghton Mifflin Harcourt, 2009.

Gates, Gary J. "How Many People Are Lesbian, Gay, Bisexual and Transgender?" Working paper, the Williams Institute UCLA School of Law, Los Angeles, CA, 2011.

Ge, Weili, Dawn Matsumoto, and Jenny L. Zhang. "Do CFOs Have Style? An Empirical Investigation of the Effect of Individual CFOs on Accounting Practices." *Contemporary Accounting Research* 28, no. 4 (2011): 1141–79.

Gibbons, Robert, and Kevin J. Murphy. "Relative Performance Evaluation for Chief Executive Officers." *Industrial and Labor Relations Review* (1990): 30S–51S.

Gipper, Brandon, Brett Lombardi, and Douglas J. Skinner. "The Politics of Accounting Standard-Setting: A Review of Empirical Research." *Australian Journal of Management* 38, no. 3 (2013): 523–51.

Glasner, Joanna. "Icahn's eBay Claims Just Tip of Iceberg for VC-Board Conflicts." *Private Markets*, March 12, 2014. Accessed March 2015. http://private1416.rssing.com/browser.php?indx=25992376&item=118.

Glassman, Cynthia. "Complexity in Financial Reporting and Disclosure Regulation." Speech given at the Twenty-fifth Annual USC Leventhal School of Accounting SEC and Financial Reporting Institute Conference, Pasadena, CA, June 8, 2006.

"Global 500: China." *Fortune*. Accessed October 2009. http://money.cnn.com/magazines/fortune/global500/2009/countries/China.html.

Goldsmith, George. Interview by Karthik Ramanna. Cambridge, MA. August 20, 2013.

Gonedes, Nicholas J., and Nicholas Dopuch. "Capital Market Equilibrium, Information Production, and Selecting Accounting Techniques: Theoretical Framework and Review of Empirical Work." *Journal of Accounting Research* 12 (1974): 48–129.

"Goodwill Hunting: What the Corus Write-Off Reveals." *Economist*, May 18, 2013. Accessed November 2013. http://www.economist.com/news/business/21578082-what-corus-write-reveals-goodwill-hunting.

Gormley, William T., Jr. "Regulatory Issue Networks in a Federal System." *Polity* 18, no. 4 (1986): 595–620.

———. "A Test of the Revolving Door Hypothesis at the FCC." *American Journal of Political Science* 23 (1979): 665–83.

Government Accountability Office. "Audits of Public Companies: Continued Concentration in Audit Market for Large Public Companies Does Not Call for Immediate Action: January 2008." Accessed January 2014. http://www.gao.gov/new.items/d08163.pdf.

———. "Public Accounting Firms: Mandated Study on Consolidation and Competition: July 2003." Accessed January 2014. http://www.gao.gov/new.items/d03864.pdf.

Governmental Accounting Standards Board. "Facts about GASB." Accessed September 2013. http://www.gasb.org.

Greenwood, Robin, and David Scharfstein. "The Growth of Finance." *Journal of Economic Perspectives* 27, no. 2 (2013): 3–28.

Grossman, Gene M., and Elhanan Helpman. *Special Interest Politics*. Cambridge, MA: MIT Press, 2001.

Güth, Werner, and Hartmut Kliemt. "The Indirect Evolutionary Approach: Bridging the Gap between Rationality and Adaptation." *Rationality and Society* 10, no. 3 (1998): 377–99.

Hanover, Alain J. "Alain J. Hanover to Financial Accounting Standards Board." Letter of Comment No. 33, file ref. 1033-201. Norwalk, CT: FASB, 1999.

Haring, John R., Jr. "Accounting Rules and 'The Accounting Establishment.'" *Journal of Business* 52 (1979): 507–19.

Harrington, George W. "George W. Harrington to Financial Accounting Standards Board." Letter of Comment No. 139, file ref. 1033-201R. Norwalk, CT: FASB, 2001.

Hawkins, David F. "The Development of Modern Financial Reporting Practices among American Manufacturing Corporations." *Business History Review* 37, no. 3 (1963): 135–68.

Hayek, Friedrich A. *The Road to Serfdom.* London: Routledge, 1951.

———. "The Use of Knowledge in Society." *American Economic Review* 35, no. 4 (1945): 519–30.

Healy, Paul M. "The Effect of Bonus Schemes on Accounting Decisions." *Journal of Accounting and Economics* 7, no. 1 (1985): 85–107.

Healy, Paul M., and Krishna G. Palepu. "The Fall of Enron." *Journal of Economic Perspectives* 17, no. 2 (2003): 3–26.

———. "Information Asymmetry, Corporate Disclosure, and the Capital Markets: A Review of the Empirical Disclosure Literature." *Journal of Accounting and Economics* 31, nos. 1–3 (2001): 405–40.

Healy, Paul M., and James M. Wahlen. "A Review of the Earnings Management Literature and Its Implications for Standard Setting." *Accounting Horizons* 13, no. 4 (1999): 365–83.

Henderson, Rebecca. "Course Objectives." Reimagining Capitalism Course No. 1524. Accessed October 2013. http://www.hbs.edu/coursecatalog/1524.html.

Henderson, Rebecca, and Karthik Ramanna. "Managers and Market Capitalism." Working paper 13-075, Harvard Business School, Boston, MA, 2013.

Hill, Charles W. L., and Thomas M. Jones. "Stakeholder-Agency Theory." *Journal of Management Studies* 29, no. 2 (1992): 131–54.

Hillman, Amy J., Gerald D. Keim, and Douglas Schuler. "Corporate Political Activity: A Review and Research Agenda." *Journal of Management* 30, no. 6 (2004): 837–57.

Hitt, Greg, and Michael Schroeder. "Enron Hoped to Extend Influence to International Accounting Group." *Wall Street Journal*, February 14, 2002. Accessed January 2014. http://online.wsj.com/news/articles/SB1013641326356372 80.

Holmstrom, Bengt. "Moral Hazard and Observability." *Bell Journal of Economics* 10, no. 1 (1979): 74–91.

Holthausen, Robert W., and Richard W. Leftwich. "The Economic Consequences of Accounting Choice: Implications of Costly Contracting and Monitoring." *Journal of Accounting and Economics* 5 (1983): 77–117.

Holthausen, Robert W., and Ross L. Watts. "The Relevance of the Value-Relevance Literature for Financial Accounting Standard Setting." *Journal of Accounting and Economics* 31, nos. 1–3 (2001): 3–75.

Holy Bible (NIV). International Bible Society, 1984. Reprint, Grand Rapids, MI: Zondervan, 1989.

"How to Become a Higher-Ambition Leader." *Forbes*, January 20, 2013. Accessed October 2013. http://www.forbes.com/sites/hbsworkingknowledge/2013/03/20/how-to-become-a-higher-ambition-leader.

Huang, Yasheng. *Capitalism with Chinese Characteristics.* Cambridge, UK: Cambridge University Press, 2004.

Huber, George P. "Organizational Learning: The Contributing Processes and the Literatures." *Organization Science* 2, no. 1 (1991): 88–115.

Human Rights Campaign. "Corporate Equality Index 2014." Accessed June 2014. http://www
    .hrc.org/campaigns/corporate-equality-index.
"Innovation: Tata Ahead of BMW, Nokia, Dell!" *Rediff Business News*, April 16, 2010. Accessed
    April 2010. http://business.rediff.com/slide-show/2010/apr/16/slide-show-1-innovation
    -tata-ahead-of-bmw-nokia-dell.htm.
International Accounting Standards Board. "IASB Simplifies Requirements for Disclosure
    of Related-Party Transactions." Accessed February 2015. http://www.ifrs.org/News/
    Press-Releases/Documents/IASBsimplifiesrequirementsfordisclosureofrelatedparty
    transactions2.pdf.
International Financial Reporting Standards. "About the IFRS Foundation and the IASB." Ac-
    cessed November 2013. http://www.ifrs.org/The-organisation/Pages/IFRS-Foundation
    -and-the-IASB.aspx.
———. "Reclassification of Financial Assets, Amendments to IAS 39 Financial Instruments:
    Recognition and Measurement and IFRS 7 Financial Instruments: Disclosures, October
    2008." Accessed November 2013. http://www.ifrs.org/News/Press-Releases/Documents/
    AmdmentsIAS39andIFRS7.pdf.
International Trade Administration. "Public Comments Received on Antidumping Methodolo-
    gies in Proceedings Involving Certain Non-Market Economies: Market-Oriented Enterprise
    (72 FR 29302)." June 25, 2007. Accessed November 2013. http://ia.ita.doc.gov/download/
    nme-moe/nme-moe-cmt-20070625-index.html.
Investment Company Institute. "Comment Letter by CEO Paul S. Stevens on the SEC's Request
    for Comment on Mark-to-Market Accounting." Accessed April 2011. http://www.ici.org/
    pdf/23068.pdf.
Israel, Jonathan I. *Radical Enlightenment: Philosophy and the Making of Modernity 1670–1750*.
    Oxford, UK: Oxford University Press, 2002.
Jensen, Michael C. "The Agency Costs of Free Cash Flow: Corporate Finance and Takeovers."
    American Economic Review 76 (1986): 323–29.
———. "Value Maximization and the Corporate Objective Function." In *Breaking the Code of
    Change*, edited by Michael Beer and Nitin Nohria, 37–58. Boston: Harvard Business School
    Press, 2000.
Jensen, Michael C., and William H. Meckling. "Theory of the Firm: Managerial Behavior, Agency
    Costs and Ownership Structure." *Journal of Financial Economics* 3, no. 4 (1976): 305–60.
Jensen, Michael C., and Kevin J. Murphy. "CEO Incentives: It's Not How Much You Pay, but
    How." *Harvard Business Review* 68, no. 3 (1990): 138–53.
———. "Performance Pay and Top Management Incentives." *Journal of Political Economy* 98,
    no. 2 (1990): 225–64.
Jensen, Michael C., and Richard S. Ruback. "The Market for Corporate Control: The Scientific
    Evidence." *Journal of Financial Economics* 11, nos. 1–4 (1983): 5–50.
Johnson, L. Todd. "Relevance and Reliability." *FASB Report*, February 28, 2005. Accessed Novem-
    ber 2013. http://www.fasb.org/articles&reports/relevance_and_reliability_tfr_feb_2005.pdf.
Jones, Jennifer J. "Earnings Management during Import Relief Investigations." *Journal of Ac-
    counting Research* 29, no. 2 (1991): 193–228.
Kallgren, Carl A., Raymond R. Reno, and Robert B. Cialdini. "A Focus Theory of Normative
    Conduct: When Norms Do and Do Not Affect Behavior." *Personality and Social Psychology
    Bulletin* 26 (2000): 1006.
Kalt, Joseph P., and Mark A. Zupan. "Capture and Ideology in the Economic Theory of Politics."
    American Economic Review 74, no. 3 (1984): 279–300.

Kamnikar, Judith, Edward Kamnikar, and Ashley Burrowes. "One Size Does Not Fit All." *Journal of Accountancy* 213, no. 1 (2012): 46–49.

Karp, Brad S., and Paul Weiss. "Second Circuit Clarifies Materiality Requirement in Securities Fraud Cases." *Harvard Law School Forum on Corporate Governance and Financial Regulation* (blog). September 10, 2011. Accessed January 2014. https://blogs.law.harvard.edu/corpgov/tag/fait-v-regions-financial.

Katz, David M. "Hot Times for Accounting Officials." *CFO*, March 11, 2008. Accessed December 2013. http://ww2.cfo.com/accounting-tax/2008/03/hot-times-for-accounting-officials.

Kellogg, Robert L. "Accounting Activities, Security Prices, and Class Action Lawsuits." *Journal of Accounting and Economics* 6, no. 3 (1984): 185–204.

Kelly, Lauren. "Corporate Management Lobbying on FAS No. 8: Some Further Evidence." *Journal of Accounting Research* 23, no. 2 (1985): 619–32.

Khanna, Tarun. *Billions of Entrepreneurs: How China and India Are Reshaping Their Futures and Yours.* Boston: Harvard Business School Press, 2008.

Khanna, Tarun, Krishna G. Palepu, and Richard J. Bullock. *House of Tata: Acquiring a Global Footprint* (HBS No. 708-446). Boston: Harvard Business School Publishing, 2009.

Kinney, William R. "Audit Technology and Preferences for Auditing Standards." *Journal of Accounting and Economics* 8 (1986): 73–89.

Kitcher, Philip. *The Ethical Project.* Cambridge, MA: Harvard University Press, 2011.

Kothari, S. P., and Rebecca Lester. "The Role of Accounting in the Financial Crisis: Lessons for the Future." *Accounting Horizons* 26, no. 2 (2012): 335–51.

Kothari, S. P., Thomas Lys, Clifford W. Smith, and Ross L. Watts. "Auditor Liability and Information Disclosure." *Journal of Accounting, Auditing and Finance* 3 (1988): 307–39.

Kothari, S. P., Karthik Ramanna, and Douglas J. Skinner. "Implications for GAAP from an Analysis of Positive Research in Accounting." *Journal of Accounting and Economics* 50, nos. 2–3 (2010): 246–86.

Kothari, S. P., Susan Shu, and Peter D. Wysocki. "Do Managers Withhold Bad News?" *Journal of Accounting Research* 47, no. 1 (2009): 241–76.

KPMG. "Additional Relief on Foreign Exchange Capitalization." 2012. Accessed December 2013. http://www.moneycontrol.com/news_html_files/news_attachment/2012/Flash%20News%20-%20Additional%20relief%20on%20foreign%20exchange%20capitalisation%20Final.pdf.

———. "KPMG to Financial Accounting Standards Board." Letter of Comment No. 58, file ref. 1250-001. Norwalk, CT: FASB, 2006.

Kroszner, Randall S., and Thomas Stratmann. "Corporate Campaign Contributions, Repeat Giving, and the Rewards to Legislator Reputation." *Journal of Law and Economics* 48, no. 1 (2005): 41–71.

———. "Interest-Group Competition and the Organization of Congress: Theory and Evidence from Financial Services' Political Action Committees." *American Economic Review* 88, no. 5 (1998): 1163–87.

LaFond, Ryan, and Ross L. Watts. "The Information Role of Conservative Financial Statements." *Accounting Review* 83, no. 2 (2008): 447–78.

Lambert, Richard A., and David F. Larcker. "An Analysis of the Use of Accounting and Market Measures of Performance in Executive Compensation Contracts." *Journal of Accounting Research* 25 (1987): 85–125.

LaPorta, Rafael, Florencio Lopez-de-Silanes, Andrei Shleifer, and Robert W. Vishny. "Investor Protection and Corporate Valuation." *Journal of Finance* 57, no. 3 (2002): 1147–70.

Larson, Magali S. *The Rise of Professionalism: A Sociological Analysis.* Berkeley, CA: University of California Press, 1977.

Laux, Christian, and Christian Leuz. "The Crisis of Fair-Value Accounting: Making Sense of the Recent Debate." *Accounting, Organizations and Society* 34, no. 6 (2009): 826–34.

———. "Did Fair-Value Accounting Contribute to the Financial Crisis?" *Journal of Economic Perspectives* 24, no. 1 (2010): 93–118.

Leaver, Clare. "Bureaucratic Minimal Squawk Behavior: Theory and Evidence from Regulatory Agencies." *American Economic Review* 99 (2009): 572–607.

Lee, Charles M. C. "Market Efficiency and Accounting Research: A Discussion of 'Capital Market Research in Accounting' by S. P. Kothari." *Journal of Accounting and Economics* 31, nos. 1–3 (2001): 233–53.

Lee, D. Scott, Donald R. Fraser, Joseph Reising, and Wanda Wallace. "Political Costs and the Fate of the FASB Proposal to Recognize the Costs of Employee Stock Options." *Journal of Financial Statement Analysis* 3 (1998): 67–79.

Leftwich, Richard W. "Accounting Information in Private Markets: Evidence from Private Lending Agreements." *Accounting Review* 58, no. 1 (1983): 23–42.

———. "The Agenda of the Financial Accounting Standards Board." Working paper, University of Chicago, Chicago, IL, 1995.

———. "Market Failure Fallacies and Accounting Information." *Journal of Accounting and Economics* 2, no. 3 (1980): 193–211.

Leland, Hayne E. "Insider Trading: Should It Be Prohibited?" *Journal of Political Economy* 100, no. 4 (1992): 859–87.

Leone, Marie. "'Spineless?' UK Pressure Targets Fair Value Weakening." *CFO*, November 11, 2008. Accessed November 2013. http://www.cfo.com/article.cfm/12586836?f=related.

Leuz, Christian. "Different Approaches to Corporate Reporting Regulation: How Jurisdictions Differ and Why." *Accounting and Business Research* 40, no. 3 (2010): 229–56.

Leuz, Christian, Dieter Pfaff, and Anthony Hopwood, eds. *The Economics and Politics of Accounting: International Perspectives on Research Trends, Policy, and Practice.* New York: Oxford University Press, 2004.

Leuz, Christian, Alexander J. Triantis, and Tracy Yue Wang. "Why Do Firms Go Dark? Causes and Economic Consequences of Voluntary SEC Deregistration." *Journal of Accounting and Economics* 45, nos. 2–3 (2008): 181–208.

Li, Kevin K., and Richard G. Sloan. "Has Goodwill Accounting Gone Bad?" Working paper, University of Toronto, Toronto, Canada, 2009.

Li, Ningzhong. "Negotiated Measurement Rules in Debt Contracts." *Journal of Accounting Research* 48, no. 5 (2010): 1103–44.

Lindbeck, Assar. "Award Ceremony Speech." Speech given at the Sveriges Riksbank Prize in Economic Sciences in Memory of Alfred Nobel, 1970. Accessed November 2013. http://www.nobelprize.org/nobel_prizes/economic-sciences/laureates/1970/press.html.

Lucchese, Cynthia L. "Cynthia L. Lucchese to Financial Accounting Standards Board." Letter of Comment No. 32A, file ref. 1033-201. Norwalk, CT: FASB, 1999.

Lucchetti, Aaron, and Serena Ng. "How Rating Firms' Calls Fueled Subprime Mess." *Wall Street Journal*, August 15, 2007. Accessed October 2013. http://online.wsj.com/news/articles/SB118714461352698015.

Lys, Thomas, and Linda Vincent. "An Analysis of Value Destruction in AT&T's Acquisition of NCR." *Journal of Financial Economics* 39, no. 2 (1995): 353–78.

Lys, Thomas, and Ross L. Watts. "Lawsuits against Auditors." *Journal of Accounting Research* 32 (1994): 65–93.

Malegam, Y. H. Interview by Karthik Ramanna. Mumbai, India. January 8, 2010.

Masters-Stout, Brenda, Michael L. Costigan, and Linda M. Lovata. "Goodwill Impairments and Chief Executive Officer Tenure." *Critical Perspectives on Accounting* 19, no. 8 (2008): 1370–83.

Mazar, Nina, On Amir, and Dan Ariely. "The Dishonesty of Honest People: A Theory of Self-Concept Maintenance." *Journal of Marketing Research* 45, no. 6 (2008): 633–44.

McAdams, Richard. "The Origin, Development, and Regulation of Norms." *Michigan Law Review* 96, no. 2 (1997): 338–433.

McCarty, Nolan, Keith T. Poole, and Howard Rosenthal. *Political Bubbles: Financial Crises and the Failure of American Democracy.* Princeton, NJ: Princeton University Press, 2013.

McGregor, Richard. "China Adopts New Accounting Standards." *Financial Times*, February 16, 2006. Accessed January 2014. http://www.ft.com/cms/s/0/c69ba44a-9e07-11da-b641-0000779e2340.html#axzz2sr2B0Mv2.

Meaning of the Holy Qur'an. Translated by Abdullah Yusuf Ali. Reprint, Beltsville, MD: Amana, 2003.

Melancon, Barry. Interview by Karthik Ramanna and Luis Viceira. Norwalk, CT. July 27, 2012.

Meulbroek, Lisa K. "An Empirical Analysis of Illegal Insider Trading." *Journal of Finance* 47, no. 5 (1992): 1661–99.

Micklethwait, John, and Adrian Wooldridge. *The Company: A Short History of a Revolutionary Idea.* New York: Modern Library, 2005.

Ministry of Finance. "British 'Financial Times': China Will Be Part of the Adoption of International Accounting Standards." February 16, 2006. Accessed November 2013. http://www.mof.gov.cn/zhuantihuigu/kjsjzzfbh/mtbd/200805/t20080519_23014.html.

———. "Wang: Chinese Language Has Been with the International Accounting Standards Convergence." February 28, 2007. Accessed November 2013. http://www.mof.gov.cn/zhengwuxinxi/caijingshidian/xinhuanet/200805/t20080519_25808.html.

Morgan, David. "Private Company Reporting Needs and Independent Board." *Accounting Today* 26, no. 1 (2012): 11.

Myers, Stewart C. "Determinants of Corporate Borrowing." *Journal of Financial Economics* 5, no. 2 (1977): 147–75.

Nelson, Kenneth, and Robert H. Strawser. "A Note on APB Opinion No. 16." *Journal of Accounting Research* 8, no. 2 (1970): 284–89.

Nelson, Mark W., John A. Elliott, and Robin L. Tarpley. "Evidence from Auditors about Managers' and Auditors' Earnings Management Decisions." *Accounting Review* 77, no. s-1 (2002): 175–202.

New York Stock Exchange. "NYSE Euronext and Greater China." Accessed September 2009. http://www.nyse.com/pdfs/NYSEEuronext_China_factsheet-CN.pdf.

Nocera, Joseph. "Auditors: Too Few to Fail." *New York Times*, June 25, 2005. Accessed September 2013. http://www.nytimes.com/2005/06/25/business/25nocera.html?pagewanted=all &_r=0.

Norris, Floyd. "Accounting Board Wants Options to Be Reported as an Expense." *New York Times*, April 1, 2004. Accessed September 2013. http://www.nytimes.com/2004/04/01/business/01options.html.

———. "Accounting Détente Delayed." *New York Times*, July 19, 2012.

———. "New Cast Enters Fight in Accounting." *New York Times*, October 22, 2010.

———. "When Accountants Act as Bankers." *New York Times*, September 12, 2013. Accessed October 2013. http://www.nytimes.com/2013/09/13/business/when-auditors-act-as-bankers .html.

Office of the Comptroller of the Currency. "About the OCC." Accessed October 2013. http:// www.occ.gov/about/what-we-do/mission/index-about.html.

Ollman v. Evans. 750 F.2d 970 (DC Cir. 1984).

Olson, Mancur. *The Logic of Collective Action: Public Goods and the Theory of Groups*. Cambridge, MA: Harvard University Press, 1965.

Organisation for Economic Co-operation and Development. "Economic Survey of China 2013." Accessed November 2013. http://www.oecd.org/economy/china-2013.

Ostrom, Elinor. "Collective Action and the Evolution of Social Norms." *Journal of Economic Perspectives* 14, no. 3 (2000): 137–58.

———. *Governing the Commons: The Evolution of Institutions for Collective Action*. Cambridge, UK: Cambridge University Press, 1990.

Paine, Lynn S. *The Fiduciary Relationship: A Legal Perspective* (HBS No. 304-064). Boston: Harvard Business School Publishing, 2009.

Palepu, Krishna G., Suraj Srinivasan, and Aldo Sesia. *New Century Financial Corporation* (HBS No. 109-034). Boston: Harvard Business School Publishing, 2009.

Palmrose, Zoe-Vonna. "An Analysis of Auditor Litigation and Audit Service Quality." *Accounting Review* 63 (1988): 55–73.

Peltzman, Sam. "Toward a More General Theory of Regulation." *Journal of Law and Economics* 19, no. 2 (1976): 211–40.

Persson, Torsten, and Guido E. Tabellini. *Political Economics: Explaining Economic Policy*. Cambridge, MA: MIT Press, 2002.

Peterson, Randall, and Sarah Ronson. "Group Norms." In *The Blackwell Encyclopedia of Management*, vol. 11, edited by Cary L. Cooper, 150–51. Malden, MA: Blackwell Publishing, 2005.

Pigou, Arthur C. *The Economics of Welfare*. 1920. Rev. ed. London: Macmillan, 1938.

Polanyi, Karl. *The Great Transformation: The Political and Economic Origins of Our Time*. Boston: Beacon Press, 1957.

Polley, Terri. Interview by Karthik Ramanna and Luis Viceira. Norwalk, CT. July 27, 2012.

Poole, Keith T. "Recovering a Basic Space from a Set of Issue Scales." *American Journal of Political Science* 42 (1998): 954–93.

Pooling Accounting: Hearing before the Committee on Banking, Housing, and Urban Affairs, United States Senate, 106th Cong., 2d session. Washington, DC: Government Printing Office, 2000.

Porter, Michael E., and Mark R. Kramer. "Creating Shared Value." *Harvard Business Review* 89, nos. 1–2 (2011): 62–77.

Porter, Michael E., and Jan W. Rivkin. "Prosperity at Risk: Findings of Harvard Business School's Survey on U.S. Competitiveness." Accessed October 2013. http://www.hbs.edu/ competitiveness/pdf/hbscompsurvey.pdf.

Posner, Richard A. "The Social Costs of Monopoly and Regulation." *Journal of Political Economy* 83, no. 4 (1975): 807–28.

———. "Social Norms and the Law: An Economic Approach." *American Economic Review* 87, no. 2 (1997): 365–69.

Powell, Dennis. "Business Combination Purchase Accounting: Goodwill Impairment Test." Appendix to minutes of Financial Accounting Standards Board meeting, FASB, Norwalk, CT, September 29, 2000.

———. "Dennis Powell to Financial Accounting Standards Board." Letter of Comment No. 25A, file ref. 1033-201. Norwalk, CT: FASB, 1999.

Power, Michael. "The Politics of Brand Accounting in the United Kingdom." *European Accounting Review* 1, no. 1 (1992): 39–68.

Press Information Bureau. "Prime Minister Addresses the Tata Centenary Celebrations." April 22, 2008. Accessed April 2010. http://www.pib.nic.in/release/release.asp?relid= 37731.

PricewaterhouseCoopers. "Point of View: Financial Reporting for Private Companies." October 2010. Accessed April 2012. http://www.pwc.com/us/en/point-of-view/private-companies -reporting.jhtml.

———. "Similarities and Differences: A Comparison of IFRS, US GAAP, and Indian GAAP." Accessed November 2013. http://www.pwc.in/assets/pdfs/india-publications-similarities -differences.pdf.

"Private Companies: The Path to a Different Standard-Setting Framework." *FASB in Focus*, July 11, 2011. Accessed April 2012. http://www.fasb.org/cs/ContentServer?site=FASB &c=Document_C&pagename=FASB%2FDocument_C%2FDocumentPage&cid= 1176158732399.

Private Company Council. "Overview of Decisions Reached on PCC Issue No. 13-01 A, 'Accounting for Identifiable Intangible Assets in a Business Combination,' and PCC Issue No. 13-01B, 'Accounting for Goodwill.'" Accessed October 2013. http://www.fasb.org/cs/ BlobServer?blobkey=id&blobnocache=true&blobwhere=1175827727994&blobheader= application%2Fpdf&blobcol=urldata&blobtable=MungoBlobs.

Public Company Accounting Oversight Board. "AU Section 328: Auditing Fair-Value Measurement and Disclosures." Accessed January 2014. http://pcaobus.org/Standards/Auditing/ Pages/AU328.aspx.

Puro, Marsha. "Audit Firm Lobbying before the Financial Accounting Standards Board: An Empirical Study." *Journal of Accounting Research* 22, no. 2 (1984): 624–46.

Quaadman, Thomas. Interview by Karthik Ramanna and Luis Viceira. Norwalk, CT. July 27, 2012.

Rajan, Raghuram G., and Luigi Zingales. *Saving Capitalism from the Capitalists*. New York: Crown, 2003.

Ramanna, Karthik. "A Framework for Research on Corporate Accountability Reporting." *Accounting Horizons* 26, no. 2 (2013): 409–32.

———. *The Future of Financial Reporting* (HBS video case No. 110-701). Boston: Harvard Business School Publishing, 2010.

———. "The Implications of Unverifiable Fair-Value Accounting: Evidence from the Political Economy of Goodwill Accounting." *Journal of Accounting and Economics* 45, nos. 2–3 (2008): 253–81.

———. "The International Politics of IFRS Harmonization." *Accounting, Economics, and Law* 3, no. 2 (2013): 1–46.

———. *The Politics and Economics of Accounting for Goodwill at Cisco Systems (A)* (HBS No. 109-002). Boston, Harvard Business School Publishing, 2008.

———. "Why 'Fair Value' Is the Rule: How a Controversial Accounting Approach Gained Support." *Harvard Business Review* 91, no. 3 (2013): 99–101.

Ramanna, Karthik, and Sugata Roychowdhury. "Elections and Discretionary Accruals: Evidence from 2004." *Journal of Accounting Research* 48, no. 2 (2010): 445–75.

Ramanna, Karthik, and Matthew Shaffer. *Tapestry Networks* (HBS No. 114-051). Boston: Harvard Business School Publishing, 2014

Ramanna, Karthik, and Ewa Sletten. "Network Effects in Countries' Adoption of IFRS." *Accounting Review* 89, no. 4 (2014): 1517–43.

———. "Why Do Countries Adopt International Financial Reporting Standards?" Working paper 09-102, Harvard Business School, Boston, MA, 2009.

Ramanna, Karthik, and Rachna Tahilyani. *Leadership in Corporate Reporting Policy at Tata Steel* (HBS No. 111-028). Boston: Harvard Business School Publishing, 2010.

Ramanna, Karthik, and Luis M. Viceira. *The Private Company Council* (HBS No. 113-045). Boston: Harvard Business School Publishing, 2013.

Ramanna, Karthik, and Ross L. Watts. "Evidence on the Use of Unverifiable Estimates in Required Goodwill Impairment." *Review of Accounting Studies* 17, no. 4 (2012): 749–80.

Ramanna, Karthik, G. A. Donovan, and Nancy Dai. *IFRS in China* (HBS No. 110-037). Boston: Harvard Business School Publishing, 2009.

Ramanna, Karthik, Karol Misztal, and Daniela Beyersdorfer. *The IASB at a Crossroads: The Future of International Financial Reporting Standards (B)* (HBS No. 113-089). Boston: Harvard Business School Publishing, 2013.

Rau, P. Raghavendra, and Theo Vermaelen. "Glamour, Value and the Post-Acquisition Performance of Acquiring Firms." *Journal of Financial Economics* 49, no. 2 (1998): 223–53.

Ray, Michael, "Tea Party Movement." *Encyclopedia Britannica Online*. Accessed October 2013. http://www.britannica.com/EBchecked/topic/1673405/Tea-Party-movement.

Rayburn, Frank R., and Ollie S. Powers. "A History of Pooling of Interests Accounting for Business Combinations in the United States." *Accounting Historians Journal* 18, no. 2 (1991): 155–92.

Reilly, David, and Michael Rapoport. "Early Exit of FASB Chairman Raises Anxiety." *Wall Street Journal*, August 25, 2010. Accessed October 2013. http://online.wsj.com/news/articles/SB10001424052748704125604575450073232699814.

Reno, Raymond R., Robert B. Cialdini, and Carl A. Kallgren. "The Transsituational Influence of Social Norms." *Journal of Personality and Social Psychology* 64, no. 1 (1993): 104–12.

Ripley, William Z. *Main Street and Wall Street*. Boston: Little, Brown, and Company, 1927.

Ritter, Jay R., Xiaohui Gao, and Zhongyan Zhu. "Where Have All the IPOs Gone?" Working paper, University of Florida, Gainesville, FL, 2012.

Rogoff, Kenneth. "The Optimal Degree of Commitment to an Intermediate Monetary Target." *Quarterly Journal of Economics* 100, no. 4 (1985): 1169–89.

Romano, Roberta. "The States as a Laboratory: Legal Innovation and State Competition for Corporate Charters." *Yale Journal on Regulation* 23, no. 2 (2006): 209–47.

Ross, Stephen A. "The Economic Theory of Agency: The Principal's Problem." *American Economic Review* 63, no. 2 (1973): 134–39.

Roychowdhury, Sugata, and Ross L. Watts. "Asymmetric Timeliness of Earnings, Market-to-Book, and Conservatism in Financial Reporting." *Journal of Accounting and Economics* 44, no. 1 (2007): 2–31.

Ryan, Stephen G. "Accounting in and for the Subprime Crisis." *Accounting Review* 83, no. 6 (2008): 1605–38.

———. "Identifying Conditional Conservatism." *European Accounting Review* 15, no. 4 (2006): 511–25.

Samuelson, Paul A. *Foundations of Economic Analysis.* Cambridge, MA: Harvard University Press, 1947.

———. "The Pure Theory of Public Expenditure." *Review of Economics and Statistics* (1954): 387–89.

Schattschneider, Elmer E. *The Semi-Sovereign People: A Realist's View of Democracy in America.* New York: Holt, Rinehart and Winston, 1960.

Schieber, Sylvester J., and John Shoven. *The Real Deal: The History and Future of Social Security.* New Haven, CT: Yale University Press, 1999.

Schipper, Katherine. "Fair Values in Financial Reporting." Presentation at the American Accounting Association Annual Meetings, San Francisco, CA, August 2005.

Scholes, Myron S., Mark A. Wolfson, Merle M. Erickson, Edward L. Maydew, and Terrence J. Shevlin. *Taxes and Business Strategy: A Planning Approach.* Upper Saddle River, NJ: Pearson Prentice Hall, 2005.

Schumpeter, Joseph A. *Capitalism, Socialism and Democracy.* New York: Harper & Row, 1942.

Scotchmer, Suzanne. *Innovation and Incentives.* Cambridge, MA: MIT Press, 2006.

Scott, Bruce R. *Capitalism: Its Origins and Evolution as a System of Governance.* Berlin: Springer-Verlag, 2011.

SDC Platinum. "M&A Activity 1980–2012." Accessed September 2013. http://thomsonreuters.com/sdc-platinum.

Securities and Exchange Commission. *Final Report of the Advisory Committee on Improvements to Financial Reporting to the United States Securities and Exchange Commission.* Accessed September 2013. http://www.sec.gov/about/offices/oca/acifr/acifr-finalreport.pdf.

———. "The Laws That Govern the Securities Industry." Accessed October 2012. http://www.sec.gov/about/laws.shtml.

———. "SEC Establishes Advisory Committee to Make U.S. Financial Reporting System More User-Friendly for Investors." June 27, 2007. Accessed January 2014. http://www.sec.gov/news/press/2007/2007-123.htm.

———. "SEC Staff Publishes Final Report on Work Plan for Global Accounting Standards." July 13, 2012. Accessed November 2013. http://www.sec.gov/news/press/2012/2012-135.htm.

———. *Work Plan for the Consideration of Incorporating International Financial Reporting Standards into the Financial Reporting System for U.S. Issuers: Final Staff Report.* Accessed November 2013. http://www.sec.gov/spotlight/globalaccountingstandards/ifrs-work-plan-final-report.pdf.

Securities and Exchange Commission Historical Society. "Accounting and Auditing in the 1930s." Accessed September 2013. http://www.sechistorical.org/museum/galleries/rca/rca02a-profession.php.

———. "In the Midst of Revolution: The SEC (1973–1981)." Accessed January 2014. http://www.sechistorical.org/museum/galleries/rev/rev04e.php.

———. "The Richard C. Adkerson Gallery on the SEC Role in Accounting Standards Setting: Accounting Principles Board (1959–1973)." Accessed September 2013. http://www.sechistorical.org/museum/galleries/rca/rca04b-fasb-organization.php.

———. "The Richard C. Adkerson Gallery on the SEC Role in Accounting Standards Setting: Financial Accounting Standards Board (1973–Present)." Accessed September 2013. http://www.sechistorical.org/museum/galleries/rca/rca04d-fasb-organization.php.

Seidman, Leslie. Interview by Karthik Ramanna and Luis Viceira. Norwalk, CT. July 27, 2012.

Seligman, Joel. *The Transformation of Wall Street,* 3rd ed. New York: Aspen Publishers, 2003.

Selvan, Kalai N. *Tata's Business and Growth Strategy*. Hyderabad, India: Icfai University Press, 2008.

Sen, Amartya. *Development as Freedom*. Oxford, UK: Oxford University Press, 1998.

———. "Markets and Freedom: Achievements and Limitations of the Market Mechanism in Promoting Individual Freedoms." *Oxford Economic Papers* 45, no. 4 (1993): 519–41.

Shleifer, Andrei, and Robert W. Vishny. "Pervasive Shortages under Socialism." *Rand Journal of Economics* 23, no. 2 (1992): 237–46.

Shleifer, Andrei, and Daniel Wolfenzon. "Investor Protection and Equity Markets." *Journal of Financial Economics* 66, no. 1 (2002): 3–27.

Shu, Lisa L., Nina Mazar, Francesca Gino, Dan Ariely, and Max H. Bazerman. "Signing at the Beginning Makes Ethics Salient and Decreases Dishonest Self-Reports in Comparison to Signing at the End." *Proceedings of the National Academy of Sciences* 109, no. 38 (2012): 15197–200.

Skinner, Douglas J. "Accounting for Intangibles—a Critical Review of Policy Recommendations." *Accounting and Business Research* 38, no. 3 (2008): 191–204.

———. "Discussion of 'the Implications of Unverifiable Fair-Value Accounting: Evidence from the Political Economy of Goodwill Accounting.'" *Journal of Accounting and Economics* 45, nos. 2–3 (2008): 282–88.

———. "Why Firms Voluntarily Disclose Bad News." *Journal of Accounting Research* 32, no. 1 (1994): 38–60.

Sloan, Richard G. "Accounting Earnings and Top Executive Compensation." *Journal of Accounting and Economics* 16, nos. 1–3 (1993): 55–100.

Smith, Adam. *An Inquiry into the Nature and Causes of the Wealth of Nations*. 1776. Reprint, Pennsylvania State College: Pennsylvania State Electronic Classics Series Publication, 2005.

Smith, Clifford W., and Jerold B. Warner. "On Financial Contracting: An Analysis of Bond Covenants." *Journal of Financial Economics* 7, no. 2 (1979): 117–61.

Snyder, James M., Jr. "Long-Term Investing in Politicians: Or, Give Early, Give Often." *Journal of Law and Economics* 35, no. 1 (1992): 15–43.

Spence, Michael. "Job Market Signaling." *Quarterly Journal of Economics* 87, no. 3 (1973): 355–74.

Spychala, Michael R. "Michael R. Spychala to Financial Accounting Standards Board." Letter of Comment No. 85, file ref. 1033-201R. Norwalk, CT: FASB, 2001.

St. Pierre, Kent, and James A. Anderson. "An Analysis of the Factors Associated with Lawsuits against Public Accountants." *Accounting Review* 59 (1984): 242–63.

Stewart, G. Bennett, III. *The Quest for Value: The EVA Management Guide*. New York: Harper Collins, 1991.

Stickney, Clyde P., Roman L. Weil, Katherine Schipper, and Jennifer Francis. *Financial Accounting*. 13th ed. Mason, OH: South–Western Cengage Learning, 2010.

Stigler, George J. *Chicago Studies in Political Economy*. Chicago: University of Chicago Press, 1988.

———. "The Theory of Economic Regulation." *Bell Journal of Economics and Management Science* 2, no. 1 (1971): 3–21.

———. *The Theory of Price*. London: Macmillan, 1946.

Stout, Lynn. *The Shareholder Value Myth: How Putting Shareholders First Hurts Investors*. San Francisco, CA: Berrett-Koehler, 2012.

Stratmann, Thomas. "Some Talk: Money in Politics. A (Partial) Review of the Literature." *Public Choice* 124, nos. 1–2 (2005): 135–56.

Sugden, Robert. "Spontaneous Order." *Journal of Economic Perspectives* 3, no. 4 (1989): 85–97.

Sunder, Shyam. "Political Economy of Accounting Standards." *Journal of Accounting Literature* 7 (1988): 31–41.

———. "Structure for Organizations of Public and Private Goods." Working paper, Carnegie Mellon University, Pittsburg, PA, 1999.

Taft, John G. *Stewardship: Lessons Learned from the Lost Culture of Wall Street*. Hoboken, NJ: Wiley, 2012.

Tang, Yunwei. "Bumpy Road Leading to Internationalization: A Review of Accounting Development in China." *Accounting Horizons* 14, no. 1 (2000): 93–102.

Tapestry Networks. "About Us." Accessed October 2013. http://www.tapestrynetworks.com/about-us.

———. "Therapeutic Area: Type 2 Diabetes." Accessed December 2013. http://www.tapestrynetworks.com/issues/healthcare/therapeutic-area-type-2-diabetes.cfm.

Tarrow, Sidney G. *Power in Movement: Social Movements and Contentious Politics*. Cambridge, UK: Cambridge University Press, 1994.

"Tata Corus Taking Big Steps to Streamline Ops." *Moneycontrol*, October 13, 2007. Accessed November 2013. http://www.moneycontrol.com/video/business/tata-corus-taking-big-steps-to-streamline-ops-_307914.html.

Tata Group. "The Quotable Jamsetji Tata." March 2008. Accessed April 2010. http://www.tata.com/aboutus/articles/inside.aspx?artid=1U2QamAhqtA=.

Tata Steel. *2007–2008 Annual Report*. Accessed May 2010. http://www.tatasteel.com/investors/annual-report-07-08/annual-report-07-08.pdf.

———. *2008–2009 Annual Report*. Accessed December 2013. http://www.tatasteel.com/media/pdf/annual-report-2008-09.pdf.

Turner, Lynn E. "Initiatives for Improving the Quality of Financial Reporting." Speech given to the New York Society of Security Analysts, New York, February 10, 1999.

Tysiac, Ken. "FAF Creates Private Company Council." *Journal of Accountancy*, July 1, 2012. Accessed October 2013. http://www.journalofaccountancy.com/Issues/2012/Jul/FAF-creates-Private-Company-Council.htm.

Valen, Leigh Van. "A New Evolutionary Law." *Evolutionary Theory* 1 (1973): 1–30.

Warner, Jerold B., Ross L. Watts, and Karen H. Wruck. "Stock Prices and Top Management Changes." *Journal of Financial Economics* 20 (1988): 461–92.

Watts, Ross L. "Conservatism in Accounting Part I: Explanations and Implications." *Accounting Horizons* 17, no. 3 (2003): 207–21.

———. "Corporate Financial Statements: A Product of the Market and Political Processes." *Australian Journal of Management* 2, no. 1 (1977): 53–75.

———. "What Has the Invisible Hand Achieved?" *Accounting and Business Research* 36, sup. (2006): 51–61.

Watts, Ross L., and Jerold L. Zimmerman. "Agency Problems, Auditing and the Theory of the Firm: Some Evidence." *Journal of Law and Economics* 26, no. 3 (1983): 613–33.

———. "Auditors and the Determination of Accounting Standards." Working paper GPB 78-06, University of Rochester, Rochester, NY, 1982.

———. *Positive Accounting Theory*. Englewood Cliffs, NJ: Prentice Hall, 1986.

———. "Towards a Positive Theory of the Determination of Accounting Standards." *Accounting Review* 53, no. 1 (1978): 112–34.

"Whatever Happened to IPOs?" *Wall Street Journal*, March 22, 2011. Accessed April 2012. http://

online.wsj.com /article /SB10001424052748704662604576203002012714150.html?mod=
googlenews_wsj.

Wheelwright, Steven C., Charles A. Holloway, Nicole Tempest, and Christian G. Kasper. *Cisco Systems, Inc.: Acquisition Integration for Manufacturing (A)* (HBS No. 600-015). Boston: Harvard Business School Publishing, 2000.

World Bank Group. "World Development Indicators." Accessed November 2013. http://data .worldbank.org/data-catalog/world-development-indicators.

World Federation of Exchanges. "Statistics." Accessed November 2013. http://www.world -exchanges.org/statistics.

World Trade Organization. "Accession of the People's Republic of China." November 10, 2001. Accessed June 2011. http://www.wto.org/english /thewto_e/acc_e/protocols_acc _membership_e.htm.

———. "Anti-Dumping." Accessed November 2013. http://www.wto.org/english /tratop_e/adp _e/adp_e.htm#statistics.

Young, Joni J. "Making up Users." *Accounting, Organizations and Society* 31, no. 6 (2006): 579–600.

Zeff, Stephen A. "The Evolution of U.S. GAAP: The Political Forces behind Professional Standards Part 1." *CPA Journal* 75 (2005): 18–27.

———. "The SEC Rules Historical Cost Accounting: 1934 to the 1970s." *Accounting and Business Research* 37, sup-1 (2007): 49–62.

Zhang, Jieying. "The Contracting Benefits of Accounting Conservatism to Lenders and Borrowers." *Journal of Accounting and Economics* 45, no. 1 (2008): 27–54.

Zingales, Luigi. "Preventing Economists' Capture." In *Preventing Regulatory Capture*, edited by Daniel Carpenter and David A. Moss, 124–51. New York: Cambridge University Press, 2014.

Index

Note: Page numbers followed by *f* and *t* refer to figures and tables, respectively.